TIME REGAINED
(LE TEMPS RETROUVÉ)

TIME REGAINED (LE TEMPS RETROUVÉ)

MARCEL PROUST,
STEPHEN HUDSON (SYDNEY SCHIFF)

ISBN: 978-93-5344-702-1

First Published: -

LECTOR HOUSE LLP
E-MAIL: lectorpublishing@gmail.com

REMEMBRANCE OF THINGS PAST
(À LA RECHERCHE DU TEMPS PERDU)
VOLUME VII

PUBLISHER'S NOTE

Marcel Proust's continuous novel À la Recherche du Temps Perdu (REMEM-BRANCE OF THINGS PAST) was originally published in eight parts, the titles and dates of which were:

Titles (Dates)	*Published in English as*
I. Du Coté de Chez Swann (1913)	SWANN'S WAY
II. À l'Ombre des Jeunes Filles en Fleurs (1918), awarded the Prix Goncourt in 1919	WITHIN A BUDDING GROVE
III. Le Côté de Guermantes, I (1920)	THE GUERMANTES WAY
IV. Le Côté de Guermantes, II - Sodome et Gomorrhe, I (1921)	CITIES OF THE PLAIN
V. Sodome et Gomorrhe, II (1922)	CITIES OF THE PLAIN
VI. La Prisonnière (1923)	THE CAPTIVE
VII.Albertine Disparue (1925)	THE SWEET CHEAT GONE
VIII. Le Temps Retrouvé (1927)	TIME REGAINED

The first seven parts were translated by C. K. Scott Moncrieff; the eighth was first translated for Chatto & Windus by Stephen Hudson.

"When to the sessions of sweet silent thought
I summon up remembrance of things past...."

"Oui, si le souvenir grâce à l'oubli, n'a pu contracter aucun lien, jeter aucun chaînon entre lui et la minute présente, s'il est resté à sa place, à sa date, s'il a gardé ses distances, son isolement dans le creux d'une vallée, où à la pointe d'un sommet, il nous fait tout à coup respirer un air nouveau, précisément parce que c'est un air qu'on a respiré autrefois, cet air plus pur que les poètes ont vainement essayé de faire régner dans le Paradis et qui ne pourrait donner cette sensation profonde de renouvellement que s'il avait été respiré déjà, car les vrais paradis sont les paradis qu'on a perdus."

TIME REGAINED
(LE TEMPS RETROUVÉ)

BY

MARCEL PROUST

TRANSLATED FROM THE FRENCH
BY
STEPHEN HUDSON (SYDNEY SCHIFF)

TRANSLATOR'S DEDICATION

TO THE MEMORY OF MY FRIEND
CHARLES SCOTT MONCRIEFF
MARCEL PROUST'S INCOMPARABLE TRANSLATOR

TRANSLATOR'S NOTE

Baffled by the phrases on page 244 of the volume of the French edition: 'La vie humaine et pensante... dans une forteresse,' an appeal to my friend Aldous Huxley brought me the reading I have almost integrally adopted. Both of us are conscious that this rendering is only approximate, the obscurity being only partly due to the elliptical nature of the passage. My belief is that there has either been an editorial misreading of Proust's manuscript or a mistake on the part of the printer, neither of which occurrences are infrequent in the series.

I have also gratefully to acknowledge valuable emendations of the text suggested by Mr. A. G. Chater.

STEPHEN HUDSON

CONTENTS

CHAPTER I

TANSONVILLE

TANSONVILLE seemed little more than a place to rest in between two walks or a refuge during a shower. Rather too countrified, it was one of those rural dwellings where every sitting-room is a cabinet of greenery, and where the roses and the birds out in the garden keep you company in the curtains; for they were old and each rose stood out so clearly that it might have been picked like a real one and each bird put in a cage, unlike those pretentious modern decorations in which, against a silver background, all the apple trees in Normandy are outlined in the Japanese manner, to trick the hours you lie in bed. I spent the whole day in my room, the windows of which opened upon the beautiful verdure of the park, upon the lilacs of the entrance, upon the green leaves of the great trees beside the water and in the forest of Méséglise. It was a pleasure to contemplate all this, I was saying to myself: "How charming to have all this greenery in my window" until suddenly in the midst of the great green picture I recognised the clock tower of the Church of Combray toned in contrast to a sombre blue as though it were far distant, not a reproduction of the clock tower but its very self which, defying time and space, thrust itself into the midst of the luminous greenery as if it were engraved upon my window-pane. And if I left my room, at the end of the passage, set towards me like a band of scarlet, I perceived the hangings of a little sitting-room which though only made of muslin, were of a scarlet so vivid that they would catch fire if a single sun-ray touched them.

During our walks Gilberte alluded to Robert as though he were turning away from her but to other women. It was true that his life was encumbered with women as masculine attachments encumber that of women-loving men, both having that character of forbidden fruit, of a place vainly usurped, which unwanted objects have in most houses.

Once I left Gilberte early and in the middle of the night, while still half-asleep, I called Albertine. I had not been thinking or dreaming of her, nor had I mistaken her for Gilberte. My memory had lost its love for Albertine but it seems there must be an involuntary memory of the limbs, pale and sterile imitation of the other, which lives longer as certain mindless animals or plants live longer than man. The legs, the arms are full of blunted memories; a reminiscence germinating in my arm had made me seek the bell behind my back, as I used to in my room in Paris and I had called Albertine, imagining my dead friend lying beside me as she so often did at evening when we fell asleep together, counting the time it would take Françoise to reach us, so that Albertine might without imprudence pull the bell I could not find.

Robert came to Tansonville several times while I was there. He was very different from the man I had known before. His life had not coarsened him as it had M. de Charlus, but, on the contrary, had given him more than ever the easy carriage of a cavalry officer although at his marriage he had resigned his commission. As gradually M. de Charlus had got heavier, Robert (of course he was much younger, yet one felt he was bound to approximate to that type with age like certain women who resolutely sacrifice their faces to their figures and never abandon Marienbad, believing, as they cannot hope to keep all their youthful charms, that of the outline to represent best the others) had become slimmer, swifter, the contrary effect of the same vice. This velocity had other psychological causes; the fear of being seen, the desire not to seem to have that fear, the feverishness born of dissatisfaction with oneself and of boredom. He had the habit of going into certain haunts of ill-fame, where as he did not wish to be seen entering or coming out, he effaced himself so as to expose the least possible surface to the malevolent gaze of hypothetical passers-by, and that gust-like motion had remained and perhaps signified the apparent intrepidity of one who wants to show he is unafraid and does not take time to think.

To complete the picture one must reckon with the desire, the older he got, to appear young, and also the impatience of those who are always bored and *blasés*, yet being too intelligent for a relatively idle life, do not sufficiently use their faculties. Doubtless the very idleness of such people may display itself by indifference but especially since idleness, owing to the favour now accorded to physical exercise, has taken the form of sport, even when the latter cannot be practised, feverish activity leaves boredom neither time nor space to develop in.

He had become dried up and gave friends like myself no evidence of sensibility. On the other hand, he affected with Gilberte an unpleasant sensitiveness which he pushed to the point of comedy. It was not that Robert was indifferent to Gilberte; no, he loved her. But he always lied to her and this spirit of duplicity, if it was not the actual source of his lies, was constantly emerging. At such times he believed he could only extricate himself by exaggerating to a ridiculous degree the real pain he felt in giving pain to her. When he arrived at Tansonville he was obliged, he said, to leave the next morning on business with a certain gentleman of those parts, who was expecting him in Paris and who, encountered that very evening near Combray, unhappily revealed the lie, Robert, having failed to warn him, by the statement that he was back for a month's holiday and would not be in Paris before. Robert blushed, saw Gilberte's faint melancholy smile, and after revenging himself on the unfortunate culprit by an insult, returned earlier than his wife and sent her a desperate note telling her he had lied in order not to pain her, for fear that when he left for a reason he could not tell her, she should think that he had ceased to love her; and all this, written as though it were a lie, was actually true. Then he sent to ask if he could come to her room, and there, partly in real sorrow, partly in disgust with the life he was living, partly through the increasing audacity of his successive pretences, he sobbed and talked of his approaching death, sometimes throwing himself on the floor as though he were ill. Gilberte, not knowing to what extent to believe him, thought him a liar on each occasion, but, disquieted by the presentiment of his approaching death and believing in a general way that he loved her, that perhaps he had some illness she knew nothing about, did not dare to oppose him or ask him to relinquish his journeys. I was unable to understand how he came to have Morel received as though he were a son of the house wherever the Saint-Loups were, whether in Paris or at Tansonville.

Françoise, knowing all that M. de Charlus had done for Jupien and Robert Saint-Loup for Morel, did not conclude that this was a trait which reappeared in certain generations of the Guermantes, but rather—seeing that Legrandin much loved Théodore—came to believe, prudish and narrow-minded as she was, that it was a custom which universality made respectable. She would say of a young man, were it Morel or Théodore: "He is fond of the gentleman who is interested in him and who has so much helped him." And as in such cases it is the protectors who love, who suffer, who forgive, Françoise did not hesitate between them and the youths they debauched, to give the former the *beau role*, to discover they had a "great deal of heart". She did not hesitate to blame Théodore who had played a great many tricks on Legrandin, yet seemed to have scarcely a doubt as to the nature of their relationship, for she added, "The young man understands he's got to do his share as he says: 'take me away with you, I will be fond of you and pet you,' and, *ma foi*, the gentleman has so much heart that Théodore is sure to find him kinder than he deserves, for he's a hot head while the gentleman is so good that I often say to Jeannette (Theodore's fiancée), 'My dear, if ever you're in trouble go and see that gentleman, he would lie on the ground to give you his bed, he is too fond of Théodore to throw him out and he will never abandon him'." It was in the course of one of these colloquies that, having inquired the name of the family with whom Théodore was living in the south, I suddenly grasped that he was the person unknown to me who had asked me to send him my article in the *Figaro* in a letter the calligraphy of which was of the people but charmingly expressed.

In the same fashion Françoise esteemed Saint-Loup more than Morel and expressed the opinion, in spite of the ignoble behaviour of the latter, that the marquis had too good a heart ever to desert him unless great reverses happened to himself.

Saint-Loup insisted I should remain at Tansonville and once let fall, although plainly he was not seeking to please me, that my visit was so great a happiness for his wife that she had assured him, though she had been wretched the whole day, that she was transported with joy the evening I unexpectedly arrived, that, in fact, I had miraculously saved her from despair, "perhaps from something worse." He begged me to try and persuade her that he loved her, assuring me that the other woman he loved was less to him than Gilberte and that he intended to break with her very soon. "And yet," he added, in such a feline way and with so great a longing to confide that I expected the name of Charlie to pop out at any moment, in spite of himself, like a lottery number, "I had something to be proud of. This woman, who has proved her devotion to me and whom I must sacrifice for Gilberte's sake, never accepted attention from a man, she believed herself incapable of love; I am the first. I knew she had refused herself to everyone, so much so that when I received an adorable letter from her, telling me there could be no happiness for her without me, I could not resist it. Wouldn't it be natural for me to be infatuated with her, were it not intolerable for me to see poor little Gilberte in tears? Don't you think there is something of Rachel in her?" As a matter of fact, it had struck me that there was a vague resemblance between them. This may have been due to a certain similarity of feature, owing to their common Jewish origin, which was little marked in Gilberte, and yet when his family wanted him to marry, drew Robert towards her. The likeness was perhaps due also to Gilberte coming across photographs of Rachel and wanting to please Robert by imitating certain of the actress's habits, such as always wearing red bows in her hair, a black ribbon on her arm and dyeing her hair to appear dark. Then, fearing her sorrows affected her appearance, she tried to remedy it by occasionally exaggerating the artifice. One day, when Robert was to come to Tansonville for twenty-four hours, I was amazed to see her come to table looking so strangely different from her present as well as from her former self, that I was as bewildered as if I were facing an actress, a sort of Theodora. I felt that in my curiosity to know what it was that was changed about her, I was looking at her too fixedly. My curiosity was soon satisfied when she blew her nose, for in spite of all her precautions, the assortment of colours upon the handkerchief would have constituted a varied palette and I saw that she was completely painted. To this was due the bleeding appearance of her mouth which she forced into a smile, thinking it suited her, while the knowledge that the hour was approaching when her husband ought to arrive without knowing whether or not he would send one of those telegrams of which the model had been wittily invented by M. de Guermantes: "Impossible to come, lie follows," paled her cheeks and ringed her eyes.

"Ah, you see," Robert said to me with a deliberately tender accent which contrasted with his former spontaneous affection, with an alcoholic voice and the inflection of an actor. "To make Gilberte happy! What wouldn't I do to secure that? You can never know how much she has done for me." The most unpleasant of all was his vanity, for Saint-Loup, flattered that Gilberte loved him, without daring to say that he loved Morel, gave her details about the devotion the violinist pretended to have for him, which he well knew were exaggerated if not altogether invented seeing that Morel demanded more money of him every day. Then confiding Gilberte to my care, he left again for Paris. To anticipate somewhat (for I am still at Tansonville), I had the opportunity of seeing him once again in society, though at a distance, when his words, in spite of all this, were so lively and charming that they enabled me to recapture the past. I was struck to see how much he was changing. He resembled his mother more and more, but the proud and well-bred manner he inherited from her and which she possessed to perfection, had become, owing to his highly accomplished education, exaggerated and stilted; the penetrating look common to the Guermantes, gave him, from a peculiar animal-like habit, a half-unconscious air of inspecting every place he passed through. Even when motionless, that colouring which was his even more than it was the other Guermantes', a colouring which seemed to have a whole golden day's sunshine in it, gave him so strange a plumage, made of him so rare a creature, so unique, that one wanted to own him for an ornithological collection; but when, besides, this bird of golden sunlight put itself in motion, when, for instance,

I saw Robert de Saint-Loup at a party, he had a way of throwing back his head so joyously and so proudly, under the golden plumage of his slightly ruffled hair, the movement of his neck was so much more supple, proud and charming than that of other men, that, between the curiosity and the half-social, half-zoological admiration he inspired, one asked oneself whether one had found him in the Faubourg Saint-Germain or in the Jardin des Plantes and whether one was looking at a *grand seigneur* crossing a drawing-room or a marvellous bird walking about in its cage. With a little imagination the warbling no less than the plumage lent itself to that interpretation. He spoke in what he believed the *grand-siècle* style and thus imitated the manners of the Guermantes, but an indefinable trifle caused them to become those of M. de Charlus. "I must leave you an instant," he said during that party, when M. de Marsantes was some distance away, "to pay court to my niece a moment." As to that love of which he never ceased telling me, there were others besides Charlie, although he was the only one that mattered to him. Whatever kind of love a man may have, one is always wrong about the number of his *liaisons*, because one interprets friendships as *liaisons*, which is an error of addition, and also because it is believed that one proved *liaison* excludes another, which is a different sort of mistake. Two people may say, "I know X's mistress," and each be pronouncing a different name, yet neither be wrong. A woman one loves rarely suffices for all our needs, so we deceive her with another whom we do not love. As to the kind of love which Saint-Loup had inherited from M. de Charlus, the husband who is inclined that way generally makes his wife happy. This is a general law, to which the Guermantes were exceptions, because those of them who had that taste wanted people to believe they were women-lovers and, advertising themselves with one or another, caused the despair of their wives. The Courvoisiers acted more sensibly. The young Vicomte de Courvoisier believed himself the only person on earth and since the beginning of the world to be tempted by one of his own sex. Imagining that the preference came to him from the devil, he fought against it and married a charming woman by whom he had several children. Then one of his cousins taught him that the practice was fairly common, even went to the length of taking him to places where he could satisfy it. M. de Courvoisier only loved his wife the more for this and redoubled his uxorious zeal so that the couple were cited as the best *ménage* in Paris. As much could not be said for Saint-Loup, because Robert, not content with invertion, caused his wife endless jealousy by running after mistresses without getting any pleasure from them.

It is possible that Morel, being exceedingly dark, was necessary to Saint-Loup, as shadow is to sunlight. In this ancient family, one could well imagine a *grand seigneur*, blonde, golden, intelligent, dowered with every prestige, acquiring and retaining in the depths of his being, a secret taste, unknown to everyone, for negroes. Robert, moreover, never allowed conversation to touch his peculiar kind of love affair. If I said a word he would answer, with a detachment that caused his eye-glass to fall, "Oh! I don't know, I haven't an idea about such things. If you want information about them, my dear fellow, I advise you to go to someone else. I am a soldier, nothing more. I'm as indifferent to matters of that kind as I am passionately interested in the Balkan Wars. Formerly the history of battles interested you. In those days I told you we should again witness typical battles, even though the conditions were completely different, such, for instance, as the great attempt of envelopment by the wing in the Battle of Ulm. Well, special as those Balkan Wars may be, Lullé Burgas is again Ulm, envelopment by the wing. Those are matters you can talk to me about. But I know no more about the sort of thing you are alluding to than I do about Sanscrit." On the other hand, when he had gone, Gilberte referred voluntarily to the subjects Robert thus disdained when we talked together. Certainly not in connection with her husband, for she was unaware, or pretended to be unaware, of everything. But she enlarged willingly upon them when they concerned other people, whether because she saw in their case a sort of indirect excuse for Robert or whether, divided like his uncle between a severe silence on these subjects and an urge to pour himself out and to slander, he had been able to instruct her very thoroughly about them. Amongst those alluded to, no one was less spared than M. de Charlus; doubtless this was because Robert, without talking to Gilberte about Morel, could not help repeating to her in one form or another what had been told him by the violinist who pursued his former benefactor with his hatred. These conversations which Gilberte affected, permitted me to ask her if in similar fashion Albertine, whose name I had for the first time heard on her lips when the two were school friends, had the same tastes. Gilberte refused to give me this information. For that matter, it had for a long time ceased to afford me the slightest interest. Yet I continued to concern myself mechanically about it, just like an old man who has lost his memory now and then wants news of his dead son.

Another day I returned to the charge and asked Gilberte again if Albertine loved women. "Oh, not at all," she answered. "But you formerly said that she was very bad form." "I said that? You must be mistaken. In any case, if I did say it—but you are mistaken—I was on the contrary speaking of little love affairs with boys and, at that age, those don't go very far."

Did Gilberte say this to hide that she herself, according to Albertine, loved women and had made proposals to her, or (for others are often better informed about our life than we think) did Gilberte know that I had loved and been jealous of Albertine and (others being apt to know more of the truth than we believe, exaggerating it and so erring by excessive suppositions, while we were hoping they were mistaken through lack of any supposition at all) did she imagine that I was so still, and was she, out of kindness, blind-folding me which one is always ready to do to jealous people? In any case, Gilberte's words, since the "bad form" of former days leading to the certificate of moral life and habits of to-day, followed an inverse course to the affirmations of Albertine, who had almost come to avowing half-relationship with Gilberte herself. Albertine had astonished me in this, as had also what Andrée told me, for, respecting the whole of that little band, I had at first, before knowing its perversity, convinced myself that my suspicions were unjustified, as happens so often when one discovers an innocent girl, almost ignorant of the realities of life, in a milieu which one had wrongly supposed the most depraved. Afterwards I retraced my steps in the contrary sense, accepting my original suspicions as true. And perhaps Albertine told me all this so as to appear more experienced than she was and to astonish me with the prestige of her perversity in Paris, as at first by the prestige of her virtue at Balbec. So, quite simply, when I spoke to her about women who loved women, she answered as she did, in order not to seem to be unaware of what I meant, as in a conversation one assumes an understanding air when somebody talks of Fourier or of Tobolsk without even knowing what these names mean. She had perhaps associated with the friend of Mlle. Vinteuil and with Andrée, isolated from them by an air-tight partition and, while they believed she was not one of them, she only informed herself afterwards (as a woman who marries a man of letters seeks to cultivate herself) in order to please me, by enabling herself to answer my questions, until she realised that the questions were inspired by jealousy when, unless Gilberte was lying to me, she reversed the engine. The idea came to me, that it was because Robert had learnt from her in the course of a flirtation of the kind that interested him, that she, Gilberte, did not dislike women, that he married her, hoping for pleasures which he ought not to have looked for at home since he obtained them elsewhere. None of these hypotheses were absurd, for in the case of women such as Odette's daughter or of the girls of the little band there is such a diversity, such an accumulation of alternating tastes, that if they are not simultaneous, they pass easily from a *liaison* with a woman to a passion for a man, so much so that it becomes difficult to define their real and dominant taste. Thus Albertine had sought to please me in order to make me marry her but she had abandoned the project herself because of my undecided and worrying disposition. It was in this too simple form that I judged my affair with Albertine at a time when I only saw it from the outside.

What is curious and what I am unable wholly to grasp, is that about that period all those who had loved Albertine, all those who would have been able to make her do what they wanted, asked, entreated, I would even say, implored me, failing my friendship, at least, to have some sort of relations with them. It would have been no longer necessary to offer money to Mme. Bontemps to send me Albertine. This return of life, coming when it was no longer any use, profoundly saddened me, not on account of Albertine whom I would have received without pleasure if she had been brought to me, not only from Touraine but from the other world, but because of a young woman whom I loved and whom I could not manage to see. I said to myself that if she died or if I did not love her any more, all those who would have been able to bring her to me would have fallen at my feet. Meanwhile, I attempted in vain to work upon them, not being cured by experience which ought to have taught me, if it ever taught anyone anything, that to love is a bad fate like that in fairy stories, against which nothing avails until the enchantment has ceased.

"I've just reached a point," Gilberte continued, "in the book which I have here where it speaks of these things. It's an old Balzac I'm raking over to be on equal terms with my uncles, *La Fille aux yeux d'Or*, but it's incredible, a beautiful nightmare. Maybe a woman can be controlled in that way by another woman, but never by a man." "You are mistaken, I knew a woman who was loved by a man who veritably succeeded in isolating her; she could never see anyone and only went out with trusted servants." "Indeed! How that must have horrified you who are so kind. Just recently Robert and I were saying you ought to get married, your wife would cure you and make you happy." "No, I've got too bad a disposition." "What nonsense." "I assure you I have. For that matter I have been engaged, but I could not marry."

I did not want to borrow *La Fille aux yeux d'Or* from Gilberte because she was reading it, but on the last evening that I stayed with her, she lent me a book which produced a lively and mingled impression upon me. It was a volume of the unpublished diary of the Goncourts. I was sad that last evening, in going up to my room, to think that I had never gone back one single time to see the Church of Combray which seemed to be awaiting me in the midst of greenery framed in the violet-hued window. I said to myself, "Well, it must be another year, if I do not die between this and then," seeing no other obstacle but my death and not imagining that of the church, which, it seemed to me, must last long after my death as it had lasted long before' my birth. When, before blowing out my candle, I read the passage which I transcribe further on, my lack of aptitude for writing—presaged formerly during my walks on the Guermantes side, confirmed during the visit of which this was the last evening, those eyes of departure, when the routine of habits which are about to end is ceasing and one begins to judge oneself—seemed to me less regrettable; it was as though literature revealed no profound truth while at the same time it seemed sad that it was not what I believed it. The infirm state which was to confine me in a sanatorium seemed less regrettable to me if the beautiful things of which books speak were no more beautiful than those I had seen. But, by a strange contradiction, now that this book spoke of them, I longed to see them. Here are the pages which I read until fatigue closed my eyes.

"The day before yesterday, who should drop in here, to take me to dinner with him but Verdurin, the former critic of the *Revue*, author of that book on Whistler in which truly the doings, the artistic atmosphere of that highly original American are often rendered with great delicacy by that lover of all the refinements, of all the prettinesses of the thing painted which Verdurin is. And while I dress myself to follow him, every now and then, he gives vent to a regular recitation, like the frightened spelling out of a confession by Fromentin on his renunciation of writing immediately after his marriage with 'Madeleine', a renunciation which was said to be due to his habit of taking morphine, the result of which, according to Verdurin, was that the majority of the habitués of his wife's salon, not even knowing that her husband had ever written, spoke to him of Charles Blanc, St. Victor, St. Beuve, and Burty, to whom they believed him completely inferior. 'You Goncourt, you well know, and Gautier knew also that my "Salons" was a very different thing from those pitiable "Maîtres d'autrefois" believed to be masterpieces in my wife's family.' Then, by twilight, while the towers of the Trocadéro were lit up with the last gleams of the setting sun which made them look just like those covered with currant jelly of the old-style confectioners, the conversation continues in the carriage on our way to the Quai Conti where their mansion is, which its owner claims to be the ancient palace of the Ambassadors of Venice and where there is said to be a smoking-room of which Verdurin talks as though it were the drawing-room, transported just as it was in the fashion of the *Thousand and One Nights*, of a celebrated Palazzo, of which I forget the name, a Palazzo with a well-head representing the crowning of the Virgin which Verdurin asserts to be absolutely the finest of Sansovinos and which is used by their guests to throw their cigar ashes into.

And, *ma foi*, when we arrive, the dull green diffusion of moonlight, verily like that under which classical painting shelters Venice and under which the silhouetted cupola of the Institute makes one think of the Salute in the pictures of Guardi, I have somewhat the illusion of being beside the Grand Canal, the illusion reinforced by the construction of the mansion, where from the first floor, one does not see the quay, and by the effective remark of the master of the house, who affirms that the name of the Rue du Bac—I am hanged if I had ever thought of it—came from the ferry upon which the religious of former days, the Miramiones, went to mass at Notre Dame. I took to reloving the whole quarter where I wandered in my youth when my Aunt de Courmont lived there on finding almost contiguous to the mansion of Verdurin, the sign of 'Petit Dunkerque', one of those rare shops surviving otherwise than vignetted in the chalks and rubbings of Gabriel de St. Aubin in which that curious eighteenth century individual came in and seated himself during his moments of idleness to bargain about pretty little French and foreign 'trifles' and the newest of everything produced by Art as a bill-head of the 'Petit Dunkerque' has it, a bill-head of which I believe we alone, Verdurin and I, possess an example and which is one of those shuttle-cock masterpieces of ornamented paper upon which, in the reign of Louis XV accounts were delivered, with its title-head representing a raging sea swarming with ships, a sea with waves which had the appearance of an illustration in the *Edition des Fermiers Généraux de l'Huître et des Plaideurs*. The mistress of the house, who places me beside her, says amiably that she has decorated her table with nothing but Japanese chrysanthemums but these chrysanthemums are disposed in vases which are the rarest works of art, one of them of bronze upon which petals of red copper seemed to be the living efflorescence of the flower. There is Cottard the doctor, and his wife, the Polish sculptor Viradobetski, Swann the collector, a Russian *grande dame*, a Princess with a golden name which escapes me, and Cottard whispers in my ear that it is she who had shot point blank at the Archduke Rudolf. According to her I have an absolutely exceptional literary position in Galicia and in the whole north of Poland, a girl in those parts never consenting to promise her hand without knowing if her betrothed is an admirer of La Faustin.

"'You cannot understand, you western people,' exclaims by way of conclusion the princess who gives me the impression, *ma foi*, of an altogether superior intelligence, 'that penetration by a writer into the intimate life of a woman.' A man with shaven chin and lips, with whiskers like a butler, beginning with that tone of condescension of a secondary professor preparing first form boys for the Saint-Charlemagne, that is Brichot, the university don. When my name was mentioned by Verdurin he did not say a word to show that he knew our books, which means for me anger, discouragement aroused by this conspiracy the Sorbonne organises against us, bringing contradiction and hostile silence even into the charming house where I am being entertained. We proceed to table and there is then an extraordinary procession of plates which are simply masterpieces of the art of the porcelain-maker. The connoisseur, whose attention is delicately tickled during the dainty repast, listens all the more complacently to the artistic chatter—while before him pass plates of Yung Tsching with their nasturtium rims yielding to the bluish centre with its rich flowering of the water-iris, a really decorative passage with its dawn-flight of kingfishers and cranes, a dawn with just that matutinal tone which I gaze at lazily when I awake daily at the Boulevard Montmorency—Dresden plates more finical in the grace of their fashioning, whether in the sleepy anemia of their roses turning to violet in the crushed wine-lees of a tulip or with their rococo design of carnation and myosotis. Plates of Sèvres trellissed by the delicate vermic- ulation of their white fluting, verticillated in gold or bound upon the creamy plane of their *pâte tendre* by the gay relief of a golden ribbon, finally a whole service of silver on which are displayed those Lucinian myrtles which Dubarry would recog- nise. And what is perhaps equally rare is the really altogether remarkable quality of the things which are served in it, food delicately manipulated, a stew such as the Parisians, one can shout that aloud, never have at their grandest dinners and which reminds me of certain *cordons bleus* of Jean d'Heurs. Even the *foie gras* has no rela- tion to the tasteless froth which is generally served under that name, and I do not know many places where a simple potato salad is thus made with potatoes having the firmness of a Japanese ivory button and the patina of those little ivory spoons with which the Chinese pour water on the fish that they have just caught. A rich red bejewelling is given to the Venetian goblet which stands before me by an amazing Léoville bought at the sale of M. Montalivet and it is a delight for the imagination and for the eye, I do not fear to say it, for the imagination of what one formerly called the jaw, to have served to one a brill which has nothing in common with that kind of stale brill served on the most luxurious tables which has received on its back the imprint of its bones during the delay of the journey, a brill not ac- companied by that sticky glue generally called *sauce blanche* by so many of the chefs in great houses, but by a veritable *sauce blanche* made out of butter at five francs the pound; to see this brill in a wonderful Tching Hon dish graced by the purple rays of a setting sun on a sea which an amusing band of lobsters is navigat- ing, their rough tentacles so realistically pictured that they seem to have been modelled upon the living carapace, a dish of which the handle is a little Chinaman catching with his line a fish which makes the silvery azure of his stomach an en- chantment of mother o' pearl. As I speak to Verdurin of the delicate satisfaction it must be for him to have this refined repast amidst a collection which no prince possesses at the present time, the mistress of the house throws me the melancholy remark: 'One sees how little you know him,' and she speaks of her husband as a whimsical oddity, indifferent to all these beauties, 'an oddity' she repeats, 'that's the word, who has more gusto for a bottle of cider drunk in the rough coolness of a Norman farm.' And the charming woman, in a tone which is really in love with the colours of the country, speaks to us with overflowing enthusiasm of that Nor- mandy where they have lived, a Normandy which must be like an enormous En- glish park, with the fragrance of its high woodlands *à la* Lawrence, with its velvet cryptomeria in their enamelled borders of pink hortensia, with its natural lawns diversified by sulphur-coloured roses falling over a rustic gateway flanked by two intertwined pear-trees resembling with its free-falling and flowering branches the highly ornamental insignia of a bronze applique by Gauthier, a Normandy which must be absolutely unsuspected by Parisians on holiday, protected as it is by the barrier of each of its enclosures, barriers which the Verdurins confess to me they did not commit the crime of removing. At the close of day, as the riot of colour was sleepily extinguished and light only came from the sea curdled almost to a skim-milk blue. 'Ah! Not the sea you know—' protests my hostess energetically in answer to my remark that Flaubert had taken my brother and me to Trouville, 'That is nothing, absolutely nothing. You must come with me, without that you will never know'—they would go back through real forests of pink-tulle flowers of the rhododendrons, intoxicated with the scent of the gardens, which gave her husband abominable attacks of asthma. 'Yes,' she insisted, 'it is true, real crises of asthma.' Afterwards, the following summer, they returned, housing a whole colony of artists in an admirable dwelling of the Middle Ages, an ancient cloister leased by them for nothing, and *ma foi*, listening to this woman who after moving in so many distinguished circles, had yet kept some of that freedom of speech of a woman of the people, a speech which shows you things with the colour imagination gives to them, my mouth watered at the thought of the life which she confessed to living down there, each one working in his cell or in the salon which was so large that it had two fireplaces. Everyone came in before luncheon for altogether superior conversation interspersed with parlour games, reminding me of those evoked by that masterpiece of Diderot, his letters to Mlle. Volland. Then after luncheon everyone went out, even on days of sunny showers, when the sparkling of the raindrops luminously filtering through the knots of a magnificent avenue of centenarian beechtrees which offered in front of the gates the vista of growth dear to the eighteenth century, and shrubs bearing drops of rain on their flowering buds suspended on their boughs, lingering to watch the delicate dabbling of a bullfinch enamoured of coolness, bathing itself in the tiny nymphembourg basin shaped like the corolla of a white rose. And as I talk to Mme. Verdurin of the landscapes and of the flowers down there, so delicately pastelled by Elstir: 'But it is I who made all that known to him,' she exclaims with an indignant lifting of the head, 'everything, you understand; wonder-provoking nooks, all his themes; I threw them in his face when he left us, didn't I, Auguste? All those themes he has painted. Objects he always knew, to be fair, one must admit that. But flowers he had never seen; no, he did not know the difference between a marsh-mallow and a hollyhock. It was I who taught him, you will hardly believe me, to recognise the jasmine.' And it is, one must admit, a strange reflection that the painter of flowers, whom the connoisseurs of to-day cite to us as the greatest, superior even to Fantin-Latour, would perhaps never have known how to paint jasmine without the woman who was beside me. 'Yes, upon my word, the jasmine; all the roses he produced were painted while he was staying with me, if I did not bring them to him myself. At our house we just called him "M. Tiche". Ask Cottard or Brichot or any of them if he was ever treated here as a great man. He would have laughed at it himself. I taught him how to arrange his flowers; at the beginning he had no idea of it. He never knew how to make a bouquet. He had no natural taste for selection. I had to say to him, "No, do not paint that; it is not worth while, paint this." Oh! If he had listened to us for the arrangement of his life as he did for the arrangement of his flowers, and if he had not made that horrible marriage!' And abruptly, with eyes fevered by their absorption in a reverie of the past, with a nerve-racked gesture, she stretched forth her arms with a frenzied cracking of the joints from the silk sleeves of her bodice, and twisted her body into a suffering pose like some admirable picture which I believe has never been painted, wherein all the pent-up revolt, all the enraged susceptibilities of a friend outraged in her delicacy and in her womanly modesty can be read. Upon that she talks to us about the admirable portrait which Elstir made for her, a portrait of the Collard family, a portrait given by her to the Luxembourg when she quarrelled with the painter, confessing that it was she who had given him the idea of painting the man in evening dress in order to obtain that beautiful expanse of linen, and she who chose the velvet dress of the woman, a dress offering support in the midst of all the fluttering of the light shades of the curtains, of the flowers, of the fruit, of the gauze dresses of the little girls like ballet-dancers' skirts. It was she, too, who gave him the idea of painting her in the act of arranging her hair, an idea for which the artist was afterwards honoured, which consisted, in short, in painting the woman, not as though on show, but surprised in the intimacy of her everyday life. 'I said to him, "When a woman is doing her hair or wiping her face, or warming her feet, she knows she is not being seen, she executes a number of interesting movements, movements of an altogether Leonardo-like grace."' But upon a sign from Verdurin, indicating that the arousing of this state of indignation was unhealthy for that highly-strung creature which his wife was, Swann drew my admiring attention to the necklace of black pearls worn by the mistress of the house and bought by her quite white at the sale of a descendant of Mme. de La Fayette to whom they had been given by Henrietta of England, pearls which had become black as the result of a fire which destroyed part of the house in which the Verdurins were living in a street the name of which I can no longer remember, a fire after which the casket containing the pearls was found but they had become entirely black. 'And I know the portrait of those pearls on the very shoulders of Mme. de La Fayette, yes, exactly so, their portrait,' insisted Swann in the face of the somewhat wonderstruck exclamations of the guests. 'Their authentic portrait, in the collection of the Duc de Guermantes. A collection which has not its equal in the world,' he asserts and that I ought to go and see it, a collection inherited by the celebrated Duc who was the favourite nephew of Mme. de Beausergent his aunt, of that Mme. de Beausergent who afterwards became Mme. d'Hayfeld, sister of the Marquise de Villeparisis and of the Princess of Hanover. My brother and I used to be so fond of him in old days when he was a charming boy called Basin, which as a matter of fact, is the first name of the Duc. Upon that, Doctor Cottard, with that delicacy which reveals the man of distinction, returns to the history of the pearls and informs us that catastrophes of that kind produce in the mind of people distortions similar to those one remarks in organic matter and relates in really more philosophical terms than most physicians can command, how the footman of Mme. Verdurin herself, through the horror of this fire where he nearly perished, had become a different man, his hand-writing having so changed that on seeing the first letter which his masters, then in Normandy, received from him, announcing the event, they believed it was the invention of a practical joker. And not only was his handwriting different, Cottard asserts that from having been a completely sober man he had become an abominable drunkard whom Mme. Verdurin had been obliged to discharge. This suggestive dissertation continued, on a gracious sign from the mistress of the house, from the dining-room into the Venetian smoking-room where Cottard told me he had witnessed actual duplications of personality, giving as example the case of one of his patients whom he amiably offers to bring to see me, in whose case Cottard has merely to touch his temples to usher him into a second life, a life in which he remembers nothing of the other, so much so that, a very honest man in this one, he had actually been arrested several times for thefts committed in the other during which he had been nothing less than a disgraceful scamp. Upon which Mme. Verdurin acutely remarks that medicine could furnish subjects truer than a theatre where the humour of an imbroglio is founded upon pathological mistakes, which from thread to needle brought Mme. Cottard to relate that a similar notion had been made use of by an amateur who is the prime favourite at her children's evening parties, the Scotchman Stevenson, a name which forced from Swann the peremptory affirmation: 'But Stevenson is a great writer, I can assure you, M. de Goncourt, a very great one, equal to the greatest.' And upon my marvelling at the escutcheoned panels of the ceiling in the room where we are smoking, panels which came from the ancient Palazzo Barberini, I express my regret at the progressive darkening of a certain vase through the ashes of our *londrès*, Swann having recounted that similar stains on the leaves of certain books attest their having belonged to Napoleon I, books owned, despite his anti-Bonapartist opinions by the Duc de Guermantes, owing to the fact that the Emperor chewed tobacco, Cottard, who reveals himself as a man of penetrating curiosity in all matters, declares that these stains do not come at all from that: 'Believe me, not at all,' he insists with authority, 'but from his habit of having always near at hand, even on the field of battle, some pastilles of Spanish liquorice to calm his liver pains. For he had a disease of the liver and it is of that he died,' concluded the doctor."

I stopped my reading there for I was leaving the following day, moreover, it was an hour when the other master claimed me, he under whose orders we are for half our time. We accomplish the task to which he obliges us with our eyes closed. Every morning he surrenders us to our other master knowing that otherwise we should be unable to yield ourselves to his service. It would be curious, when our spirit has reopened its eyes, to know what we could have been doing under that master who clouds the minds of his slaves before putting them to his immediate business. The most cunning, before their task is finished, try to peep out surreptitiously. But slumber speedily struggles to efface the traces of what they long to see. And, after all these centuries we know little about it. So I closed the Goncourt journal. Glamour of literature! I wanted to see the Cottards again, to ask them so many details about Elstir, I wanted to go and see if the "Petit Dunkerque" shop still existed, to ask permission to visit that mansion of the Verdurins where I had dined. But I experienced a vague apprehension. Certainly I did not disguise from myself that I had never known how to listen nor, when I was with others, to observe; to my eyes no old woman exhibited a pearl necklace and my ears heard nothing that was said about it. Nevertheless, I had known these people in my ordinary life, I had often dined with them; whether it was the Verdurins, or the Guermantes, or the Cottards, each had seemed to me as commonplace as did that Basin to my grandmother who little supposed he was the beloved nephew, the charming young hero, of Mme. de Beausergent. All had seemed to me insipid; I remembered the numberless vulgarities of which each one was composed....

"Et que tout cela fît un astre dans la nuit!"

I resolved to put aside provisionally the objections against literature which these pages of Goncourt had aroused in me. Apart from the peculiarly striking naïvete of the memoir-writer, I was able to reassure myself from different points of view. To begin with, in regard to myself, the inability to observe and to listen of which the journal I have quoted had so painfully reminded me was not complete. There was in me a personage who more or less knew how to observe but he was an intermittent personage who only came to life when some general essence common to many things which are its nourishment and its delight, manifested itself. Then the personage remarked and listened, but only at a certain depth and in such a manner that observation did not profit. Like a geometrician who in divesting things of their material qualities, only sees their linear substratum, what people said escaped me, for that which interested me was not what they wanted to say but the manner in which they said it in so far as it revealed their characters or their absurdities. Or rather that was an object which had always been my particular aim because I derived specific pleasure from identifying the denominator common to one person and another. It was only when I perceived it that my mind—until then dozing even behind the apparent activity of my conversation the animation of which masked to the outside world a complete mental torpor—started all at once joyously in chase, but that which it then pursued—for example the identity of the Verdurin's salon at diverse places and periods—was situated at half-depth, beyond actual appearance, in a zone somewhat withdrawn. Also the obvious transferable charm of people escaped me because I no longer retained the faculty of confining myself to it, like the surgeon who, beneath the lustre of a female abdomen, sees the internal disease which is consuming it. It was all very well for me to go out to dinner. I did not see the guests because when I thought I was observing them I was radiographing them. From that it resulted that in collating all the observations I had been able to make about the guests in the course of a dinner, the design of the lines traced by me would form a unity of psychological laws in which the interest pertaining to the discourse of a particular guest occupied no place whatever. But were my portraits denuded of all merit because I did not compose them merely as portraits? If in the domain of painting one portrait represents truths relative to volume, to light, to movement, does that necessarily make it inferior to another quite dissimilar portrait of the same person in which, a thousand details omitted in the first will be minutely related to each other, a second portrait from which it would be concluded that the model was beautiful while that of the first would be considered ugly, which might have a documentary and even historical importance but might not necessarily be an artistic truth. Again my frivolity the moment when I was with others, made me anxious to please and I desired more to amuse people with my chatter than to learn from listening unless I went out to interrogate someone upon a point of art or unless some jealous suspicion preoccupied me. But I was incapable of seeing a thing unless a desire to do so had been aroused in me by reading; unless it was a thing of which I wanted a previous sketch to confront later with reality. Even had that page of the Goncourts not enlightened me, I knew how often I had been unable to give my attention to things or to people, whom afterwards, once their image had been presented to me in solitude by an artist, I would have gone leagues and risked death to rediscover. Then my imagination started to work, had begun to paint. And the very thing I had yawned at the year before I desired when I again contemplated it and with anguish said to myself, "Can I never see it again? What would I not give for it?" When one reads articles about people, even about mere society people, qualifying them as "the last representatives of a society of which there is no other living witness", doubtless some may exclaim, "to think that he says so much about so insignificant a person and praises him as he does", but it is precisely such a man I should have deplored not having known if I had only read papers and reviews and if I had never seen the man himself and I was more inclined, in reading such passages in the papers, to think, "What a pity! And all I cared about then was getting hold of Gilberte and Albertine and I paid no attention to that gentleman whom I simply took for a society bore, for a pure façade, a marionnette." The pages of the Goncourt Journal that I had read made me regret that attitude. For perhaps I might have concluded from them that life teaches one to minimise the value of reading and shows us that what the writer exalts for us is not worth much; but I could equally well conclude the contrary, that reading enhances the value of life, a value we have not realised until books make us aware of how great that value is. Strictly, we can console ourselves for not having much enjoyed the society of a Vinteuil or of a Bergotte, because the awkward middleclassness of the one, the unbearable defects of the other prove nothing against them, since their genius is manifested by their works; and the same applies to the pretentious vulgarity of an Elstir in early days. Thus the journal of the Goncourts made me discover that Elstir was none other than the "M. Tiche" who had once inflicted upon Swann such exasperating lectures at the Verdurins. But what man of genius has not adopted the irritating conversational manner of artists of his own circle before acquiring (as Elstir did, though it happens rarely) superior taste. Are not the letters of Balzac, for instance, smeared with vulgar terms which Swann would rather have died than use? And yet, it is probable that Swann, so sensitive, so completely exempt from every dislikeable idiosyncrasy, would have been incapable of writing *Cousine Bette* and *Le Curé de Tours*. Therefore, whether or no memoirs are wrong to endow with charm a society which has displeased us, is a problem of small importance, since, even if the writer of these memoirs is mistaken, that proves nothing against the value of a society which produces such genius and which existed no less in the works of Vinteuil, of Elstir and of Bergotte.

Quite at the other extremity of experience, when I remarked that the very curious anecdotes which are the inexhaustible material of the journal of the Goncourts and a diversion for solitary evenings, had been related to him by those guests whom in reading his pages we should have envied him knowing, it was not so very difficult to explain why they had left no trace of interesting memory in my mind. In spite of the ingenuousness of Goncourt, who supposed that the interest of these anecdotes lay in the distinction of the man who told them, it can very well be that mediocre people might have experienced during their lives or heard tell of curious things which they related in their turn. Goncourt knew how to listen as he knew how to observe, and I do not. Moreover, it was necessary to judge all these happenings one by one. M. de Guermantes certainly had not given me the impression of that adorable model of juvenile grace whom my grandmother so much wanted to know and set before my eyes as inimitable according to the *Mémoires of Mme. de Beausergent*. One must remember that Basin was at that time seven years old, that the writer was his aunt and that even husbands who are going to divorce their wives a few months later are loud in praise of them. One of the most charming poems of Sainte-Beuve is consecrated to the apparition beside a fountain of a young child crowned with gifts and graces, the youthful Mlle. de Champlâtreux who was not more than ten years old. In spite of all the tender veneration felt by that poet of genius, the Comtesse de Noailles, for her mother-in-law the Duchesse de Noailles, born Champlâtreux, it is possible, if she were to paint her portrait, that it would contrast rather piquantly with the one Sainte-Beuve drew fifty years earlier.

What may perhaps be regarded as more disturbing, is something in between, personages in whose case what is said implies more than a memory which is able to retain a curious anecdote yet without one's having, as in the case of the Vinteuils, the Bergottes, the resource of judging them by their work; they have not created, they have only—to our great astonishment, for we found them so mediocre—inspired. Again it happens that the salon which, in public galleries, gives the greatest impression of elegance in great paintings of the Renaissance and onwards, is that of a little ridiculous bourgeoise whom after seeing the picture, I might, if I had not known her, have yearned to approach in the flesh, hoping to learn from her precious secrets that the painter's art did not reveal to me in his canvas, though her majestic velvet train and laces formed a passage of painting comparable to the most splendid of Titians. If only in bygone days I had understood that it is not the wittiest man, the best educated, the man with the best social relationships who becomes a Bergotte but he who knows how to become a mirror and is thereby enabled to reflect his own life, however commonplace, (though his contemporaries might consider him less gifted than Swann and less erudite than Bréauté) and one can say the same, with still more reason, of an artist's models. The awakening of love of beauty in the artist who can paint everything may be stimulated, the elegance in which he could find such beautiful motifs may be supplied, by people rather richer than himself—at whose houses he would find what he was not accustomed to in his studio of an unknown genius selling his canvases for fifty francs; for instance, a drawing-room upholstered in old silk, many lamps, beautiful flowers and fruit, handsome dresses—relatively modest folk, (or who would appear that to people of fashion who are not even aware of the others' existence) who for that very reason are more in a position to make the acquaintance of an obscure artist, to appreciate him, to invite him and buy his pictures, than aristocrats who get themselves painted like a Pope or a Prime Minister by academic painters. Would not the poetry of an elegant interior and of the beautiful dresses of our period be discovered by posterity in the drawing-room of the publisher Charpentier by Renoir rather than in the portrait of the Princesse de Sagan or of the Comtesse de La Rochefoucauld by Cotte or Chaplin? The artists who have given us the most resplendent visions of elegance have collected the elements at the homes of people who were rarely the leaders of fashion of their period; for the latter are seldom painted by the unknown depositary of a beauty they are unable to distinguish on his canvases, disguised as it is by the interposition of a vulgar burlesque of superannuated grace which floats before the public eye in the same way as the subjective visions which an invalid believes are actually before him. But that these mediocre models whom I had known could have inspired, advised certain arrangements which had enchanted me, that the presence of such an one of them in the picture was less that of a model, than of a friend whom a painter wishes to figure in his canvas, was like asking oneself whether we regret not having known all these personages because Balzac painted them in his books or dedicated his books to them as the homage of his admiration, to whom Sainte-Beuve or Baudelaire wrote their loveliest verses, still more if all the Récamiers, all the Pompadours would not have seemed to me insignificant people, whether owing to a temperamental defect which made me resent being ill and unable to return and see the people I had misjudged, or because they might only owe their prestige to the illusory magic of literature which forced me to change my standard of values and consoled me for being obliged from one day to the other, on account of the progress which my illness was making, to break with society, renounce travel and going to galleries and museums in order that I could be nursed in a sanatorium. Perhaps, however, this deceptive side, this artificial illumination, only exists in memoirs when they are too recent, too close to reputations, whether intellectual or fashionable, which will quickly vanish, (and if erudition then tries to react against this burial, will it succeed in dispelling one out of a thousand of these oblivions which keep on accumulating?)

These ideas tending some to diminish, others to increase my regret that I had no gift for literature, no longer occupied my mind during the long years I spent as an invalid in a sanatorium far from Paris and I had altogether renounced the project of writing until the sanatorium was unable to find a medical staff at the beginning of 1916. I then returned, as will be seen, to a very different Paris from the Paris where I returned in August, 1914, when I underwent medical examination, after which I went back to the sanatorium.

CHAPTER II

M. DE CHARLUS DURING THE WAR, HIS OPIN-IONS, HIS PLEASURES

ON one of the first evenings after my return to Paris in 1916, wanting to hear about the only thing that interested me, the war, I went out after dinner to see Mme. Verdurin, for she was, together with Mme. Bontemps, one of the queens of that Paris of the war which reminded one of the Directory. As the leavening by a small quantity of yeast appears to be a spontaneous germination, young women were running about all day wearing cylindrical turbans on their heads as though they were contemporaries of Mme. Tallien, As a proof of public spirit they wore straight Egyptian tunics, dark and very "warlike" above their short skirts, they were shod in sandals, recalling Talma's buskin or high leggings like those of our beloved combatants. It was, they said, because they did not forget it was their duty to rejoice the eyes of those combatants that they still adorned themselves not only with *flou* dresses but also with jewels evoking the armies by their decorative theme if indeed their material did not come from the armies and had not been worked by them. Instead of Egyptian ornaments recalling the campaign of Egypt, they wore rings or bracelets made out of fragments of shell or beltings of the "seventy-fives", cigarette-lighters consisting of two English half-pennies to which a soldier in his dug-out had succeeded in giving a patina so beautiful that the profile of Queen Victoria might have been traced on it by Pisanello. It was again, they said, because they never ceased thinking of their own people, that they hardly wore mourning when one of them fell, the pretext being that he was proud to die, which enabled them to wear a close bonnet of white English crêpe (graceful of effect and encouraging to aspirants) while the invincible certainty of final triumph enabled them to replace the earlier cashmire by satins and silk muslins and even to wear their pearls "while observing that tact and discretion of which it is unnecessary to remind French women."

The Louvre and all the museums were closed and when one read at the head of an article "Sensational Exhibition" one might be certain it was not an exhibition of pictures but of dresses destined to quicken "those delicate artistic delights of which Parisian women have been too long deprived." It was thus that elegance and pleasure had regained their hold; fashion, in default of art, sought to excuse itself, just as artists exhibiting at the revolutionary salon in 1793 proclaimed that it would be a mistake if it were regarded as "inappropriate by austere Republicans that we should be engaged in art when coalesced Europe is besieging the territory of liberty." The dressmakers acted in the same spirit in 1916 and asserted with the self-conscious conceit of the artist, that "to seek what was new, to avoid banality, to prepare for victory, by disengaging a new formula of beauty for the generations after the war, was their absorbing ambition, the chimera they were pursuing as would be discovered by those who came to visit their salons delightfully situated in such and such a street, where the exclusion of the mournful preoccupations of the moment with the restraint imposed by circumstances and the substitution of cheerfulness and brightness was the order of the day. The sorrows of the hour might, it is true, have got the better of feminine» energy if we had not such lofty examples of courage and endurance to meditate. So, thinking of our combatants in the trenches who dream of more comfort and coquetry for the dear one at home, let us unceasingly labour to introduce into the creation of dresses that novelty which responds to the needs of the moment. Fashion, it must be conceded, is especially associated with the English, consequently with allied firms and this year the really smart thing is the *robe-tonneau* the charming freedom of which gives to all our young women an amusing and distinguished *cachet*. 'It will indeed be one of the happiest consequences of this sad war' the delightful chronicler added (while awaiting the recapture of the lost provinces and the rekindling of national sentiment)'to have secured such charming results in the way of dress with so little material and to have created coquetry out of nothing without ill-timed luxury and bad style. At the present time dresses made at home are preferred to those made in several series by great dress-makers, because each one is evidence of the intelligence, taste and individuality of the maker.'" As to charity, when we remember all the unhappiness born of the invasion, of the many wounded and mutilated, obviously it should become "ever more ingenious" and compel the ladies in the high turbans to spend the afternoon taking tea at the bridge-table commenting on the news from the front while their automobiles await them at the door with a handsome soldier on the seat conversing with the *chasseur*. For that matter it was not only the high cylindrical hats which were new but also the faces they surmounted. The ladies in the new hats were young women come one hardly knew whence, who had become the flower of fashion, some during the last six months, others during the last two years, others again during the last four. These differences were as important for them as, when I made my first appearance in society, were those between two families like the Guermantes and the Rochefoucaulds with three or four centuries of ancient lineage. The lady who had known the Guermantes since 1914 considered another who had been introduced to them in 1916 a parvenue, gave her the nod of a dowager duchess while inspecting her through her *lorgnon*, and avowed with a significant gesture that no one in society knew whether the lady was even married. "All this is rather sickening," concluded the lady of 1914, who would have liked the cycle of the newly-admitted to end with herself. These newcomers whom young men considered decidedly elderly and whom certain old men who had not been exclusively in the best society, seemed to recognise as not being so new as all that, did something more than offer society the diversions of political conversation and music in suitable intimacy; it had to be they who supplied such diversions for, so that things should seem new, whether they are so or not, in art or in medicine as in society, new names are necessary (in certain respects they were very new indeed). Thus Mme. Verdurin went to Venice during the war and like those who want at any cost to avoid sorrow and sentiment, when she said it was "épatant", what she admired was not Venice nor St. Mark's nor the palaces, all that had given, me delight and which she cheapened, but the effect of the search-lights in the sky, searchlights about which she gave information supported by figures. (Thus from age to age a sort of realism is reborn out of reaction against the art which has been admired till then.)

The Sainte-Euverte salon was a back number and the presence there of the greatest artists or the most influential ministers attracted no one. On the other hand, people rushed to hear a word uttered by the Secretary of one Government, by the Under-Secretary of another, at the houses of the new ladies in turbans whose winged and chattering invasions filled Paris. The ladies of the first Directory had a queen who was young and beautiful called Mme. Tallien; those of the second had two who were old and ugly and who were called Mme. Verdurin and Mme. Bontemps. Who reproached Mme. Bontemps because her husband had been bitterly criticised by the *Echo de Paris* for the part he played in the Dreyfus affair? As the whole Chamber had at an earlier period become revisionist, it was necessarily among the old revisionists and the former socialists that the party of social order, of religious toleration and of military efficiency had to be recruited. M. Bontemps would have been detested in former days because the anti-patriots were then given the name of Dreyfusards, but that name had soon been forgotten and had been replaced by that of the adversary of the three-year law. M. Bontemps on the other hand, was one of the authors of that law, therefore he was a patriot. In society (and this social phenomenon is only the application of a much more general psychological law) whether novelties are reprehensible or not, they only excite consternation until they have been assimilated and defended by reassuring elements. As it had been with Dreyfusism, so it was with the marriage of Saint-Loup and Odette's daughter, a marriage people protested against at first. Now that people met everyone they knew at the Saint-Loups', Gilberte might have had the morals of Odette herself, people would have gone there just the same and would have agreed with Gilberte in condemning undigested moral novelties like a dowager-duchess. Dreyfusism was now integrated in a series of highly respectable and customary things. As to asking what it amounted to in itself, people now thought as little about accepting as formerly about condemning it. It no longer shocked anyone and that was all about it. People remembered it as little as they do whether the father of a young girl they know was once a thief or not. At most they might say: "The man you're talking about is the brother-in-law or somebody of the same name, there was never anything against this one." In the same way there had been different kinds of Dreyfusism and the man who went to the Duchesse de Montmorency's and got the Three-Year Law passed could not be a bad sort of man. In any case, let us be merciful to sinners. The oblivion allotted to Dreyfus was *a fortiori* extended to Dreyfusards. Besides, there was no one else in politics, since everyone had to be Dreyfusards at one time or another if they wanted to be in the Government, even those who represented the contrary of what Dreyfusism had incarnated when it was new and dreadful (at the time that Saint-Loup was considered to be going wrong) namely, anti-patriotism, irreligion, anarchy, etc. Thus M. Bontemps' Dreyfusism, invisible and contemplative like that of all politicians, was as little observable as the bones under his skin. No one remembered he had been Dreyfusard, for people of fashion are absentminded and forgetful and also because time had passed which they affected to believe longer than it was and it had become fashionable to say that the pre-war period was separated from the war-period by a gulf as deep, implying as much duration, as a geological period; and even Brichot the nationalist in; alluding to the Dreyfus affair spoke of "those pre-historic days". The truth is that the great change brought about by the war was in inverse ratio to the value of the minds it touched, at all events, up to a certain point; for, quite at the bottom, the utter fools, the voluptuaries, did not bother about whether there was a war or not; while quite at the top, those who create their own world, their own interior life, are little concerned with the importance of events. What profoundly modifies the course of their thought is rather something of no apparent importance which overthrows the order of time and makes them live in another period of their lives. The song of a bird in the Park of Montboissier, or a breeze laden with the scent of mignonette, are obviously matters of less importance than the great events of the Revolution and of the Empire; nevertheless they inspired in Chateaubriand's *Mémoires d'outre tombe* pages of infinitely greater value.

M. Bontemps did not want to hear peace spoken of until Germany had been divided up as it was during the Middle Ages, the doom of the house of Hohenzollern pronounced, and William II sentenced to be shot. In a word, he was what Brichot called a Diehard; this was the finest brevet of citizenship one could give him. Doubtless, for the three first days Mme. Bontemps had been somewhat bewildered to find herself among people who asked Mme. Verdurin to present her to them, and it was in a slightly acid tone that Mme. Verdurin replied: "the Comte, my dear," when Mme. Bontemps said to her, "Was that not the Duc d'Haussonville you just introduced to me?" whether through entire ignorance and failure to associate the name of Haussonville with any sort of tide, or whether, on the contrary, by excess of knowledge and the association of her ideas with the *Parti des Ducs* of which she had been told M. d'Haussonville was one of the Academic members. After the fourth day she began to be firmly established in the Faubourg Saint-Germain. Sometimes she could be observed among the fragments of an obscure society which as little surprised those who knew the egg from which Mme. Bontemps had been hatched as the debris of a shell around a chick. But after a fortnight, she shook them off and by the end of the first month, when she said, "I am going to the Lévi's," everyone knew, without her being more precise, that she was referring to the Lévis-Mirepoix and not a single duchesse who was there would have gone to bed without having first asked her or Mme. Verdurin, at least by telephone, what was in the evening's communiqué, how things were going with Greece, what offensive was being prepared, in a word, all that the public would only know the following day or later and of which, in this way, they had a sort of dress rehearsal. Mme. Verdurin, in conversation, when she communicated news, used "we" in speaking of France: "Now, you see, we exact of the King of Greece that he should retire from the Peloponnese, etc. We shall send him etc." And in all her discourses G.H.Q. occurred constantly ("I have telephoned to G.H.Q., etc.") an abbreviation in which she took as much pleasure as women did formerly who, not knowing the Prince of Agrigente, asked if it was "Gri-gri" people were speaking of, to show they were *au courant*, a pleasure known only to society in less troubled times but equally enjoyed by the masses at times of great crisis. Our butler, for instance, when the King of Greece was discussed, was able, thanks to the papers, to allude to him like William II, as "Tino", while until now his familiarity with kings had been more ordinary and invented by himself when he called the King of Spain "Fonfonse". One may further observe that the number of people Mme. Verdurin named "bores" diminished in direct ratio with the social importance of those who made advances to her. By a sort of magical transformation, every bore who came to pay her a visit and solicited an invitation, suddenly became agreeable and intelligent. In brief, at the end of a year the number of "bores" was reduced to such proportions that "the dread and unendurableness of being bored" which occurred so often in Mme. Verdurin's conversation and had played such an important part in her life, almost entirely disappeared. Of late, one would have said that this unendurableness of boredom (which she had formerly assured me she never felt in her first youth) caused her less pain, like headaches and nervous asthmas, which lose their strength as one grows older; and the fear of being bored would doubtless have entirely abandoned Mme. Verdurin owing to lack of bores, if she had not in some measure replaced them by other recruits amongst the old "faithfuls". Finally, to have done with the duchesses who now frequented Mme. Verdurin, they came there, though they were unaware of it, in search of exactly the same thing as during the Dreyfus period, a fashionable amusement so constituted that its enjoyment satisfied political curiosity and the need of commenting privately upon the incidents read in the newspapers. Mme. Verdurin would say, "Come in at five o'clock to talk about the war," as she would have formerly said "to talk about *l'affaire* and in the interval you shall hear Morel." Now Morel had no business to be there for he had not been in any way exempted. He had simply not joined up and was a deserter, but nobody knew it. Another star of the Salon, "Dans-les-choux", had, in spite of his sporting tastes, got himself exempted. He had become for me so exclusively the author of an admirable work about which I was constantly thinking, that it was only when, by chance, I established a transversal current between two series of souvenirs, that I realised it was he who had brought about Albertine's departure from my house. And again this transversal current ended, so far as those reminiscent relics of Albertine were concerned, in a channel which was dammed in full flow several years back. For I never thought any more about her. It was a channel unfrequented by memories, a line I no longer needed to follow. On the other hand the works of "Dans-les-choux" were recent and that line of souvenirs was constantly frequented and utilised by my mind.

I must add that acquaintance with the husband of Andrée was neither very easy nor very agreeable and that the friendship one offered him was doomed to many disappointments. Indeed he was even then very ill and spared himself fatigues other than those which seemed likely to give him pleasure. He only thus classified meeting people as yet unknown to him whom his vivid imagination represented as being potentially different from the rest. He knew his old friends too well, was aware of what could be expected of them and to him they were no longer worth a dangerous and perhaps fatal fatigue. He was in short a very bad friend. Perhaps, in his taste for new acquaintances, he regained some of the mad daring which he used to display in sport, gambling and the excesses of the table in the old days at Balbec. Each time I saw Mme. Verdurin, she wanted to introduce me to Andrée, apparently unable to admit that I had known her long before. As it happened, Andrée rarely came with her husband but she remained my excellent and sincere friend. Faithful to the aesthetic of her husband, who reacted against Russian ballets, she remarked of the Marquis de Polignac, "He has had his house decorated by Bakst. How can one sleep in it? I should prefer Dubufe."

Moreover the Verdurins, through that inevitable progress of aestheticism which ends in biting one's own tail, declared that they could not stand the modern style (besides, it came from Munich) nor white walls and they only liked old French furniture in a sombre setting.

It was very surprising at this period when Mme. Verdurin could have whom she pleased at her house, to see her making indirect advances to a person she had completely lost sight of, Odette, One thought the latter could add nothing to the brilliant circle which the little group had become. But a prolonged separation, in soothing rancour, sometimes revives friendship. And the phenomenon which makes the dying utter only names formerly familiar to them and causes old people's complaisance with childish memories, has its social equivalent. To succeed in the enterprise of bringing Odette back to her, it must be understood that Mme. Verdurin did not employ the "ultras" but the less faithful *habitués* who had kept a foot in each salon. To them she said, "I don't know why she doesn't come here any more. Perhaps she has quarrelled with me, I haven't quarrelled with her. What have I ever done to her? It was at my house she met both her husbands. If she wants to come back, let her know that my doors are open to her." These words, which might have cost the pride of *"the patronne"* a good deal if they had not been dictated by her imagination, were passed on but without success. Mme. Verdurin awaited Odette but the latter did not come until certain events which will be seen later brought her there for quite other reasons than those which could have been put forward by the embassy of the faithless, zealous as it was; few successes are easy, many checks are decisive.

Things were so much the same, although apparently different, that one came across the former expressions "right thinking" and "ill-thinking" quite naturally. And just as the former communards had been anti-revisionist, so the strongest Dreyfusards wanted everybody to be shot with the full support of the generals just as at the time of the Affaire they had been against Galliffet. Mme. Verdurin invited to such parties some rather recent ladies, known for their charitable works, who at first came strikingly dressed, with great pearl necklaces. Odette possessed one as fine as any and formerly had rather overdone exhibiting it but now she was in war dress, and imitating the ladies of the faubourg, she eyed them severely. But women know how to adapt themselves. After wearing them three or four times, these ladies observed that the dresses they considered *chic* were for that very reason proscribed by the people who were *chic* and they laid aside their golden gowns and resigned themselves to simplicity.

Mme. Verdurin said, "It is deplorable, I shall telephone to Bontemps to do what is necessary to-morrow. They have again 'censored' the whole end of Norpois' article simply because he let it be understood that they had '*limogé*' Percin." For all these women got glory out of using the shibboleth current at the moment and believed they were in the fashion, just as a middle-class woman, when M. de Bréauté or M. de Charlus was mentioned, exclaimed: "Who's that you're talking about? Babel de Bréauté, Mémé de Charlus?" For that matter, duchesses got the same pleasure out of saying "*limogé*", for like *roturiers un peu poètes* in that respect, it is the name that matters but they express themselves in accordance with their mental category in which there is a great deal that is middle-class. Those who have minds have no regard for birth.

All those telephonings of Mme. Verdurin were not without ill-effects. We had forgotten to say that the Verdurin salon though continuing in spirit, had been provisionally transferred to one of the largest hotels in Paris, the lack of coal and light having rendered the Verdurin receptions somewhat difficult in the former very damp abode of the Venetian ambassadors. Nevertheless, the new salon was by no means unpleasant. As in Venice the site selected for its water supply dictates the form the palace shall take, as a bit of garden in Paris delights one more than a park in the country, the narrow dining-room which Mme. Verdurin had at the hotel was a sort of lozenge with the radiant white of its screen-like walls against which every Wednesday, and indeed every day, the most various and interesting people and the smartest women in Paris stood out, happy to avail themselves of the luxury of the Verdurins, thanks to their fortune increasing at a time when the richest were restricting their expenditure owing to difficulty in getting their incomes. This somewhat modified style of reception enchanted Brichot who, as the social relations of the Verdurins developed, obtained additional satisfaction from their concentration in a small area, like surprises in a Christmas stocking. On certain days guests were so numerous that the dining-room of the private apartment was too small and dinner had to be served in the enormous dining-room of the hotel below where the "faithful", while hypocritically pretending to miss the intimacy of the upper floor, were in reality delighted (constituting a select group as formerly in the little railway) to be a spectacular object of envy to neighbouring tables. In peace-time a society paragraph, surreptitiously sent to the *Figaro* or the *Gaulois*, would doubtless have announced to a larger audience than the dining-room of the Majestic could hold that Brichot had dined with the Duchesse de Duras, but since the war, society reporters having discontinued that sort of news (they got home on funerals, investitures and Franco-American banquets), the only publicity attainable was that primitive and restricted one, worthy of the dark ages prior to the discovery of Gutenberg, of being seen at the table of Mme. Verdurin. After dinner, people went up to the Pattonne's suite and the telephoning began again. Many of the large hotels were at that time full of spies, who daily took note of the news telephoned by M. Bontemps with an indiscretion fortunately counterbalanced by the complete inaccuracy of his information which was always contradicted by the event.

Before the hour when afternoon-teas had finished, at the decline of day, one could see from afar in the still, clear sky, little brown spots which, in the twilight, one might have taken for gnats or birds. Just as, when we see a mountain far away which we might take for a cloud, we are impressed because we know it really to be solid, immense and resistant, so I was moved because the brown spots in the sky were neither gnats nor birds but aeroplanes piloted by men who were keeping watch over Paris. It was not the recollection of the aeroplanes I had seen with Albertine in our last walk near Versailles that affected me for the memory of that walk had become indifferent to me.

At dinner-time the restaurants were full and if, passing in the street, I saw a poor fellow home on leave, freed for six days from the constant risk of death, fix his eyes an instant upon the brilliantly illuminated windows, I suffered as at the hotel at Balbec when the fishermen looked at us while we dined. But I suffered more because I knew that the misery of a soldier is greater than that of the poor for it unites all the miseries and is still more moving because it is more resigned, more noble, and it was with a philosophical nod of his head, without resentment, that he who was ready to return to the trenches, observing the *embusqués* elbowing each other to reserve their tables, remarked: "One would not say there was a war going on here."

At half-past nine, before people had time to finish their dinner, the lights were suddenly put out on account—of police regulations and at nine-thirty-five there was a renewed hustling of *embusqués* seizing their overcoats from the hands of the *chasseurs* of the restaurant where I had dined with Saint-Loup one evening of his leave, in a mysterious interior twilight like that in which magic lantern slides are shown or films at one of those cinemas towards which men and women diners were now hurrying. But after that hour, for those who, like myself, on the evening of which I am speaking, had remained at home for dinner and went out later to see friends, certain quarters of Paris were darker than the Combray of my youth; visits were like those one made to neighbours in the country. Ah! if Albertine had lived, how sweet it would have been, on the evenings when I dined out, to make an appointment with her under the arcades. At first I should have seen nobody, I should have had the emotion of believing she would not come, when all at once I should have seen one of her dear grey dresses in relief against the black wall, her smiling eyes would have perceived me and we should have been able to walk arm-in-arm without anyone recognising or interfering with us and to have gone home together. Alas, I was alone and it was as though I were making a visit to a neighbour in the country, one of those calls such as Swann used to pay us after dinner, without meeting more passers-by in the obscurity of Tansonville as he walked down that little twisting path to the street of St. Esprit, than I encountered this evening in the alley between the Rue Clothilde and the Rue Bonaparte, now a sinuous, rustic path. And as sections of countryside played upon by rough weather are unspoiled by a change in their setting, on evenings swept by icy winds, I felt myself more vividly on the shore of an angry sea than when I was at that Balbec of which I so often dreamed. And there were other elements which had not before existed in Paris and made one feel as though one had arrived from the train for a holiday in the open country, such as the contrast of light and shade at one's feet on moonlit evenings. Moonlight produces effects unknown to towns even in full winter; its rays played on the snow of the Boulevard Haussman unswept by workmen as on an Alpine glacier. The outlines of the trees were sharply reflected against the golden-blue snow as delicately as in certain Japanese pictures or in some backgrounds by Raphael. They lengthened on the ground at the foot of the trees as in nature when the setting sun reflects the trees which rise at regular intervals in the fields. But by a refinement of exquisite delicacy, the meadow upon which these shadows of ethereal trees were cast, was a field of Paradise, not green but of a white so brilliant on account of the moon shedding its rays on the jade-coloured snow, that one would have said it was woven of petals from the blossoms of pear-trees. And in the squares the divinities of the public fountains holding a jet of ice in their hands seemed made of a two-fold substance and, as though the artist had married bronze to crystal to produce it. On such rare days all the houses were black; but in spring, braving the police regulation once in a while, a particular house, perhaps only one floor of a particular house, or even only one room on that floor, did not close its shutters and seemed suspended by itself on impalpable shadows like a luminous projection, like an apparition without consistency. And the woman one's raised eyes perceived, isolated in the golden penumbra of the night in which oneself seemed lost, in which she too seemed abandoned, was endowed with the veiled, mysterious charm of an Eastern vision. At length one passed on and no living thing interrupted the rhythm of monotonous and hygienic tramping in the darkness.

* * *

I was reflecting that it was a long time since I had seen any of the personages with whom this work has been concerned. In 1914, during the two months I passed in Paris, I had once perceived M. de Charlus and had met Bloch and Saint-Loup, the latter only twice. It was certainly on the second occasion that he seemed to be most himself, and to have overcome that unpleasant lack of sincerity I had noticed at Tansonville to which I referred earlier. On this occasion, I recognised all his lovable qualities of former days. The first time I had seen him was at the beginning of the week that followed the declaration of war and while Bloch displayed extremely chauvinistic sentiments, Saint-Loup alluded to his own failure to join up with an irony that rather shocked me. Saint-Loup was just back from Balbec. "All who don't go and fight," he exclaimed with forced gaiety, "whatever reason they give, simply don't want to be killed, it's nothing but funk." And with a more emphatic gesture than when he alluded to others, "And if I don't rejoin my regiment, it's for the same reason." Before that, I had noticed in different people that the affectation of laudable sentiments is not the only disguise of unworthy ones, that a more original way is to exhibit the latter so that, at least, one does not seem to be disguising them. In Saint-Loup this tendency was strengthened by his habit, when he had done something for which he might have been censured, of proclaiming it as though it had been done on purpose, a habit he must have acquired from some professor at the War School with whom he had lived on terms of intimacy and for whom he professed great admiration. So I interpreted this outbreak as the affirmation of sentiments he wanted to exhibit as having inspired his evasion of military service in the war now beginning. "Have you heard," he asked as he left me, "that my Aunt Oriane is about to sue for divorce? I know nothing about it myself. People have often said it before and I've heard it announced so often that I shall wait until the divorce is granted before I believe it. I may add that it isn't surprising; my uncle is a charming man socially and to his friends and relations and in one way he has more heart than my aunt. She's a saint, but she takes good care to make him feel it. But he's an awful husband; he has never ceased being unfaithful to his wife, insulting her, ill-treating her and depriving her of money into the bargain. It would be so natural if she left him that it's a reason for its being true and also for its not being true just because people keep on saying so. And after all, she has stood it for so long.... Of course, I know there are ever so many false reports which are denied and afterwards turn out to be true." That made me ask him whether, before he married Gilberte, there had ever been any question of his marrying Mlle. de Guermantes. He started at this and assured me it was not so, that it was only one of those society rumours born, no one knows how, which disappear as they come, the falsity of which does not make those who believe them more cautious, for no sooner does another rumour of an engagement, of a divorce or of a political nature arise than they give it immediate credence and pass it on. Forty-eight hours had not passed before certain facts proved that my interpretation of Robert's words was completely wrong when he said, "All those who are not at the front are in a funk." Saint-Loup had only said this to show off and appear psychologically original while he was uncertain whether his services would be accepted. But at that very moment he was moving heaven and earth to be accepted, showing less originality in the sense he had given to that word, but that he was more profoundly French, more in conformity with all that was best in the French of St. André-des-Champs, gentlemen, bourgeois, respectable servants of gentlemen, or those in revolt against gentlemen, two equally French divisions of the same family, a Françoise offshoot and a Sauton offshoot, from which two arrows flew once more to the same target which was the frontier. Bloch was delighted to hear this avowal of cowardice by a Nationalist (who, in truth, was not much of a Nationalist) and when Saint-Loup asked him if he was going to join up, he made a grimace like a high-priest and replied "shortsighted." But Bloch had completely changed his opinion about the war when he came to see me in despair some days later for, although he was shortsighted, he had been passed for service. I was taking him back to his house when we met Saint-Loup. The latter had an appointment with a former officer, M. de Cambremer, who was to present him to a colonel at the Ministry of War, he told me. "Cambremer is an old acquaintance of yours, you know Cancan as well as I do." I replied that, as a fact, I did know him and his wife too, but that I did not greatly appreciate them. Yet I was so accustomed, ever since I first made their acquaintance, to consider his wife an unusual person with a thorough knowledge of Schopenhauer who had access to an intellectual *milieu* closed to her vulgar husband, that I was at first surprised when Saint-Loup remarked: "His wife is an idiot, you can have her; but he's an excellent fellow, gifted and extremely agreeable," By the idiocy of the wife, no doubt Saint-Loup meant her mad longing to get into the best society which that society severely condemned and, by the qualities of the husband, those his niece implied when she called him the best of the family. Anyhow, he did not bother himself about duchesses but that sort of intelligence is as far removed from the kind that characterises thinkers as is the intelligence the public respects because it has enabled a rich man "to make his pile." But the words of Saint-Loup did not displease me since they recalled that pretentiousness is closely allied to stupidity and that simplicity has a subtle but agreeable flavour. It is true I had no occasion to savour that of M. de Cambremer. But that is exactly why one being is so many different beings apart from differences of opinion. I had only known the shell of M. de Cambremer and his charm, attested by others, was unknown to me. Bloch left us in front of his door, overflowing with bitterness against Saint-Loup, telling him that those "beautiful red tabs" parading about at Staff Headquarters run no risk and that he, an ordinary second class private had no wish to "get a bullet through his skin for the sake of William." "It seems that the Emperor William is seriously ill," Saint-Loup answered. Bloch, like all those people who have something to do with the Stock Exchange, received any sensational news with peculiar credulity added, "it is said even that he is dead." On the Stock Exchange every, sovereign who is ill, whether Edward VII or William II, is dead; every city on the point of being besieged, is taken. "It is only kept secret," Bloch went on, "so that German public opinion should not be depressed. But he died last night. My father has it from 'the best sources'." "The best sources" were the only ones of which M. Bloch senior took notice, when, through the luck of possessing certain "influential connections" he received the as yet secret news that the Exterior Debt was going to rise or de Beers fall. Moreover, if at that very moment there was a rise in de Beers or there were offers of Exterior Debt, if the market of the first was "firm and active" and that of the second "hesitating and weak", "the best sources" remained nevertheless "the best sources." Bloch too announced the death of the Kaiser with a mysteriously important air, but also with rage. He was particularly exasperated to hear Robert say the "Emperor William." I believe under the knife of the guillotine Saint-Loup and M. de Guermantes would not have spoken of him otherwise. Two men in society who were the only living souls on a desert island where they would not have to give proof of good breeding to anyone, would recognise each other by those marks of breeding just as two Latinists would recognise each other's qualifications through correct quotations from Virgil. Saint-Loup would never, even under torture, have said other than "Emperor William"; yet the *savoir vivre* is all the same a bondage for the mind. He who cannot reject it remains a mere man of society. Yet elegant mediocrity is charming—especially for the generosity and unexpressed heroism that go with it—in comparison with the vulgarity of Bloch, at once braggart and mountebank, who shouted at Saint-Loup: "Can't you say simply 'William'? That's it, you're in a funk, even here you're ready to crawl on your stomach to him. Pshaw! they'll make nice soldiers at the front, they'll lick the boots of the Boches. You red-tabs are fit to parade in a circus, that's all."

"That poor Bloch will have it that I can do nothing but parade," Saint-Loup remarked with a smile when we left our friend. And I felt that parading was not at all what Robert was after, though I did not then realise his intention as I did later when the cavalry being out of action, he applied to serve as an infantry officer, then as a *Chasseur à pied* and finally when the sequel came which will be read later. But Bloch had no idea of Robert's patriotism simply because the latter did not express it. Though Bloch made professions of nefarious anti-militarism once he had been passed for service, he had declared the most chauvinistic opinions when he believed he would be exempted for shortsightedness. Saint-Loup would have been incapable of making such declarations, because of a certain moral delicacy which prevents one from expressing the depth of sentiments which are natural to us. My mother would not have hesitated a second to sacrifice her life for my grandmother's and would have suffered intensely from being unable to do so. Nevertheless I cannot imagine retrospectively a phrase on her lips such as "I would give my life for my mother." Robert was equally silent about his love for France and in that he seemed to me much more Saint-Loup (as I imagined his father to have been) than Guermantes. He would also have been incapable of such expressions owing to his mind having a certain moral bias. Men who do their work intelligently and earnestly have an aversion to those who want to make literature out of what they do, to make it important. Saint-Loup and I had not been either at the Lycée or at the Sorbonne together, but each of us had separately attended certain lectures by the same masters and I remember his smile when he alluded to those who, because, undeniably, their lectures were exceptional tried to make themselves out men of genius by giving ambitious names to their theories. Little as we spoke of it, Robert laughed heartily. Our natural predilection was not for the Cottards or Brichots, though we had a certain respect for those who had a thorough knowledge of Greek or medicine and did not for that reason consider they need play the charlatan. Just as all my mother's actions were based upon the feeling that she would have given her life for her mother, as she had never formulated this sentiment which in any case she would have considered not only useless and ridiculous but indecent and shameful to express to others, so it was impossible to imagine Saint-Loup (speaking to me of his equipment, of the different things he had to attend to, of our chances of victory, of the little value of the Russian army, of what England would do) enunciating one of those eloquent periods to which even the most sympathetic minister is inclined to give vent when he addresses deputies and enthusiasts. I cannot, however, deny, on this negative side which prevented his expressing the beautiful sentiments he felt that there was a certain effect of the "Guermantes spirit" of which so many examples were afforded by Swann. For if I found him a Saint-Loup more than anything else, he remained a Guermantes as well and owing to that, among the many motives which excited his courage there were some dissimilar to those of his Doncières friends, those young men with a passion for their profession with whom I had dined every evening and of whom so many were killed leading their men at the Battle of the Marne or elsewhere. Such young socialists as might have been at Doncières when I was there, whom I did not know because they were not in Saint-Loup's set, were able to satisfy themselves that the officers in that set were in no way "aristos" in the arrogantly proud and basely pleasure-loving sense which the "populo" officers from the ranks, and the Freemasons, gave to the word. And equally, the aristocratic officer discovered the same patriotism amongst those Socialists whom when I was at Doncières in the midst of the Affair Dreyfus, I heard them accuse of being anti-patriotic. The deep and sincere patriotism of soldiers had taken a definite form which they believed intangible and which it enraged them to see aspersed, whereas the Radical-Socialists who were, in a sense, unconscious patriots, independents, without a defined religion of patriotism, did not realise what a profound reality underlay what they believed to be vain and hateful formulas. Without doubt, Saint-Loup, like them, had grown accustomed to developing as the truest part of himself, the exploration and the conception of better schemes in view of greater strategic and tactical success, so that for him as for them the life of the body was of relatively small importance and could be lightly sacrificed to that inner life, the vital kernel around which personal existence had only the value of a protective epidermis. I told Saint-Loup about his friend, the director of the Balbec Grand Hotel, who, it appeared had, at the outbreak of war, alleged that there had been disaffection in certain French regiments which he called "defectuosity" and had accused what he termed "Prussian militarists" of provoking it, remarking with a laugh, "My brother's in the trenches. They're only thirty meters from the Boches" until it was discovered that he was a Boche himself and they put him in a concentration camp. "Apropos of Balbec, do you remember the former lift-boy of the hotel?" Saint-Loup asked me in the tone of one who seems not to know much about the person concerned and was counting upon me for enlightenment. "He's joining up and wrote me to get him entered in the aviation corps." Doubtless the lift-boy was tired of going up and down in the closed cage of the lift and the heights of the staircase of the Grand Hotel no longer sufficed for him. He was going to "get his stripes" otherwise than as a concierge, for our destiny is not always what we had believed. "I shall certainly support his application," Saint-Loup said, "I told Gilberte again this morning, we shall never have enough aeroplanes. It is through them we shall observe what the enemy is up to; they will deprive him of the chief advantage in an attack, surprise; the best army will perhaps be the one that has the best eyes. Has poor Françoise succeeded in getting her nephew exempted?" Françoise who had for a long while done everything in her power to get her nephew exempted, on a recommendation through the Guermantes to General de St. Joseph being proposed to her, had replied despairingly: "Oh! That would be no use there's nothing to be done with that old fellow, he's the worst sort of all, he's patriotic!" From the beginning of the war, Françoise whatever sorrow it had brought her, was of opinion that the "poor Russians" must not be abandoned since we were "allianced". The butler, persuaded that the war would not last more than ten days and would end by the signal victory of France, would not have dared, for fear of being contradicted by events, to predict a long and indecisive one, nor would he have had enough imagination. But, out of this complete and immediate victory he tried to extract beforehand whatever might cause anxiety to Françoise. "It may turn out pretty rotten; it appears there are many who don't want to go to the front, boys of sixteen are crying about it." He also tried to provoke her by saying all sorts of disagreeable things, what he called "pulling her leg" by "pitching an apostrophe at her" or "flinging her a pun." "Sixteen years old! Sainted Mary!" exclaimed Françoise, and then, with momentary suspicion, "But they said they only took them after they were twenty, they're only children at sixteen." "Naturally, the papers are ordered to say that. For that matter, the whole youth of the country will be at the front and not many will come back. In one way that will be a good thing, a good bleeding is useful from time to time, it makes business better. Yes, indeed, if some of these boys are a bit soft and chicken-hearted and hesitate, they shoot them immediately, a dozen bullets through the skin and that's that. In a way it's got to be done and what does it matter to the officers? They get their *pesetas* all the same and that's all they care about." Françoise got so pale during these conversations that one might well fear the butler would cause her death from heart disease. But she did not on that account lose her defects. When a girl came to see me, however much the old servant's legs hurt her, if ever I went out of my room for a moment I saw her on the top of the steps, in the hanging cupboard, in the act, she pretended, of looking for one of my coats to see if the moths had got into it, in reality to spy upon us. In spite of all my remonstrances, she kept up her insidious manner of asking indirect questions and for some time had been making use of the phrase "because doubtless." Not daring to ask me, "Has that lady a house of her own?" she would say with her eyes lifted timidly like those of a gentle dog, "Because doubtless that lady has a house of her own," avoiding the flagrant interrogation in order to be polite and not to seem inquisitive. And further, since those servants we most care for—especially if they can no longer render us much service or even do their work—remain, alas, servants and mark more clearly the limits (which we should like to efface) of their caste in proportion to the extent to which they believe they are penetrating ours, Françoise often gave vent to strange comments about my person (in order to tease me, the butler would have said) which people in our own world would not make. For instance, with a delight as dissimulated but also as deep as if it had been a case of serious illness, if I happened to be hot and the perspiration (to which I paid no attention) was trickling down my forehead, she would say, "My word! You're drenched" as though she were astonished by a strange phenomenon, smiling with that contempt for something indecorous with which she might have remarked, "Why, you're going out without your collar!" while adopting a concerned tone intended to cause one discomfort. One would have thought I was the only person in the universe who had ever been "drenched". For, in her humility, in her tender admiration for beings infinitely inferior to her, she adopted their ugly forms of expression. Her daughter complained of her to me, "She's always got something to say, that I don't close the doors properly and *patatipatali et patat-apatala*." Françoise doubtless thought it was only her insufficient education that had deprived her until now of this beautiful expression. And on her lips, on which formerly flowered the purest French, I heard several times a day, "*Et patati patall patata patala*." As to that it is curious how little variation there is not only in the expressions but in the thoughts of the same individual. The butler, being accustomed to declare that M. Poincaré had evil motives, not of a venal kind but because he had absolutely willed the war, repeated this seven or eight times a day before the same ever interested audience, without modifying a single word or gesture or intonation. Although it only lasted about two minutes, it was invariable like a performance. His mistakes in French corrupted the language of Françoise quite as much as the mistakes of her daughter.

She hardly slept, she hardly ate, she had the communiqués read to her, though she did not understand them, by the butler who understood them little better and in whom the desire to torment Françoise was often dominated by a superficial sort of patriotism; he remarked with a sympathetic chuckle when speaking of the

Germans, "That will stir them up a bit, our old Joffre is planning a comet to fall on them." Françoise did not understand what comet he was talking about but felt none the less that this phrase was one of those charming and original extravagances to which a well-bred person must reply, so with good humour and urbanity, shrugging her shoulders with the air of saying "He's always the same," she tempered her tears with a smile. At all events she was happy that her new butcher boy who in spite of his calling was somewhat timorous, (although he had begun in the slaughter-house) was too young to join up; otherwise, she would have been capable of going to the Minister of War about him. The butler could not believe the communiqués were other than excellent and that the troops were not approaching Berlin, as he had read, "We have repulsed the enemy with heavy losses on their side," actions that he celebrated as though they were new victories. For my part, I was horrified by the rapidity with which the theatre of these victories approached Paris and I was astonished that even the butler, who had seen in a communiqué that an action had taken place close to Lens, had not been alarmed by reading in the next day's paper that the result of this action had turned to our advantage at Jouy-le-Vicomte to which we firmly held the approaches. The butler very well knew the name of Jouy-le-Vicomte which was not far from Combray. But one reads the papers as one wants to with a bandage over one's eyes without trying to understand the facts, listening to the soothing words of the editor as to the words of one's mistress. We are beaten and happy because we believe ourselves unbeaten and victorious.

I did not stay long in Paris and returned fairly soon to my sanatorium. Though in principle the doctor treated his patients by isolation, I had received on two different occasions letters from Gilberte and from Robert. Gilberte wrote me (about September, 1914) that much as she would have liked to remain in Paris in order to get news from Robert more easily, the perpetual "taube" raids over Paris had given her such a fright, especially on her little girl's account, that she had fled from Paris by the last train which left for Combray, that the train did not even reach Combray and it was only thanks to a peasant's cart upon which she had made a ten hours journey in atrocious discomfort that she had at last been able to get to Tansonville. "And what do you think awaited your old friend there?" Gilberte closed her letter by saying. "I had left Paris to get away from the German aeroplanes, imagining that at Tansonville I should be sheltered from everything. I had not been there two days when what do you think happened! The Germans were invading the region after beating our troops near La Fère and a German staff, followed by a regiment, presented themselves at the gate of Tansonville and I was obliged to take them in without a chance of escaping, not a train, nothing." Had the German staff behaved well or was one supposed to read into the letter of Gilberte the contagious effect of the spirit of the Guermantes who were of Bavarian stock and related to the highest aristocracy in Germany, for Gilberte was inexhaustible about the perfect behaviour of the staff and of the soldiers who had only asked "permission to pick one of the forget-me-nots which grew at the side of the lake," good behaviour she contrasted with the unbridled violence of the French fugitives who had traversed the estate and sacked everything before the arrival of the German generals. Anyhow, if Gilberte's letter was, in certain respects, impregnated with the "Guermantes spirit,"—others would say it was her Jewish interna-tionalism, which would probably not be true, as we shall see—the letter I received some months later from Robert was much more Saint-Loup than Guermantes for it reflected all the liberal culture he had acquired and was altogether sympathetic. Unhappily he told me nothing about the strategy as he used to in our conversa-tions at Doncières and did not mention to what extent he considered the war had confirmed or disproved the principles which he then exposed to me. The most he told me was that since 1914, several wars had succeeded each other, the lessons of each influencing the conduct of the following one. For instance, the theory of the "break through" had been completed by the thesis that before the "break through" it was necessary to overwhelm the ground occupied by the enemy with artillery. Later it was discovered, on the contrary, that this destruction made the advance of infantry and artillery impossible over ground so pitted with thousands of shell-holes that they became so many obstacles. "War," he said, "does not escape the laws of our old Hegel. It is a state of perpetual becoming." This was little enough of all I wanted to know. But what disappointed me more was that he had no right to give me the names of the generals. And indeed, from what little I could glean from the papers, it was not those of whom I was so much concerned to know the value in war, who were conducting this one. Geslin de Bourgogne, Galliffet, Négri-er were dead, Pau had retired from active service almost at the beginning of the war. We had never talked about Joffre or Foch or Castlenau or Pétain. "My dear boy," Robert wrote, "if you saw what these soldiers are like, especially those of the people, the working class, small shopkeepers who little knew the heroism of which they were capable and would have died in their beds without ever being suspect-ed of it, facing the bullets to succour a comrade, to carry off a wounded officer and, themselves struck, smile at the moment they are going to die because the staff surgeon tells them that the trench had been re-captured from the Germans; I can assure you, my dear boy, that it gives one a wonderful idea of what a Frenchman is and makes us understand the historic epochs which seemed rather extraordi-nary to us when we were at school. The epic is so splendid that, like myself, you would find words useless to describe it. In contact with such grandeur the word "poilu" has become for me something which I can no more regard as implying an allusion or a joke than when we read the word "chouans". I feel that the word "poilu" is awaiting great poets like such words as "Deluge" or "Christ" or "Bar-barians" which were saturated with grandeur before Hugo, Vigny and the rest used them. To my mind, the sons of the people are the best of all but everyone is fine. Poor Vaugoubert, the son of the Ambassador, was wounded seven times be-fore being killed and each time he came back from an expedition without being "scooped," he seemed to be excusing himself and saying that it was not his fault. He was a charming creature. We had seen a great deal of each other and his poor parents obtained permission to come to his funeral on condition that they didn't wear mourning nor stop more than five minutes on account of the bombardment. The mother, a great horse of a woman, whom you perhaps know, may have been very unhappy but one would not have thought so. But the father was in such a state, I assure you, that I, who have become almost insensible through getting ac-customed to seeing the head of a comrade I was talking to shattered by a bomb or severed from his trunk, could hardly bear it when I saw the collapse of poor Vaugoubert who was reduced to a rag. It was all very well for the general to tell him it was for France that his son died a hero's death, that only redoubled the sobs of the poor man who could not tear himself away from his son's body. Well, that is why we can say, 'they will not get through.' Such men as these, my poor valet or Vaugoubert, have prevented the Germans from getting through. Perhaps you have thought we do not advance much, but that is not the way to reason; an army feels itself victorious by intuition as a dying man knows he is done for. And we know that we are going to be the victors and we will it so that we may dictate a just peace, not only for ourselves, but a really just peace, just for the French and just for the Germans". As heroes of mediocre and banal mind, writing poems during their convalescence, placed themselves, in order to describe the war, not on the level of the events which in themselves are nothing, but on the level of the banal aesthetic of which they had until then followed the rules, speaking as they might have done ten years earlier of the "bloody dawn," of the "shuddering flight of victory," Saint-Loup, himself much more intelligent and artistic, remained intelligent and artistic and for my benefit noted with taste the landscapes while he was immobilised at the edge of a swampy forest, just as though he had been shooting duck. To make me grasp contrasts of shade and light which had been "the enchantment of the morning," he referred to certain pictures we both of us loved and alluded to a page of Romain Rolland or of Nietzsche with the independence of those at the front who unlike those at the rear, were not afraid to utter a German name, and with much the same coquetry that caused Colonel du Paty de Clam to declaim in the witnesses' room during the Zola affair as he passed by Pierre Quillard, a Dreyfusard poet of the extremest violence whom he did not know, verses from the latter's symbolic drama "La Fille aux Mains coupées," Saint-Loup, when he spoke to me of a melody of Schumann gave it its German title and made no circumlocution to tell me, when he had heard the first warble at the edge of a forest, that he had been intoxicated as though the bird of that "sublime Siegfried" which he hoped to hear again after the war, had sung to him. And now on my second return to Paris I had received on the day following my arrival another letter from Gilberte who without doubt had forgotten the one she had previously written me, to which I have alluded above, for her departure from Paris at the end of 1914 was represented retrospectively in quite different fashion. "Perhaps you do not realise, my dear friend," she wrote me, "that I have now been at Tansonville two years. I arrived there at the same time as the Germans. Everybody wanted to prevent me going, I was treated as though I were mad. 'What,' they said to me, 'you are safe in Paris and you want to leave for those invaded regions just as everybody else is trying to get away from them?' I recognised the justice of this reasoning but what was to be done? I have only one quality, I am not a coward or, if you prefer, I am faithful, and when I knew that my dear Tansonville was menaced I did not want to leave our old steward there to defend it alone; it seemed to me that my place was by his side. And it is, in fact, thanks to that resolution that I was able to save the Château almost completely—when all the others in the neighbourhood, abandoned by their terrified proprietors, were destroyed from roof to cellar—and not only was I able to save the Château but also the precious collections which my dear father so much loved."

In a word, Gilberte was now persuaded that she had not gone to Tansonville, as she wrote me in 1914, to fly from the Germans and to be in safety, but, on the contrary, in order to meet them and to defend her Château from them. As a matter of fact, they (the Germans) had not remained at Tansonville, but she did not cease to have at her house a constant coming and going of officers which much exceeded that which reduced Françoise to tears in the streets of Combray and to live, as she said this time with complete truth, the life of the front. Also she was referred to eulogistically in the papers because of her admirable conduct and there was a proposal to give her a decoration. The end of her letter was perfectly accurate: "You have no idea of what this war is, my dear friend, the importance of a road, a bridge or a height. How many times, during these days in this ravaged countryside, have I thought of you, of our walks you made so delightful, while tremendous fights were going on for the capture of a hillock you loved and where so often we had been together. Probably you, like myself, are unable to imagine that obscure Roussainville and tiresome Méséglise, whence our letters were brought and where one went to fetch the doctor when you were ill, are now celebrated places. Well, my dear friend, they have for ever entered into glory in the same way as Austerlitz or Valmy. The Battle of Méséglise lasted more than eight months, the Germans lost more than one hundred thousand men there, they destroyed Méséglise but they have not taken it. The little road you so loved, the one we called the stiff hawthorn climb, where you professed to be in love with me when you were a child, when all the time I was in love with you, I cannot tell you how important that position is. The great wheatfield in which it ended is the famous 'slope 307' the name you have so often seen recorded in the communiqués. The French blew up the little bridge over the Vivonne which, you remember, did not bring back your childhood to you as much as you would have liked. The Germans threw others across; during a year and a half, they held one half of Combray and the French the other." The day following that on which I received this letter, that is to say the evening before the one when, walking in the darkness, I heard the sound of my foot-steps while reflecting on all these memories, Saint-Loup, back from the front and on the point of returning there, had paid me a visit of a few minutes only, the mere announcement of which had greatly stirred me. Françoise at first was going to throw herself upon him, hoping she would be able to get the butcher boy exempted; his class was going to the front in a year's time. But she restrained herself, realising the uselessness of the effort, since, for some time the timid animal-killer had changed his butcher-shop and, whether the owner of ours feared she would lose our custom, or whether it was simply in good faith, she declared to Françoise that she did not know where this boy "who for that matter would never make a good butcher" was employed. Françoise had looked everywhere for him, but Paris is big, there are a large number of butchers' shops and however many she went into she never was able to find the timid and blood-stained young man.

When Saint-Loup entered my room I had approached him with that diffidence, with that sense of the supernatural one felt about those on leave as we feel in approaching a person attacked by a mortal disease, who nevertheless gets up, dresses himself and walks about. It seemed that there was something almost cruel in these leaves granted to combatants, at the beginning especially, for, those who had not like myself lived far from Paris, had acquired the habit which removes from things frequently experienced the root-deep impression which gives them their real significance. The first time one said to oneself, "They will never go back, they will desert"—and indeed they did not come from places which seemed to us unreal merely because it was only through the papers we had heard of them and where we could not realise they had been taking part in Titanic combats and had come back with only a bruise on the shoulder—they came back to us for a moment from the shores of death itself and would return there, incomprehensible to us, filling us with tenderness, horror and a sentiment of mystery like the dead who appear to us for a second and whom, if we dare to question them, at most reply, "You cannot imagine." For it is extraordinary, in those who have been resurrected from the front, for, among the living that is what men on leave are, or in the case of the dead whom a hypnotised medium evokes, that the only effect of this contact with the mystery is to increase, were that possible, the insignificance of our intercourse with them. Thus, approaching Robert who had a scar on his forehead more august and mysterious to me than a footprint left upon the earth by a giant, I did not dare ask him a question and he only said a few simple words. And those words were little different from what they would have been before the war, as though people, in spite of the war, continued to be what they were; the tone of intercourse remains the same, the matter differs and even then—? I gathered that Robert had found resources at the front which had made him little by little forget that Morel had behaved as badly to him as to his uncle. Nevertheless he had preserved a great friendship for him and now and then had a sudden longing to see him again which he kept on postponing. I thought it more considerate towards Gilberte not to inform Robert, if he wanted to find Morel, he had only to go to Mme. Verdurin's. On my remarking to Robert with a sense of humility how little one felt the war in Paris, he said that even there it was sometimes "rather extraordinary". He was alluding to a raid of zeppelins there had been the evening before and asked me if I had had a good view of it in the same way as he would formerly have referred to a piece of great aesthetic beauty at the theatre. One can imagine that at the front there is a sort of coquetry in saying, "It's marvellous! What a pink—and that pale green!" when at that instant one can be killed, but it was not that which moved Saint-Loup about an insignificant raid on Paris. When I spoke to him about the beauty of the aeroplanes rising in the night, he replied, "And perhaps the descending ones are still more beautiful. Of course they are marvellous when they soar upwards, when they're about to form *constellation* thus obeying laws as precise as those which govern astral constellations, for what is a spectacle to you is the assemblage of squadrons, orders being given to them, their despatch on scout duty, etc. But don't you prefer the moment when, mingling with the stars, they detach themselves from them to start on a chase or to return after the maroon sounds, when they 'loop the loop', even the stars seem to change their position. And aren't the sirens rather Wagnerian, as they should be, to salute the arrival of the Germans, very like the national hymn, very 'Wacht am Rhein' with the Crown Prince and the Princesses in the Imperial box; one wonders whether aviators or Walkyries are up there." He seemed to get pleasure out of comparing aviators with Walkyries, and explained them on entirely musical principles.

"*Dame*! the music of sirens is like the prancing of horses; we shall have to await the arrival of the Germans to hear Wagner in Paris." From certain points of view the comparison was not false. The city seemed a formless and black mass which all of a sudden passed from the depth of night into a blaze of light, and in the sky, where one after another, the aviators rose amidst the shrieking wail of the sirens while, with a slower movement, more insidious and therefore more alarming, for it made one think they were seeking ah object still invisible but perhaps close to us, the searchlights swept unceasingly, scenting the enemy, encircling him with their beams until the instant when the pointed planes flashed like arrows in his wake. And in squadron after squadron the aviators darted from the city into the sky like Walkyries. Yet close to the ground, at the base of the houses, some spots were in high light and I told Saint-Loup, if he had been at home the evening before, he would have been able, while he contemplated the apocalypse in the sky, to see on the earth, as in the burial of the Comte d'Orgaz by Greco, where those contrasting planes are parallel, a regular vaudeville played by personages in night-gowns, whose Well-known names ought to have been sent to some successor of that Ferrari whose fashionable notes it had so often amused him and myself to parody. And we should have done so again that day as though there had been no war, although about a very "war-subject", the dread of zeppelins realised, the Duchesse de Guermantes superb in her night-dress, the Duc de Guermantes indescribable in his pink pyjamas and bath-gown, etc., etc. "I am sure," he said, "that in all the large hotels one might have seen American Jewesses in their chemises hugging to their bursting breasts pearl necklaces which would buy them a 'busted' duke. On such nights, the Hotel Ritz must resemble an exchange and mart emporium."

I asked Saint-Loup if this war had confirmed our conclusions at Doncières about war in the past. I reminded him of the proposition which he had forgotten, for instance about the parodies of former battles by generals of the future. "The feint," I said to him, "is no longer possible in these operations where the advance is prepared with such accumulation of artillery and what you have since told me about reconnaissance by aeroplane which obviously you could not have foreseen, prevents the employment of Napoleonic ruses." "How mistaken you are," he answered, "obviously this war is new in relation to former wars for it is itself composed of successive wars of which the last is an innovation on the preceding one. It is necessary to adapt oneself to the enemy's latest formula so as to defend oneself against him; then he starts a fresh innovation and yet, as in other human things, the old tricks always come off. No later than yesterday evening the most intelligent of our military critics wrote: 'When the Germans wanted to deliver East Prussia they began the operation by a powerful demonstration in the south against Warsaw, sacrificing ten thousand men to deceive the enemy. When at the beginning of 1915 they created the mass manœuvre of the Arch-Duke Eugène in order to disengage threatened Hungary, they spread the report that this mass was destined for an operation against Serbia. Thus, in 1800 the army which was about to operate against Italy was definitely indicated as a reserve army which was not to cross the Alps but to support the armies engaged in the northern theatres of war. The ruse of Hindenburg attacking Warsaw to mask the real attack on the Mazurian Lakes, imitates the strategy of Napoleon in 1812.' You see that M. Bidou repeats almost the exact words of which you remind me and which I had forgotten. And as the war is not yet finished, these ruses will be repeated again and again and will succeed because they are never completely exposed and what has done the trick once will do it again because it was a good trick." And in fact, for a long time after that conversation with Saint-Loup, while the eyes of the Allies were fixed upon Petrograd against which capital it was believed the Germans were marching, they were preparing a most powerful offensive against Italy. Saint-Loup gave me many other examples of military parodies or, if one believes that there is not a military art but a military science, of the application of permanent laws. "I will not say, there would be contradiction in the words," added Saint-Loup, "that the art of war is a science. And if there is a science of war there is diversity, dispute and contradiction between its professors, diversity partly projected into the category of Time. That is rather reassuring, for, as far as it goes, it indicates that truth rather than error is evolving." Later he said to me, "See in this war the ideas on the possibility of the break-through, for instance. First it is believed in, then we come back to the doctrine of invulnerability of the fronts, then again to the possible but risky break-through, to the necessity of not making a step forward until the objective has been first destroyed (the dogmatic journalist will write that to assert the contrary is the greatest foolishness), then, on the contrary, to that of advancing with a very light preparation by artillery, then to the invulnerability of the fronts as a principle in force since the war of 1870, from that the assertion that it is a false principle for this war and therefore only a relative truth. False in this war because of the accumulation of masses and of the perfecting of engines (see Bidou of the 2nd July, 1918), an accumulation which at first made one believe that the next war would be very short, then very long, and finally made one again believe in the possibility of decisive victories. Bidou cites the Allies on the Somme, the Germans marching on Paris in 1918. In the same way, at each victory of the Germans, it is said:'the ground gained is nothing, the towns are nothing, what is necessary is to destroy the military force of the adversary.' Then the Germans in their turn adopt this theory in 1918 and Bidou curiously explains (and July, 1918) that the capture of certain vital points, certain essential areas, decides the victory. It is moreover a particular turn of his mind. He has shown how, if Russia were blockaded at sea, she would be defeated and that an army enclosed in a sort of vast prison camp is doomed to perish."

Nevertheless, if the war did not modify the character of Saint-Loup, his intelligence, developed through an evolution in which heredity played a great part, had reached a degree of brilliancy which I had never seen in him before. How far away was the young golden-haired man formerly courted or who aspired to be, by fashionable ladies and the dialectician, the doctrinaire who was always playing with words. To another generation of another branch of his family, much as an actor taking a part formerly played by Bressant or Delaunay, he, blonde, pink and golden was like a successor to M. de Charlus, once dark, now completely white. However much he failed to agree with his uncle about the war, identified as he was with that part of the aristocracy which was for France first and foremost whereas M. de Charlus was fundamentally a defeatist, to those who had not seen the original "creator of the part" he displayed his powers as a controversialist.

"It seems that Hindenburg is a revelation," I said to him. "An old revelation of tit-for-tat or a future one. They ought, instead of playing with the enemy, to let Mangin have his way, beat Austria and Germany to their knees and Europeanise Turkey instead of Montenegrinising France." "But we shall have the help of the United States," I suggested. "At present all I see is the spectacle of Divided States. Why not make greater concessions to Italy and frighten them with dechristianising France?" "If your Uncle Charlus could hear you!" I said. "Really you would not be sorry to offend the Pope a bit more and he must be in despair about what may happen to the throne of Francis Joseph. For that matter he's in the tradition of Talleyrand and the Congress of Vienna." "The era of the Congress of Vienna has gone full circle;" he answered; "one must substitute concrete for secret diplomacy. My uncle is at bottom an impenitent monarchist who would swallow carps like Mme. Molé or scarps like Arthur Meyer as long as his carps and scarps were cooked *à la Chambord*. Through hatred of the tricolour flag I believe he would rather range himself under the red rag, which he would accept in good faith instead of the white standard." Of course, these were only words and Saint-Loup was far from having the occasionally basic originality of his uncle. But his disposition was as affable and delightful as the other's was suspicious and jealous and he remained, as at Balbec, charming and pink under his thick golden hair. The only thing in which his uncle would not have surpassed him was in that mental attitude of the faubourg Saint-Germain with which those who believe themselves the most detached from it are saturated and which simultaneously gives them respect for men of intelligence who are not of noble birth (which only flourishes in the nobility and makes revolution so unjust) and silly self-complacency. It was through this mixture of humility and pride, of acquired curiosity of mind and inborn sense of authority, that M. de Charlus and Saint-Loup by different roads and holding contrary opinions had become to a generation of transition, intellectuals interested in every new idea and talkers whom no interrupter could silence. Thus a rather commonplace individual would, according to his disposition, consider both of them either dazzling or bores.

While recalling Saint-Loup's visit I had made a long-detour on my way to Mme. Verdurin's and I had nearly reached the bridge of the Invalides. The lamps (few and far between, on account of Gothas) were lighted a little too early, for the change of hours had been prematurely determined for the summer season (like the furnaces which are lighted and extinguished at fixed dates) while night still came quickly and above the partly-illumined city, in one whole part of the sky—a sky which ignored summer and winter and did not deign to observe that half-past eight had become half-past nine—it still continued to be daylight. In all that part of the city, dominated by the towers of the Trocadero, the sky had the appearance of an immense turquoise-tinted sea, which, at low-tide, revealed a thin line of black rocks or perhaps only fishermen's nets aligned next each other and which were tiny clouds. A sea, now the colour of turquoise which was bearing unknowing man with it in the immense revolution of an earth upon which they are mad enough to continue their own revolutions, their vain wars such as this one now drenching France in blood. In fact one became giddy looking at the lazy, beautiful sky which deigned not to change its time-table and prolonged in its blue tones the lengthened day above the lighted city; it was no longer a spreading sea, but a vertical gradation of blue glaciers. And the towers of the Trocadéro seeming so close to those turquoise heights were in reality as far away from them as those twin towers in a town of Switzerland which, from far away, seem to neighbour the mountain-slopes. I retraced my steps but as I left the Bridge of the Invalides behind me there was no more day in the sky, nor scarcely a light in all the city and stumbling here and there against the dust-bins, mistaking my road, I found myself, unexpectedly and after following a labyrinth of obscure streets, upon the Boulevards. There the impression of the East renewed itself and to the evocation of the Paris of the Directoire succeeded that of the Paris of 1815. As then, the disparate procession of uniforms of Allied troops, Africans in baggy red trousers, white-turbaned Hindus, created for me, out of that Paris where I was walking, an exotic imaginary city in an East minutely exact in costume and colour of the skins but arbitrarily chimerical in scenery, just as Carpaccio made of his own city a Jerusalem or a Constantinople by assembling therein a crowd whose marvellous medley of colour was not more varied than this. Walking behind two Zouaves who did not seem to notice him, I perceived a great stout man in a soft, felt hat and a long cloak, to whose mauve coloured face I hesitated to put the name of an actor or of a painter equally well-known for innumerable sodomite scandals. In any case feeling certain I did not know the promenader, I was greatly surprised, when his glance met mine, to notice that he was embarrassed and made as though to stop and speak to me, like one who wants to show you that you are not surprising him in an occupation he would rather have kept secret. For a second I asked myself who was saying good-evening to me. It was M. de Charlus. One could say of him that the evolution of his disease or the revolution of his vice had reached that extreme point where the small primitive personality of the individual, his ancestral qualities, were entirely obscured by the interposition of the defect or generic evil which accompanied them. M. de Charlus had gone as far as it was possible for him to go, or rather, he was so completely marked by what he had become, by habits that were not his alone but also those of many other inverts, that, at first, I had taken him for one of these following the zouaves on the open boulevard; in fact, for another of their kind who was not M. de Charlus, not a *grand seigneur*, not a man of mind and imagination and who only resembled the baron through that appearance common to them all and to him as well which, until one looked closer, had covered everything. It was thus that, having wanted to go to Mme. Verdurin's, I met M. de Charlus. And certainly I should not have found him as I used to at her house; their quarrel had only become accentuated and Mme. Verdurin often made use of present conditions to discredit him further. Having said for a long time that he was used up, finished, more old-fashioned in his pretended audacities than the most pompous nonentities, she now comprised that condemnation in a general indictment by saying that he was "pre-war". According to the little clan, the war had placed between him and the present, a gulf which relegated him to a past that was completely dead. Moreover — and that concerned rather the political world which was less well-informed — Mme. Verdurin represented him as done for, as complete a social as an intellectual outsider. "He sees no one, no one receives him," she told M. Bontemps, whom she easily convinced. Moreover there was some truth in what she said. The situation of M. de Charlus had changed. Caring less and less about society, having quarrelled with everybody owing to his petulant disposition and, having through conviction of his own social importance, disdained to reconcile himself with most of those who constituted the flower of society, he lived in a relative isolation which, unlike that in which Mme. de Villeparisis died, was not caused by the ostracism of the aristocracy but by something which appeared to the eyes of the public worse, for two reasons. M. de Charlus' bad reputation, now well-known, caused the ill-informed to believe that that accounted for people not frequenting his society, while actually it was he who, of his own accord, refused to frequent them, so that the effect of his own atrabilious humour appeared to be that of the hostility of those upon whom he exercised it. Besides that, Mme. de Villeparisis had a great rampart; her family. But M. de Charlus had multiplied the quarrels between himself and his family, which, moreover appeared to him uninteresting, especially the old faubourg side, the Courvoisier set. He who had made so many bold sallies in the field of art, unlike the Courvoisiers, had no notion that what would have most interested a Bergotte was his relationship with that old faubourg, his having the means of describing the almost provincial life lived by his cousins in the Rue de la Chaise or in the Place du Palais Bourbon and the Rue Garancière. A point of view less transcendent and more practical was represented by Mme. Verdurin who affected to believe that he was not French. "What is his exact nationality? Is he not an Austrian?" M. Verdurin innocently inquired. "Oh, no, not at all," answered the Comtesse Molé, whose first gesture rather obeyed her good sense than her rancour. "Nothing of the sort, he's a Prussian," pronounced *la Patronne*: "I know, I tell you. He told us often enough he was a hereditary peer of Prussia and a 'Serene Highness'." "All the same, the Queen of Naples told me—" "As to her, you know she's an awful spy," exclaimed Mme. Verdurin who had not forgotten the attitude which the fallen sovereign had displayed at her house one evening. "I know it most positively. She only lives by spying. If we had a more energetic Government, all those people would be in a concentration camp. And in any case you would do well not to receive that charming kind of society, for I happen to know that the Minister of the Interior has got his eye on them and your house will be watched. Nothing will convince me that during two years Charlus was not continually spying at my house." And thinking probably, that there might be some doubt as to the interest the German Government might take, even in the most circumstantial reports on the organisation of the "little clan", Mme. Verdurin, with the soft, confidential manner of a person who knows the value of what she is imparting and that it seems more significant if she does not raise her voice, "I tell you, from the first day I said to my husband,'the way in which this man has inveigled himself into our house is not to my liking. There's something suspicious about it.' Our estate was on a very high point at the back of a bay. I am certain he was entrusted by the Germans to prepare a base there for their submarines. Certain things surprised me and now I understand them. For instance, at first he would not come by train with the other guests. I had offered in the nicest way to give him a room in the château. Well, not a bit of it, he preferred living at Doncières where there were an enormous number of troops. All that stank in one's nostrils of espionage." As to the first of these accusations directed against the Baron de Charlus, that of being out of fashion, society people were quite ready to accept Mme. Verdurin's point of view. This was ungrateful of them for M. de Charlus who had been, up to a point their poet, had the art of extracting from social surroundings a sort of poetry into which he wove history, beauty, the picturesque, comedy and frivolous elegance. But fashionable people, incapable of understanding poetry, of which they saw none in their own lives, sought it elsewhere and placed a thousand feet above M. de Charlus men infinitely inferior to him, who affected to despise society and, on the other hand, professed social and political-economic theories. M. de Charlus delighted in an unprofessedly lyrical form of wit with which he described the knowing grace of the Duchesse of X—'s dresses and alluded to her as a sublime creature. This caused him to be looked upon as an idiot by those women in society who thought that the Duchesse of X— was an uninteresting fool, that dresses are made to be worn without drawing attention to them and who, thinking themselves more intelligent, rushed to the Sorbonne or to the Chamber if Deschanel was going to speak. In short, people in society were disillusioned with M. de Charlus, not because they had got through him but because they had never grasped his rare intellectual value. He was considered pre-war, old-fashioned, just because those least capable of judging merit, most readily accept the edicts of passing fashion; so far from exhausting, they have hardly even skimmed the surface of men of quality in the preceding generation whom they now condemn en bloc because they are offered the label of a new generation they will understand just as little. As to the second accusation against M. de Charlus, that of Germanism, the happy-medium mentality of people in society made them reject it, but they encountered an indefatigable and particularly cruel interpreter in Morel, who, having managed to retain in the press and even in society the position which M. de Charlus had succeeded in getting him by expending twice as much trouble as he would have taken in depriving him of it, pursued the Baron with implacable hatred; this was not only cruel on the part of Morel, but doubly wrong, for whatever his relations with the Baron might have been, Morel had experienced the rare kindness his patron hid from so many people. M. de Charlus had treated the violinist with such generosity, with such delicacy, had shown such scruple about not breaking his word, that the idea of him which Charlie had retained was not at all that of a vicious man (at most he considered the Baron's vice a disease) but of one with the noblest ideas and the most exquisite sensibility he had ever known, a sort of saint. He denied it so little that though he had quarrelled with him he said sincerely enough to his relations, "You can confide your son to him, he would only have the best influence upon him." Indeed when he tried to injure him by his articles, in his mind he jeered, not at his vices but, at his virtues. Before the war, certain little broad-sheets, transparent to what are called the "initiates", had begun to do the greatest harm to M. de Charlus. Of one of these entitled *The Misadventure of a pedantic Duchess, the Old Age of the Baroness* Mme. Verdurin had bought fifty copies, in order to lend them to her acquaintances, and M. Verdurin, declaring that Voltaire himself never wrote anything better, read them aloud to his friends. Since the war it was not the invertion of the Baron alone that was denounced, but also his alleged Germanic nationality. "Frau Bosch", "Frau voh der Bosch" were the customary surnames of M. de Charlus. One effusion of poetic character had borrowed from certain dance melodies in Beethoven, the title "Une Allemande". Finally, two little novels, *Oncle d'Amérique et Tante de Francfort*, and *Gaillard d'arrière*, read in proof by the little clan, had given delight to Brichot himself who remarked, "Take care the most noble and puissant Anastasia doesn't do us in." The articles themselves were better done than their ridiculous titles would have led one to suppose. Their style derived from Bergotte but in a way which perhaps only I could recognise, for this reason. The writings of Bergotte had had no influence upon Morel. Fecundation had occurred in so peculiar and exceptional a fashion that I must register it here. I have indicated in its place the special way Bergotte had of selecting his words and pronouncing them when he talked. Morel, who had met him in early days, gave imitations of him at the time in which he mimicked his speech perfectly, using the same words as Bergotte would have used. So now Morel transcribed conversations *à la Bergotte* but without transmuting them into what would have represented Bergotte's style of writing. As few people had talked with Bergotte, they did not recognise the tonality which was quite different from his style. That oral fertilisation is so rare that I wanted to mention it here; for that matter, it produces only sterile flowers.

Morel, who was at the Press Bureau and whose irregular situation was unknown, made the pretence, with his French blood boiling in his veins like the juice of the grapes of Combray, that to work in an office during the war was not good enough and that he wanted to join up (which he could have done at any moment he pleased) while Mme. Verdurin did everything in her power to persuade him to remain in Paris. Certainly she was indignant that M. de Cambremer, in spite of his age, had a staff job, and she remarked about every man who did not come to her house, "Where has he found means of hiding?" And if anyone affirmed that so and so had been in the front line from the first day she answered, lying unscrupulously or from the mere habit of falsehood, "Not a bit of it, he has never stirred from Paris, he is doing something about as dangerous as promenading around the Ministries. I tell you I know what I am talking about because I have got it from someone who has seen him." But in the case of "the faithful" it was different. She did not want them to go and alluded to the war as a "boring business" that took them away from her; and she took all possible steps to prevent them going which gave her the double pleasure of having them at dinner and, when they did not come or had gone, of abusing them behind their backs for their pusillanimity. The "faithful" had to lend themselves to this *embusquage* and she was distressed when Morel pretended to be recalcitrant and told him, "By serving in the Press Bureau you are doing your bit, and more so than if you were at the front. What is required is to be useful, really to take part in the war, to be of it. There are those who are of it and *embusqués*; you are of it and don't you bother, everyone knows you are and no one can have a word to say against you." Under different circumstances, when men were not so few and when she was not obliged as now to have chiefly women, if one of them lost his mother she did not hesitate to persuade him that he could unhesitatingly continue to go to her receptions. "Sorrow is felt in the heart. If you were to go to a ball (she never gave any) I should be the first to advise you not to, but here at my little Wednesdays or in a box at the theatre, no one can be shocked. Everybody knows how grieved you are." Now, however, men were fewer, mourning more frequent, she did not have to prevent them from going into society, the war saw to that. But she wanted to persuade them that they were more useful to France by stopping in Paris, in the same way as she would formerly have persuaded them that the defunct would have been more happy to see them enjoying themselves. All the same she got very few men, and sometimes, perhaps, she regretted having brought about the rupture with M. de Charlus, which could never be repaired.

But if M. de Charlus and Mme. Verdurin no longer saw each other, each of them—with certain minor differences—continued as though nothing had changed, Mme. Verdurin to receive and M. de Charlus to go about his own pleasures. For example, at Mme. Verdurin's house, Cottard was present at the receptions in the uniform of a Colonel of *l'Ile du Rève* rather similar to that of a Haitian Admiral, and upon the lapel of which a broad sky-blue ribbon recalled that of the *Enfants de Marie*; as to M. de Charlus, finding himself in a city where mature men who had up to then been his taste had disappeared, he had, like certain Frenchmen who run after women when they are in France but who live in the Colonies, at first from necessity, then from habit, acquired a taste for little boys.

Furthermore, one of the characteristic features of the Salon Verdurin disappeared soon after, for Cottard died "with his face to the enemy" the papers said, though he had never left Paris; the fact was he had been overworked for his time of life and he was followed shortly afterwards by M. Verdurin, whose death caused sorrow to one person only—would one believe it?—Elstir. I had been able to study his work from a point of view which was in a measure final. But, as he grew older, he associated it superstitiously with the society which had supplied his models and, after the alchemy of his intuitions had transmuted them into works of art, gave him his public. More and more inclined to the belief that a large part of beauty resides in objects as, at first, he had adored in Mme. Elstir that rather heavy type of beauty he had studied in tapestries and handled in his pictures, M. Verdurin's death signified to him the disappearance of one of the last traces of the perishable social framework, falling into limbo as swiftly as the fashions in dress which form part of it—that framework which supports an art and certifies its authenticity like the revolution which, in destroying the elegancies of the eighteenth century, would have distressed a painter of *fêtes galantes* or afflicted Renoir when Montmartre and the Moulin de la Galette disappeared. But, above all, with M. Verdurin disappeared the eyes, the brain, which had had the most authentic vision of his painting, wherein that painting lived, as it were, in the form of a cherished memory. Without doubt young men had emerged who also loved painting, but another kind of painting, and they had not, like Swann, like M. Verdurin, received lessons in taste from Whistler, lessons in truth from Monet, which enabled them to judge Elstir with justice! Also he felt himself more solitary when M. Verdurin, with whom he had, nevertheless, quarrelled years ago, died and it was as though part of the beauty of his work had disappeared with some of that consciousness of beauty which had until then, existed in the world.

The change which had been effected in M. de Charlus' pleasures remained intermittent. Keeping up a large correspondence with the front, he did not lack mature men home on leave. Therefore, in a general way, Mme. Verdurin continued to receive and M. de Charlus to go about his pleasures as if nothing had happened. And still for two years the immense human entity called France, of which even from a purely material point of view one can only feel the tremendous beauty if one perceives the cohesion of millions of individuals who, like cellules of various forms fill it like so many little interior polygons up to the extreme limit of its perimeter, and if one saw it on the same scale as infusoria or cellules see a human body, that is to say, as big as Mont Blanc, was facing a tremendous collective battle with that other immense conglomerate of individuals which is Germany. At a time when I believed what people told me, I should have been tempted to believe Germany, then Bulgaria, then Greece when they proclaimed their pacific intentions. But since my life with Albertine and with Françoise had accustomed me to suspect those motives they did not express, I did not allow any word, however right in appearance of William II, Ferdinand of Bulgaria or Constantine of Greece to deceive my instinct which divined what each one of them was plotting. Doubtless my quarrels with Françoise and with Albertine had only been little personal quarrels, mattering only to the life of that little spiritual cellule which a human being is. But in the same way as there are bodies of animals, human bodies, that is to say, assemblages of cellules, which, in relation to one of them alone, are as great as a mountain, so there exist enormous organised groupings of individuals which we call nations; their life only repeats and amplifies the life of the composing cellules and he who is not capable of understanding the mystery, the reactions and the laws of those cellules, will only utter empty words when he talks about struggles between nations. But if he is master of the psychology of individuals, then these colossal masses of conglomerate individuals facing one another will assume in his eyes a more formidable beauty than a fight born only of a conflict between two characters, and he will see them on the scale on which the body of a tall man would be seen by infusoria of which it would require more than ten thousand to fill one cubic millimeter. Thus for some time past the great figure of France, filled to its perimeter with millions of little polygons of various shapes and the other figure of Germany filled with even more polygons were having one of those quarrels which, in a smaller measure, individuals have.

But the blows that they were exchanging were regulated by those numberless boxing-matches of which Saint-Loup had explained the principles to me. And because, even in considering them from the point of view of individuals they were gigantic assemblages, the quarrel assumed enormous and magnificent forms like the uprising of an ocean which with its millions of waves seeks to demolish a secular line of cliffs or like giant glaciers which, with their slow and destructive oscillation, attempt to disrupt the frame of the mountain by which they are circumscribed. In spite of this, life continued almost the same for many people who have figured in this narrative, notably for M. de Charlus and for the Verdurins, as though the Germans had not been so near to them; a permanent menace in spite of its being concentrated in one immediate peril leaving us entirely unmoved if we do not realise it. People pursue their pleasures from habit without ever thinking, were etiolating and moderating influences to cease, that the proliferation of the infusoria would attain its maximum, that is to say, making a leap of many millions of leagues in a few days and passing from a cubic millimeter to a mass a million times larger than the sun, at the same time destroying all the oxygen of the substances upon which we live, that there would no longer be any humanity or animals or earth, and, without any notion that an irremediable and quite possible catastrophe might be determined in the ether by the incessant and frantic energy hidden behind the apparent immutability of the sun, they go on with their business, without thinking of these two worlds, one too small, the other too large for them to perceive the cosmic menace which hovers around us. Thus the Verdurins gave their dinners (soon, after the death of M. Verdurin, Mme. Verdurin alone) and M. de Charlus went about his pleasures, without realising that the Germans—immobilised, it is true, by a bleeding barrier which was always being renewed—were at an hour's automobile drive from Paris. One might say the Verdurins did, nevertheless, think about it, since they had a political salon where the situation of the armies and of the fleets was discussed every day. As a matter of fact, they thought about those hecatombs of annihilated regiments, of engulfed seafarers, but an inverse operation multiplies to such a degree what concerns our welfare and divides by such a formidable figure what does not concern it, that the death of millions of unknown people hardly affects us more unpleasantly than a draught. Mme. Verdurin, who suffered from headaches on account of being unable to get *croissants* to dip into her coffee, had obtained an order from Cottard which enabled her to have them made in the restaurant mentioned earlier. It had been almost as difficult to procure this order from the authorities as the nomination of a general. She started her first *croissant* again on the morning the papers an-announced the wreck of the *Lusitania*. Dipping it into her coffee, she arranged her newspaper so that it would stay open without her having to deprive her other hand of its function of dipping, and exclaimed with horror, "How awful! It's more frightful than the most terrible tragedies." But those drowning people must have seemed to her reduced a thousand-fold, for, while she indulged in these saddening reflections, she was filling her mouth and the expression on her face, induced, one supposes, by the savour of the *croissant*, precious remedy for her headache, was rather that of placid satisfaction.

M. de Charlus went beyond not passionately desiring the victory of France; without avowing it, he wanted, if not the triumph of Germany, at least that she should not, as everybody desired, be destroyed. The reason of this was that in quarrels the great assemblages of individuals called nations behave, in a certain measure, like individuals. The logic which governs them is within them and is perpetually remoulded by passion like that of people engaged in a love-quarrel or in some domestic dispute, such as that of a son with his father, of a cook with her mistress, of a woman with her husband. He who is in the wrong believes himself in the right, as was the case with Germany, and he who is in the right supports it with arguments which only appear irrefutable to him because they respond to his anger. In these quarrels between individuals, in order to be convinced that one of the parties is in the right—the surest plan is to be that party; no onlooker will ever be so: completely convinced of it. And an individual, if he be an integral part of a nation, is himself merely a cellule of an individual which is the nation. Stuffing people's heads full of words means nothing. If, at a critical period in the war, a

Frenchman had been told that his country was going to be beaten, he would have been desperate as though he were himself about to be killed by the "Berthas". Really, one fills one's own head with hope which is a sort of instinct of self-preservation in a nation if one is really an integral member of it. To remain blind to what is false in the claims of the individual called Germany, to see justice in every claim of the individual called France, the surest way was not for a German to lack judgment and for a Frenchman to possess it but for both to be patriotic. M. de Charlus, who had rare moral qualities, who was accessible to pity, generous, capable of affection and of devotion, was in contrast, for various reasons, amongst them that a Bavarian duchess had been his mother, without patriotism. In consequence he belonged as much to the body of Germany as to the body of France. If I had been devoid of patriotism myself, instead of feeling myself one of the cellules in the body of France, I think my way of judging the quarrel would not have been the same as formerly. In my adolescence, when I believed exactly what I was told, doubtless, on hearing the German Government protest its good faith, I should have been inclined to believe it, but now for a long time I had realised that our thoughts do not always correspond with our words.

But actually I can only imagine what I should have done if I had not been a member of the agent, France, as in my quarrels with Albertine, when my sad appearance and my choking throat were, as parts of my being, too passionately interested on my own behalf for me to reach any sort of detachment. That of M. de Charlus was complete. Since he was only a spectator, everything had the inevitable effect of making him Germanophile because, though not really French, he lived in France. He was very keen-witted and in all countries fools outnumber the rest; no doubt, if he had lived in Germany the German fools defending an unjust cause with passionate folly would—have equally irritated him; but living in France, the French fools, defending a just cause with passionate folly, irritated him no less. The logic of passion, even in the service of justice, is never irrefutable by one who remains dispassionate. M. de Charlus acutely noted each false argument of the patriots. The satisfaction a brainless fool gets out of being in the right and out of the certainty of success, is particularly irritating. M. de Charlus was maddened by the triumphant optimism of people who did not know Germany and its power as he did, who every month were confident that she would be crushed the following month, and when a year had passed were just as ready to believe in a new prognostic as if they had not with equal confidence credited the false one they had forgotten, or if they were reminded of it, replied that, "it was not the same thing." M. de Charlus, whose mind contained some depth, might perhaps not have understood in Art that the "it isn't the same thing" offered as an argument by the detractors of Monet in opposition to those who contended that "they said the same thing about Delacroix", corresponded to the same mentality. And then M. de Charlus was merciful, the idea of a vanquished man pained him, he was always for the weak, and could not read the accounts of trials in the papers without feeling in his own flesh the anguish of the prisoner and a longing to assassinate the judge, the executioner and the mob who delighted in "seeing justice done". In any case, it was now certain that France could not be beaten and he knew that the Germans were famine-stricken and would be obliged sooner or later to surrender at discretion. This idea was also more unpleasant to him owing to his living in France. His memories of Germany were, after all, dimmed by time, whereas the French who unpleasantly gloated in the prospect of crushing Germany, were people whose defects and antipathetic countenances were familiar to him. In such a case we feel more compassionate towards those unknown to us, whom we can only imagine, than towards those whose vulgar daily life is lived close to us, unless we feel completely one of them, one flesh with them; patriotism works this miracle, we stand by our country as we do by ourselves in a love quarrel. The war, too, acted on M. de Charlus as an extraordinarily fruitful culture of those hatreds of his which were born from one instant to another, lasted a very short time, but during it were exceedingly violent. Reading the papers, the triumphant tone of the articles daily representing Germany laid low, "the beast at bay, reduced to impotence", at a time when the contrary was only too true, drove him mad with rage by their irresponsible and ferocious stupidity. The papers were in part edited at that time by well-known people who thus found a way of "doing their bit"; by the Brichots, the Norpois, by the Legrandins. M. de Charlus longed to meet and pulverise them with his bitterest irony. Always particularly well informed about sexual taints, he recognised them in others who, imagining themselves unsuspected, delighted in denouncing the sovereigns of the "Empires of prey", Wagner et cetera as culprits in this respect. He yearned to encounter them face to face so that he could rub their noses in their own vices before the world and leave these insulters of a fallen foe demolished and dishonoured. Finally M. de Charlus had a still further reason for being the Germanophile he was. One was that as a man of the world he had lived much amongst people in society, amongst men of honour who will not shake hands with a scamp; he knew their niceties and also their hardness, he knew they were insensible to the tears of a man they expel from a club, with whom they refuse to fight a duel, even if their act of "moral purity" caused the death of the black sheep's mother. Great as his admiration had been for England, that impeccable England incapable of lies preventing corn and milk from entering Germany was in a way a nation of chartered gentlemen, of licensed witnesses and arbiters of honour, whilst to his mind some of Dostoevski's disreputable rascals were better. But I never could understand why he identified such characters with the Germans since the latter do not appear to us to have displayed the goodness of heart which, in the case of the former, lying and deceit failed to prejudice. Finally, a last trait will complete the Germanophilism of M. de Charlus, which he owed through a peculiar reaction to his "Charlisme". He considered Germans very ugly, perhaps because they were a little too close to his own blood, he was mad about Moroccans but above all about Anglo-Saxons whom he saw as living statues of Phidias. In him sexual gratification was inseparable from the idea of cruelty and (how strong this was I did not then realise) the man who attracted him seemed like a kind of delightful executioner. He would have thought, if he had sided against the Germans, that he was acting as he only did in his hours of self-indulgence, that is, in a sense contrary to his naturally merciful nature, in other words, impassioned; by seductive evil and desiring to crush virtuous ugliness. He was like that at the time of the murder of Rasputine at a supper party *a la* Dostoevski, which impressed people by its strong Russian flavour (an impression which would have been much stronger if the public had been aware of all that M. de Charlus knew), because life deceives us so much that we come to believing that literature has no relation with it and we are astonished to observe that the wonderful ideas books have presented to us are gratuitously exhibited in everyday life, without risk of being spoilt by the writer, that for instance, a murder at a supper-party, a Russian incident, should have something Russian about it.

The war continued indefinitely and those who had announced years ago from a reliable source that negotiations for peace had begun, specifying even the clauses of the armistice, did not take the trouble, when they talked with you, to excuse themselves for their false information. They had forgotten it and were ready sincerely to circulate other information which they would forget equally quickly. It was the period when there were continuous raids of Gothas. The air perpetually quivered with the vigilant and sonorous vibration of the French aeroplanes. But sometimes the siren rang forth like a harrowing appeal of the Walkyries, the only German music one had heard since the war—until the hour when the firemen announced that the alarm was finished, while the maroon, like an invisible newsboy, communicated the good news at regular intervals and cast its joyous clamour into the air.

M. de Charlus was astonished to discover that even men like Brichot who, before the war, had been militarist and reproached France for not being sufficiently so, were not satisfied with blaming Germany for the excesses of her militarism, but even condemned her for admiring her army. Doubtless, they changed their view when there was a question of slowing down the war against Germany and rightly denounced the pacifists. Yet Brichot, as an example of inconsistency, having agreed in spite of his failing sight, to give lectures on certain books which had appeared in neutral countries, exalted the novel of a Swiss in which two children, who fell on their knees in admiration of the symbolic vision of a dragoon, are denounced as the seed of militarism. There were other reasons why this denunciation should displease M. de Charlus, who considered that a dragoon can be exceedingly beautiful. But still more he could not understand the admiration of Brichot, if not for the book which the baron had not read, at all events for its spirit which was so different from that which distinguished Brichot before the war. Then everything that was soldierlike was good, whether it was the irregularities of a General de Boisdeffre, the travesties and machinations of a Colonel du Paty de Clam or the falsifications of Colonel Henry. But by that extraordinary *volte-face* (which was in reality only another face of that most noble passion, patriotism, necessarily militarised when it was fighting against Dreyfusism which then had an anti-militarist tendency and now was almost anti-militarist since it was fighting against Germany, the super-militarist country), Brichot now cried: "Oh! What an admirable exhibition, how seemly, to appeal to youth to continue brutality for a century, to recognise no other culture than that of violence: a dragoon! One can imagine the sort of vile soldiery we can expect of a generation brought up to worship these manifestations of brute force." "Now, look here," M. de Charlus said to me, "you know Brichot and Cambremer. Every time I see them, they talk to me about the extraordinary lack of psychology in Germany. Between ourselves, do you believe that until now they have cared much about psychology or that even now they are capable of proving they possess any? But, believe me, I am not exaggerating. Even when the greatest Germans are in question, Nietzsche or Goethe, you will hear Brichot say 'with that habitual lack of psychology which characterises the Teutonic race'. Obviously there are worse things than that to bear but you must admit that it gets on one's nerves. Norpois is more intelligent, I admit, though he has never been other than wrong from the beginning. But what is one to say about those articles which excite universal enthusiasm? My dear Sir, you know as well as I do what Brichot's value is, and I have a liking for him even since the feud which has separated me from his little tabernacle, on account of which I see him much less. Still, I have a certain respect for this college dean, a fine speaker and an erudite, and I avow that it is extremely touching, at his age and in bad health as he is, for he has become sensibly so in these last years, that he should have given himself up to what he calls service. But whatever one may say, good intention is one thing, talent another and Brichot never had talent. I admit that I share his admiration for certain grandeurs of the war. At most, however, it is extraordinary that a blind partisan of antiquity like Brichot, who never could be ironical enough about Zola seeing more beauty in a workman's home, in a mine than in historic palaces or about Goncourt putting Diderot above Homer and Watteau above Raphael, should repeat incessantly that Thermopylae or Austerlitz were nothing in comparison with Vauquois. This time the public, which resisted the modernists of Art and Literature, follows those of the war, because it's the fashion to think like that and small minds are not overwhelmed by the beauty but by the enormous scale of the war. They never write Kolossal without a K but at bottom what they bow down to is indeed colossal."

"It is a curious thing," added M. de Charlus, with that little high voice he adopted at times, "I hear people who look quite happy all day long and drink plenty of excellent cocktails, say they will never be able to see the war through, that their hearts aren't strong enough, that they cannot think of anything else and that they will die suddenly, and the extraordinary thing is that it actually happens; how curious! Is it a matter of nourishment, because they only eat things which are badly cooked or because, to prove their zeal, they harness themselves to some futile task which interferes with the diet that preserved them? Anyhow, I have registered a surprising number of these strange premature deaths, premature at all events, so far as the desire of the dead person was concerned. I do not remember exactly what I was saying to you about Brichot and Norpois admiring this war but what a singular way to talk about it. To begin with, have you remarked that pullulation of new idioms used by Norpois which, exhausted by daily use — for really he is indefatigable and I believe the death of my Aunt Villeparisis gave him a second youth — are immediately replaced by others that are in general use. Formerly, I remember you used to be amused by noting these modes of language which appear, are kept going for a time, and then disappear: 'He who sows the wind shall reap the whirlwind', 'The dog barks, the caravan passes', 'Find me a good politic and I shall produce good finance for you, said Baron Louis'. These are symptoms which it would be exaggerated to take too tragically but which must be taken seriously, 'To work for the King of Prussia', (for that matter this last has been revived as was inevitable). Well, since, alas, I have seen so many of them die we have had the 'Scrap of paper', 'the Robber Empires', 'the famous Kultur which consists in assassinating defenceless women and children', 'Victory, as the Japanese say, will be to him who can endure a quarter of an hour longer than the other', 'The Germano-Turanians', 'Scientific barbarity', 'if we want to win the war in accordance with the strong expression of Mr. Lloyd George', in fact, there are no end of them; the *mordant* of the troops, and the *cran* of the troops. Even the sentiments of the excellent Norpois undergo, owing to the war, as complete a modification as the composition of bread or the rapidity of transport. Have you observed that the excellent man, anxious to proclaim his desires as though they were a truth on the point of being realised, does not, all the same, dare to use the future tense which might be contradicted by events, but has adopted instead the verb 'know'." I told M. de Charlus that I did not understand what he meant. I must observe here that the Duc de Guermantes did not in the least share the pessimism of his brother. He was, moreover, as Anglophile as M. de Charlus was Anglophobe. For instance, he considered M. Caillaux a traitor who deserved to be shot a thousand times over. When his brother asked him for proofs of this treason, M. de Guermantes answered that if one only condemned people who signed a paper on which they declared "I have betrayed", one would never punish the crime of treason. But in case I should not have occasion to return to it, I will also remark that two years later the Duc de Guermantes, animated by pure anti-Caillauxism, made the acquaintance of an English military attaché and his wife, a remarkably well-read couple, with whom he made friends as he did with the three charming ladies at the time of the Dreyfus Affair and that from the first day he was astounded, in talking of Caillaux, whose conviction he held to be certain and his crime patent, to hear one of the charming and well-read couple remark, "He will probably be acquitted, there is absolutely nothing against him." M. de Guermantes tried to allege that M. de Norpois, in his evidence had exclaimed, looking the fallen Caillaux in the face, "You are the Giolitti of France, yes, M. Caillaux, you are the Giolitti of France." But the charming couple smiled and ridiculed M. de Norpois, giving examples of his senility and concluded that he had thus addressed a M. Caillaux overthrown according to the *Figaro*, but probably in reality a very sly M. Caillaux. The opinions of the Duc de Guermantes soon changed. To attribute this change to the influence of an English woman is not as extreme as it might have seemed if one had prophesied even in 1919, when the English called the Germans Huns and demanded a ferocious sentence on the guilty, that their opinion was to change and that every decision which could sadden France and help Germany would be supported by them. To return to M. de Charlus. "Yes," he said, in reply to my not understanding him, "'to know' in the articles of Norpois takes the place of the future tense, that is, expresses the wishes of Norpois, all our wishes, for that matter," he added, perhaps not with complete sincerity. "You understand that if 'know' had not replaced the simple future tense one might, if pressed, admit that the subject of this verb could be a country. For instance, every time Brichot said 'America "would not know" how to remain indifferent to these repeated violations of right,' 'the two-headed Monarchy "would not know" how to fail to mend its ways', it is clear that such phrases express the wishes of Norpois (his and ours) but, anyhow, the word can still keep its original sense in spite of its absurdity, because a country can 'know', America can 'know', even the two-headed Monarchy itself can 'know' (in spite of its eternal lack of psychology) but that sense can no longer be admitted when Brichot writes 'the systematic devastations "would not know" how to persuade the neutrals', or 'the region of the Lakes "would not know" how to avoid shortly falling into the hands of the Allies', or 'the results of the elections in the neutral countries "would not know" how to reflect the opinion of the great majority in those countries'. Now it is clear that these devastations, these Lakes and these results of elections are inanimate things which cannot 'know'. By that formula Norpois is simply addressing his injunctions to the neutrals (who, I regret to observe, do not seem to obey him) to emerge from their neutrality or exhorts the Lakes no longer to belong to the 'Boches'." (M. de Charlus put the same sort of arrogance into his tone in pronouncing the word *boches* as he did formerly in the train to Balbec when he alluded to men whose taste is not for women,) "Moreover, did you observe the tricks Norpois made use of in opening his articles on neutrals ever since 1914? He begins by declaring emphatically that France has no right to mix herself up in the politics of Italy, Roumania, Bulgaria, et cetera. It is 'for those powers alone to decide with complete independence, consulting only their national interests, whether or not they are to abandon their neutrality.' But if the preliminary declarations of the article (which would formerly have been called the exordium) are so markedly disinterested, what follows is generally much less so. Anyhow, as he goes on M. de Norpois says substantially, 'it follows that those powers only who have allied themselves with the side of Right and Justice will secure material advantages from the conflict. It cannot be expected that the Allies will compensate those nations which, following the line of least resistance, have not placed their sword at the service of the Allies, by granting them territories from which, for centuries the cry of their oppressed brethren has been raised in supplication'. Norpois, having taken this first step towards advising intervention, nothing stops him and he now offers advice more and more thinly disguised, not only as to the principle but also as to the appropriate moment for intervention. 'Naturally,' he says, playing as he would himself call it, the good apostle, 'it is for Italy, for Roumania alone to decide the proper hour and the form under which it will suit them to intervene. They cannot, however, be unaware that if they delay too long, they run the risk of missing the crucial moment. Even now Germany trembles at the thud of the Russian cavalry. It is obvious that the nations which have only flown to help in the hour of victory of which the resplendent dawn is already visible, can in no wise have a claim to the rewards they can still secure by hastening, et cetera, et cetera'. It is like at the theatre when they say,'the last remaining seats will very soon be gone. This is a warning to the dilatory', an argument which is the more stupid that Norpois serves it up every six months and periodically admonishes Roumania: 'The Hour has come for Roumania to make up her mind whether she desires or not to realise her national aspirations. If she waits much longer, she will risk being too late'. And though he has repeated the admonition for two years, the 'too late' has not yet come to pass and they keep on increasing their offers to Roumania. In the same way he invites France et cetera to intervene in Greece as a protective power because the treaty which bound Greece to Serbia has not been maintained. And, really and truly, if France were not at war and did not desire the assistance of the benevolent neutrality of Greece, would she think of intervening as a protective power and would not the moral sentiment which inspires her reprobation of Greece for not keeping her engagements with Serbia, be silenced the moment the question arose of an equally flagrant violation in the case of Roumania and Italy who, like Greece, I believe with good reason, have not fulfilled their obligations, which were less imperative and extensive than is supposed, as Allies of Germany. The truth is that people see everything through their newspaper and how can they do otherwise, seeing that they themselves know nothing about the peoples or the events in question. At the time of the 'Affaire' which stirred all passions during that period from which it is now the right thing to say we are separated by centuries, for the war-philosophers have agreed that all links with the past are broken, I was shocked at seeing members of my own family give their esteem to anti-clericals and former Communists whom their paper represented as anti-Dreyfusards and insult a general of high birth and a Catholic who was a revisionist. I am no less shocked to see the whole French people execrate the Emperor Francis Joseph, whom they used rightly to venerate; I am able to assure you of this, for I used to know him well and he honoured me by treating me as his cousin. Ah! I have not written to him since the war," he added as though avowing a fault for which he knew he could not be blamed. "Yes, let me see, I did write once, only the first year. But it doesn't matter. It doesn't in the least change my respect for him, but I have many young relatives fighting in our lines and they would, I know, consider that I was acting very badly if I kept up a correspondence with the head of a nation at war with us. Let him who wishes criticise me," he added, as if he were boldly exposing himself to my reproof; "I did not want a letter signed Charlus to arrive at Vienna in such times as these. The chief criticism that I should direct against the old sovereign is that a *Seigneur* of his rank, head of one of the most ancient and illustrious houses in Europe, should have allowed himself to be led by the nose by that little upstart of a country squire very intelligent for that matter but a pure *parvenu* like William of Hohenzollern. That is not the least shocking of the anomalies of this war." And as, once he adopted the nobiliary point of view which for him overshadowed everything else, M. de Charlus was capable of the most childish extravagances, he told me, in the same serious tone as if he were speaking of the Marne or of Verdun, that there were most interesting and curious things which should not be excluded by any historian of this war. "For instance," he said, "people are so ignorant that no one has observed this remarkable point: the Grand-Master of the Order of Malta, who is a pure-bred Boche, does not on that account cease living at Rome where, as Grand-Master of our Order he enjoys exterritorial privileges. Isn't that interesting?" he added with the air of saying, "You see you have not wasted your evening by meeting me." I thanked him and he assumed the modest air of one who is not asking for payment. "Ah! What was I telling you? Oh, yes, that people now hated Francis Joseph according to their paper. In the cases of the King Constantine of Greece and the Czar of Bulgaria the public has wavered between aversion and sympathy according to reports that they were going to join the Entente or what Norpois calls 'the Central Empires'. It is like when he keeps on telling us every moment that the hour of Venizelos is going to strike. I do not doubt that Venizelos is a man of much capacity but how do we know that his country wants him so much? He desired, we are informed, that Greece should keep her engagements with Serbia. So we ought to know what those engagements were and if they were more binding than those which Italy and Roumania thought themselves justified in violating. We display an anxiety about the way in which Greece executes her treaties and respects her constitution that we certainly should not have were it not to our interest. If there had been no war, do you believe that the guaranteeing powers would even have paid the slightest attention to the dissolution of the Chamber? I observe that one by one they are withholding their support from the King of Greece so as to be able to throw him out or imprison him the day that he has no army to defend him. I was telling you that the public only judges the King of Greece and the Czar of Bulgaria by the papers, and how could they do otherwise since they do not know them? I used to see a great deal of them and knew them well. When Constantine of Greece was Crown Prince he was a marvel of beauty. I have always believed that the Emperor Nicholas had a great deal of sentiment for him. *Honi soit qui mal y pense,* of course. Princess Christian spoke of it openly, but she's a fiend. As to the Czar of the Bulgarians, he's a sly hussy, a regular show-figure, but very intelligent, a remarkable man. He's very fond of me."

M. de Charlus, who could be so pleasant, became odious when he touched on these subjects. His self-complacency irritated one like an invalid who keeps on assuring you how well he is. I have often thought that the "faithful" who so much wanted the avowals withheld by the tortuous personage of Balbec, could not have put up with his ostentatious but uneasy display of his mania and would have felt as uncomfortable as if a morphinomaniac took out his syringe in front of them; probably they would soon have had enough of the confidences they thought they would relish. Besides, one got sick of hearing everybody relegated without proof to a category to which he belonged himself though he denied it. In spite of his intelligence, he had constructed for himself in that connection a narrow little philosophy (at the base of which there was perhaps a touch of that peculiar way of looking at life which characterised Swann) which attributed everything to special causes and, as always happens when a man is conscious of bordering on his own particular defect, he was unworthy of himself and yet unusually self-satisfied. So it came about that so earnest, so noble-minded a man could wear that idiotic smile when he enunciated: "as there are strong presumptions of the same character in regard to Ferdinand of Coburg's relations with the Emperor William, that might be the reason why Czar Ferdinand placed himself by the side of the Robber-Empires. *Dame,* after all, that is quite comprehensible. One is generous to one's sister, one doesn't refuse her anything. To my mind it would be a very charming explanation of the alliance of Germany and Bulgaria." And M. de Charlus laughed as long over this stupid explanation as though it had been an ingenious one which, even if there had been any justification for it, was as puerile as the observations he made about the war when he judged it from the feudal point of view of from that of a Knight of the Order of Jerusalem. He finished with a sensible observation: "It is astonishing that the public, though it only judges men and things in the war by the papers, is convinced that it is exercising its own initiative." M. de Charlus was right about that. I was told that Mme. de Forcheville's silences and hesitations were worth witnessing for the sake of her facial expression when she announced with deep personal conviction: "No, I do not believe that they will take Warsaw", "I am under the impression that it will not last a second winter." "What I do not want is a lame peace." "What alarms me, if you care for my opinion, is the Chamber." "Yes, I believe, all the same, they can break through." In enunciating these phrases, Odette's features assumed a knowing look which was emphasised when she remarked: "I don't say that the German armies don't fight well, but they lack that *cran* as we call it." In using that expression (or the word *mordant* in connection with the troops) she made a gesture of kneading with her hand, putting her head on one side and half-closing her eyes like an art-student. Her language bore more traces than ever of her admiration for the English whom she was no longer content to call as she used to "our neighbours across the Channel", or "our friends the English", but nothing less than "our loyal allies". Unnecessary to say that she never neglected to use in all contexts the expression "fair play" in order to show that the English considered the Germans unfair players. "Fair play is what is needed to win the war, as our brave allies say." And she rather awkwardly associated the name of her son-in-law with everything that concerned the English soldiers and alluded to the pleasure he found in living on intimate terms with the Australians, as also with the Scottish, the New Zealanders and the Canadians. "My son-in-law, Saint-Loup, knows the slang of all those brave 'tommies'. He knows how to make himself understood by those who came from the far 'Dominions' and he would just as soon fraternise with the most humble private as with the general commanding the base."

Let this digression about Mme. de Forcheville, while I am walking along the boulevard side by side with M. de Charlus, justify a longer one, to elucidate the relations of Mme. Verdurin with Brichot at this period. If poor Brichot, like Norpois, was judged with little indulgence by M. de Charlus (because the latter was at once extremely acute and, unconsciously, more or less Germanophile) he was actually treated much worse by the Verdurins. The latter were, of course, chauvinist, and they ought to have liked Brichot's articles which, for that matter, were not inferior to many publications considered delectable by Mme. Verdurin. The reader will, perhaps, recall that, even in the days of La Raspelière, Brichot had become, instead of the great man they used to think him, if not a Turk's head like Saniette, at all events the object of their thinly disguised raillery. Nevertheless, he was still one of the "faithfuls" which assured him some of the advantages tacitly allotted by the statutes to all the foundation and associated members of the little group. But as, gradually, perhaps owing to the war or through the rapid crystallisation of the long-delayed fashionableness with which all the necessary but till then invisible elements had long since saturated the Verdurin Salon, that salon had been opened to a new society and as the "faithfuls", at first the bait for this new society, had ended by being less and less frequently invited, so a parallel phenomenon was taking place in Brichot's case. In spite of the Sorbonne, in spite of the Institute, his fame had, until the war, not outgrown the limits of the Verdurin salon. But when almost daily he began writing articles embellished with that false brilliance we have so often seen him lavishly dispensing for the benefit of the "faithful" and as he possessed a real erudition which, as a true Sorbonian, he did not seek to hide under some of the graces he gave to it, society was literally dazzled. For once, moreover, it accorded its favour to a man who was far from being a nonentity and who could claim attention owing to the fertility of his intelligence and the resources of his memory. And while three duchesses went to spend the evening at Mme. Verdurin's, three others contested the honour of having the great man at their table; and when the invitation of one of them was accepted, she felt herself the freer because Mme. Verdurin, exasperated by the success of his articles in the Faubourg Saint-Germain, had taken care not to have him at her house when there was any likelihood of his encountering there some brilliant personage whom he did not yet know and who would hasten to capture him. Brichot in his old age was satisfied to bestow on journalism in exchange for liberal emoluments, all the distinction he had wasted gratis and unrecognised in the Verdurins' salon (for his articles gave him no more trouble than his conversation, so good a talker and so learned was he) and this might have brought him unrivalled fame and at one moment seemed on the eve of doing so, had it not been for Mme. Verdurin. Certainly Brichot's articles were far from being as remarkable as society people believed them to be. The vulgarity of the man was manifest at every instant under the pedantry of the scholar. And over and above imagery which meant nothing at all ("the Germans can no longer look the statue of Beethoven in the face", "Schiller must have turned in his grave", "the ink which initialled the neutrality of Belgium was hardly dry", "Lenin's words mean no more than the wind over the steppes") there were trivialities such as "Twenty thousand prisoners, that's something like a figure". "Our Command will know how to keep its eyes open once for all". "We mean to win; one point, that's all". But mixed up with that nonsense, there were so much knowledge, intelligence and good reasoning. Now Mme. Verdurin never began one of Brichot's articles without the anticipatory satisfaction of expecting to find absurdities in it and read it with concentrated attention so as to be certain not to let any of them escape her. Unfortunately there always were some, one hardly had to wait. The most felicitous quotation from an almost unknown author, unknown at all events, by the writer of the work Brichot referred to, was made use of to prove his unjustifiable pedantry and Mme. Verdurin awaited the dinner-hour with impatience so that she could let loose her guests' shrieks of laughter, "Well! What about our Brichot this evening? I thought of you when I was reading the quotation from Cuvier. Upon my word, I believe he's going crazy." "I haven't read it yet," said a "faithful". "What, you haven't read it yet? You don't know the delights in store for you. It's so perfectly idiotic that I nearly died of laughing." And delighted that someone or other had not yet read the particular article so that she could expose Brichot's absurdities herself, Mme. Verdurin told the butler to bring the *Temps* and began to read it aloud, emphasising the most simple phrases. After dinner, throughout the evening, the anti-Brichot campaign continued, but with a pretence of reserve. "I'm not reading this too loud because I'm afraid that down there," she pointed at the Comtesse Molé, "there's a lingering admiration for this rubbish. Society people are simpler than one would think." While they wanted Mme. Molé to hear what they were saying about her, they pretended the contrary by lowering their voices, and she, in cowardly fashion, disowned Brichot whom in reality she considered the equal of Michelet. She agreed with Mme. Verdurin and yet, so as to end on a note which seemed to her incontrovertible, added, "One cannot deny that it is well written." "You call that well written," rejoined Mme. Verdurin, "I consider that it's written like a pig," a sally which raised a society laugh, chiefly because Mme. Verdurin, rather abashed by the word "pig", had uttered it in a whisper, with her hand over her lips. Her vindictiveness towards Brichot increased the more because he naïvely displayed satisfaction at his success in spite of ill-humour provoked by the censorship each time, as he said, with his habitual use of slang to show he was not too don-like, it had *caviardé* a part of his article. To his face Mme. Verdurin did not let him perceive how poor an opinion she had of his articles except by a sullen demeanour which would have enlightened a more perceptive man. Once only she reproached him with using "I" so often. As a matter of fact he did so, partly from professional habit; expressions like: "I admit that", "I am aware that the enormous development of the fronts necessitates", et cetera, et cetera imposed themselves on him but still more because as a former militant anti-Dreyfusard who had surmised the German preparations long before the war, he had grown accustomed to continually writing: "I have denounced them since 1897", "I pointed it out in 1901", "I. warned them in my little brochure, very scarce to-day *'habent sua fata libelli'*" and thus the habit had taken root. He blushed deeply at Mme. Verdurin's bitter observation. "You are right, madame. One who loved the Jesuits as little as M. Combes, before he had been privileged with a preface by our charming master in delightful scepticism, Anatole France, who, unless I err, was my adversary—before the deluge, said that the 'I' was always detestable." From that moment Brichot replaced "I" by "we", but "we" did not prevent the reader from seeing that the writer was speaking about himself, on the contrary it enabled him never to cease talking about himself, making a running commentary out of his least significant sentences and composing an article simply on a negation, invariably protected by "we". For instance, Brichot had stated, maybe, in another article that the German armies had lost some of their value, he would then begin as follows: "'We' are not going to disguise the truth. 'We' have said that these German armies had lost some of their value. 'We' have not said that they were not still of great value. Still less shall 'we' say that they have no value at all, any more than 'we' should say that ground is gained which is not gained, et cetera, et cetera." In short, Brichot would have been able, merely by enunciating everything he would not say and by recalling everything that he had been saying for years and what Clausewitz, Ovid, Apollonius of Tyana had said so and so many centuries ago, easily to constitute the material of a large volume. It is a pity he did not publish it because those articles crammed with erudition are now difficult to obtain. The Faubourg Saint-Germain, instructed by Mme. Verdurin, began laughing at Brichot at her house, but, once they got away from the little clan, they continued to admire him. Then laughing at him became the fashion as it had been the fashion to admire him, and even those ladies who continued to be secretly interested in him, had no sooner read one of his articles, than they stopped and laughed at them in company, so as not to appear less intelligent than others. Brichot had never been so much talked about in the little clan as at this period, but with derision. The criterion of the intelligence of every newcomer was his opinion of Brichot's articles; if he responded unsatisfactorily the first time, they soon taught him how to judge people's intelligence. "Well, my dear friend," continued M. de Charlus, "all this is appalling and there's a good deal more to deplore than tiresome articles. They talk about vandalism, about the destruction of statues, but is not the destruction of so many wonderful young men who were polychrome statues of incomparable beauty also vandalism? Is not a city in which there are no more beautiful men like a city in which all the statuary has been destroyed? What pleasure can I have in going to dinner at a restaurant where I am served by old moss-grown pot-bellies who look like Père Didon, if not by women in mob caps who make me think I am at a Bouillon Duval. Exactly, my dear fellow, and I think I have the right to say so, for the Beautiful is as much the Beautiful in living matter. A fine pleasure to be served by rickety creatures with spectacles the reason of whose exemption can be read in their faces. Nowadays, if one wants to gratify one's eyes with the sight of a good-looking person in a restaurant, one must no longer seek him among the waiters but among the customers. And one may see a servant again, often as they are changed, but what about that English lieutenant who has been to the restaurant for the first time and will perhaps be killed to-morrow? When Augustus of Poland, as Morand, the delightful author of *Clarisse* narrates, exchanged one of his regiments against a collection of Chinese pots, in my opinion he did a bad business. To think that all those splendid footmen six feet high, who adorned the monumental staircases of our beautiful lady friends, have all been killed, most of them having joined up because people kept on telling them that the war would only last two months. Ah! little did they know, as I did, the power of Germany, the valour of the Prussian race," he added, forgetting himself. And then, noticing that he had allowed his point of view to be too clearly seen, he continued: "It is not so much Germany as the war itself that I fear for France. People imagine that the war is only a gigantic boxing-match at which they are gazing from afar, thanks to the papers. But that is completely untrue. It is a disease which, when it seems cured at one spot crops up in another. To-day, Noyon will be relieved, to-morrow we shall have neither bread nor chocolate, the day after, he who believed himself safe and would, if needs must, be ready to die an unimagined death, will be horrified to read in the papers that his class has been called up. As to monuments, the destruction of a unique masterpiece like Rheims is not so terrible to me as to witness the destruction of such numbers of *ensembles* which made the smallest village of France instructive and charming." Immediately I began thinking of Combray and how in former days I had thought myself diminished in the eyes of Mme. de Guermantes by avowing the modest situation which my family occupied there. I wondered if it had not been revealed to the Guermantes and to M. de Charlus whether by Legrandin or Swann or Saint-Loup or Morel. But that this might have been divulged was less painful to me than retrospective explanations. I only hoped that M. de Charlus would not allude to Combray. "I do not want to speak ill of the Americans, Monsieur," he continued, "it seems they are inexhaustibly generous and, since there has been no orchestral conductor in this war and each entered the dance considerably after the other and the Americans began when we were almost finished, they may have an ardour which four years of war has quenched among us. Even before the war they loved our country and our art and paid high prices for our masterpieces of which they have many now. But it is precisely this deracinated art, as M. Barrés would say, which is the reverse of everything which made the supreme charm of France. The Chateau explained the church which in its turn, because it had been a place of pilgrimage, explained the *chanson de geste*. As an illustration, I need not elaborate my own origin and my alliances; for that matter we are not concerned with that, but recently I had to settle some family interests and in spite of a certain coolness which exists between myself and the Saint-Loup family, I had to pay a visit to my niece who lives at Combray. Combray was only a little town like so many others, but our ancestors were represented as patrons in many of the painted windows of the church, in others our arms were inscribed. We had our chapel there and our tombs. This church was destroyed by the French and by the English because it served as an observation post for the Germans. All that medley of surviving history and of art which was France is being destroyed and it is not over yet. Of course I am not so ridiculous as to compare for family reasons the destruction of the Church of Combray with that of the Cathedral of Rheims which was a miracle of a Gothic cathedral in its spontaneous purity of unique statuary, or that of Amiens. I do not know if the raised arm of St. Firmin is smashed to atoms to-day. If it is, the the most noble affirmation of faith and of energy has disappeared from this world." "The symbol of it, Monsieur," I answered, "I love symbols as you do, but it would be absurd to sacrifice to the symbol the reality which it symbolises. The cathedrals must be adored until the day when in order to preserve them, it would be necessary to deny the truths which they teach. The raised arm of St. Firmin, with an almost military gesture, said: 'Let us be broken if honour demands it. Do not sacrifice men to stones whose beauty arises from having for a moment established human verities.'". "I understand what you mean," answered M. de Charlus, "and M. Barrés who alas! has been the cause of our making too many pilgrimages to the statue of Strasbourg and to the tomb of M. Deroulède, was moving and graceful when he wrote that the Cathedral of Rheims itself was less dear to us than the life of one of our infantrymen. This assertion makes the rage of our newspapers against the German general who said that the Cathedral of Rheims was less precious to him than the life of a German soldier, rather ridiculous. And what is so exasperating and harrowing is that every country says the same thing. The reasons given by the industrialist associations of Germany for retaining possession of Belfort as indispensable for the preservation of their country against our ideas of revenge are the same as those of Barrés exacting Mayence to protect us against the velleities of invasion by the Boches. How is it that the restitution of Alsace-Lorraine appeared to France an insufficient motive for a war and yet a sufficient motive for continuing it and for declaring it anew each year? You seem to believe the victory of France certain; I hope so with all my heart, you don't doubt that, but ever since, rightly or wrongly, the Allies believe that their own victory is assured (for my own part, of course, I should be delighted with such a solution, but I observe a great many paper victories, pyrrhic victories at a cost not revealed to us) and that the Boches are no longer confident of victory, we see Germany seeking peace and France wanting to prolong the war; that just France rightly desiring to make the voice of justice heard should be also France the compassionate, and make words of pity heard, were it only for the sake of her children, so that when spring-days come round and flowers bloom again, they will brighten other things than tombs. Be frank, my dear friend, you yourself exposed the theory to me that things only exist thanks to a perpetually renewed creation. You used to say that the creation of the world did not take place once and for all, but necessarily continues day by day. Well, if you said that in good faith you cannot except the war from that theory. It is all very well for our excellent Norpois to write (trotting out one of those rhetorical accessories he loves, like 'the dawn of victory' and 'General Winter') 'now that Germany has wanted war, the die is cast' the truth is that every day war is declared anew. Therefore he who wants to continue it is as culpable as he who began it, perhaps more, for the latter could not perhaps foresee all its horrors. And there is nothing to show that so prolonged a war, even if it has a victorious issue, will not have perils. It is difficult to talk about things which have no precedent and of repercussions on the organism of an operation which is attempted for the first time. Generally, it is true, we get over these novelties we're alarmed about quite well. The shrewdest Republican thought it mad to bring about the Disestablishment of the Church and it passed like a letter through the post. Dreyfus was rehabilitated, Picquart was made Minister of War without anybody saying a word. Nevertheless, what may not happen after such an exhaustion as that induced by an uninterrupted war lasting for several years? What will the men do when they come back? Will they be tired out? Will fatigue have broken them or driven them mad? All this may turn out badly, if not for France, at least for the Government and perhaps for the form of Government. Formerly you made me read the admirable Aimée de Coigny by Maurras. I should be much surprised if some Aimée de Coigny did not anticipate from the war which our Republic is making, developments expected by Aimée de Coigny in 1812 from the war the Empire was then making. If that Aimée de Coigny actually does exist, will her hopes be realised? I hope not. To return to the war itself: did the Emperor William begin it? I strongly doubt it and if so, what act has he committed that Napoleon, for instance, did not commit? Acts I, personally, consider abominable but I am astonished they should inspire so much horror in the Napoleonic incense-burners, in those who, on the day of the declaration of war, shrieked like General X—: 'I have been awaiting this day for forty years. It is the greatest day of my life;' Heaven knows if anyone protested more loudly than I when society gave a disproportionate position to the Nationalists, to soldiers, when every friend of the Arts was accused of doing things which were injurious to the Fatherland, when every unwarlike civilisation was considered deleterious. Hardly an authentic social figure counted in comparison with a general, Some crazy woman or other nearly introduced me to M. Syveton! You will tell me that all I was concerned to uphold were laws of society; but, in spite of their apparent frivolity, they might perhaps have prevented many excesses. I have always honoured those who defend grammar and logic and it is only realised fifty years later that they have averted great dangers. And our Nationalists are the most Germanophobe, the most diehard of men, but during the last fifteen years their philosophy has entirely changed. As a fact, they are now urging the continuation of the war but it is only to exterminate a belligerent race and from love of peace. For the warlike civilisation they thought so beautiful fifteen years ago now horrifies them; not only they reproach Prussia with having allowed the military element in her country to predominate, but they consider that at all periods military civilisations were destructive of everything they have now discovered to be precious, including in the Arts that of gallantry. It suffices for one of their critics to be converted to nationalism for him to become at once a friend of peace; he is persuaded that in all warlike civilisations women play a humiliating and lowly part. One does not venture to reply that the ladies of the Knights in the Middle Ages and Dante's Beatrice were perhaps placed on a throne as elevated as M. Becque's heroines. I am expecting one of these days to find myself placed at table below a Russian revolutionary or perhaps only below one of our generals who make war because of their horror of war and in order to punish a people for cultivating an ideal which they themselves considered the only invigorating one fifteen years ago. The unhappy Czar was still honoured some months ago because he called the Conference of the Hague, but now that we are saluting free Russia we forget her only title to glory, thus the wheel of the world turns. And yet Germany uses so many of the same expressions as France that one might think that she's copying her. She never stops saying that she is fighting for her existence. When I read: 'We are fighting against an implacable and cruel enemy until we have obtained a peace which will guarantee our future against all aggression and in order that the blood of our brave soldiers should not have been shed in vain,' or 'who is not with us is against us', I do not know if this phrase is Emperor William's or M. Poincaré's, for each one has used the same words with variations twenty times, though to tell you the truth I must confess that the Emperor in this case was the imitator of the President of the Republic. France would not perhaps have held to prolonging the war if she had remained weak, but neither would Germany perhaps have been in such a hurry to finish it if she had not ceased to be strong, I mean, to be as strong as she was, for you will see she is still strong enough." He had got into the habit of talking very loud from nervousness, from seeking relief from impressions which, having never cultivated any art, he felt impelled to cast forth, as an aviator his bombs, into an open field where his words struck no one, and especially in society where they fell haphazard and where he was listened to with attention owing to snobbishness and where he so tyrannised his audience that one could say it was intimidated. On the boulevards this harangue was, moreover, a mark of his scorn for passers-by on whose account he no more lowered his voice than he would have moved aside for them. But there his voice exploded and astounded, and, especially when his remarks were sufficiently intelligible for passers-by to turn round, the latter might have had us arrested as defeatists. I drew M. de Charlus' attention to this but succeeded only in exciting his hilarity: "Admit that it really would be funny," he said. "After all, one never knows, anyone of us risks every evening being in the news-column the following day; and, if it comes to that, why shouldn't I be shot in the ditch of Vincennes? The same thing happened to my great-uncle the Duc d'Enghien, Thirst for noble blood delights the populace which in this respect displays more refinement than lions. As to those animals, you know, if Mme. Verdurin only had a scratch on her nose, she'd say they had sprung upon, what in my youth one would have called her *pif*." And he began to laugh with his mouth wide open as though he had been alone in a room. At moments, seeing certain rather suspicious individuals emerging from a gloomy passage near where M. de Charlus was passing and congregating at some distance from him, I wondered whether he would prefer me to leave him alone or stay with him. Thus, one who met an old man subject to epileptic fits whose incoherent behaviour foreshadowed the probable imminence of an attack, would ask himself whether his company is desired as a support or feared as that of a witness from whom he might wish to hide the attack and whose mere presence perhaps might induce it whereas complete quiet might prevent it, while the possible event from which he cannot decide whether to fly or not, is revealed by the zigzag walk of the patient, similar to that of a drunken man. In the present case of M. de Charlus, the various divergent positions, signs of a possible incident of which I was not sure whether he wished it to happen or feared that my presence would prevent it, were, by an ingenious setting, not assumed by the baron himself who was walking straight on, but by a whole company of actors. All the same I think he preferred avoiding the encounter for he drew me into a side street more obscure than the boulevard and where there was a constant stream of soldiers of every army and of every nation, a juvenile influx compensating and consoling M. de Charlus for the reflux of all those men to the frontier which had caused that frightful void in Paris in the first days of the mobilisation. M. de Charlus unceasingly admired the brilliant uniforms passing before us which made Paris as cosmopolitan as a port, as unreal as a painted scene composed of architectural forms making a background for the most varied and seductive costumes. He retained all his respect and affection for certain *grandes dames* who were accused of defeatism, just as he did for those who had formerly been accused of Dreyfusism. He only regretted that in condescending to be political, they should have given a hold to "the polemics of journalists." His view was unchanged so far as they were concerned. For his frivolity was so systematic that birth combined with beauty and other glamours was the lasting thing, and the war, like the Dreyfus Affair, a vulgar and fugitive fashion. Had the Duchesse de Guermantes been shot as an overture to a separate peace with Austria, he would have considered it heroic and no more degrading than it seems to-day that Marie Antoinette was sentenced to decapitation. At that moment, M. de Charlus, looking as noble as a St. Vallier or a St. Mégrin, was erect, rigid, solemn, spoke gravely, making none of those gestures and movements which reveal those of his kind. Yet why is it there are none whose voice is just right? At the very moment when he was talking of the most serious things, there was still that false note which needed tuning. And M. de Charlus literally did not know which way to look next, raising his head as though he felt the need of an opera-glass, which, however, would not have been much use to him, for, on account of the zeppelin raid of the previous day having aroused the vigilance of the public authorities, there were soldiers right up to the sky. The aeroplanes I had seen some hours earlier, like insects or brown spots upon the evening blue, continued to pass into the night deepened still more by the partial extinction of the street lamps like luminous faggots. The greatest impression of beauty given us by these flying human stars was perhaps that of making us look at the sky whither one rarely turned one's eyes in that Paris of which in 1914 I had seen the almost defenceless beauty awaiting the menace of the approaching enemy. Certainly there was now, as then, the ancient unchanged splendour of a moon cruelly, mysteriously serene, which poured upon the still intact monuments the useless loveliness of her light, but, as in 1914, and more than in 1914, there was something else, other lights and intermittent beams which, one realised, whether they came from aeroplanes or from the searchlights of the Eiffel Tower, were directed by an intelligent will, by a protective vigilance which caused that same emotion, inspired that same gratitude and calm I had experienced in Saint-Loup's room, in the cell of that military cloister where so many fervent and disciplined hearts were being prepared for the day when without a single hesitation they were to consummate their sacrifice in the fullness of youth.

During the raid of the evening before the sky was more agitated than the earth, but when it was over, the sky became comparatively calm but, like the sea after a tempest, not completely so. Aeroplanes rose like rockets into the sky to rejoin the stars and searchlights moved slowly across the sky divided into sections by their pale star dust like wandering Milky Ways. The aeroplanes so mingled with the stars that one could almost imagine oneself in another hemisphere looking at new constellations. M. de Charlus expressed his admiration for these aviators and, as he could no more help giving free play to his Germanophilism than to his other inclinations, although he denied both, said to me: "Moreover, I must add that I admire the Germans in their Gothas just as much. And think of the courage that is needed to go in those zeppelins. They are simply heroes. And if they do throw their bombs upon civilians, don't our batteries fire upon theirs? Are you afraid of Gothas and cannon?" I avowed that I was not, but perhaps I was wrong. Having got into the habit, through idleness, of postponing my work from day to day, I doubtless supposed death might deal in the same way with me. How could one be afraid of a shell which you are convinced will not strike you that day? Moreover, these isolated ideas of bombs thrown, of possible death, added nothing tragic to the image I had formed of the passing German airships, until, one evening, I might see a bomb thrown towards us from one of them as it was tossed and segmented in the storm-clouds or from an aeroplane which, though I knew its murderous errand, I had till then regarded as celestial. For the ultimate reality of danger is only perceived through something new and irreducible to what one has previously known which we call an impression and which is often, as was the case now, summed up in a line, a line which would disclose a purpose, a line in which there was a latent power of action which modified it; thus upon the Pont de la Concorde around the menacing and pursued aeroplane, as though the fountains of the Champs Elysées, of the Place de la Concorde, of the Tuileries, were reflected in the clouds, searchlights like jets of luminous water pierced the sky like arrows, lines full of purpose, the foreseeing and protective purpose of powerful and wise men towards whom I felt that same gratitude as on the night in quarters at Doncières when their power deigned to watch over us with such splendid precision.

The night was as beautiful as in 1914 when Paris was equally menaced. The moonbeams seemed like soft, continuous magnesium-light offering for the last time nocturnal visions of beautiful sites such as the Place Vendôme and the Place de la Concorde, to which my fear of shells which might destroy them lent a contrasting richness of as yet untouched beauty as though they were offering up their defenceless architecture to the coming blows. "You are not afraid?" repeated M.

de Charlus. "Parisians do not seem to realise their danger. I am told that Mme. Verdurin gives parties every day. I only know it by hearsay for I know absolutely nothing about them; I have entirely broken with them," he added, lowering not only his eyes as if a telegraph boy had passed by, but also his head and his shoulders and lifting his arms with a gesture that signified: "I wash my hands of them!" "At least I can tell you nothing about them," (although I had not asked him). "I know that Morel goes there a great deal" (it was the first, time he had spoken to me about him). "It is suggested that he much regrets the past, that he wants to make it up with me again," he continued, showing simultaneously the credulity of a suburban who remarks: "It is commonly said that France is negotiating more than ever with Germany, even that *pourparlers* are taking place" and of the lover whom the worst rebuffs cannot discourage. "In any case, if he wants to, he has only to say so. I am older than he is and it is not for me to take the first step." And indeed the uselessness of his saying so was abundantly evident. But, besides, he was not even sincere and for that reason one was embarrassed about M. de Charlus because, when he said it was not for him to take the first step, he was, on the contrary, making one and was hoping that I should offer to bring about a reconciliation. Certainly I knew the naïve or assumed credulity of those who care for someone or even who are simply not invited by him, and impute to that person a wish he has never expressed in spite of fulsome importunities.

It must here be noted, that, unhappily, the very next day, M. de Charlus suddenly found himself face to face with Morel in the street. The latter in order to excite his jealousy took him by the arm and told him some tales that were more or less true and when M. de Charlus, bewildered and urgently wanting Morel to stay with him that evening, entreated him not to go away, the other, catching sight of a friend, said good-bye. M. de Charlus, in a fury, hoping that the threat which, as may be imagined, he was never likely to execute, would make Morel remain with him, said to him: "Take care, I shall be revenged," and Morel turned away with a laugh, smacking his astonished friend on the back and putting his arm round him. From the sudden tremulous intonation with which M. de Charlus, in talking of Morel, had emphasised his words, from the pained expression in the depth of his eyes, I had the impression that there was something more behind his words than ordinary insistence. I was not mistaken and I will relate at once the two incidents which later proved it. (I am anticipating by many years in regard to the second of these incidents, which was after the death of M. de Charlus and that only occurred at a much later period. We shall have occasion to see him again several times, very different from the man we have hitherto known and in particular, when we see him the last time, it will be at a period when he had completely forgotten Morel). The first of these events happened only two years after the evening when I was walking down the boulevards, as I say, with M. de Charlus. I met Morel. Immediately I thought of M. de Charlus, of the pleasure it would give him to see the violinist, and I begged the latter to go and see him, were it only once. "He has been good to you," I told Morel. "He is now old, he might die, one must liquidate old quarrels and efface their memory." Morel appeared entirely to share my view as to the desirability of a reconciliation. Nevertheless, he refused categorically to pay a single visit to M. de Charlus. "You are wrong," I said to him. "Is it obstinacy or indolence or perversity or ill-placed pride or virtue (be sure that won't be attacked), or is it coquetry?" Then the violinist, distorting his face into an avowal which no doubt cost him dear, answered with a shiver: "No, it is none of those reasons. As to virtue, I don't care a damn, as to perversity, on the contrary, I'm beginning to pity him, nor is it from coquetry, that would be futile. It is not from idleness, there are days together when I do nothing but twiddle my thumbs. No, it has nothing to do with all that, it is—I beg you tell no one, and it is folly for me to tell you—it's— it's because I'm afraid." He began trembling in all his limbs. I told him I did not understand what he meant. "Don't ask me; don't let us say any more about it. You don't know him as I do. I could tell you things you've no idea of." "But what harm could he do you? Less still if there were no resentment between you. And, besides, you know at bottom he is very kind." "Yes, indeed, I know it. I know that he is kind and full of delicacy and right feeling. But leave me alone, don't talk about it, I beg you, I'm ashamed that I'm afraid of him." The second incident dates from after the death of M. de Charlus. There were brought to me several *souvenirs* which he had left me and a letter enclosed in three envelopes written at least ten years before his death. But he had at that time been so seriously ill that he had made his will, then he had partially recovered before falling into the condition in which we shall see him later on the day of an afternoon party at the Princesse de Guermantes'. The letter had remained in a casket with objects he had left to certain friends, for seven years; seven years during which he had completely forgotten Morel. The letter written in a very fine yet firm hand was as follows: "My dear friend, the ways of Providence are sometimes inscrutable. It makes use of the sin of an inferior individual to prevent a just man's fall from virtue. You know Morel, you know where he came from, from what fate I wanted to raise him, so to speak, to my own level. You know that he preferred to return, not merely to the dust and ashes from which every man, for man is veritably a phoenix, can be reborn, but into the slime and mud where the viper has its being. He let himself sink and thus preserved me from falling into the pit. You know that my arms contain the device of Our Lord Himself: '*Inculcabis super leonem et aspidem*', with a man represented with a lion and a serpent at his feet as a heraldic support. Now if the lion in me has permitted itself to be trampled on, it is because of the serpent and its prudence which is sometimes too lightly called a defect, because the profound wisdom of the Gospel has made of it a virtue, at least a virtue for others. Our serpent whose hisses were formerly harmoniously modulated when he had a charmer—himself greatly charmed for that matter—was not only a musical reptile but possessed to the point of cowardice that virtue which I now hold for divine, prudence.. It was this divine prudence which made him resist the appeals which I sent him to come and see me. And I shall have neither peace in this world nor hope of forgiveness in the next if I do not make this avowal to you. It is he who in this matter was the instrument of divine wisdom, for I had resolved that he should not leave me alive. It was necessary that one or the other of us should disappear. I had decided to kill him. God himself inspired his prudence to preserve me from a crime. I do not doubt but that the intercession of the Archangel Michael, my patron saint, played a great part in this matter, and I implore him to forgive me for having so much neglected him during many years and for having requited him so ill for the innumerable bounties he has shown me, especially in my fight against evil. I owe to his service, I say it from the fulness of my faith and my intelligence, that the Celestial Father inspired Morel not to come and see me. And now it is I who am dying. Your faithful and devoted *Semper idem*, P. G. Charlus." Then I understood Morel's fear. Certainly there were both pride and literature in that letter, but the avowal was true. And Morel knew better than I did that "almost mad side" which Mme. de Guermantes recognised in her brother-in-law and which was not limited, as I had supposed until then, to momentary outbursts of superficial and futile passion.

But we must retrace our steps. I am still walking down the boulevards beside M. de Charlus, who is using me as a vague intermediary for overtures of peace between him and Morel. Observing that I did not reply, he thus continued: "As to that, I do not know why he doesn't play any more. Apparently there is no more music, under the pretext of the war, but they dance and dine out. These fêtes represent what will be perhaps, if the Germans advance further, the last days of our Pompeii. It only needs the lava of some German Vesuvius (their naval guns are not less terrible than a volcano) to surprise them at their toilet and eternalise their gesture by interrupting it; children will later on be educated by illustrations of Mme. Molé about to put the last layer of paint on her face before going to dine with her sister-in-law, or Sosthène de Guermantes finishing painting her false eyebrows. It will be lecturing material for the Brichots of the future; the frivolity of a period after ten centuries is worthy of the most serious erudition, especially if it has been preserved intact by a volcanic irruption in which matter akin to lava was thrown by bombardment. What documents for future history! When asphyxiating gases analogous to those emitted by Vesuvius and earthquakes like those which buried Pompeii will preserve intact all the remaining imprudent women who have not fled to Bayonne with their pictures and their statues. Moreover, has it not been Pompeii, a bit at a time every evening, for more than a year? These people flying to their cellars, not to bring out an old bottle of Mouton-Rothschild or of St. Emilion, but to hide themselves and their most precious possessions like the priests of Herculaneum surprised by death at the moment when they were carrying off the sacred vessels. Attachment to an object always brings death to the possessor. Paris was not, like Herculaneum, founded by Hercules. But what similarities force themselves upon one and that lucidity which has come to us is not only of our period, every period possessed it. If we think that to-morrow we may share the fate of the cities of Vesuvius, the women of those days believed they were menaced with the fate of the Cities of the Plain. They have discovered on the walls of one of the houses of Pompeii the inscription: 'Sodom and Gomorra.'" I do not know if it was this name of Sodom and the ideas which it aroused in him, or whether it was that of the bombardment which made M. de Charlus lift for an instant his eyes to Heaven, but he soon brought them down to earth again. "I admire all the heroes of this war," he said. "My dear fellow, take all those English soldiers whom I thought of somewhat lightly at the beginning of the war as mere football-players presumptuous enough to measure themselves against professionals—and what professionals! Well, merely aesthetically they are athletes of Greece, yes, of Greece, my dear fellow, these are the youths of Plato or rather of the Spartans. A friend of mine went to their camp at Rouen and saw marvels of which one has no idea. It is no longer Rouen, it is another town. Of course there is still the old Rouen with the emaciated saints of the Cathedral. That is beautiful also, but it is another thing. And our *poilus*! I cannot tell you what a savour I find in our *poilus*, in our little '*parigots*.' There, like that one who is passing so free and easy in that droll, wide-awake manner. I often stop and have a word with them. What quick intelligence, what good sense! And the boys from the Provinces, how nice they are with their rolling 'r's and their country jargon. I have always lived a great deal in the country, I have slept in the farms, I know how to talk to these people. But our admiration for the French must not allow us to underestimate our enemies, that diminishes ourselves. And you don't know what a German soldier is, you've never seen them as I have, on parade doing the goose-step in 'Unter den Linden.'" In returning to the ideal of virility he had touched on at Balbec which in the course of time had taken a philosophic form, he made use of absurd arguments and at moments, even when he showed superiority, these forced one to perceive the limitations of a mere man of fashion, even though he was an intelligent man of fashion; "You see," he said, "that superb fellow, the German soldier, is a strong, healthy being, who only thinks of the greatness of his country, 'Deutschland über Alles' which isn't as stupid as it sounds, and while they prepare themselves in virile fashion we are steeped in dilettantism." That word probably signified to M. de Charlus something analogous to literature, for immediately, recalling without doubt that I loved literature and, for a time, had the intention of devoting myself to it, he tapped me on the shoulder (taking the opportunity of leaning on it until I felt as bad as I used to during my military service from the recoil of a "76") and remarked, as though to soften the reproach: "Yes, we have ruined ourselves by dilettantism, all of us, you too, remember, you can repeat your *mea culpa* like me. We have all been too dilettante." Through surprise at the reproach, lack of the spirit of repartee, deference towards my interlocutor and touched by his friendly kindness, I replied, as though, at his invitation, I ought also to strike my breast. And this was perfectly senseless, for I had not a shadow of dilettantism to reproach myself with. "Well," he said, "I'll leave you," the knot of men which had escorted us some distance having at last disappeared, "I'm going home to bed like an old gentleman, the war seems to have changed all our habits—one of Norpois' aphorisms." As to that, I knew that M. de Charlus would not be less surrounded by soldiers because he was at home for he had transformed his mansion into a military hospital, yielding in that less to his obsession than to his good heart.

It was a clear, still night and, in my imagination, the Seine, flowing between its circular bridges, circular through a combination of structure and reflection, re-sembled the Bosphorus, the moon symbolising, may-be, that invasion which the defeatism of M. de Charlus predicted or the cooperation of our Musulman broth-ers with the armies of France, thin and curved like a sequin, seemed to be placing the Parisian sky under the oriental sign of the crescent. For an instant longer M. de Charlus stopped, facing a Senegalese and, in farewell took my hand and crushed it, a German habit, peculiar to people of the baron's sort, continuing for some minutes to knead it, as Cottard would have said, as though the baron wanted to impart to my joints a suppleness they had not lost. In the case of blind people touch supplements the vision to a certain extent; I hardly know which sense this kneading took the place of. Perhaps he believed he was only pressing my hand, as, no doubt, he also believed he was only glancing at the Senegalese who passed into the shadows and did not deign to notice he was being admired. But in both cases M. de Charlus made a mistake; there was an excess of contact and of staring. "Is not the whole Orient of Decamps, of Fromentin, of Ingres, of Delacroix in all this?" he remarked, still immobilised by the departure of the Senegalese. "You know that I am never interested in things and people except as a painter or as a philosopher. Besides, I'm too old. But what a pity, to complete the picture, that one of us two is not an odalisque."

It was not the Orient of Decamps or even of Delacroix which began haunting my imagination when the baron left me, but the old Orient of the *Thousand and One Nights* which I had so much loved. Losing myself more and more in the network of black streets, I was thinking of the Caliph Haroun Al Raschid in quest of adventures in the lost quarters of Bagdad. Moreover, heat, due to the weather and to my walking, had made me thirsty, but all the bars had been closed long since and on account of the shortage of petrol the few taxis I met, driven by Levantines or negroes, did not even trouble to respond to my signs. The only place where I could have obtained something to drink and have regained the strength to return home, would have been a hotel. But in the street, rather far from the centre, I had now reached, all the hotels had been closed since the Gothas began hurling their bombs on Paris. The same applied to nearly all the shops whose proprietors, owing to the dearth of employees or because they themselves had taken fright and had fled to the country, had left upon their doors the usual notice, written by hand, announcing their reopening at a distant and problematical date. Those establishments which survived, announced in the same fashion they they would only open twice a week, and one felt that misery, desolation and fear inhabited the whole quarter. I was the more surprised to observe, amongst these abandoned houses, one where, in contrast, life seemed to have conquered fear and failure and which seemed to be full of activity and opulence. Behind the closed shutters of every window, lights, shaded to conform to police regulations, revealed complete indifference to economy and every few moments the door opened to admit some new visitor. This hotel must have excited the jealousy of the neighbouring shopkeepers (on account of the money which its owners must be making) and my curiosity was aroused on noticing an officer emerge from it at a distance of some fifteen paces which was too far for me to be able to recognise him in the darkness.

Yet something about him struck me. It was not his face for I could not see it nor was it his uniform which was disguised in an ample cloak, it was the extraordinary disproportion between the number of different points past which his body flitted and the minute number of seconds employed in an exit, which resembled an attempted sortie by someone besieged. This made me believe, though I could not formally recognise him—whether by his outline, his slimness or his gait, or—even by his velocity but by a sort of ubiquity peculiar to him—that it was Saint-Loup. Who-ever he was, the officer with this gift of occupying so many different points in space in so short a time, had disappeared, without noticing me, in a cross street, and I stood asking myself whether or not I should enter this hotel the modest appearance of which made me doubt if it was really Saint-Loup who had emerged from it. I now remembered that Saint-Loup had got himself unhappily mixed up in an espionage affair owing to the appearance of his name in some letters seized upon a German officer. Full justice had been rendered him by the military authority but in spite of myself I related that fact to what I now saw. Was that hotel used as a meeting-place by spies? The officer had been gone some moments when I saw several privates of various arms enter and this added to my suspicions; and I was extremely thirsty. "It is probable I can get something to drink here," I said to myself and I took advantage of that to try and satisfy my curiosity in spite of my apprehensions. I do not think, however, that it was curiosity which decided me to climb up the several steps of the little staircase at the end of which the door of a sort of vestibule was open, no doubt on account of the heat. I believed at first that I should not be able to satisfy it for I saw several people come and ask for rooms, to whom the reply was given that there was not a single one vacant. Soon I grasped that all the people of the place had against them was that they did not belong to that nest of spies, for an ordinary sailor presented himself and they immediately gave him No. 28. I was able, thanks to the darkness, without being seen myself, to observe several soldiers and two men of the working class who were talking quietly in a small, stuffy room showily decorated with coloured portraits of women out of magazines and illustrated reviews. The men were expressing patriotic opinions: "There's no help for it, one must do like the rest," said one. "Certainly, I don't think I'm going to be killed," another said in answer to a wish I had not heard, and who, I gathered, was leaving the following day for a dangerous post. "Just think of it, at twenty-two! It would be pretty stiff after only doing six months!" he cried in a tone revealing, more even than a desire to live, the justice of his reasoning as though being only twenty-two ought to give him a better chance of not being killed, in fact, that it was impossible he should be. "In Paris it's wonderful," said another, "one wouldn't think there was a war on. Are you joining up, Julot?" "Of course I'm joining up. I want to go and have a smack at those dirty Boches." "That Joffre! He's a chap who slept with Minister's wives, he's not done anything." "It's rotten to hear that sort of stuff," interrupted an aviator who was somewhat older, turning towards the last speaker, a workman. "I advise you not to talk like that when you get to the front or the *poilus* will very soon have you out of it." The banality of this conversation gave me no great desire to hear more and I was about to go up or down when my attention was roused by hearing the following words which made me tremble. "It is extraordinary that the *patron* has not come back yet, at this time of night. I don't know where he'll find those chains." "But the other is already chained up." "Yes, of course he's chained — in a way. If I were chained like that I'd pretty soon free myself." "But the padlock is locked." "Oh! It's locked all right but if one tried, one could force it open. The trouble is the chains aren't long enough. You aren't going to explain that sort of thing to me, considering I was beating him the whole night till my hands bled." "Well, you'll have to take a turn at it to-night." "No, it's not my turn, it's Maurice's. It will be my turn on Sunday. The patron promised me." Now I knew why the sailor's strong arms were needed. If peaceful citizens had been refused admittance, it was not because the hotel was a nest of spies. An atrocious crime was going to be consummated if someone did not arrive in time to discover it and have the guilty arrested. On this threatened yet peaceful night all this seemed like a dream story and I deliberately entered the hotel with the determination of one who wants to see justice done with the enthusiasm of a poet. I lightly touched my hat and those present, without disturbing themselves, answered my salute more or less politely. "Will you please tell me whom I can ask for a room and for something to drink?" "Wait a minute, the *patron* has gone out." "But the chief is upstairs," suggested one of them. "You know perfectly well you can't disturb him." "Do you think they'll give me a room?" "Yes, I believe so, 43 must be free," said the young man who was sure of not being killed because he was only twenty-two, making room for me on the sofa beside him. "It would be a good thing to open the window, there's an awful lot of smoke here," said the aviator, and indeed each of them had a pipe or a cigarette. "Yes, that's all right, but shut the shutters first; you know lights are forbidden on account of zeppelins." "There won't be any more zeppelins, the papers said that they'd all been shot down." "They won't come! They won't come! What do you know about it? When you've been fifteen months at the front as I have, when you've shot down your five German aeroplanes, then you'll be able to talk. It's absurd to believe the papers. They were over Compiègne yesterday and killed a mother with her two children." The young man who hoped not to be killed and who had an energetic, open and sympathetic face spoke with ardent eyes and with profound pity. "There's no news of big Julot. His godmother hasn't had a letter from him for eight days and it's the first time he has been so long without giving her any news." "Who's his godmother?" "The lady who keeps the place of convenience below Olympia." "Do they sleep together?" "What are you talking about, she's a perfectly respectable married woman. She sends him money every week because she's got a good heart. She's a jolly good sort." "So you know big Julot?" "Do I know him?" The young man of twenty-two answered hotly. "He's one of my most intimate friends. There aren't many I think as much of as I do of him, he's a good pal, always ready to do one a turn. It would be a bad look out if anything happened to him." Someone proposed a game of dice and from the fevered fashion in which the young man cast them and called out the results with his eyes starting out of his head, it was easy to see that he had the temperament of a gambler. I could not quite grasp what someone else said to him just then but he suddenly cried in a tone of deep resentment. "Julot a pimp! He may say he is but he bloody well isn't. I've seen him pay his women. Yes I have. I don't say that Algerian Jeanne hasn't ever given him a bit. But never more than five francs, a woman in a house, earning more than fifty francs a day. To think of a man letting a woman give him only five francs. And now she's at the front, she's having a pretty hard life, I admit, but she earns what she likes and she never sends him anything. Julot a pimp, indeed there'd be plenty of pimps at that rate. Not only he isn't a pimp, but I think he's a fool into the bargain." The oldest of the party, whom no doubt the *patron* had entrusted with keeping a certain amount of order, having gone out for a moment, only heard the end of the conversation but he stared at me and seemed visibly annoyed at the effect which it might have produced upon me. Without specially addressing the young man of twenty-two who had been exposing and developing his theory of venal love, he remarked in a general way: "You're talking too much and too loud The window is open. People are asleep at this hour. You know, if the *patron* heard you, there would be trouble." Just at that moment there was a sound of a door, opening, and everybody kept quiet, thinking it was the *patron*. But it was only a foreign chauffeur, whom everybody welcomed. When the young man of twenty-two, seeing the superb watch-chain extending across the new-comer's waistcoat, bestowed on him a questioning and laughing glance followed by a frown of his eyebrows at the same time giving me a severe wink, I understood that the first glance meant "Hullo! Where did you steal that? All my congratulations!" and the second "Don't say anything. We don't know this chap, so look out." Suddenly the *patron* came in sweating, carrying several yards of heavy chains, strong enough to chain up several prisoners and said: "I've got a nice load here. If all of you were not so lazy, I shouldn't be obliged to go myself." I told him I wanted a room for some hours only, "I could not find a carriage and I am not very well, but I should like to have something taken up to my room to drink." "Pierrot, go to the cellar and fetch some cassis and tell them to prepare No. 43. There's No. 7 ringing. They say they're ill! Nice sort of illness! They're after cocaine, they look half-doped. They ought to be chucked out. Have a pair of sheets been put in No. 22? There you are, there's No. 7 ringing again. Run and see. What are you doing there, Maurice? You know very well you're expected, go up to 14 his, and look sharp!" Maurice went out rapidly, following the *patron* who was evidently annoyed that I had seen his chains. "How is it you're so late?" inquired the young man of twenty-two of the chauffeur. "What do you mean, so late, I'm an hour too early. But it's too hot to walk about, my appointment's only at midnight." "But who are you here for?" "For Pamela la Charmeuse," answered the oriental chauffeur, whose laugh disclosed beautiful white teeth. "Ah!" exclaimed the young man of twenty-two. Soon I was shown up to No. 43 but the atmosphere was so unpleasant and my curiosity so great that, having drunk my cassis, I descended the stairs, then, seized with another idea, I went up again and, without stopping at the floor where my room was, I went right up to the top. All of a sudden, from a room which was isolated at the end of the corridor, I seemed to hear stifled groans. I went rapidly towards them and applied my ear to the door. "I implore you, pity, pity, unloose me, unchain me, do not strike me so hard," said a voice. "I kiss your feet, I humiliate myself, I won't do it again, have pity." "I won't, you blackguard," replied another voice, "and as you're screaming and dragging yourself about on your knees like that, I'll tie you to the bed. No mercy!" And I heard the crack of a cat-o'nine-tails, probably loaded with nails for it was followed by cries of pain. Then I perceived that there was a lateral peep-hole in the room, the curtain of which they had forgotten to draw. Creeping softly in that direction, I glided up to the peep-hole and there on the bed, like Prometheus bound to his rock, squirming under the strokes of a cat-o-nine-tails, which was, as a fact, loaded with nails, wielded by Maurice, already bleeding and covered with bruises which proved he was not submitting to the torture for the first time, I saw before me M. de Charlus. All of a sudden the door opened and someone entered who, happily, did not see me. It was Jupien. He approached the Baron with an air of respect and an intelligent smile. "Well! Do you need me?" The Baron requested Jupien to send Maurice out for a moment. Jupien put him out with the greatest heartiness. "We can't be heard, I suppose?"

asked the Baron. Jupien assured him that they could not. The Baron knew that Jupien, though he was as intelligent as a man of letters, had no sort of practical sense, and talked in front of designing people with hidden meanings that deceived no one, mentioning surnames everyone knew. "One second," interrupted Jupien who had heard a bell ring in room No. 3. It was a Liberal Deputy who was going away. Jupien did not need to look at the number of the bell, he knew the sound of it, as the deputy came after luncheon every day. That particular day he had been obliged to change his hour because he had to attend his daughter's marriage at mid-day at St. Pierre de Chaillot So he had come in the evening, but wanted to get away in good time because of his wife who got anxious if he came home late, especially in these times of bombardment. Jupien made a point of accompanying him to the door so as to show deference towards the honourable gentleman without any eye to his own advantage. For while the deputy repudiating the exaggerations of the Action Française (he would for that matter have been incapable of understanding a line of Charles Maurras or of Léon Daudet), was on good terms with Ministers who were flattered at being invited to his shooting parties, Jupien would never have dared to solicit the slightest help from him in his occasional difficulties with the police. He fully understood, if he had risked talking about such matters to the wealthy and timid legislator, he would not have been spared the most harmless raid but would instantly have lost the most generous of his customers. Having accompanied the deputy to the door, the latter pulled his hat over his eyes, raised his collar and gliding rapidly away as he did in his electoral campaigns, believed he was hiding his face. Jupien—going up again to M. de Charlus, said: "It was M. Eugène." At Jupien's, as in lunatic asylums, people were only called by their first names, but, to satisfy the curiosity of the habitués and increase the prestige of his house, he took care to add the surnames in a whisper. Sometimes, however, Jupien did not know the identity of his clients, so he invented them and said that this one was a stockbroker, another a man of title or an artist; trifling and amusing mistakes so far as those whom he wrongly named were concerned. He finally quite resigned himself to ignorance as to the identity of M. Victor. Jupien further had the habit of pleasing the Baron by doing the contrary of what is considered the right thing at certain parties: "I am going to introduce M. Lebrun to you" (in his ear: "he calls himself M. Lebrun but in reality he's a Russian Grand-Duke.)" In another sense, Jupien did not think it interesting enough to introduce a milkman to M. de Charlus, but, with a wink: "He's a sort of milkman, but over and above that he's one of the most dangerous *apaches* in Belleville." (The rollicking way in which Jupien said "*apache*" was worth seeing). And as though this observation were not enough, he added others such as: "He has been sentenced several times for stealing and burgling houses. He was sent to Fresnes for fighting (the same jolly air) with people in the street whom he half crippled and he has been in an African battalion where he killed his sergeant."

The Baron was slightly annoyed with Jupien because he knew that everybody more or less in that house he had charged his factotum to buy and have run by an underling, owing to the indiscretions of the uncle of Mlle. d'Oloran late Mme. de Cambremer, was aware of his personality and his name, (fortunately many believed it was a pseudonym and so deformed it that the Baron was protected by their stupidity, not by Jupien's discretion). Eased by the knowledge that they could not be overheard, the Baron said to him: "I did not want to speak before that little fellow. He's very nice and does his best but he's not brutal enough. His face pleases me but he calls me a low debauchee as though he had learnt it by heart." "Oh dear no! No one has said a word to him," Jupien answered without realising the unlikelihood of the assertion. "As a matter of fact he was mixed up in the murder of a concierge in La Villette." "Indeed? That is rather interesting," said the Baron with a smile. "But I've just secured a butcher, a slaughterer, who looks rather like him; by a bit of luck he happened to look in. Would you like to try him?" "Yes, with pleasure." I watched the man of the slaughter-house enter. He did look a little like "Maurice" but, what was more curious, both of them were of a type that I had never been able to define but which I then realised was also exemplified in Morel; if not in his face as I knew it, at least in a cast of features that the eyes of love, seeing Morel differently from me, might have fitted into his countenance. From the moment that I had made within myself a model with features borrowed from my recollections of what Morel might represent to someone else, I realised that those two young men, of whom one was a jeweller's boy and the other a hotel-employee, were vaguely his successors. Must one conclude that M. de Charlus, at all events on one side of his love-affairs, was always faithful to the same type and that the lust which caused him to select these two young men was the same which had caused him to stop Morel on the platform of the station of Doncières, that all three resembled a little that youth whose form, engraved in the sapphire eyes of M. de Charlus, gave to his gaze the peculiar something which had frightened me on that first day at Balbec. Or, was it that his love for Morel had modified the type he favoured and he was now seeking men who resembled Morel to console himself for the latter's desertion? Another supposition was that perhaps in spite of appearances there had never been between Morel and himself any relations but those of friendship and that M. de Charlus had made Jupien procure these young men because they sufficiently resembled Morel for him to have the illusion that Morel was taking pleasure with him. It is true, bearing in mind all that M. de Charlus had done for Morel, that this supposition seems improbable, if one did not know that love forces great sacrifices from us for the being we love and sometimes the sacrifice of our very desire which, moreover, is the less easily exorcised because the being we love feels that we love him the more. What takes away the likelihood of such a supposition was the highly strung and profoundly passionate temperament of M. de Charlus, similar in that respect to Saint-Loup, which might at first have played the same part in his relations with Morel, though a more decent and negative part, as his nephew's early relations with Rachel. The relations one has with a woman one loves (and that can apply also to love for a youth) can remain platonic for other reasons than the chastity of the woman or the unsensual nature of the love she inspires. The reason may be that the lover is too impatient and by the very excess of his love is unable to await the moment when he will obtain his desires by sufficient pretence of indifference. Continually, he returns to the charge, he never ceases writing to her whom he loves, he is always trying to see her, she refuses herself, he becomes desperate. From that time she knows, if she grants him her company, her friendship, that these benefits will seem so considerable to one who believed he was going to be deprived of them, that she need grant nothing more and that she can take advantage of the moment when he can no longer bear being unable to see her and when, at all costs, he must put an end to the struggle by accepting a truce which will impose upon him a platonic relationship as its preliminary condition. Moreover, during all the time that preceded this truce, the lover, in a constant state of anxiety, ceaselessly hoping for a letter, a glance, has long ceased thinking of the physical desire which at first tormented him but which has been exhausted by waiting and has been replaced by another order of longings more painful still if left unsatisfied. The pleasure formerly anticipated from caresses will later be accorded but transmuted into friendly words and promises of intercourse which brings delicious moments after the strain of uncertainty or after a look impregnated with such coldness that it seemed to remove the loved one beyond hope of his ever seeing her again. Women divine all this and know they can afford the luxury of never yielding to those who, from the first, have betrayed their inextinguishable desire. A woman is enchanted if, without giving anything, she can receive more than she generally gets when she does give herself. On that account highly-strung men believe in the chastity of their idol. And the halo with which they surround her is also a product, but, as we see, an indirect one, of their excessive love. There is in woman something of the unconscious function of drugs which are cunning without knowing it, like morphine. They are not indispensable in the case of those to whom they give the blessings of sleep and real well-being. By such they will not be bought at their weight in gold, taken in exchange for everything the sick man possesses, it is by those other unfortunates (they may, indeed, be the same but altered in the course of years) to whom the drug brings no sleep, gives them no pleasure but who, without it, are a prey to an agitation to which they must at all costs put an end, even though to do so means death. And M. de Charlus, whose case, with the slight difference due to the similarity of sex, can be included in the general laws of love, though he belonged to a family more ancient than the Capets themselves, rich and sought after by the most exclusive society, while Morel was nobody, might say to him as he had said to me: "I am a prince and I desire your welfare," nevertheless Morel was his master if he did not yield to him. And perhaps, to know he was loved was sufficient to make him determine not to. The disgust of distinguished people for snobs who want to force themselves upon them, the virile man has for the invert, the woman for every man who is too much in love with her. M. de Charlus not only had every advantage, he might perhaps have offered immense bribes to Morel, yet it is likely that they would have been unavailing in opposition to the latter's will. M. de Charlus had something in common with the Germans to whom he belonged by his origin and who, in the war now proceeding, were, as the Baron too often repeated, conquerors on every front. But what use were their victories since each one left the Allies more resolved than ever to refuse them the peace and reconciliation they wanted. Thus Napoleon invaded Russia and magnanimously invited the authorities to present themselves to him. But no one came.

I went downstairs and entered the little ante-room where Maurice, uncertain whether they would call him back or not and whom Jupien had told to wait, was about to join in a game of cards with one of his friends. They were much excited about a croix-de-guerre which had been found on the floor and did not know who had lost it or to whom to send it back so that the rightful owner should not be worried about it. They then started talking about the bravery of an officer who had been killed trying to save his orderly. "All the same there are good people amongst the rich. I would have got killed with pleasure for such a man as that!" exclaimed Maurice who evidently only managed to inflict his ghastly flagellations on the Baron from mechanical habit, ignorance, need of money and preference for making it without working although, perhaps, it gave him more trouble. And as M. de Charlus had feared, he was possibly a good-hearted fellow, and certainly he seemed plucky. Tears almost came into his eyes when he spoke of the death of the officer and the young man of twenty-two was equally moved. "Ah! They're fine fellows! Poor devils like us have nothing to lose. But a gentleman who's got lots of stuff, who can go and take his *aperitif* every day at six o'clock, it's really a bit thick. One can jaw as much as one likes, but when one sees chaps like that die, really it's pretty stiff. God oughtn't to let rich people like that die, besides, they're useful to working people. The damned Boches ought to be killed to the last man of them for doing in a man like that. And look what they've done at Louvain, cutting off the heads of little children! I don't know, I am not any better than anyone else but I'd rather have my throat cut than obey savages like that; they aren't men, they are out and out savages, you can't deny it." In fact all these boys were patriots. One, only slightly wounded in the arm, was not on such a high level as the others as he said, having shortly to return to the front: "Damn it, I wish it had been a proper wound" (one which procures exemption) just as Mme. Swann formerly used to say, "I've succeeded in catching a tiresome influenza." The door opened again for the chauffeur who had gone to take the air for a moment. "Hullo!" he said, "is it over already? It wasn't long!" noticing Maurice who, he supposed, was engaged in whipping the man they nick-named after a newspaper of that period, "The man in chains." "It may not seem long to you who've been out for a walk," answered Maurice, annoyed for it to be known that he had not pleased the customer upstairs, "but if you'd been obliged to keep on whipping like me in this heat! If it weren't for the fifty francs he gives—!" "Besides, he's a man who talks well, one feels he's had an education. Did he say it would soon be over?" "He said we shan't get them, that it will end without either side winning." "*Bon sang de bon sang*! He must be a Boche." "I told you you were talking too loud," said a man older than the others, noticing me. "Have you done with your room?" "Shut up, you're not master here." "Yes, I've finished and I've come to pay." "You'd better pay the *patron*. Maurice, go and fetch him." "I don't want to disturb you." "It doesn't disturb me." Maurice went upstairs and came back. "The *patron* is coming down," he said. I gave him two francs for his trouble. He blushed with pleasure: "Thank you very much. I shall send them to my brother who's a prisoner. No, he's all right, it depends on the camp." Meanwhile, two extremely elegant customers in dress coats and white ties under their overcoats, they seemed Russians from their slight accent, were standing in the doorway deliberating if they should enter. It was visibly the first time they had come there. They must have been told where the place was and seemed divided between desire, temptation and extreme fright. One of the two, a handsome young man, kept repeating every minute to the other, with a half-questioning, half-persuasive smile, "After all, we don't care a damn." He might say he did not mind the consequences, but he was not so indifferent as his words suggested for his remark did not result in his entering but on the contrary, in another glance at his friend, followed by the same smile and the same, "After all we don't care a damn." It was this "we don't care a damn," an example among thousands of that expressive language so different from what we generally speak, in which emotion makes us vary what we meant to say and in its place make use of phrases emerging from an unknown lake where live expressions without relation to one's thought and for that very reason reveal it. I remember that Albertine once, when Françoise noiselessly entered the room just at the moment when my friend was lying beside me nude, exclaimed in spite of herself, to warn me: "Ah! here's that beauty Françoise." Françoise, whose sight was not good, and who was crossing the room some distance from us, apparently saw nothing. But the abnormal words "that beauty Françoise" which Albertine had never used in her life, spontaneously revealed their origin; Françoise knew they had escaped Albertine through emotion and understanding without seeing, went off muttering in her patois, the word *"poutana"*. Much later on, when Bloch having become the father of a family, married one of his daughters to a Catholic, an ill-bred person informed her that he had heard she was the daughter of a Jew and asked her what her name had been. The young woman who had been Miss Bloch since her birth, answered, pronouncing Bloch in the German fashion as the Duc de Guermantes might have done, that is, pronouncing the Ch not like "K" but with the Germanic "ch".

To go back to the scene of the hotel, (into which the two Russians had finally decided to penetrate—"after all we don't care a damn") the *patron* had not yet come back when Jupien entered and rated them for talking too loud, saying that the neighbours would complain. But he stood dumbfounded on seeing me. "Get out all of you this instant!" he cried. Immediately all of them jumped up, whereupon I said: "It would be better if these young men stayed here and I went outside with you a moment." He followed me, much troubled, and I explained to him why I had come. One could hear customers asking the *patron* if he could not introduce them to a footman, a choir boy, a negro chauffeur. All professions interested these old madmen; soldiers of all arms and the allies of all nations. Some especially favoured Canadians, feeling the charm of their accent which was so slight that they did not know whether it was of old France or of England. On account of their kilts and because of the lacustrine dreams associated with such lusts, Scotchmen were at a premium, and as every mania owes its peculiar character, if not its aggravation, to circumstances, an old man, whose prurient cravings had all been sated, demanded with insistence to be made acquainted with a mutilated soldier. Steps were heard on the stairs. With the indiscretion which was natural to him, Jupien could not resist telling me it was the Baron who was coming down, that he must not on any account see me but if I would enter the little room contiguous to the passage where the young men were, he would open the shutter, a trick he had invented for the Baron to see and hear without being seen and which would now operate in my favour against him. "Only don't make a noise," he said. And half pushing me into the darkness, he left me. Moreover, he had no other room to offer me, his hotel, in spite of the war, being full. The room I had just left had been taken by the Vicomte de Courvoisier who, having been able to leave the Red Cross at X— — for two days, had come to amuse himself for an hour in Paris before returning to the Chateau de Courvoisier where he would tell the Vicomtesse he had been unable to catch the last train. He had no notion that M. de Charlus was only a few yards away from him and the former had as little, never having encountered his cousin at Jupien's house, the latter being ignorant of the carefully disguised identity of the Vicomte. The Baron soon came in, walking with some difficulty on account of his bruises which he must, nevertheless, have got used to. Although his debauch was finished and he was only going in to give Maurice the money he owed him, he directed a circular glance upon the young men gathered there which was at once tender and inquisitive and evidently expected to have the pleasure of a quite platonic but amorously prolonged chat with each of them. I noticed in all the lively frivolity he displayed towards the harem by which he seemed almost intimidated, those twistings of the body and tossings of the head, those sensitive glances I had noticed on the evening of his first arrival at La Raspelière, graces inherited from one of his grandmothers whom I had not known and which, masked in ordinary life by more virile expressions, were coquettishly displayed when he wanted to please an inferior audience by appearing a *grande dame*. Jupien had recommended them to the goodwill of the Baron by telling him they were hooligans of Belleville and that they would go to bed with their own sisters for a louis. In actual fact, Jupien was both lying and telling the truth. Better and more sensitive than he told the Baron they were, they did not belong to a class of miscreants. But those who believed them so talked to them with entire good faith as if these terrible fellows were doing the same. However, much a sadist may believe he is with an assassin, his own pure sadist soul is not on that account changed and he is hypnotised by the lies of these fellows who aren't in the least assassins but who, wanting to turn an easy penny, wordily bring their father, their mother or their sister to life and kill them again, turn and turn about, because they get interrupted in their conversation with the customer they are trying to please. The customer is bewildered in his simplicity and, in his absurd conception of the guilty gigolo revelling in mass-murders, is astounded at the culprit's lies and contradictions. All of them seemed to know M. de Charlus who stayed some time talking to each of them in what he thought was his vernacular, from pretentious affectation of local colour and also from the sadistic pleasure of mixing himself up in a crapulous life. "It's disgusting," he said, "I saw you in front of Olympia with two street-women, just to get some coppers out of them. That's a nice way of deceiving me." Happily for the young man who was thus addressed, he had no time to declare that he had never accepted coppers from a woman which would have diminished the excitement of M. de Charlus and he reserved his protest for the end of the latter's sentence, replying, "Oh, no! I do not deceive you." These words caused M. de Charlus a lively pleasure and as, in his own despite, his natural intelligence prevailed over his affectation, he turned to Jupien: "It's nice of him to say that and he says it so charmingly, one would think it was true. And, after all, what does it matter whether it's true or not if he makes one believe it. What sweet little eyes he's got. Come here, boy, I'm going to give you two big kisses for your trouble. You'll think of me in the trenches, won't you? Is it very hard?" "Oh, my God. There are days when a shell passes close to you!" and the young man began imitating the noise of a shell, of aeroplanes and so on. "But one must do like the rest and you can be sure we shall go on to the end." "Till the end," replied the pessimistic Baron in a melancholy tone. "Haven't you read in the papers that Sarah Bernhardt said France would go on till the end. The French will let themselves be killed to the last man." "I don't doubt for a single instant that the French will bravely be killed to the last man," M. de Charlus answered as though it were the most natural thing in the world, in spite of his having no intention of doing anything whatever, but with the intention of correcting any impression of pacifism he might give in moments of forgetfulness, "I don't doubt it, but I am asking myself to what extent Mme. Sarah Bernhardt is qualified to speak in the name of France—Ah, I seem to know this charming young man," pointing at another whom he had probably never seen. He saluted him as he would have saluted a prince at Versailles and, so as to profit by the opportunity and have a supplementary pleasure gratis, like when I was small and went with my mother to give an order to Boissier or Gouache and one of the ladies offered me a bonbon from one of the glass vases in the midst of which she presided, he took the hand of the charming young man and pressed it for a long time in his Prussian fashion, fixing his eyes upon him and smiling for the interminable time photographers used to take in posing us when the light was bad. "Monsieur, I am charmed, I am enchanted to make your acquaintance. He has such lovely hair," he said, turning to Jupien. Then he moved over to Maurice to give him his fifty francs and put his arm round his waist. "You never told me you had lined an old Belleville bitch," M. de Charlus guffawed with ecstasy, sticking his face close to that of Maurice. "Oh, Monsieur le Baron," protested the gigolo whom they had forgotten to warn, "how can you believe such a thing?" Whether it was false or whether the alleged culprit really thought it was an abominable thing he had to deny, the boy went on: "To touch my own kind, even a German as it is war is one thing, but a woman and an old woman at that!" This declaration of virtuous principles had the effect of a cold water douche upon the Baron, who moved coldly away from Maurice, none the less giving him his money, but with the air of one who is "put off", someone who has been "done" but who doesn't want to make a fuss, one who pays but is dissatisfied.

The bad impression produced upon the Baron was, moreover, increased by the way in which the beneficiary thanked him: "I am going to send this to my old people and I shall keep a little for my pal at the front." These touching sentiments disappointed M. de Charlus almost as much as did his rather conventional peasant-like expression. Jupien sometimes warned them that they had to be "more vicious". Then one of them with the air of confessing something satanic would adventure: "I'll tell you something, Baron, but you won't believe me. When I was a boy I looked through the key-hole and saw my parents embracing each other. Isn't that vicious? You seem to believe that I'm drawing the long bow but I swear I'm not. It's the exact truth." This fictitious attempt at perversity which only revealed stupidity and innocence, exasperated M. de Charlus. The most determined burglar, robber or assassin would not have satisfied him for they do not talk about their crimes, and, moreover, there is in the sadist—good as he may be, indeed the better he is—a thirst for evil that malefactors cannot satisfy. The handsome young man, realising his mistake, might say, "he'd let him have it hot and heavy," and push audacity to the point of telling the Baron to "bloody well make a date" with him, the charm was dissipated. The humbug was as transparent as in books whose authors insist on writing slang. In vain the young man gave him details of all his obscenities with his women, M. de Charlus was only struck by how little they amounted to. For that matter that was not only the result of insincerity, for nothing is more limited than vice. In that sense one can really use a common expression and say that one is always turning in the same vicious circle.

"How simple he is, one would never say he was a Prince," the habitués commented when M. de Charlus had gone escorted downstairs by Jupien to whom the Baron did not cease complaining about the decency of the young man. From the dissatisfied manner of Jupien, he had been trying to train the young man in advance and one felt that the false assassin would presently get a good dressing down. "He's quite contrary to what you told me," added the Baron so that Jupien should profit by the lesson for another time. "He seems to have a nice nature, he expresses sentiments of respect for his family." "All the same, he doesn't get on with his father at all," objected Jupien, "they live together but each goes to a different bar." Obviously that was rather a feeble crime in comparison with assassination but Jupien found himself taken aback. The Baron said nothing more because, though he wanted his pleasures prepared for him, he also needed the illusion that they were not prepared. "He's an out-and-out ruffian, he told you all that to take you in, you're too simple," Jupien added, to exculpate himself but in so doing only wounded the pride of M. de Charlus the more. While talking of M. de Charlus being a prince the young men in the establishment were deploring the death of someone about whom the gigolos said, "I don't know his name but it appears he is a baron," and who was no other than the Prince de Foux (the father of Saint-Loup's friend). While the Prince's wife believed he was spending most of his time at the Club, in reality he was spending hours with Jupien chattering and telling stories about society in the presence of blackguards. He was a fine, handsome man like his son. It is extraordinary that M. de Charlus did not know that he shared his tastes; doubtless this was because the, Baron had only seen him in society. People went so far as to say that he had actually gone to the length of practising these tastes upon his son when he was still at College, which was probably false. On the other hand, very well-informed about habits many are ignorant of, he kept a careful watch upon the people his son frequented. One day a man of low extraction followed the young Prince de Foux as far as his father's mansion and threw a missive through a window which the father had picked up. But though this follower was not, aristocratically speaking, of the same society as M. de Foux, he was from another point of view, and he had no difficulty in finding among their common associates an intermediary who made M. de Foux hold his tongue by proving that it was the young man who had provoked the advance from a man much older than himself. And that was quite credible, the Prince de Foux having succeeded in protecting his son from bad company outside, but not from his heredity. It may be added that young Prince de Foux, like his father, unsuspected in this respect by people in society, went to extreme lengths with another class.

"He's said to have a million a year to spend," said the young man of twenty-two to whom this statement did not seem incredible. Soon the sound of M. de Charlus' carriage was heard. At that moment I perceived someone accompanied by a soldier leaving a neighbouring room with a slow step, a person who looked to me like an old lady in a black dress. I soon saw my mistake, it was a priest; that rare and in France extremely exceptional thing, a bad priest. Apparently the soldier was chaffing his companion about the incompatability of his conduct with his cloth for the priest, holding his finger in front of his hideous face with the grave gesture of a doctor of theology, answered sententiously: "Well, what do you expect of me, I am not" (I was expecting him to say a saint) "an angel." There was nothing for him to do but go and he took leave of Jupien, who, having returned from escorting the Baron, was going upstairs, but, owing to his bewilderment, the bad priest had forgotten to pay for his room. Jupien, whose presence of mind never abandoned him, rattling the box in which the customers' contributions were put remarked: "For the expenses of the service, Monsieur l'Abbé." The repulsive personage apologised, handed over his money and departed. Jupien came and fetched me from the obscure cavern whence I had not dared move. "Go into the vestibule for a moment where the young men are sitting—it's quite all right as you're a lodger—while I go and shut up your room." The *patron* was there and I paid him. At that moment, a young man in a dinner-jacket entered and with an air of authority demanded of the *patron*: "Can I have Léon to-morrow morning at a quarter to eleven instead of eleven because I'm lunching out?" "That depends on how long the Abbé keeps him," the *patron* answered. This appeared to dissatisfy the young man in the dinner-jacket who seemed about to curse the Abbé but his anger took another form when he perceived me. Going straight up to the *patron*, he asked in an angry voice: "Who's that? What does this mean?" The *patron*, much embarrassed, explained that my presence was of no importance, I was merely a lodger. The young man in the dinner-jacket was by no means appeased by this explanation and kept on repeating: "This is extremely unpleasant; it's the sort of thing that ought not to happen. You know I hate it and I shan't put my foot inside this place again." The execution of the threat did not seem, however, to be imminent for though he went away in a rage, he again expressed the wish that Léon should be free at a quarter to eleven if not at half-past ten. Jupien returned and took me downstairs. "I don't want you to have a bad opinion of me," he said, "this house doesn't bring in as much money as you might think. I'm obliged to have respectable lodgers, though, if I depended only on them, I should lose money. Here to the contrary of the Mount Carmels, it is thanks to vice that virtue can exist. If I've taken this house, or rather, if I have had it taken by the *patron* whom you've seen, it's only to render service to the Baron and to distract his old age." Jupien did not want to talk only about sadistic performances like those I had seen or about the Baron's vices. The latter even for conversation, for company or to play cards with, now only liked common people who exploited him. Doubtless, snobbishness about low company is just as comprehensible as the opposite. In the case of M. de Charlus, the two kinds had long been interchangeable; no one in society was smart enough to associate with and in the underworld, no one was base enough. "I hate anything middling," he said, "the bourgeois comedy is irksome. Give me either princesses of classical tragedy or broad farce, no half-and-half, Phèdre or Les Saltimbanques. But, talk as he might, the equilibrium between these two forms of snobbery had been upset. Whether owing to an old man's fatigue or the extension of sensuality to the most banal intercourse, the Baron only lived now with inferiors. Thus unconsciously he was accepting succession from such of his great ancestors as the Duc de La Rochefoucauld, the Prince d'Harcourt, the Duc de Berry whom Saint-Simon exhibits as spending their lives with their lackeys who got enormous sums out of them, to such a point that when people went to see these great gentlemen they were shocked to find them familiarly playing cards and drinking with their servants. "It's chiefly," added Jupien, "to save him being bored, because, you see, the Baron is a great baby. Even now, when he has got everything here he wants, he must run after adventures and play the villain. And, generous though he is, some time or other this behaviour may lead to trouble. Only the other day the *chasseur* of a hotel nearly died of fright because of the money the Baron offered him. Fancy! To come to his house, what imprudence! This lad, who only liked women, was very relieved when he understood what the Baron wanted. The Baron's promises of money made the lad believe he was a spy and he was consoled when he knew that he was not being asked to betray his country but only to surrender his body which is perhaps not any more moral but less dangerous and certainly easier." Listening to Jupien I said to myself: "What a pity M. de Charlus is not a novelist or a poet, not in order to describe what he sees, but the stage reached by M. de Charlus in relation to desire causes scandals to arise round him, forces him to take life seriously, to emotionalise pleasure, prevents him from becoming static through taking a purely ironical and exterior view of things, reopens in him a constant source of pain. Almost every time he makes overtures, he risks outrage if not prison. Not the education of children but that of poets is accomplished by blows. Had M. de Charlus been a novelist, the protection the house controlled by Jupien afforded him (though a police raid was always on the cards) by reducing the risks he ran from casual street encounters, would have been a misfortune for him. But M. de Charlus was only a dilettante in Art who did not dream of writing and had no gift for it. "Moreover, I'll admit to you," continued Jupien, "that I haven't much scruple about making money out of this sort of job. I can't disguise from you that I like it, that it's to my taste. And is it a crime to get a salary for things one doesn't consider wrong? You are better educated than I am and doubtless you will tell me that Socrates did not consider he was justified in receiving money for his lessons. But in our day professors of philosophy are not like that nor are doctors nor painters nor playwrights nor theatrical managers. Don't imagine that this business forces one to associate only with low people. It is true that the manager of an establishment of this kind, like a great courtesan, only receives men but he receives men who are important in all sorts of ways and who are generally on equal terms with the most refined, the most sensitive and the most amiable of their kind. This house might easily be transformed, I assure you, into an intellectual bureau and a news agency." But I was still occupied with thinking of the blows I had seen M. de Charlus receive. And, to tell the truth when one knew M. de Charlus, his pride, his satiation with social amusements, his caprices which changed so readily into passion for men of the worst class and of the lowest kind, one could easily understand that he was glad to possess the large fortune which, when enjoyed by a parvenu, enables him to marry his daughter to a duke and to invite Highnesses to his shooting parties, and permitted him to exercise authority in one, perhaps in several, establishments where there were permanently young men with whom he took his pleasure. Perhaps, indeed, he did not need to be vicious for that. He was the successor of so many great gentlemen and princes of the blood or dukes who, Saint-Simon tells us, never associated with anyone fit to speak to. "Meanwhile," I said to Jupien: "this house is something very different, it is rather a pandemonium than a mad house, since the madness of the lunatics who are there is placed upon the stage and visually reconstituted. I believed, like the Caliph in the *Thousand and One Nights*, that I had, at the critical moment, come to the rescue of a man who was being ill-treated and another story of the *Thousand and One Nights* was realised before my eyes, in which a woman is changed into a dog and allows herself to be beaten in order to regain her former shape." Jupien, realising that I had seen the Baron being whipped, was much concerned. He remained silent a moment, then, suddenly, with that pretty wit of his own that had so often struck me when he greeted Françoise or myself in the court-yard of our house with such graceful phrases: "You talk of stories in the *Thousand and One Nights*" he said. "I know one which is not without relevance to the title of a book which I caught sight of at the Baron's house" (he was alluding to a translation of Ruskin's *Sesame and Lilies* which I had sent to M. de Charlus). "If you ever wanted one evening to see, I won't say forty but ten thieves, you have only to come here; to be sure I'm there, you have only to look up and if my little window is left open and the light is on, it will mean that I am there and that you can come in; that is my Sesame. I only refer to Sesame; as to the Lilies, if you're seeking for them I advise you to look elsewhere," and saluting me somewhat cavalierly, for an aristocratic connection and a band of young men whom he controlled like a pirate-chief had given him a certain familiarity, he took leave of me. He had hardly left me when blasts of a siren were immediately followed by violent barrage firing. It was evident that a German aviator was hovering close over our heads and suddenly a violent explosion proved that he had hurled one of his bombs.

Many who had not wanted to run away had collected in the same room at Jupien's. Though they did not know each other they belonged more or less to the same wealthy and aristocratic society. The aspect of each inspired a repugnance due, doubtless, to their indulging in degrading vices. The face of one of them, an enormous fellow, was covered with red blotches like a drunkard's. I afterward learnt that, at first, he was not one but enjoyed making youths drink and that, later on, in fear of being mobilised, (though he seemed to be over fifty) as he was very fat, he started to drink without stopping until he exceeded the weight of a hundred kilos, beyond which men were exempted. And now the trick had turned into a passion, and however much people tried to prevent him, he always went back to the liquor-merchant. But the moment he spoke one could see, in spite of his mediocre intelligence, that he was a man of considerable education and culture. Another young society man of remarkably distinguished appearance, came in. In his case, there were as yet no exterior stigmata of vice but, what was worse, there were internal ones. Tall, with an attractive face, his manner of speech indicated a different order of intelligence to that of his alcoholic neighbour, indeed, without exaggeration, a very remarkable one. But whatever he said was accompanied by a facial expression suited to a different remark. Though he owned a complete storehouse of human expressions, he might have lived in another world, for he used them in the wrong order and seemed to scatter smiles and glances haphazard without relation to the remarks he was making or hearing. I hope for his sake if, as seems likely, he is still alive, that he was not the victim of an organic disease but of a passing disorder. Probably, if those men had been ordered to produce their visiting cards one would have been surprised to observe that they all belonged to the upper class of society. But every sort of vice and the greatest vice of all, lack of will which prevents a man from resisting it, brought them together there, in separate rooms, it is true, but every evening, I was told, so that if ladies in society still knew their names, they were gradually forgetting their faces. They still received invitations but habit always brought them back to that composite resort of evil repute. They concealed it but little from themselves, being in this respect different from the little chasseurs, workmen, et cetera, who ministered to their pleasure. And besides many obvious reasons this can be explained by the following one. For a commercial employee or a servant to go there was like a respectable woman going to a place of assignation. Some of them who had been there refused ever again to do so and Jupien himself telling lies to save their reputation or to prevent competition, declared: "Oh, no, he doesn't come to my place and he wouldn't want to." For men in society it is of less importance, in that other people in society do not go to such places and neither know anything about them nor concern themselves with other people's business.

At the beginning of the alarm I had left Jupien's house. The streets had become entirely dark. Only now and then an enemy aeroplane which was flying low enough cast a light on the spot where he was going to throw a bomb. I could no longer find my way and thought of that day when going to La Raspelière I had met an aviator like a god reining back his horse. I was thinking that this time the encounter would have a different end, that the God of Evil would kill me. I hurried my steps to escape like a traveller pursued by a water-spout, yet I turned in a circle round dark places from which I could not escape. At last the flames of a fire lighted me and I was able to rediscover my road whilst the cannon boomed unceasingly. But my thought turned elsewhere. I thought of Jupien's house now reduced perhaps to cinders for a bomb had fallen quite close to me just as I was coming out of that house upon which M. de Charlus might prophetically have written "Sodom" as an unknown inhabitant of Pompeii had done with no less prescience when, possibly, as a prelude to the catastrophe, the volcanic eruption began. But what did sirens or Gothas matter to those who had come there bent on gratifying their lusts? We never think of the framework of nature which surrounds our passion. The tempest rages on the sea, the ship heaves and pitches on every side, avalanches fall from the windswept sky and, at most, we allow ourselves to pause a moment, to ward off an inconvenience caused us by that immense scene, in which both we and the human body we desire, are the tiniest atoms. The premonitory siren of the bombs troubled the inhabitants of Jupien's house as little as would an iceberg. More than that, the menace of a physical danger freed them from the fear by which they had been so long unhealthily obsessed. It is false to believe that the scale of fears corresponds to that of the dangers which inspire them. One might be frightened of sleeplessness and yet not of a duel, of a rat and not of a lion. For some hours the police would be concerned only for the lives of the population, a matter of small consequence, for it did not threaten to dishonour them.

Some of the habitués, recovering their moral liberty were the more tempted by the sudden darkness in the streets. Some of these Pompeians upon whom the fire of Heaven was already pouring, descended into the Métro passages which were as dark as catacombs. They knew, of course, that they would not be alone there. And the darkness which bathes everything as in a new element had the effect, an irresistibly tempting one for certain people, of eliminating the first phase of lust and enabling them to enter, without further ado the domain of caresses which as a rule, demands preliminaries. Whether the libidinous aim is directed towards a woman or a man, assuming that approach is easy and that the sentimentalities that go on eternally in a drawing-room in the day time can be dispensed with, even in the evening however ill-lit the street, there must, at least, be a preamble when only the eyes can devour the corn within the ear, when the fear of passers-by or even of the one pursued prevents the follower getting further than vision and speech. But in darkness the whole bag of tricks goes by the board, hands, lips, bodies, come into immediate play. Then there is the excuse of the darkness itself and of the mistakes it engenders if a bad reception is met with, but if on the contrary, there is the immediate response of a body which, instead of withdrawing, comes closer, the inference that the woman or the man approached is equally licentious and vicious, adds the additional thrill of being able to bite into the fruit without lusting after it with the eyes and without asking permission. And still the darkness continued. Plunged in this new element Jupien's habitués imagined themselves travellers witnessing a phenomenon of nature such as a tidal-wave or an eclipse and instead of indulgence in a pre-arranged debauch, were seeking fortuitous adventures in the unknown, and celebrating, to the accompaniment of the volcanic thunder of bombs—as though in a Pompeian brothel—secret rites in the tenebrous shadows of the catacombs. To such events the Pompeian paintings at Jupien's were appropriate for they recalled the end of the French Revolution at the somewhat similar period of the Directoire which was now beginning. Already in the anticipation of peace, new dances organised in darkness so as not too openly to infringe police regulations, were rioting in the night. And as an accompaniment certain artistic opinions, less anti-German than during the first years of the war, enabled stifled minds to expand though a brevet of civic virtue was needed by him who ventured to express them. A professor wrote a remarkable book on Schiller of which the papers took notice. But before mentioning the author, the publishers inscribed the volume with a statement like a printing licence, to the effect that he had been at the Marne and at Verdun, that he had had five mentions, and two sons killed. Upon that, there was loud praise of the lucidity and depth of the author's work upon Schiller, who could be qualified as great as long as he was alluded to as a great Boche and not as a great German, and thus the articles were passed by the Censor. As I approached my home I was meditating on how quickly the consciousness ceases to collaborate with our habits, leaving them to develop on their own account without further concerning itself with them and how astonished we are, when we base our judgment of an individual merely on externals as though they comprehended the whole of him, at the actions of a man whose moral or intellectual value may develop independently in a completely different direction. Obviously it was a fault of upbringing or the entire lack of upbringing combined with a preference for earning money in the easiest way (many different kinds of work might be easier as it happens, but does not a sick man fabricate a far more painful existence out of manifold privations and remedies than the often comparatively mild illness against which he thinks he is thus defending himself?) or at all events, in the least laborious way, which had caused these youths, so to speak, in complete innocence and for small pay to do things which gave them no pleasure and must at first have inspired them with the strongest repugnance. Accordingly one might consider them fundamentally rotten but they were not only wonderful soldiers in the war, brave to a degree, but often good-hearted fellows if not decent people in civil life. They no longer realised what was moral or immoral in the life they led because it was that of their surroundings. Thus, in studying certain periods of ancient history we are sometimes amazed to observe that people who were individually good, participated without scruple in mass assassinations and human sacrifices, which probably seemed to them perfectly natural things. For him who reads the history of our period two thousand years hence, it will in the same way seem to have allowed gentle and pure consciences to be plunged in a vital environment to which they adapted themselves though it will then appear just as monstrously pernicious. And what is more, I knew no man more gifted with intelligence and sensibility than Jupien for those charming acquisitions which constituted the intellectual fabric of his discourse, did not come to him from school instruction or from university culture which might have made him remarkable, while so many young men in society got no profit from them whatever. It was his spontaneous, innate sense, his natural taste which enabled him from occasional haphazard and unguided readings in his spare moments to compose his way of speaking so rightly that all the symmetries of language were set off and showed their beauty in it. Yet the business in which he was engaged could with good reason be considered, if one of the most lucrative, one of the lowest imaginable. As to M. de Charlus, disdain as he might "what people say", how was it that a feeling of personal dignity and self-respect had not forced him to resist sensual indulgences for which the only excuse was complete insanity? It could only be that in his case, as in that of Jupien, the habit of isolating morality from a whole order of actions (which, for that matter, must occur in a function such as that of a judge, sometimes in that of a statesman and others) had been acquired so long ago that, no longer demanding his judgment or moral sentiment, it had become aggravated from day to day until it had reached a point where this consenting Prometheus had allowed himself to be nailed by force to the rock of pure matter. Certainly I realised that therein a new phase declared itself in the disease of M. de Charlus which, ever since I first perceived and judged it as stage by stage it revealed itself to my eyes, had continued to evolve with ever-increasing speed. The poor Baron could not now be far distant from the final term, from death, if indeed that was not preceded, according to the predictions and hopes of Mme. Verdurin, by a poisoning which at his age could only hasten his death. Nevertheless, perhaps I used an inaccurate expression in saying rock of pure matter. It is possible that a little mind still survived in that pure matter. This madman knew, in spite of everything, that he was mad, that he was the prey at such moments of insanity, since he knew perfectly well that the man who was beating him was no wickeder than the little boys in battle-games who draw lots to decide which of them is to play the Prussian and upon whom all the others fall in true patriotic ardour and pretended hatred. A prey to insanity into which, nevertheless, some of M. de Charlus' personality entered; for even in its aberrations, human nature (as in our loves and in our journeys) still betrays the need of faith through the exactions of truth. When I told Françoise about a church in Milan—a city she would probably never see—or about the Cathedral of Rheims—even about that of Arras!—which she would never be able to see since they had been more or less destroyed, she envied the rich people who were able to afford the sight of such treasures and cried with nostalgic regret: "Ah, how wonderful it must be!" Yet she, who had lived in Paris so many years, had never had the curiosity to go and see Notre Dame! It was just because Notre Dame belonged to Paris, to the city where her daily life was spent and where in consequence it was difficult for our old servant (as it would have been for me if the study of architecture had not modified in certain respects Combray instincts) to situate the objects of her dreams. There is imminent in those we love a certain dream which we cannot always discern but which we pursue. It was my belief in Bergotte and in Swann which made me love Gilberte, my belief in Gilbert the Bad which had made me fall in love with Mme. de Guermantes. And what a great sweep of ocean had been included in my love, the saddest, the most jealous the most personal ever, for Albertine. In that love of one creature towards whom one's whole being is urged, there is already something of aberration. Arid are not the very diseases of the body, at least those closely associated with the nervous system, in some measure peculiar tastes or peculiar fears contracted by our organs, by our articulation, which thus discover for themselves a horror of certain climates as inexplicable and as obstinate as the fancy certain men display for a woman who wears an eyeglass, or for circus-riders? Who shall ever say with what lasting and curious dream that desire aroused time after time at the sight of a circus rider, is associated; as unconscious and as mysterious as is, for example, the influence of a certain town, in appearance similar to others but in which a lifelong sufferer from asthma is able, for the first time, to breathe freely.

Aberrations are like passions which a morbid strain has overlaid, yet, in the craziest of them love can still be recognised. M. de Charlus' insistence that the chains which bound his feet and hands should be of attested strength, his demand to be tried at the bar of justice and, from what Jupien told me, for ferocious accessories there was great difficulty in obtaining even from sailors (the punishment they used to inflict having been abolished even where the discipline is strictest, on ship-board), at the base of all this there was M. de Charlus' constant dream of virility proved, if need be, by brutal acts and all the illumination the reflections of which within himself though to us invisible, he projected on judicial and feudal tortures which embellished an imagination coloured by the Middle Ages. This sentiment was in his mind each time he said to Jupien: "There won't be any alarm this evening anyhow, for I can already see myself reduced to ashes by the fire of Heaven like an inhabitant of Sodom," and he affected to be frightened of the Gothas not because he really had the smallest fear of them but to have a pretext the moment the sirens sounded of dashing into the shelter of the Métropolitain, where he hoped to get a thrill from midnight frictions associated in his mind with vague dreams of prostrations and subterranean dungeons in the Middle Ages. Finally his desire to be chained and beaten revealed, with all its ugliness, a dream as poetic as the desire of others to go to Venice or to keep dancing girls. And M. de Charlus held so much to the illusion of reality which this dream gave him that Jupien was compelled to sell the wooden bed which was in room No. 43, and replace it by one of iron which went better with the chains.

At last the maroon sounded as I arrived home. The noise of approaching firemen was announced by a small boy and I met Françoise coming up from the cellar with the butler. She had thought me dead. She told me that Saint-Loup had excused himself for coming in to see if he had not let his *croix de guerre* fall when calling that morning. He had only just noticed he had lost it and having to rejoin his regiment the next day had wanted at all costs to see if it was not at my house. He and Françoise had searched everywhere without success. Françoise believed he must have lost it before coming to see me, for, she said, she could almost have sworn he did not have it on when she saw him; in this she was mistaken, which shows the value of witnesses and of recollections. I felt immediately by the unenthusiastic way they spoke of him that Saint-Loup had not produced a good impression on Françoise and the butler. Saint-Loup's efforts to court danger were the exact opposite of those made by the butler's son and Françoise's nephew to get themselves exempted, but judging from their own standpoint, Françoise and the butler could not believe that. They were convinced that rich people are always protected. For that matter had they even known the truth about Robert's heroic bravery, they would not have been moved by it. He never talked of "Boches", he praised the bravery of the Germans, he had not attributed our failure to secure victory from the first day, to treason. That was what they wanted to hear and that was what they would have considered a mark of courage. So, while they continued searching for the *croix de guerre*, I, who had not much doubt as to where that cross had been lost, found them cold on the subject of Robert. Though Saint-Loup had been amusing himself in equivocal fashion that evening, it was only while awaiting news of Morel; he had been seized with longing to see him again, and had made use of all his connections to discover the corps Morel was in, supposing him to have joined up, but, so far, he had received only contradictory answers. I advised Françoise and the butler to go to bed but the latter was never in any hurry to leave Françoise since, thanks to the war, he had found a still more efficacious way of tormenting her than telling her about the expulsion of the nuns and the Dreyfus affair. That evening and whenever I was near them during the time I spent in Paris, I heard the butler say to poor, frightened Françoise: "They're not in a hurry, of course; they're waiting for the ripe pear, the day that they take Paris they'll have no mercy." "My God! Blessed Virgin Mary!" cried Françoise, "isn't it enough for them to have conquered poor Belgium. She suffered enough at the time of her 'invahition'." "Belgium, Françoise. Why! What they did to Belgium is nothing to what they'll do here." The war having thrown upon the people's conversation-market a number of new expressions which they only knew visually through reading the papers without being able to pronounce them, the butler added, "You'll see, Françoise they are preparing a new attack of a greater *enverjure* than ever before." In protest, if not out of pity for Françoise or from strategic common-sense, at least for grammar's sake, I told them that the right way to pronounce the word was *envergure*, but I only succeeded in making Françoise repeat the terrible word every time I entered the kitchen. The butler, much as he enjoyed frightening his fellow-servant, was equally pleased to show his master, though he was only a former gardener of Combray and now a butler, that he was a good Frenchman of the order of St. André-dès-Champs and possessed the privilege, since the declaration of the rights of man, to pronounce *enverjure*, with complete independence and not to accept orders on a matter which had nothing to do with his service and, in regard to which, in consequence of the Revolution, no one had any right to correct him, since he was my equal. I had, therefore, the irritation of hearing Françoise talk about an operation of great *enverjure* with an insistence which was intended to prove to me that that pronunciation was, in fact, not that of ignorance but of maturely-considered determination. The butler indiscriminately applied a suspicious "they" to the Government and the papers: "They talk of the losses of the Boches, they don't talk of ours which, it appears, are ten times greater. They tell us that they're at the last gasp, that they've got nothing to eat. I believe they've got a hundred times more to eat than we have. It's all very well but they've no right to humbug us like that. If they had nothing to eat they wouldn't be able to fight like the other day when they killed a hundred thousand youngsters less than twenty years old." He thus continually exaggerated the triumphs of the Germans as he did formerly those of the Radicals, and told tales of their atrocities so as to make the victories of the enemy still more painful to Françoise who kept on exclaiming: "Sainted Mother of Angels! Sainted Mother of God!" Sometimes he tried being unpleasant to her in another way by saying: "For that matter, we're no better than they are. What we're doing in Greece is no nicer than what they did in Belgium. You'll see, we shall have the whole world against us and we shall have to fight the lot," while, actually, the exact contrary was the truth. On days when news was good he revenged himself on Françoise by assuring her the war would last thirty-five years and that if, by chance, a possible peace came, it would not last more than a few months and would be succeeded by battles in comparison with which those of to-day were child's play and that after them nothing would be left of France. The victory of the Allies if not close at hand, seemed at any rate assured, and unfortunately it must be admitted that this displeased the butler. For, having identified the world-war and the rest of it with his campaign against Françoise (whom he liked, all the same, just as one likes a person whom one daily enrages by defeating him at dominoes) victory was represented to him in terms of the first conversation he would have with her thereafter when he would be irritated by hearing her say: "Well, it's finished at last, and they'll have to give us a great deal more than we gave them in '71." Really, he always believed this must happen in the end for an unconscious patriotism made him think, like all Frenchmen, who were victims of an illusion similar to my own ever since I had been ill, that victory like my recovery was coming to-morrow. He took the upper hand of Françoise by announcing that though victory might come about, her heart would bleed from it, because a revolution would swiftly follow and then invasion. "Ah! That bloody old war, the Boches will be the ones to recover quick from it! Why, Françoise! They've already made hundreds of millions out of it. But don't you imagine they're going to give us a penny of it. They may put that in the papers," he added for prudence sake and to be on the safe side, "to keep people quiet just as they've been saying for three years that the war would be finished the next day. I can't understand how people can be such fools as to believe it." Françoise was the more worried by his comments because, as a matter of fact, she had believed the optimists in preference to the butler and had seen that the war, which was to end in a fortnight in spite of the "invahition of poor Belgium," lasted for ever, that there was no advance, a phenomenon of fixation of the fronts the sense of which she could not understand, and that one of her innumerable godsons to whom she gave everything she received from us, had told her that this, that and the other things were concealed from the public. "All that will fall upon the working-class," the butler remarked in conclusion, "and they'll take your field from you, Françoise." "Oh, my God!" But he preferred miseries that were close at hand and devoured the papers, hoping to announce a defeat to Françoise, and awaited news like Easter eggs, which should be bad enough to terrify Françoise without his suffering material disadvantages therefrom. Thus a Zeppelin-raid enchanted him because he could watch Françoise hiding in the cellar while he felt convinced that in so large a city as Paris, bombs would not just fall upon our house. Then Françoise began to get back her Combray pacifism. She even began doubting the "German atrocities". "At the beginning of the war they told us the Germans were assassins, brigands, regular bandits—*bbboches*." (If she put several 'b's to Boches it was because it seemed plausible enough to accuse the Germans of being assassins but to call them Boches seemed almost impossible in its enormity). Still, it was rather difficult to grasp what mysteriously horrible sense Françoise gave to the word Boche since she was talking about the beginning of the war and uttered the word so doubtfully. For the doubt that the Germans were criminals might be ill-founded in fact but did not in itself contain a contradiction from a logical point of view but how could anyone doubt that they were Boches since that word in the popular tongue means German and nothing else. Perhaps she was merely repeating violent comments she had heard at the time when a particular emphasis was given to the word Boche. "I used to believe all that," she said, "but I'm now wondering if we aren't really just as big rogues as they are." This blasphemous thought had been cunningly fostered in Françoise by the butler who, observing that his fellow-servant had a certain weakness for King Constantine of Greece, continually represented that we did not allow him to have any food until he surrendered. The abdication of the sovereign had further moved Françoise to declare: "We're no better than they are. If we were in Germany we should do the same." I did not see much of her at that time as she often went to stay with cousins of hers about whom my mother one day said to me: "You know, they're richer than you are." In that connection a very beautiful thing happened, frequent enough at that period throughout the country, which, had there been historians to perpetuate its memory, would have borne witness to the grandeur of France, to the grandeur of her soul, that grandeur of St. André-des-Champs which was displayed no less by civilians at the rear than by the soldiers who fell at the Marne. A nephew of Françoise had been killed at Berry-au-Bac who was also a nephew of those millionaire cousins of Françoise, former café proprietors long since retired with a fortune. This young man of twenty-five, himself the proprietor of a little café, without other means, was called up and left his young wife to keep the little bar alone, hoping to return in a few months. He was killed and the following happened. These millionaire cousins of Françoise upon whom this young woman, widow of their nephew, had no claim whatever, left their home in the country to which they had retired ten years previously and again took over the café but without taking a penny. Every morning at six o'clock the millionaire wife, a true gentlewoman, dressed herself as did her young lady daughter to assist their niece and cousin by marriage, and for three years they washed glasses and served meals from early morning till half-past-nine at night without a day of rest. In this book in which there is not a single event which is not fictitious, in which there is not a single personage *"a clef"*, where I have invented everything to suit the requirements of my presentation, I must, in homage to my country, mention as personages who did exist in real life, these millionaire relations of Françoise who left their retirement to help their bereaved niece. And, persuaded that their modesty will not be offended for the excellent reason that they will never read this book, it is with childlike pleasure and deeply moved, that, unable to give the names of so many others who acted similarly and, thanks to whom France has survived, I here transcribe their name, a very French one, Larivière. If there were certain contemptible *embusqués* like the imperious young man in the dinner-jacket whom I saw at Jupien's and whose sole preoccupation was to know whether he could have Léon at half-past-ten because he was lunching out, they are more than made up for by the innumerable mass of Frenchmen of St. André-des-Champs, by all those superb soldiers beside whom I place the Larivières. The butler, to quicken the anxieties of Françoise showed her some old *Readings for All* he had discovered somewhere, on the cover of which (the copies dated from before the war) figured "The Imperial Family of Germany". "Here is our master of to-morrow," said the butler to Françoise, showing her "Guillaume". She opened her eyes wide, then pointing at the feminine personage beside him in the picture, she added, "And there is the Guillaumesse."

My departure from Paris was retarded by news which, owing to the pain it caused me, rendered me incapable of moving for some time. I had learnt, in fact, of the death of Robert Saint-Loup, killed, protecting the retreat of his men, on the day following his return to the front. No man less than he, felt hatred towards a people (and as to the Emperor, for special reasons which may have been mistaken, he believed that William II had rather sought to prevent war than to unleash it). Nor did he hate Germanism; the last words I heard him utter six days before, were those at the beginning of a Schumann song which he hummed to me in German on my staircase; indeed on account of neighbours I had to ask him to keep quiet. Accustomed by supreme good breeding to refrain from apologies, invective and phrase, in the face of the enemy he had avoided, as he did at the moment of mobilisation, whatever might have preserved his life by a self-effacement in action which his manners symbolised, even to his way of closing my cab-door when he saw me out, standing bare-headed every time I left his house. For several days I remained shut up in my room thinking about him. I recalled his arrival at Balbec that first time when in his white flannels and his greenish eyes moving like water he strolled through the hall adjoining the large dining-room with its windows open to the sea. I recalled the uniqueness of a being whose friendship I had then so greatly desired. That desire had been realised beyond my expectation, yet it had given me hardly a moment's pleasure, and afterwards I had realised all the qualities as well as other things which were hidden under that elegant appearance. He had bestowed all, good and bad, without stint, day by day, and on the last he stormed a trench with utter generosity, putting all he possessed at the service of others, just as one evening he had run along the sofas of the restaurant so as not to inconvenience me. That I had, after all, seen him so little in so many different places, under so many different circumstances separated by such long intervals, in the hall of Balbec, at the café of Rivebelle, in the Doncières Cavalry barracks and military dinners, at the theatre where he had boxed a journalist's ears, at the Princesse de Guermantes', resulted in my retaining more striking and sharper pictures of his life, feeling a keener sorrow at his death than one often does in the case of those one has loved more but of whom one has seen so much that the image we retain of them is but a sort of vague average of an infinite number of pictures hardly different from each other and also that our sated affection has not preserved, as in the case of those we have seen for limited moments in the course of meetings unfulfilled in spite of them and of ourselves, the illusion of greater potential affection of which circumstances alone had deprived us. A few days after the one on which I had seen Saint-Loup tripping along behind his eye-glass and had imagined him so haughty in the hall of Balbec there was another figure I had seen for the first time upon the Balbec beach and who now also existed only as a memory—Albertine—walking along the sand that first evening indifferent to everybody and as akin to the sea as a seagull. I had so soon fallen in love with her that, not to miss being with her every day I never left Balbec to go and see Saint-Loup. And yet the history of my friendship with him bore witness also to my having ceased at one time to love Albertine, since, if I had gone away to stay with Robert at Doncières, it was out of grief that Mme. de Guermantes did not return the sentiment I felt for her. His life and that of Albertine so late known to me, both at Bal-bec and both so soon ended, had hardly crossed each other; it was he, I repeated to myself, visualising that the flying shuttle of the years weaves threads between memories which seemed at first to be completely independent of each other, it was he whom I sent to Mme. Bontemps when Albertine left me. And then it happened that each of their two lives contained a parallel secret I had not suspected. Saint-Loup's now caused me more sadness than Albertine's for her life had become to me that of a stranger. But I could not console myself that hers like that of Saint-Loup had been so short. She and he both often said when they were seeing to my comfort: "You are so ill," and yet it was they who were dead, they whose last presentment I can visualise, the one facing the trench, the other after her accident, separated by so short an interval from the first, that even Albertine's was worth no more to me than its association with a sunset on the sea. Françoise received the news of Saint-Loup's death with more pity than Albertine's. She immediately adopted her rôle of mourner and bewailed the memory of the dead with lamentations and despairing comments. She manifested her sorrow and turned her face away to dry her eyes only when I let her see my own tears which she pretended not to notice. Like many highly-strung people the agitation of others horrified her, doubtless because it was too like her own. She wanted to draw attention to the slightest stiff-neck or giddiness she had managed to get afflicted with. But if I spoke of one of my own pains she became stoical and grave and made a pretence of not hearing me. "Poor marquis!" she would say, although she could not help thinking he had done everything in his power not to go to the front and once there to escape danger. "Poor lady!" she would say, alluding to Mme. de Marsantes, "how she must have wept when she heard of the death of her son! If only she had been able to see him again! But perhaps it was better she was not able to because his nose was cut in two. He was completely disfigured." And the eyes of Françoise filled with tears through which nevertheless the cruel curiosity of the peasant peered. Without doubt Françoise condoled with Mme. de Marsantes with all her heart but she was sorry not to witness the form her grief had taken and that she could not luxuriate in the spectacle of her affliction. And as she liked crying and liked me to see her cry, she worked herself up by saying: "I feel it dreadfully." And she observed the traces of sorrow in my face with an eagerness which made me pretend to a kind of hardness when I spoke of Robert. In a spirit of imitation and because she had heard others say so, for there are *clichés* in the servants' quarters just as in coteries, she repeated, not without the complaisance of the poor: "All his wealth did not prevent his dying like anyone else and it's no good to him now." The butler profited by the opportunity to remark to Françoise that it was certainly sad but that it scarcely counted compared with the millions of men who fell every day in spite of all the efforts of the Government to hide it. But this time the butler did not succeed in causing Françoise more pain as he had hoped, for she answered: "It's true they died for France too, but all of them are unknown and it's always more interesting when one has known people." And Françoise who revelled in her tears, added: "Be sure and let me know if the death of the marquis is mentioned in the paper."

Robert had often said to me with sadness long before the war: "Oh, don't let us talk about my life, I am doomed in advance." Was he then alluding to the vice which he had until then succeeded in hiding from the world, the gravity of which he perhaps exaggerated as young people do who make love for the first time or who even earlier seek solitary gratification and imagine themselves like plants which cannot disseminate their pollen without dying? Perhaps in Saint-Loup's case this exaggeration arose as in that of children from the idea of an unfamiliar sin, a new sensation possessing an almost terrifying power which later on is attenuated. Or had he, owing to his father's early death, the presentiment of his premature end. Such a presentiment seems irrational and yet death seems subject to certain laws. One would think, for instance, that people born of parents who died very old or very young are almost forced to die at the same age, the former sustaining sorrows and incurable diseases till they are a hundred, the latter carried off, in spite of a happy, healthy existence at the inevitable and premature date by a disease so timely and accidental (however deep its roots in the organism) that it seems to be a formality necessary to the actuality of death. And is it not possible that accidental death itself—like that of Saint-Loup, linked as it was with his character in more ways than I have been able to say—is also determined beforehand, known only to gods invisible to man, but revealed by a special and semi-conscious sadness (and even expressed to others as sincerely as we announce misfortunes which, in our inmost hearts, we believe we shall escape and which nevertheless happen) in him who bears the fatal date and perceives it continuously within himself, like a device.

He must have been very beautiful in those last hours, he who in this life had seemed always, even when he sat or walked about in a drawing-room, to contain within himself the dash of a charge and to disguise smilingly the indomitable will-power centred in his triangle-shaped head when he charged for the last time. Disencumbered of its books, the feudal turret had become warlike again and that Guermantes was more himself in death—he was more of his breed, a Guermantes and nothing more and this was symbolised at his funeral in the church of Saint-Hilaire-de-Combray hung with black draperies where the "G" under the closed coronet divested of initials and titles betokened the race of Guermantes which he personified in death. Before going to the funeral which did not take place at once I wrote to Gilberte. Perhaps I ought to have written to the Duchesse de Guermantes but I imagined that she would have accepted the death of Robert with the indifference I had seen her display about so many others who had seemed so closely associated with her life, and perhaps even that, with her Guermantes spirit, she would want to show that superstition about blood ties meant nothing to her. I was too ill to write to everybody. I had formerly believed that she and Robert liked each other in the society sense, which is the same as saying that they exchanged affectionate expressions when they felt so disposed. But when he was away from her, he did not hesitate to say that she was a fool and if she sometimes found a selfish pleasure in his society, I had noticed that she was incapable of giving herself the smallest trouble, of using her power in the slightest degree to render him a service or even to prevent some misfortune happening to him. The spitefulness she had shown in refusing to recommend him to General Saint-Joseph when Robert was going back to Morocco proved that her goodwill towards him when he married was only a sort of compromise that cost her nothing. So that I was much surprised when I heard that, owing to her being ill when Robert was killed, her people considered it necessary to hide the papers from her for several days (under fallacious pretexts) for fear of the shock that would have been caused her by their announcement of his death. But my surprise was greater when I learnt that after she had been told the truth, the Duchesse de Guermantes wept the whole day, fell ill and took a long time—more than a week, which was long for her—to console herself. When I heard about her grief, I was touched and it enabled everyone to say, as I do, that there was a great friendship between them. But when I remember how many petty slanders, how much ill-will entered into that friendship, I realise how small a value society attaches to it. Moreover somewhat later, under circumstances which were historically more important though they touched my heart less, Mme. de Guermantes appeared, in my opinion, in a still more favourable light. It will be remembered that as a girl she had displayed audacious impertinence towards the Imperial family of Russia and after her marriage, spoke about them with a freedom amounting to social tactlessness, yet she was perhaps the only person, after the Russian Revolution, who gave proof of extreme devotion to the Grand-Dukes and Duchesses. The very year which preceded the war she had annoyed the Grande-Duchesse Vladimir by calling the Comtesse of Hohenfelsen, the morganatic wife of the Grand-Duc Paul, the "Grande-Duchesse Paul". But, no sooner had the Russian Revolution broken out, than our Ambassador at St. Petersburg, M. Paléologue ("Paléo" for diplomatic society which, like the other, has its pseudo-witty abbreviations), was harassed by telegrams from the Duchesse de Guermantes who wanted news of the Grande-Duchesse Maria Pavlovna and for a long time the only marks of sympathy and respect which that Princess received came to her exclusively from Mme. de Guermantes.

Saint-Loup caused, if not by his death, at least by what he had done in the weeks that preceded it, troubles greater than those of the Duchesse. What happened was that the day following the evening when I had seen M. de Charlus, the day on which he had said to Morel: "I shall be revenged," Saint-Loup's hunt for Morel had ended, by the general, under whose orders Morel ought to have been, discovering that he was a deserter and having him sought out and arrested. To excuse himself to Saint-Loup for the punishment which was going to be inflicted on a person he had been interested in, the general had written to inform Saint-Loup of it. Morel was convinced that his arrest was due to the rancour of M. de Charlus. He remembered the words "I shall be revenged" and, thinking this was the revenge, he demanded to be heard. "It is true," he declared, "that I deserted but, if I have been influenced to evil courses, is it altogether my fault?" Without compromising himself, he gave accounts of M. de Charlus and of M. d'Argencourt with whom he had also quarrelled, concerning matters which these two, with the twofold exuberance of lovers and of inverts, had told him, which caused the simultaneous arrest of M. de Charlus and M. d'Argencourt. This arrest caused, perhaps, less distress to these two than the knowledge that each had been the unwilling rival of the other and the proceedings disclosed an enormous number of other and more obscure rivals picked up daily in the street. They were, moreover, quickly released as was Morel because the letter written to Saint-Loup by the general was returned to him with the mention: "Dead on the field of honour." The general, in honour of the dead, decided that Morel should simply be sent to the front; he there behaved bravely, escaped all dangers and, when the war was over, returned with the cross which, earlier, M. de Charlus had vainly solicited for him and which he thus got indirectly through the death of Saint-Loup. I have since often thought, when recalling the croix-de-guerre lost at Jupien's, that if Saint-Loup had survived he would have been easily able to get elected deputy in the election which followed the war, thanks to the frothy idiocy and to the halo of glory which it left behind it, thanks also to centuries of prejudice being, on that account, abolished and if the loss of a finger procured a brilliant marriage and entrance into an aristocratic family, the croix-de-guerre, though it were won in an office, took the place of a profession of faith and ensured a triumphant election to the Chamber of Deputies, almost to the French Academy. The election of Saint-Loup would, on account of his "sainted" family, have made M. Arthur Meyer pour out floods of tears and ink. But perhaps Saint-Loup loved the people too sincerely to gain their suffrages although they would, doubtless, have forgiven him his democratic ideas for the sake of his noble birth. Saint-Loup would perhaps have exposed the former with success before a chamber composed of aviators and those heroes would have understood him as would have done a few other elevated minds. But owing to the pacifying effect of the *Bloc National*, a lot of old political rascals had been fished up and were always elected. Those who were unable to enter a Chamber of aviators went about soliciting the votes of Marshals, of a President of the Republic, of a President of the Chamber, etc. in the hope of at least becoming members of the French Academy. They would not have favoured Saint-Loup but they did another of Jupien's customers, that deputy of Liberal Action, and he was re-elected unopposed. He did not stop wearing his territorial officer's uniform although the war had been over a long time. His election was joyfully welcomed by all the newspapers who had formed the Coalition on the strength of his name, with the help of rich and noble ladies who wore rags out of conventional sentimentality and fear of taxes, while men on the Stock Exchange ceaselessly bought diamonds, not for their wives but because, having no confidence in the credit of any country, they sought safety in tangible wealth, and incidentally made de Beers go up a thousand francs. Such imbecility was somewhat irritating but one was less indignant with the *Bloc National* when, suddenly, the Victims of Bolshevism appeared on the scene; Grand-Duchesses in tatters whose husbands and sons had been in turn assassinated. Husbands in wheelbarrows, sons stoned and deprived of food, forced to labour amidst jeers and finally thrown into pits and buried alive because they were said to be sickening of the plague and might infect the community. The few who succeeded in escaping suddenly reappeared and added new and terrifying details to this picture of horror.

CHAPTER III

AN AFTERNOON PARTY AT THE HOUSE OF THE PRINCESSE DE GUERMANTES

THE new sanatorium to which I then retired did not cure me any more than the first one and a long time passed before I left it. During my railway-journey back to Paris the conviction of my lack of literary gifts again assailed me. This conviction which I believed I had discovered formerly on the Guermantes side, that I had recognised still more sorrowfully in my daily walks at Tansonville with Gilberte before going back to dinner or far into the night, and which on the eve of departure I had almost identified, after reading some pages of the Mémoires of the Goncourts, as being synonymous with the vanity and lie of literature, a thought less sad perhaps but still more dismal if its reason was not my personal incompetence but the non-existence of an ideal in which I had believed, that conviction which had not for long re-entered my mind, struck me anew and with more lamentable force than ever. It was, I remember, when the train stopped in open country and the sun lit half-way down their stems the line of trees which ran alongside the railway. "Trees," I thought, "you have nothing more to tell me, my cold heart hears you no more. I am in the midst of Nature, yet it is with boredom that my eyes observe the line which separates your luminous countenance from your shaded trunks. If ever I believed myself a poet I now know that I am not one. Perhaps in this new and barren stage of my life, men may inspire me as Nature no longer can and the years when I might perhaps have been able to sing her beauty will never return." But in offering myself the consolation that possible observation of humanity might take the place of impossible inspiration, I was conscious that I was but seeking a consolation which I knew was valueless. If really I had the soul of an artist, what pleasure should I not be now experiencing at the sight of that curtain of trees lighted by the setting sun, of those little field-flowers lifting themselves almost to the foot-board of the railway carriage, whose petals I could count and whose colours I should not dare describe as do so many excellent writers, for can one hope to communicate to the reader a pleasure one has not felt? A little later I had observed with the same indifference, the lenses of gold and of orange into which the setting sun had transformed the windows of a house; and then, as the hour advanced, I had seen another house which seemed made of a strange pink substance. But I had made these various observations with the indifference I might have felt if, when walking in a garden with a lady, I had remarked a leaf of glass and further on an object like alabaster the unusual colour of which would not have distracted me from agonising boredom but which I had pointed at out of politeness to the lady and to show her that I had noticed them though they were coloured glass and stucco. In the same way as a matter of conscience I registered within myself as though to a person who was accompanying me and who would have been capable of getting more pleasure than I from them, the fiery reflections in the window-panes and the pink transparence of the house. But that companion whose notice I had drawn to these curious effects was doubtless of a less enthusiastic nature than many well disposed people whom such a sight would have delighted, for he had observed the colours without any sort of joy.

Since my name was on their visiting-lists, my long absence from Paris had not prevented old friends from sending me invitations and when, on getting home, I found together with an invitation for the following day to a supper given by La Berma in honour of her daughter and her son-in-law, another for an afternoon reception at the Prince de Guermantes', my sad reflections in the train were not the least of the motives which counselled me to go there. I told myself it really was not worth while to deprive myself of society since I was either not equipped for or not up to the precious "work" to which I had for so long been hoping to devote myself "to-morrow" and which, may be, corresponded to no reality. In truth, this reasoning was negative and merely eliminated the value of those which might have kept me away from this society function. But what made me go was that name of Guermantes which had so far gone out of my head that, when I saw it on the invitation card, it awakened a beam of attention and laid hold of a fraction of the past buried in the depths of my memory, a past associated with visions of the forest domain, its rich luxuriance once again assuming the charm and significance of the old Combray days when, before going home, I passed into the Rue de l'Oiseau and saw from outside, like dark lacquer, the painted window of Gilbert le Mauvais, Sire of Guermantes. For a moment the Guermantes seemed once more utterly different from society people, incomparable with them or with any living beings, even with a king, beings issuing from gestation in the austere and virtuous atmosphere of that sombre town of Combray where my childhood was spent, and from the whole past represented by the little street whence I gazed up at the painted window. I longed to go to the Guermantes' as though it would bring me back my childhood from the deeps of memory where I glimpsed it. And I continued to re-read the invitation until the letters which composed the name, familiar and mysterious as that of Combray itself, rebelliously recaptured their independence and spelled to my tired eyes a name I did not know.

My mother was going to a small tea-party with Mme. Sazerat so I had no scruple about attending the Princesse de Guermantes' reception. I ordered a carriage to take me there for the Prince de Guermantes no longer lived in his former mansion but in a magnificent new one which he had had built in the Avenue du Bois. One of the mistakes of people in society is that they do not realise, if they want us to believe in them, that they must first believe in themselves or at least that they must have some respect for the elements essential to our belief. At a time when I made myself believe even though I knew the contrary, that the Guermantes lived in their palace by virtue of hereditary privilege, to penetrate into the palace of a magician or a fairy, to have those doors open before me which are closed until the magical formula has been uttered seemed to me as difficult as to obtain an interview with the sorcerer and the fairy themselves. Nothing was easier than to convince myself that the old servant engaged the previous day at Potel and Chabot's was the son or grandson or descendant of those who served the family long before the revolution and I had infinite good will in calling the picture which had been bought the preceding month at Bernheim junior's the portrait of an ancestor. But the charm must not be decanted, memories cannot be isolated and now that the prince de Guermantes had himself destroyed my illusion by going to live in the Avenue du Bois, there was little of it left. Those ceilings which I had feared would fall at the sound of my name and under which so much of my former awe and fantasy might still have lingered, now sheltered the evening parties of an American woman of no interest to me. Of course things have no power in themselves and since it is we who impart it to them, some middle-class school-boy might at this moment be standing in front of the mansion in the Avenue du Bois and feeling as I did formerly about the earlier one. And this because he would still be at the age of faith which I had left far behind; I had lost that privilege as one loses the child's power to digest milk which we can only consume in small quantities whilst babies can suck it down indefinitely without taking breath. At least the Guermantes' change of domicile had the advantage for me that the carriage which had come to take me there and in which I was making these reflections had to pass through the streets which go towards the Champs Elysées. Those streets were at the time very badly paved, yet the moment the carriage entered them I was detached from my thoughts by a sensation of extreme sweetness; it was as though, all at once, the carriage was rolling along easily and noiselessly, like, when the gates of a park are opened, one seems to glide along a drive covered with fine gravel or dead leaves. There was nothing material about it but suddenly I felt emancipated from exterior obstacles as though I need no longer make an effort to adapt my attention as we do almost unconsciously when faced with something new; the streets through which I was then passing were those long forgotten ones which Françoise and I used to take when we were going to the Champs Elysées. The road itself knew where it was going, its resistance was overcome. And like an aviator who rolls painfully along the ground until, abruptly, he breaks away from it, I felt myself being slowly lifted towards the silent peaks of memory. Those particular streets of Paris, will, for me, always be composed of a different substance from others. When I reached the corner of the Rue Royale where formerly an open-air street-seller used to display the photographs beloved of Françoise, it seemed to me that the carriage accustomed in the course of years to turning there hundreds of times was compelled to turn of itself. I was not traversing the same streets as those who were passing by, I was gliding through a sweet and melancholy past composed of so many different pasts that it was difficult for me to identify the cause of my melancholy. Was it due to those pacings to and fro awaiting Gilberte and fearing she would not come? Was it that I was close to a house where I had been told that Albertine had gone with Andrée or was it the philosophic significance a street seems to assume when one has used it a thousand times while one was obsessed with a passion which has come to an end and borne no fruit like when after luncheon I made fevered expeditions to gaze at the play-bills of *Phèdre* and of the *Black Domino* while they were still moist with the bill-sticker's paste? Reaching the Champs Elysées and not much wanting to hear the whole of the concert at the Guermantes', I stopped the carriage and was able to get out of it to walk a few steps, when I noticed a carriage likewise about to stop. A man with glazed eyes and bent body was deposited rather than sitting in the back of it, and was making efforts to hold himself straight such as a child makes when told to behave nicely. An untouched forest of snow-white hair escaped from under his straw hat while a white beard like those snow attaches to statues in public gardens depended from his chin. It was M. de Charlus sitting beside Jupien (prodigal of attentions), convalescing from an attack of apoplexy (of which I was ignorant; all I had heard being that he had lost his eyesight, a passing matter, for he now saw clearly). He seemed, unless until then he had been in the habit of dyeing his hair and that he had been forbidden to do so because of the fatigue it involved, to have been subjected to some sort of chemical precipitation which had the effect of making his hair shine with such a brilliant and metallic lustre that the locks of his hair and beard spouted like so many geysers of pure silver and clad the aged and fallen prince with the Shakespearean majesty of a King Lear. The eyes had not remained unaffected by this total convulsion, this metallurgical alteration of the head; but by an inverse phenomenon they had lost all their lustre. What was most moving was the feeling that the lustre had been lent to them by moral pride and that owing to this having been lost, the physical and even the intellectual life of M. de Charlus survived his aristocratic hauteur which one had supposed to be embodied in it. At that very moment there passed in a victoria, doubtless also going to the Prince de Guermantes', Mme. de Sainte-Euverte whom formerly the Baron did not consider smart enough to be worth knowing. Jupien, who was taking care of him like a child, whispered in his ear that it was a personage he knew, Mme. de Sainte-Euverte. Immediately, with infinite trouble and with the concentration of an invalid who wants to appear capable of movements still painful to him, M. de Charlus uncovered, bowed and wished Mme. de Sainte-Euverte good-day with the respect he might have shown if she had been the Queen of France. The very difficulty of thus saluting her may have been the reason of it, through realising the poignancy of doing something painful and therefore doubly meritorious on the part of an invalid and doubly flattering to the lady to whom it was addressed. Like kings, invalids exaggerate politeness. Perhaps also there was a lack of co-ordination in the Baron's movements caused by disease of the marrow and brain and his gestures exceeded his intention. For myself I rather perceived therein a sort of quasi-physical gentleness, a detachment from the realities of life which strikes one in those about to enter the shadows of death. The profuse exposure of his silver-flaked head revealed a change less profound than this unconscious worldly humility which, reversing all social relationships, brought low in the presence of Mme. de Sainte-Euverte, would have brought low — showing thereby its debility — in the presence of the least important American woman (who might at last have secured from the Baron a consideration until then withheld) a snobbishness which had seemed the most arrogant. For the Baron still lived, could still think; his intelligence survived. And, more than a chorus of Sophocles on the humbled pride of Oedipus, more even than death itself or any funeral speech, the Baron's humble and obsequious greeting of Mme. de Sainte-Euverte proclaimed the perishable nature of earthly grandeurs and of all human pride. M. de Charlus who, till then, would not have consented to dine with Mme. de Sainte-Euverte now bowed down to the ground before her. It may, of course, be that he thus bowed to her through ignorance of her rank (for the rules of the social code can be obliterated by a stroke like any other part of the memory) perhaps by an inco-ordination which transposed to the plane of apparent humility his uncertainty—which might otherwise have been haughty—regarding the identity of the passing lady. He saluted her, in fact, with the timid politeness of a child told by its mother to say good-morning to grown-up people. And a child he had become, without a child's pride. For Mme. de Sainte-Euverte to receive the homage of M. de Çharlus was a world of gratified snobbery as, formerly, it was a world of snobbery for the Baron to refuse it her. And M. de Charlus had, at one blow, destroyed that precious and inaccessible character which he had succeeded in making Mme. de Sainte-Euverte believe was an essential part of himself by the concentrated timidity, the frightened eagerness with which he raised his hat and let loose the foaming torrents of his silver hair as he stood uncovered before her with the eloquent deference of a Bossuet. After Jupien had assisted the Baron to descend, I saluted him and he began speaking to me very fast and so indistinctly that I could not understand him and when, for the third time, I asked him to repeat what he said, it provoked a gesture of impatience which surprised me because of the previous impassiveness of his face which was doubtless due to the effects of paralysis. But when I succeeded in grasping his whispered words I realised that the invalid's intelligence was completely intact. There were moreover two M. de Charluses without counting others. Of the two the intellectual one spent the whole time complaining that he was approaching amnesia, that he was constantly pronouncing one word or one letter instead of another. But coincidentally, the other M. de Charlus, the subconscious one which wanted to be envied as much as the other to be pitied, stopped, like the leader of an orchestra at the beginning of a passage in which his musicians are floundering, and with infinite ingeniousness attached what followed to the word he had wrongly used but which he wanted one to believe he had deliberately chosen. Even his memory was uninjured; indeed he indulged in the exceedingly fatiguing coquetry of resuscitating some ancient and insignificant recollection in connexion with myself to prove to me that he had preserved or recovered all his mental acuteness. For instance, without moving his head or his eyes and without varying his inflection, he said to me: "Look! There's a post on which there's a notice exactly like the one where I was standing the first time I saw you at Avranches—no at Balbec, I mean." And it was actually an advertisement of the same product. At first I had difficulty in understanding what he said, as at first, one is unable to see in a darkened room, but like eyes which become accustomed to the dusk, my ears soon became accustomed to his pianissimo. I believe too that it got stronger as he went on speaking, whether because the weakness came partly from nervous apprehension which diminished while he was being distracted by someone or whether, on the contrary, the weakness was real and the strength of his voice was temporarily stimulated by excitement which was injurious to him and made strangers say: "He's getting better, he mustn't think about his illness," whereas, on the contrary, it made him worse. Be this as it may, the Baron, at this particular moment, cast up his words with greater vigour like the tide does its waves in bad weather. An effect of his recent stroke was to make his voice sound like stones rolling under his words. And as he went on talking to me of the past, no doubt to show he had not lost his memory, he evoked it funereally, yet without sadness. He kept on enumerating the various members of his family or of his set who were dead, apparently less because he was sorry they had departed than because of his satisfaction at having survived them; in reminding himself of their death, he seemed to become more conscious of his own recovery. He enumerated almost triumphantly but in a monotonous tone accompanied by a slight stammer and with a sort of sepulchral resonance: "Hannibal de Bréauté, dead! Antoine de Mouchy, dead! Charles Swann, dead! Adalbert de Montmorency, dead! Baron de Talleyrand, dead! Sosthène de Doudeauville, dead!" And each time the word "dead" seemed to fall upon the defunct like a shovelful of earth, the heavier for the gravedigger wanting to press them ever deeper into the tomb.

The Duchesse de Létourville, who was not going to the reception of the Princesse de Guermantes because she had been ill for a long time, at that moment passed by us on foot and noticing the Baron whose attack she had not heard about, stopped to say good-day to him. But the illness from which she had been suffering did not make her better understand the illness of others which she bore with an impatience and nervous irritation in which there was perhaps a good deal of pity. Hearing the Baron's defective pronunciation and the mistakes in some of his words and observing the difficulty with which he moved his arm, she glanced in turn at Jupien and at me as though she were asking the explanation of such a shocking phenomenon. As we did not answer she directed a long, sad, reproachful stare at M. de Charlus himself, apparently vexed at his being seen out with her in a condition as unusual as if he were wearing neither tie nor shoes. When the Baron made another mistake in his pronunciation, the distress and indignation of the Duchesse increased, and she cried at the Baron: "Palamède?" in the interrogatory and exasperated tone of neurasthenic people who cannot bear waiting a moment and who, if one asks them in immediately and apologises for not being completely dressed, remark bitterly, not to excuse themselves but to accuse you: "Oh, I see I'm disturbing you!" as though the person they are disturbing had done something wrong. Finally, she left us with a still more concerned air, saying to the Baron: "You'd better go home."

M. de Charlus wanted to sit down and rest in a chair while Jupien and I took a few steps together, and painfully extracted a book from his pocket which seemed to me to be a prayer-book. I was not sorry to learn some details about the Baron's health from Jupien. "I am glad to talk to you, Monsieur," said Jupien, "but we won't go further than the Rond-Point. Thank God, the Baron is better now, but I don't dare leave him long alone. He's always the same, he's too good-hearted, he'd give everything he has to others and that isn't all, he remains as much of a *coureur* as if he were a young man and I'm obliged to keep my eye on him." "The more so," I replied, "as he has recovered his own. I was greatly distressed when I was told that he had lost his eye-sight." "His paralysis did, indeed, have that effect, at first he couldn't see at all. Just think that during the cure which, as a matter of fact, did him a lot of good, for several months he couldn't see any more than if he'd been blind from birth." "At least, that must have made part of your supervision unnecessary." "Not the least in the world! We had hardly arrived at a hotel than he asked me what such and such a person on the staff was like. I assured him they were all awful, but he knew it couldn't be as universal as I said and that I must be lying about some of them. There's that *petit polisson* again! And then he got a sort of intuition, perhaps from a voice, I don't know, and managed to send me away on some urgent commission. One day—excuse me for telling you all this, but as you once by chance entered the temple of impurity, I have nothing to hide from you" (for that matter he always got a rather unpleasant satisfaction out of revealing secrets) "I came back from one of those pretended urgent commissions quickly because I thought it had been arranged on purpose, when just as I approached the Baron's room I heard a voice ask: 'What?' and the Baron's answer: 'Do you mean to say it's the first time?' I entered without knocking and what was my horror! The Baron, misled by the voice which was indeed more mature than is habitual at that age (and at that time he was completely blind) he, who formerly only liked grown men, was with a child not ten years old."

I was told that at that period he was nearly every day a prey to attacks of mental depression characterised not exactly by divagation but by confessing at the top of his voice—in front of third parties whose presence and censoriousness he had forgotten—opinions he usually hid, such as his Germanophilism. So, long after the end of the war he was bewailing the defeat of the Germans, amongst whom he included himself and said bitterly: "We shall have to be revenged. We have proved the power of our resistance and we were the best organised," or else his confidences took another form and he exclaimed in a rage: "Don't let Lord X— or the Prince of X—, come and tell me again what they said the other day for it was all I could do to prevent myself replying, 'You know, because you're one of them, at least, as much as I am.'" Needless to add that when M. de Charlus thus gave vent at times when he was, as they say, not all there, to these Germanophile and other avowals, people in his company such as Jupien or the Duchesse de Guermantes were in the habit of interrupting his imprudent words and giving to the third party who was less intimate and more indiscreet a forced but honourable interpretation of his words. "Oh, my God," called Jupien, "I had good reason not to want to go far away. There he is starting a conversation with a gardener boy. Good-day, sir, it's better I should go, I can't leave my invalid alone a moment; he's nothing but a great baby."

I got out of the carriage again a little before reaching the Princesse de Guermantes' and began thinking again of that lassitude, that weariness with which I had tried the evening before to note the railway line which separated the shadow from the light upon the trees in one of the most beautiful countrysides in France. Certainly such intellectual conclusions as I had drawn from these thoughts did not affect my sensibility so cruelly to-day, but they remained the same, for, as always happened when I succeeded in breaking away from my habits, going out at an unaccustomed hour to some new place, I derived a lively pleasure from it.

To-day, the pleasure of going to a reception at Mme. de Guermantes', seemed to me purely frivolous, but since I now knew that I could expect to have no other than frivolous pleasures, what was the use of my not accepting them? I repeated to myself that in attempting this description I had experienced none of that enthusiasm which I is not the only but the first criterion of talent. I began now to draw on my memory for "snapshots", notably snapshots it had taken at Venice but the mere mention of the word made Venice as boring to me as a photographic exhibition and I was conscious of no more taste or talent in visualising what I had formerly seen than yesterday in describing what I had observed with a meticulous and mournful eye. In a few minutes so many charming friends I had not seen for so long would doubtless be asking me not to cut myself off and to spend some time with them. I had no reason to refuse them since I now had the proof that I was good for nothing, that literature could no longer give me any joy whether because of my lack of talent or because it was a less real thing than I had believed.

When I remembered what Bergotte had said to me: "You are ill but one cannot be sorry for you because you possess the delights of the mind," I saw how much he had been mistaken. How little delight I got out of this sterile lucidity. I might have added that if sometimes I had tasted pleasures—not those of the mind—I had always exhausted them with a different woman so that even if destiny were to grant me a hundred years of healthy life it would only be adding successive lengths to an existence already in a straight line which there was no object in lengthening further. As to the "delights of the mind", could I thus name those cold and sterile reflections which my clear-sighted eye or my logical reasoning joylessly summarised? But sometimes illumination comes to our rescue at the very moment when all seems lost; we have knocked at every door and they open on nothing until, at last, we stumble unconsciously against the only one through which we can enter the kingdom we have sought in vain a hundred years—and it opens.[1]

Reviewing the painful reflections of which I have just been speaking, I had entered the courtyard of the Guermantes' mansion and in my distraction I had not noticed an approaching carriage; at the call of the link-man I had barely time to draw quickly to one side, and in stepping backwards I stumbled against some unevenly placed paving stones behind which there was a coach-house. As I recovered myself, one of my feet stepped on a flagstone lower than the one next it. In that instant all my discouragement disappeared and I was possessed by the same felicity which at different moments of my life had given me the view of trees which seemed familiar to me during the drive round Balbec, the view of the belfries of Martinville, the savour of the madeleine dipped in my tea and so many other sensations of which I have spoken and which Vinteuil's last works had seemed to synthesise. As at the moment when I tasted the madeleine, all my apprehensions about the future, all my intellectual doubts, were dissipated. Those doubts which had assailed me just before, regarding the reality of my literary gifts and even regarding the reality of literature itself were dispersed as though by magic. This time I vowed that I should not resign myself to ignoring why, without any fresh reasoning, without any definite hypothesis, the insoluble difficulties of the previous in-

---

[1] In the French text of Le Temps Retrouvé, vol. I ends here.

stant had lost all importance as was the case when I tasted the madeleine. The felicity which I now experienced was undoubtedly the same as that I felt when I ate the madeleine, the cause of which I had then postponed seeking. There was a purely material difference in the images evoked. A deep azure intoxicated my eyes, a feeling of freshness, of dazzling light enveloped me and in my desire to capture the sensation, just as I had not dared to move when I tasted the madeleine because of trying to conjure back that of which it reminded me, I stood, doubtless an object of ridicule to the link-men, repeating the movement of a moment since, one foot upon the higher flagstone, the other on the lower one. Merely repeating the movement was useless; but if, oblivious of the Guermantes' reception, I succeeded in recapturing the sensation which accompanied the movement, again the intoxicating and elusive vision softly pervaded me as though it said "Grasp me as I float by you, if you can, and try to solve the enigma of happiness I offer you." And then, all at once, I recognised that Venice which my descriptive efforts and pretended snapshots of memory had failed to recall; the sensation I had once felt on two uneven slabs in the Baptistry of St. Mark had been given back to me and was linked with all the other sensations of that and other days which had lingered expectant in their place among the series of forgotten years from which a sudden chance had imperiously called them forth. So too the taste of the little madeleine had recalled Combray. But how was it that these visions of Combray and of Venice at one and at another moment had caused me a joyous certainty sufficient without other proofs to make death indifferent to me? Asking myself this and resolved to find the answer this very day, I entered the Guermantes' mansion, because we always allow our inner needs to give way to the part we are apparently called upon to play and that day mine was to be a guest. On reaching the first floor a footman requested me to enter a small boudoir-library adjoining a buffet until the piece then being played had come to an end, the Princesse having given orders that the doors should not be opened during the performance. At that very instant a second premonition occurred to reinforce the one which the uneven paving-stones had given me and to exhort me to persevere in my task. The servant in his ineffectual efforts not to make a noise had knocked a spoon against a plate. The same sort of felicity which the uneven paving-stones had given me invaded my being; this time my sensation was quite different, being that of great heat accompanied by the smell of smoke tempered by the fresh air of a surrounding forest and I realised that what appeared so pleasant was the identical group of trees I had found so tiresome to observe and describe when I was uncorking a bottle of beer in the railway carriage and, in a sort of bewilderment, I believed for the moment, until I had collected myself, so similar was the sound of the spoon against the plate to that of the hammer of a railway employee who was doing something to the wheel of the carriage while the train was at a standstill facing the group of trees, that I was now actually there. One might have said that the portents which that day were to rescue me from my discouragement and give me back faith in literature, were determined to multiply themselves, for a servant, a long time in the service of the Prince de Guermantes, recognised me and, to save me going to the buffet, brought me some cakes and a glass of orangeade into the library. I wiped my mouth with the napkin he had given me and immediately, like the personage in the *Thousand and*

One Nights who unknowingly accomplished the rite which caused the appearance before him of a docile genius, invisible to others, ready to transport him far away, a new azure vision passed before my eyes; but this time it was pure and saline and swelled into shapes like bluish udders. The impression was so strong that the moment I was living seemed to be one with the past and (more bewildered still than I was on the day when I wondered whether I was going to be welcomed by the Princesse de Guermantes or whether everything was going to melt away), I believed that the servant had just opened the window upon the shore and that everything invited me to go downstairs and walk along the sea-wall at high tide; the napkin upon which I was wiping my mouth had exactly the same kind of starchiness as that with which I had attempted with so much difficulty to dry myself before the window the first day of my arrival at Balbec and within the folds of which, now, in that library of the Guermantes mansion, a green-blue ocean spread its plumage like the tail of a peacock. And I did not merely rejoice in those colours, but in that whole instant which produced them, an instant towards which my whole life had doubtless aspired, which a feeling of fatigue or sadness had prevented my ever experiencing at Balbec but which now, pure, disincarnated and freed from the imperfections of exterior perceptions, filled me with joy. The piece they were playing might finish at any moment, and I should be obliged to enter the drawing room. So I forced myself to try to penetrate as quickly as possible into the nature of those identical sensations I had felt three times within a few minutes so as to extract the lesson I might learn from them. I did not stop to consider the extreme difference which there is between the true impression which we have had of a thing and the artificial meaning we give to it when we employ our will to represent it to ourselves, for I remembered with what relative indifference Swann had been able to speak formerly of the days when he was loved, because beneath the words, he felt something else than them, and the immediate pain Vinteuil's little phrase had caused him by giving him back those very days themselves as he had formerly felt them, and I understood but too well that the sensation the uneven paving-stones, the taste of the madeleine, had aroused in me, bore no relation to that which I had so often attempted to reconstruct of Venice, of Balbec and of Combray with the aid of a uniform memory. Moreover, I realised that life can be considered commonplace in spite of its appearing so beautiful at particular moments because in the former case one judges and underrates it on quite other grounds than itself, upon images which have no life in them. At most I noted additionally that the difference there is between each real impression—differences which explain why a uniform pattern of life cannot resemble it—can probably be ascribed to this: that the slightest word we have spoken at a particular period of our life, the most insignificant gesture to which we have given vent, were surrounded, bore upon them the reflection of things which logically were unconnected with them, were indeed isolated from them by the intelligence which did not need them for reasoning purposes but in the midst of which—here, the pink evening-glow upon the floral wall-decoration of a rustic restaurant, a feeling of hunger, sexual desire, enjoyment of luxury—there, curling waves beneath the blue of a morning sky enveloping musical phrases which partly emerge like mermaids' shoulders—the most simple act or gesture remains enclosed as though in a thousand jars of which each would be filled with things of different colours, odours and temperature; not to mention that those vases placed at intervals during the growing years throughout which we ceaselessly change, if only in dream or in thought, are situated at completely different, levels and produce the impression of strangely varying climates. It is true that these changes have occurred to us without our being aware of them; but the distance between the memory which suddenly returns and our present personality as similarly between two memories of different years and places, is so great that it would suffice, apart from their specific uniqueness, to make comparison between; them impossible. Yes, if a memory, thanks to forgetfulness, has been unable to contract any tie, to forge any link between itself and the present, if it has remained in its own place, of its own date, if it has kept its distance, its isolation in the hollow of a valley or on the peak of a mountain, it makes us suddenly breathe an air new to us just because it is an air we have formerly breathed, an air purer than that the poets have vainly called Paradisiacal, which offers that deep sense of renewal only because it has been breathed before, inasmuch as the true paradises are paradises we have lost. And on the way to it, I noted that there would be great difficulties in creating the work of art I now felt ready to undertake without its being consciously in my mind, for I should have to construct each of its successive parts out of a different sort of material. The material which would be suitable for memories at the side of the sea would be quite different from those of afternoons at Venice which would demand a material of its own, a new one, of a special transparency and sonority, compact, fresh and pink, different again if I wanted to describe evenings at Rivebelle where, in the dining-room open upon the garden, the heat was beginning to disintegrate, to descend and come to rest on the earth, while the rose-covered walls of the restaurant were lighted up by the last ray of the setting sun and the last water-colours of daylight lingered in the sky. I passed rapidly over all these things, being summoned more urgently to seek the cause of that happiness with its peculiar character of insistent certainty, the search for which I had formerly adjourned. And I began to discover the cause by comparing those varying happy impressions which had the common quality of being felt simultaneously at the actual moment and at a distance in time, because of which common quality the noise of the spoon upon the plate, the unevenness of the paving-stones, the taste of the madeleine, imposed the past upon the present and made me hesitate as to which time I was existing in. Of a truth, the being within me which sensed this impression, sensed what it had in common in former days and now, sensed its extra-temporal character, a being which only appeared when through the medium of the identity of present and past, it found itself in the only setting in which it could exist and enjoy the essence of things, that is, outside Time. That explained why my apprehensions on the subject of my death had ceased from the moment when I had unconsciously recognised the taste of the little madeleine because at that moment the being that I then had been was an extra-temporal being and in consequence indifferent to the vicissitudes of the future. That being had never come to me, had never manifested itself except when I was inactive and in a sphere beyond the enjoyment of the moment, that was my prevailing condition every time that analogical miracle had enabled me to escape from the present. Only that being had the power of enabling me to recapture former days,

Time Lost, in the face of which all the efforts of my memory and of my intelligence came to nought.

And perhaps, if just now I thought that Bergotte had spoken falsely when he referred to the joys of spiritual life it was because I then gave the name of spiritual life to logical reasonings which had no relation with it, which, had no relation with what now existed in me—just as I found society and life wearisome because I was judging them from memories without Truth while now that a veritable moment of the past had been born again in me three separate times, I had such a desire to live.

Nothing but a moment of the past? Much more perhaps; something which being common to the past and the present, is more essential than both.

How many times in the course of my life reality had disappointed me because at the moment when I perceived it, my imagination, which was my only means of enjoying beauty, could not be applied to it by virtue of the inevitable law which only allows us to imagine that which is absent. And now suddenly the effect of this hard law had become neutralised, held in suspense by a marvellous expedient of nature which had caused a sensation to flash to me—sound of a spoon and of a hammer, uneven paving-stones—simultaneously in the past which permitted my imagination to grasp it and in the present in which the shock to my senses caused by the noise had effected a contact between the dreams of the imagination and that of which they are habitually deprived, namely, the idea of existence—and thanks to that stratagem had permitted that being within me to secure, to isolate and to render static for the duration of a lightning flash that which it can never wholly grasp, a fraction of Time in its pure essence. When, with such a shudder of happiness, I heard the sound common, at once, to the spoon touching the plate, to the hammer striking the wheel, to the unevenness of the paving-stones in the court-yard of the Guermantes' mansion and the Baptistry of St. Mark's, it was because that being within me can only be nourished on the essence of things and finds in them alone its subsistence and its delight. It languishes in the observation by the senses of the present sterilised by the intelligence awaiting a future constructed by the will out of fragments of the past and the present from which it removes still more reality, keeping that only which serves the narrow human aim of util-itarian purposes. But let a sound, a scent already heard and breathed in the past be heard and breathed anew, simultaneously in the present and in the past, real without being actual, ideal without being abstract, then instantly the permanent and characteristic essence hidden in things is freed and our true being which has for long seemed dead but was not so in other ways awakes and revives, thanks to this celestial nourishment. An instant liberated from the order of time has recre-ated in us man liberated from the same order, so that he should be conscious of it. And indeed we understand his faith in his happiness even if the mere taste of a madeleine does not logically seem to justify it; we understand that the name of death is meaningless to him for, placed beyond Time, how can he fear the future? But that illusion which brought near me a moment of the past incongruous to the present, would not last. Certainly we can prolong the visions of memory by willing it which is no more than turning over an illustrated book. Thus former-ly, when I was going for the first time to the Princesse de Guermantes' from the sun-lit court of our house in Paris, I had lazily focused my mind at one moment on the square where the church of Combray stood, at another on the sea shore of Balbec, as I might have amused myself by turning over a folio of water-colours of different places I had visited and cataloguing these mnemonic illustrations with the egotistical pleasure of a collector, I might have said: "After all, I have seen some beautiful things in my life." Doubtless, in that event, my memory would have been asserting different sensations but it would only have been combining their homogeneous elements. That was a different thing from the three memories I had just experienced which, so far from giving me a more flattering notion of my personality, had, on the contrary, almost made me doubt its very existence. Thus, on the day when I dipped the madeleine in the hot infusion, in the heart of that place where I happened to be (whether that place was, as then, my room in Paris or, as to-day, the Prince de Guermantes' library) there had been the irradiation of a small zone within and around myself, a sensation (taste of the dipped madeleine, metallic sound, feeling of the uneven steps) common to the place where I then was and also to the other place (my Aunt Léonie's room, the railway carriage, the Baptistry of St. Mark's). And, at the very moment when I was thus reasoning, the strident sound of a water-pipe, exactly like those long screeches which one heard on board excursion steamers at Balbec, made me experience (as had happened to me once in a large restaurant in Paris at the sight of a luxurious dining-room half empty, summerlike and hot) something more than a mere sensation like one I had, one late afternoon at Balbec, when, all the tables symmetrically laid with linen and silver, the large bow-windows wide open to the sun slowly setting on the sea with its wandering ships, I had only to step across the window-frame hardly higher than my ankle, to be with Albertine and her friends who were walking on the sea-wall. It was not only the echo, the duplication of a past sensation that the water-conduit had caused me to experience, it was the sensation itself. In that case as in all the preceding ones, the common sensation had sought to recreate the former place around itself whilst the material place in which the sensation occurred, opposed all the resistance of its mass to this immigration into a Paris mansion of a Norman seashore and a railway-embankment. The marine dining-room of Balbec with its damask linen prepared like altar cloths to receive the setting sun had sought to disturb the solidity of the Guermantes' mansion, to force its doors, and had made the sofas round me quiver an instant as on another occasion the tables of the restaurant in Paris had done. In all those resurrections, the distant place engendered by the sensation common to them all, came to grips for a second with the material place, like a wrestler. The material place was always the conqueror and always the conquered seemed to me the more beautiful, so much so that I remained in a state of ecstasy upon the uneven pavement as I did with my cup of tea, trying to retain with the moment of their appearance, to make reappear as they escaped, that Combray, that Venice, that Balbec, invading, yet repelled, which came before my eyes only immediately to abandon me in the midst of a newer scene which yet was penetrable by the past. And if the material place had not been at once the conqueror I think I should have lost consciousness; for these resurrections of the past, for the second that they last, are so complete that they not only force our eyes to cease seeing the room which is before them in order to see the railway bordered by trees or the rising tide, they force our nostrils to breathe the air of those places which are, nevertheless, so far away, our will to choose between the diverse alternatives it offers us, our whole personality to believe itself surrounded by them, or at least to stumble between them and the material world, in the bewildering uncertainty we experience from an ineffable vision on the threshold of sleep.

So, that which the being within me, three or four times resurrected, had experienced, were perhaps fragments of lives snatched from time which, though viewed from eternity, were fugitive. And yet I felt that the happiness given me at those rare intervals in my life was the only fruitful and authentic one. Does not the sign of unreality in others consist in their inability to satisfy us, as, for instance, in the case of social pleasures which, at best, cause that discomfort which is provoked by unwholesome food, when friendship is almost a pretence, since, for whatever moral reasons he may seek it, the artist who gives up an hour of work to converse for that time with a friend knows that he is sacrificing a reality to an illusion (friends being friends only in the sense of a sweet madness which overcomes us in life and to which we yield, though at the back of our minds we know it to be the error of a lunatic who imagines the furniture to be alive and talks to it) owing to the sadness which follows its satisfaction—like that I felt the day I was first introduced to Albertine when I gave myself the trouble, after all not great, to obtain something—to make the acquaintance of the girl—which only seemed to me unimportant because I had obtained it. Even a deeper pleasure such as that which I might have felt when I loved Albertine was in reality only perceived by contrast with my anguish when she was no longer there, for when I was sure she would return as on the day when she came back from the Trocadéro, I only experienced a vague boredom whereas the deeper I penetrated into the sound of the spoon on the plate or the taste of tea, the more exalted became my delight that my Aunt Léonie's chamber and later the whole of Combray and both its sides had entered my room. And now I was determined to concentrate my mind on that contemplation of the essence of things, to define it to myself, but how and by what means? Doubtless at the moment when the stiffness of the table-napkin had brought back Balbec to me and, for an instant, caressed my imagination not only with a view of the sea as it was that morning but with the scent of the room, with the swiftness of the wind, with an appetite for breakfast, with wavering between various walks, all those things attached to a sensation of space like winged wheels in their delirious race, doubtless at the moment when the unevenness of the two pavements had prolonged in all directions and dimensions my arid and crude visions of Venice and St. Mark's, and all the emotions I had then experienced, relating the square to the church, the landing-stage to the square, the canal to the landing-stage, to everything the eye saw, to that whole world of longings which is in reality only perceived by the spirit, I had been tempted to set forth if not to Venice because of the inclement season, at least, to Balbec. But I did not stop an instant at that thought; not only did I realise that countries were not that which their name pictured to me and my imagination represented them but that it was only in my dreams, and hardly then, that a place consisting of pure matter, was spread out before me clear and distinct from those common things one can see and touch. But even in regard to those images of another kind, of the memory, I knew that I had not found any beauty in Balbec when I went there and that the beauty memory had left in me was no longer the same at my second visit. I had too clearly proved the impossibility of expecting from reality that which was within myself. It was not in the Square of St. Mark any more than during my second visit to Balbec or on my return to Tansonville to see Gilberte that I should find Lost Time and the journey which once more tempted me with the illusion that these old impressions existed outside myself and were situated in a certain spot could not be the means I was seeking. I would not allow myself to be lured again; it was necessary for me to know at last, if indeed it were possible to attain that which, disappointed as I had always been by places and people, I had (in spite of a concert-piece by Vinteuil which had seemed to say the contrary) believed unrealisable. I was not, therefore, going to attempt another experience on the road which I had long known to lead nowhere. Impressions such as those which I was attempting to render permanent could only vanish at the contact of a direct enjoyment which was powerless to give birth to them. The only way was to attempt to know them more completely where they existed, that is, within myself and by so doing to illuminate them in their depths. I had never known any pleasure at Balbec any more than I had in living with Albertine except what was perceptible afterwards. And if in recapitulating the disappointments of my life as I had so far lived it, they led me to believe that its reality must reside elsewhere than in action and, if, in following the vicissitudes of my life, I did not summarise them as a matter of pure hazard, I well knew that the disappointment of a journey and the disappointment of love were not different disappointments but varying aspects which, according to the conditions to which they apply, are inflicted upon us by the impotence, difficult for us to realise, of material pleasure and effective action. Again reflecting on that extra-temporal delight caused whether by the sound of the spoon or by the taste of the madeleine, I said to myself: "Was this the happiness suggested by the little phrase of the Sonata, which Swann was deceived into identifying with the pleasure of love and was not endowed to find in artistic creation; that happiness which had made me respond as to a presentiment of something more supraterrestrial still than the little phrase of the Sonata, to the red and mysterious appeal of that septet which Swann did not know, having died like so many others, before the truth, meant for them, had been revealed?" Moreover, it would have done him no good, for that phrase might symbolise an appeal but it could not create the force which would have made of Swann the writer he was not. And yet I reminded myself after a moment and after having thought over those resurrections of memory, that in another way, obscure impressions had sometimes, as far back as Combray and on the Guermantes' side, demanded my thought, in the same way as those mnemonic resurrections, yet they did not contain an earlier experience but a new truth, a precious image which I was trying to discover by efforts of the kind one makes to remember something as though our loveliest ideas were like musical airs which might come to us without our having ever heard them and which we force ourselves to listen to and write down. I reminded myself with satisfaction, (because it proved that I was the same then and that it represented a fundamental quality of my nature) and also with sadness in the thought that since then I had made no progress, that, as far back as at Combray, I was attempting to concentrate my mind on a compelling image, a cloud, a triangle, a belfry, a flower, a pebble, believing that there was perhaps something else under those symbols I ought to try to discover, a thought which these objects were expressing in the manner of hieroglyphic characters which one might imagine only represented material objects. Doubtless such deciphering was difficult, but it alone could yield some part of the truth. For the truths which the intelligence apprehends through direct and clear vision in the daylight world are less profound and less necessary than those which life has communicated to us unconsciously through an intuition which is material only in so far as it reaches us through our senses and the spirit of which we can elicit. In fact, in this case as in the other, whether it was a question of impressions given me by a view of the Martinville belfry or memories like those of the two uneven paving-stones or the taste of the madeleine, it was necessary to attempt to interpret them as symbols of so many laws and ideas, by trying to think, that is, by trying to educe my sensation from its obscurity and con-vert it into an intellectual equivalent. And what other means were open to me than the creation of a work of art? Already the consequences pressed upon my spirit; for whether it was a question of memories like the sound of the spoon and the taste of the madeleine or of those verities expressed in forms the meaning of which I sought in my brain, where, belfries, wild herbs, what not, they composed a complex illuminated scroll, their first characteristic was that I was not free to choose them, that they had been given to me as they were. And I felt that that must be the seal of their authenticity. I had not gone to seek the two paving-stones in the courtyard against which I had struck. But it was precisely the fortuitousness, the inevitability of the sensation which safeguarded the truth of the past it revived, of the images it set free, since we feel its effort to rise upwards to the light and the joy of the real recaptured. That fortuitousness is the guardian of the truth of the whole series of contemporary impressions which it brings in its train, with that infallible proportion of light and shade, of emphasis and omission, of memory and forgetfulness, of which the conscious memory or observation are ignorant.

That book of unknown signs within me (signs in relief it seemed, for my concentrated attention, as it explored my unconscious in its search, struck against them, circled round them like a diver sounding) no one could help me read by any rule, for its reading consists in an act of creation in which no one can take our place and in which no one can collaborate. And how many turn away from writing it, how many tasks will one not assume to avoid that one! Every event, whether it was the Dreyfus affair or the war, furnished excuses to writers for not deciphering that book; they wanted to assert the triumph of Justice, to recreate the moral unity of the nation and they had no time to think of literature. But those were only excuses because either they did not possess or had ceased to possess genius, that is, instinct. For it is instinct which dictates duty and intelligence which offers pretexts for avoiding it. But excuses do not exist in art, intentions do not count there, the artist must at all times follow his instinct, which makes art the most real thing, the most austere school in life and the true last judgment. That book which is the most arduous of all to decipher is the only one which reality has dictated, the only one printed within us by reality itself. Whatever idea life has left in us, its material shape, mark of the impression it has made on us, is still the necessary pledge of its truth. The ideas formulated by the intellect have only a logical truth, a possible truth, their selection is arbitrary. Our only book is that one not made by ourselves whose characters are already imaged. It is not that the ideas we formulate may not be logically right but that we do not know if they are true. Intuition alone, however tenuous its consistency, however improbable its shape, is a criterion of truth and, for that reason, deserves to be accepted by the mind because it alone is capable, if the mind can extract that truth, of bringing it to greater perfection and of giving it pleasure without alloy. Intuition for the writer is what experiment is for the learned, with the difference that in the case of the learned the work of the intelligence precedes and in the case of the writer it follows. That which we have not been forced to decipher, to clarify by our own personal effort, that which was made clear before, is not ours. Only that issues from ourselves which we ourselves extract from the darkness within ourselves and which is unknown to others. And as art exactly recomposes life, an atmosphere of poetry surrounds those truths within ourselves to which we attain, the sweetness of a mystery which is but the twilight through which we have passed. An oblique ray from the setting sun brings instantly back to me a time of which I had never thought again, when, in my childhood, my Aunt Léonie had a fever which Dr. Percepied had feared was typhoid and they had made me stop for a week in the little room Eulalie had in the church square, where there was only a matting on the floor and a dimity curtain at the window humming in the sunlight to which I was unaccustomed. And when I think how the memory of that little room of an old servant suddenly added to my past life an extension so different from its other side and so delightful, I remember, as a contrast, the nullity of impressions left on my mind by the most sumptuous parties in the most princely mansions. The only thing that was distressing in Eulalie's room was that owing to the proximity of the viaduct, one heard the noise of passing trains at night. But as I knew that this roaring proceeded from regulated machines, it did not terrify me as much as the roars of a mammoth, prowling near by in savage freedom, would have done in prehistoric days.

Thus I had already reached the conclusion that we are in no wise free in the presence of a work of art, that we do not create it as we please but that it pre-exists in us and we are compelled as though it were a law of nature to discover it because it is at once hidden from us and necessary. But is not that discovery, which art may enable us to make, most precious to us, a discovery of that which for most of us remains for ever unknown, our true life, reality as we have ourselves felt it and which differs so much from that which we had believed that we are filled with delight when chance brings us an authentic revelation of it? I was sure of this from the very falsity of so-called realistic art which would not be so deceptive if we had not in the course of life, contracted the habit of giving what we feel an expression so different that, after a time, we believe it to be reality itself. I felt that it was not necessary for me to incommode myself with the diverse literary theories which had for a time troubled me—notably those that criticism had developed at the time of the Dreyfus affair and which had again resumed their sway during the war, which tended to "make the artist come out of his ivory tower" and, instead of using frivolous or sentimental subjects as his material, to picture great working-class movements or if not the crowd, at all events rather than insignificant idlers—("I avow," said Bloch, "that the portraits of these futile people are indifferent to me")—noble intellectuals or heroes. Before even considering their logical content, these theories seemed to me to denote amongst those who entertained them, a proof of inferiority like a well brought-up child, who, being sent out to lunch at a friend's house, hearing someone say: "We speak out, we are frank," realises that the words signify a moral quality inferior to a pure and simple good act about which nothing is said. Authentic art does not proclaim itself for it is achieved in silence. Moreover, those who thus theorise, use ready-made expressions which singularly resemble those of the imbeciles they castigate. And perhaps it is rather by the quality of the language than by the particular aesthetic that we can judge the level which intellectual and moral work has reached. But inversely this quality of language (and we can study the laws of character equally well in a serious as in a frivolous subject as an anatomist can study the laws of anatomy on the body of an imbecile just as well as on that of a man of talent; the great moral laws as well as those which govern the circulation of the blood or renal elimination making small difference between the intellectual value of individuals) with which theorists think they can dispense, those who admire theorists believe to be of no great intellectual value and in order to discern it, require it to be expressed in direct terms because they are unable to infer it from the beauty of imagery. Hence that vulgar temptation of an author to write intellectual works. A great indelicacy. A work in which there are theories is like an object upon which the price is marked. Further, this last only expresses a value which, in literature, is diminished by logical reasoning. We reason, that is, our mind wanders, each time our courage fails to force us to pursue an intuition through all the successive stages which end in its fixation, in the expression of its own reality. The reality that must be expressed resides, I now realised, not in the appearance of the subject but in the degree of penetration of that intuition to a depth where that appearance matters little, as symbolised by the sound of the spoon upon the plate, the stiffness of the table-napkin, which were more precious for my spiritual renewal than many humanitarian, patriotic, international conversations. More style, I had heard said in those days, more literature of life. One can imagine how many of M. de Norpois' simple theories "against flute-players" had flowered again since the war. For all those who, lacking artistic sensibility, that is, submission to the reality within, may be equipped with the faculty of reasoning for ever about art, and even were they diplomatists or financiers associated with the "realities" of the present into the bargain, they will readily believe that literature is a sort of intellectual game which is destined to be eliminated more and more in the future. Some of them wanted the novel to be a sort of cinematographic procession. This conception was absurd. Nothing removes us further from the reality we perceive within ourselves than such a cinematographic vision. Just now as I entered this library, I remembered what the Goncourts say about the beautiful original editions it contains and I promised myself to have a look at them whilst I was shut in here. And still following my argument, I took up one after another of the precious volumes without paying much attention to them when, inattentively opening one of them, *François le Champi,* by George Sand, I felt myself disagreeably affected as by some impression out of harmony with my thoughts, until I suddenly realised with an emotion which nearly brought tears to my eyes how much that impression was in harmony with them. It was as at the moment when in the mortuary vault the undertakers' men are lowering the coffin of a man who has rendered services to his country and his son pressing the hands of the last friends who file past the tomb, suddenly hearing a flourish of trumpets under the windows, would be horrified by what he supposed a mockery designed to insult his sorrow, while another who had controlled himself until then, would be unable to restrain his tears because he realised that what he heard was the music of a regiment which was sharing his mourning and wanting to render homage to the remains of his father. Such was the painful impression I had experienced in reading the title of a book in the Prince de Guermantes' library, a title which communicated the idea to me that literature really does offer us that world of mystery I had no longer found in it. And yet, *François le Champi* was not a very remarkable book but the name, like the name of Guermantes, was unlike those I had known later. The memory of what had seemed incomprehensible when my mother read it to me, was aroused by its title and in the same way that the name of Guermantes (when I had not seen the Guermantes' for a long time) contained for me the whole of feudalism, —so *François le Champi* contained the whole essence of the novel—dispossessing for an instant the commonplace ideas of which the stuffy novels of George Sand are composed. At a dinner party where thought is always superficial I might no doubt have spoken of *François le Champi* and the Guermantes' as though neither were associated with Combray. But when, as at this moment, I was alone, I plunged to a greater depth. At that time the idea that a particular individual whose acquaintance I had made in society was the cousin of Mme. de Guermantes, that is to say, the cousin of a personage on a magic lantern slide, seemed to me incomprehensible and just as much, that the finest books I had read should be, I do not even say superior which they nevertheless were but equal to this extraordinary *François le Champi*. This was an old childish impression with which my memories of childhood and of my family were tenderly associated and which at first I had not recognised. At the first instant I had angrily asked myself who this stranger was who had done me a violence and the stranger was myself, the child I once was whom the book had revived in me, for recognising only the child in me, the book had at once summoned him, wanting only to be seen with his eyes, only to be loved with his heart and only to talk to him. And that book my mother had read aloud to me almost until morning at Combray, retained for me all the charm of that night. Certainly "the pen" of George Sand, to use one of Brichot's expressions, (he loved to say that a book was written by "a lively pen") did not appear to me a magical pen as it so long did to my mother before she modelled her literary tastes on mine. But it was a pen I had unconsciously electrified, as schoolboys sometimes amuse themselves by doing, and now a thousand trifles of Combray which I had not for so long seen, leaped lightly and spontaneously forth and came and hung on head over heels to the magnet in an endless chain vibrating with memories. Certain minds which love mystery like to believe that objects preserve something of the eyes which have looked at them, that monuments and pictures are seen by us under an impalpable veil which the contemplative love of so many worshippers has woven about them through the centuries. That chimera would become true if they transposed it into the domain of the only reality there is for us all, into the domain of their own sensibility.

Yes, in that sense and only in that sense; but much more so, for if we see again a thing which we looked at formerly it brings back to us, together with our past vision, all the imagery with which it was instinct. This is because objects—a book bound like others in its red cover—as soon as they have been perceived by us become something immaterial within us, partake of the same nature as our pre-occupations or our feelings at that time and combine, indissolubly with them. A name read in a book of former; days contains within its syllables the swift wind and the brilliant sun of the moment when we read it. In the slightest sensation conveyed by the humblest aliment, the smell of coffee and milk, we recover that vague hope of fine weather which enticed us when the day was dawning and the morning sky uncertain; a sun-ray is a vase filled with perfumes, with sounds, with moments, with various humours, with climates. It is that essence which art worthy of the name must express and if it fails, one can yet derive a lesson from its failure (while one can never derive anything from the successes of realism) namely that that essence is in a measure subjective and incommunicable.

More than this, a thing we saw at a certain period, a book we read, does not remain for ever united only with what was then around us; it remains just as faith-fully one with us as we then were and can only be recovered by the sensibility restoring the individual as he then was. If, ever in thought, I take up *François le Champi* in the library, immediately a child rises within me and replaces me, who alone has the right to read that title *François le Champi* and who reads it as he read it then with the same impression of the weather out in the garden, with the same old dreams about countries and life, the same anguish of the morrow. If I see a thing of another period, another young man will emerge. And my personality of to-day is only an abandoned quarry which believes that all it contains is uniform and monotonous, but from which memory, like a sculptor of ancient Greece, pro-duces innumerable statues. I say, everything we see again, for books, behaving in that respect like things, through the way their cover opens, through the quality of the paper, can preserve within themselves as vivid a memory of how I then imagined Venice or of the wish I had to go there, as the sentences themselves. More vivid even, for the latter are sometimes an impediment like the photograph of a friend whom one recalls less after looking at it than when one contents one-self with thinking of him. Certainly in the case of many books of my youth, even, alas, those by Bergotte himself, when I happened to take them up on an evening I was tired, it was as though I had taken a train in the hope of obtaining repose by seeing different scenes and by breathing the atmosphere of former days. It often happens that the desired evocation is hindered by prolonged reading. There is one of Bergotte's books (the copy in this library contained a toadying and most plati-tudinous dedication to the Prince) which I read through one winter day some time ago when I could not see Gilberte, and I failed to discover those pages I formerly so much loved. Certain words made me think they were those pages but they were not. Where was the beauty I then found in them? Yet the snow which covered the Champs Èlysées on the day I read it still covers the volume. I see it still. And for that reason, had I been tempted to become a bibliophile like the Prince de Guermantes, I should only have been one in a way of my own, one who seeks a beauty independent of the value proper to the book and which consists for collectors in knowing the libraries through which it has passed, that it was given when such and such an event occurred to such and such a sovereign, to such and such a celebrity, in following its life from sale to sale; that beauty of a book which is in a sense historical, would not have been lost upon me. But I should extract that beauty with better will from the history of my own life, that is to say, not as a book-fancier; and it would often happen that I attached that beauty, not to the material volume itself but to a work such as this *François le Champi* contemplated for the first time in my little room at Combray during that night, perhaps the sweetest and the saddest of my life, when, alas, (at a time when the mysterious Guermantes seemed very inaccessible to me) I had wrung from my parents that first abdication from which I was able to date the decline of my health and of my will, my renunciation of a difficult task which every ensuing day made more painful—a task reassumed to-day in the library of those very Guermantes, on the most wonderful day when not only the former gropings of my thought but even the aim of my life and perhaps that of art were illuminated. Moreover, I should have been capable of interesting myself in the copies of books themselves in a living sense. The first edition of a work would have been more precious to me than the others but I should have understood by the first edition the one I read for the first time. I should seek original editions but by that I should mean books from which I got an original impression. For the impressions that follow are no longer original. I should collect the bindings of novels of former days, but they would be the days when I read my first novels, the days when my father repeated so often "Sit up straight". Like the dress in which we have seen a woman for the first time, they could help me to recover my love of then, the beauty which I had supplanted by so many images, ever less loved; in order to find it again, I who am no longer the self who felt it, must give place to the self I then was in order that he shall recall what he alone knew, what the self of to-day does not know. The library which I should thus collect would have a greater value still, for the books I read formerly at Combray, at Venice, enriched now by memory with spacious illuminations representing the church of Saint-Hilaire, the gondola moored at the foot of San Giorgio Maggiore on the Grand Canal incrusted with flashing sapphires, would have become worthy of those medallioned scrolls and historic bibles which the collector never opens in order to read the text but only to be again enchanted by the colours with which some competitor of Fouquet has embellished them and which constitute all the value of the work. And yet to open those books read formerly only to look at the images which did not then adorn them would seem to me so dangerous that even in that sense, the only one I understand, I should not be tempted to become a bibliophile. I know too well how easily the images left by the mind are effaced by the mind. It replaces the old ones by new which have not the same power of resurrection. And if I still had the *François le Champi* which my mother selected one day from the parcel of books my grandmother was to give me for my birthday, I would never look at it; I should be too much afraid that, little by little, my impressions of to-day would insert themselves in it and blot out the earlier ones, I should be too fearful of its becoming so much a thing of the present that when I asked it to evoke again the child who spelt out its title in the little room at Combray, that child, unable to recognise its speech, would no longer respond to my appeal and would be for ever buried in oblivion.

The idea of a popular art like that of a patriotic art, even if it were not dangerous, seems to me absurd. If it were a matter of making it accessible to the masses one would have to sacrifice the delicacies of form "suitable for idle people"; and I had frequented people in society enough to know that it is they who are the veritable unlettered not the working electricians. In that respect a popular art-form should rather be intended for members of the Jockey Club than for those of the General Confederation of Labour; as to subjects, popular novels intoxicate the people like books written for children. They seek distraction through reading, and workmen are as inquisitive about princes as princes are about workmen. From the beginning of the war M. Barrés said that the artist (such as Titian) must above all work for the glory of his country. But he could only serve it as an artist, that is to say, on the condition, when he studies the laws of art, serves his apprenticeship and makes discoveries as intricate as those of science, that he must think of nothing—were it even his fatherland—except the truth he has to face. Do not let us imitate the revolutionaries who on account of their civic spirit despised when they did not destroy the works of Watteau and La Tour, painters who did more for the honour of France than all who took part in the Revolution. A soft-hearted person would not, perhaps, of his own accord choose anatomy as a subject of study. It was not the goodness of his virtuous heart, great though that was, which made Choderlos de Laclos write *Liaisons dangereuses* nor was it Flaubert's preference for the small or great *bourgeoisie* which made him select "Madame Bovary" and "*L'Education sentimentale*" as subjects. Some people say that the art of a period of speed must be brief like those who said the war would be short before it had taken place. By the same reasoning, the railway should have killed contemplation. Yet it was vain to regret the period of stage-coaches for the automobile, in taking their place, still stops for tourists in front of abandoned churches.

A picture of life brings with it multiple and varied sensations. The sight, for instance, of the cover of a book which has been read spins from the character of its title the moonbeams of a distant summer-night. The taste of our morning coffee brings us that vague hope of a fine day which formerly so often smiled at us in the unsettled dawn from a fluted bowl of porcelain which seemed like hardened milk. An hour is not merely an hour, it is a vase filled with perfumes, with sounds, with projects, with climates. What we call reality is a relation between those sensations and those memories which simultaneously encircle us—a relation which a cinematographic vision destroys because its form separates it from the truth to which it pretends to limit itself—that unique relation which the writer must discover in order that he may link two different states of being together for ever in a phrase. In describing objects one can make those which figure in a particular place succeed each other indefinitely; the truth will only begin to emerge from the moment that the writer takes two different objects, posits their relationship, the analogue in the world of art to the only relationship of causal law in the world of science, and encloses it within the circle of fine style. In this, as in life, he fuses a quality common to two sensations, extracts their essence and in order to withdraw them from the contingencies of time, unites them in a metaphor, thus chaining them together with the indefinable bond of a verbal alliance. Was not nature herself from this point of view, on the track of art, was she not the beginning of art, she who often only permitted me to realise the beauty of an object long afterwards in another, mid-day at Combray only through the sound of its bells, mornings at Doncières only through the groans of our heating apparatus. The relationship may be of little interest, the objects commonplace, the style bad, but unless there is that relationship, there is nothing. A literature which is content with "describing things", with offering a wretched summary of their lines and surfaces, is, in spite of its prétention to realism, the furthest from reality, the one which impoverishes us and saddens us the most, however much it may talk of glory and grandeur, for it abruptly severs communication between our present self, the past of which objects retain the essence and the future in which they encourage us to search for it again. But there is more. If reality were that sort of waste experience approximately identical in everyone because when we say: "bad weather", "war", "cab-stand", "lighted restaurant", "flower garden", everybody knows what we mean—if reality were that, no doubt a sort of cinematographic film of these things would suffice and "style", "literature" isolating itself from that simple datum would be an artificial *hors d'œuvre*. But is it so in reality? If I tried to render conscious to myself what takes place in us at the moment a circumstance or an event makes a certain impression, if, on the day I crossed the Vivonne bridge, the shadow of a cloud on the water made me jump for joy and ejaculate "hullo!" if, listening to a phrase of Bergotte, all I could make of my impression were an expression such as "Admirable!" which did not specially apply to it, if, annoyed by somebody's bad behaviour, Bloch uttered words with no particular relevance to so sordid an adventure: such as "I consider it fantastic for a man to behave like that", or if flattered at being well received by the Guermantes and perhaps a little drunk on their wine, I could not help saying to myself in an undertone as I left them: "After all, they're charming people whom it would be delightful to spend one's life with," I perceived that to express those impressions, to write that essential book, which is the only true one, a great writer does not, in the current meaning of the word, invent it, but, since it exists already in each one of us, interprets it. The duty and the task of a writer are those of an interpreter.

And if, where an inaccurate mode of expression inspired by the writer's self-esteem is concerned, the straightening-out of the oblique inner utterance (which diverges more and more from the original mental impression) until it makes one with the straight line which should have issued from that impression, if that straightening-out is an uneasy process against which our idleness rebels, there are other cases, of love, for instance, where that same straightening-out becomes painful. All our feigned indifferences, all our natural indignation at its inevitable lies, so like our own, in a word, all that we constantly said when we were unhappy or deceived, not only to the being we loved but even to ourselves while awaiting her, sometimes aloud in the silence of our chamber, marked by: "No, really such behaviour is unbearable," and "I've decided to see you for the last time. I can't deny the pain it causes," to bring back what was really and truly felt from where it had strayed, is to abolish everything we most clung to, the matter of our passionate self-communion during fevered moments when, face to face with ourselves, we asked what letter we could write, what should be our next step.

Even when we seek artistic delights for the sake of the impression they make on us, we manage quickly to dispense with the impression itself and to fix our attention on that element in it which enables us to experience pleasure without penetrating to its depth, and thinking we can communicate it to others in conversation because we shall be talking to them about something common to them and to us, the personal root impression is eliminated. In the very moments when we are the most disinterested spectators of nature, of society, of love, of art itself—as all impression is two-fold, half-sheathed in the object, prolonged in ourselves by another half which we alone can know—we hasten to neglect the latter, that is to say, the only one on which we should concentrate and fasten merely on the other half which, being unfathomable because it is exterior to ourselves, causes us no fatigue; we consider the effort to perceive the little groove which a musical phrase or the view of a church has hollowed in ourselves too arduous. But we play the symphony over and over again, we go back to look at the church until—in that flight far away from our own life which we have not the courage to face called erudition—we get to know them as well, and in the same way as the most accomplished musical or archaeological amateur. And how many stop at that point, get nothing from their impression, and ageing useless and unsatisfied, remain sterile celibates of art! To them come the same discontents as to virgins and idlers whom the fecundity of labour would cure. They are more exalted when they talk about works of art than real artists, for their enthusiasm, not being an incentive to the hard task of penetrating to the depths, expands outwards, heats their conversation and empurples their faces; they think they are doing something by shrieking at the tops of their voices: "Bravo! Bravo!" after the performance of a composition they like. But these manifestations do not force them to clarify the character of their admiration, so they learn nothing. Nevertheless, this futile admiration overflows in their most ordinary conversation and causes them to make gestures, grimaces and movements of the head when they talk of art: "I was at a concert where they were playing music which I can assure you did not thrill me. Then they began the quartette. Ah! My word! That changed it! (The face of the amateur at that moment expresses anxious apprehension as if he were thinking: 'I see sparks flying, there's a smell of burning, there's a fire!') Bless my soul! This is maddening! It's badly composed but it's flabbergasting! This is no ordinary work." But laughable as those amateurs may be, they are not altogether to be despised. They are the first attempts of nature to create an artist, as formless and unviable as the antediluvian animals which preceded those of to-day and which were not created to endure. These whimsical and sterile amateurs affect us much as did those first mechanical contrivances which could not leave the earth, in which, though the secret means remained to be discovered, was contained the aspiration of flight. "And, old fellow," adds the amateur, taking you by the arm, "it's the eighth time I've heard it and I swear to you it won't be the last." And in truth since they do not assimilate from art what is really nourishing, they perpetually need artistic stimulus, because they are a prey to a craving which can never be assuaged. So they will go on applauding the same work for a long time to come, believing that their presence is a duty, such as others fulfil at a board-meeting or a funeral. Then come other works whether of literature, of painting or of music which create opposition. For the faculty of starting ideas or systems and above all of assimilating them has always been much more frequent even amongst those who create, than real taste, but has been extended since the reviews, the literary papers, have multiplied (and with them the artificial profession of writers and artists). Thus the best of the young, the most intelligent, the most intense, preferred works of an elevated moral, sociological or religious tendency. They imagined that such considerations constitute the value of a work, thus renewing the error of the Davids, the Chenavards, the Brunetières; they prefer to Bergotte whose lightest phrases really exacted a much deeper return to oneself, writers who seemed more profound only because they wrote less well. The complexity of Bergotte's writing was only meant for society people, was the comment of these democrats, who thus did society people an honour they did not deserve. But from the moment that works of art are judged by reasoning, nothing is stable or certain, one can prove anything one likes. Whereas the reality of genius is a benefaction, an acquisition for the world at large, the presence of which must first be identified beneath the more obvious modes of thought and style, criticism stops at this point and assesses writers by the form instead of the matter. It consecrates as a prophet a writer who, while expressing in arrogant terms his contempt for the school which preceded him, brings no new message. This constant aberration of criticism has reached a point where a writer would almost prefer to be judged by the general public (were it not that it is incapable of understanding the researches an artist has been attempting in a sphere unknown to it). For there is more analogy between the instinctive life of the public and the genius of a great writer which is itself but instinct, realised and perfected, to be listened to in a religious silence imposed upon all others, than there is in the superficial verbiage and changing criteria of self-constituted judges. Their wrangling renews itself every ten years for the kaleidoscope is not composed only of groups in society but of social, political and religious ideas which obtain a momentary expansion, thanks to their refraction in the masses but survive only so long as their novelty influences minds which exact little in the way of proof. Again, parties and schools succeed each other, always catering to the same mentalities, men of relative intelligence prone to extravagances from which minds more scrupulous and more difficult to convince, abstain. Unhappily, just because the former are only half-minds they require action to complete themselves and as through this they exercise more influence than superior minds, they impose themselves on the mass and create a constituency not merely of unmerited reputations and unjustifiable rancours but also of civil and exterior warfare from which a little self-criticism might have saved them. Now the enjoyment a well-balanced mind, a heart which is really alive, gets from the beautiful thought of a master, is undoubtedly wholesome, but valuable as are those who properly appreciate that thought (how many are there in twenty years?) they are reduced by their very enjoyment to being no more than the enlarged consciousness of another. A man may have done everything in his power to be loved by a woman who would only make him unhappy but has not succeeded, in spite of all his attempts during years, in obtaining an assignation with her. Instead of seeking to express his sufferings and the danger from which he has escaped, he ceaselessly re-reads this thought of Labruyère making it represent a thousand implications and the most moving memories of his own life: "Men often want to love and I do not know how to, they seek defeat without being able to encounter it and, if I may say so, are forced to remain free." Whether this thought had this meaning or not for him who wrote it (for it to have that meaning he ought to have said "to be loved" instead of "to love" and it would have been more beautiful), it is certain that this sensitive man of letters endows the thought with life, swells it with significance until it bursts within him and he cannot repeat it without a feeling of immense satisfaction, so completely true and beautiful does it seem to him, although, after all, he has added nothing to it and it remains simply a thought of Labruyère.

How can a literature of notations have any value since it is beneath the little things it notes that the reality exists (the grandeur in the distant sound of an aeroplane, in the outline of the belfry of Saint-Hilaire, the past in the savour of a madeleine) these being without significance in themselves if one does not disengage it from them. Accumulated little by little in the memory, the chain of all the obscure impressions where nothing! of what we actually experienced remains, constitutes our thought, our life, reality and it is that lie which a so-called "lived art" would only reproduce, an art as crude as life, without beauty, a reproduction so wearisome and futile of what our eyes have seen and our intelligence has observed, that one asks oneself how he who makes that his aim can find in it the exultant stimulus which gives zest to work. The grandeur of veritable art, to the contrary of what M. de Norpois called "a dilettante's amusement", is to recapture, to lay hold of, to make one with ourselves that reality far removed from the one we live in, from which we separate ourselves more and more as the knowledge which we substitute for it acquires a greater solidity and impermeability, a reality we run the risk of never knowing before we die but which is our real, our true life at last revealed and illumined, the only life which is really lived and which in one sense lives at every moment in all men as well as in the artist. But they do not see it because they do not seek to illuminate it. And thus their past is encumbered with innumerable "negatives" which remain useless because the intelligence has not "developed" them. To lay hold of our life; and also the life of others; for a writer's style and also a painter's are matters not of technique but of vision. It is the revelation, impossible by direct and conscious means, of the qualitative difference there is in the way in which we look at the world, a difference which, without art, would remain for ever each man's personal secret. By art alone we are able to get outside ourselves, to know what another sees of this universe which for him is not ours, the landscapes of which would remain as unknown to us as those of the moon. Thanks to art, instead of seeing one world, our own, we see it multiplied and as many original artists as there are, so many worlds are at our disposal, differing more widely from each other than those which roll round the infinite and which, whether their name be Rembrandt or Ver Meer, send us their unique rays many centuries after the hearth from which they emanate is extinguished. This labour of the artist to discover a means of apprehending beneath matter and experience, beneath words, something different from their appearance, is of an exactly contrary nature to the operation in which pride, passion, intelligence and habit are constantly engaged within us when we spend our lives without self-communion, accumulating as though to hide our true impressions, the terminology for practical ends which we falsely call life. In short, this complex art is precisely the only living art. It alone expresses for others and makes us see, our own life, that life which cannot observe itself, the outer forms of which, when observed, need to be interpreted and often read upside down, in order to be laboriously deciphered. The work of our pride, our passion, our spirit of imitation, our abstract intelligence, our habits must be undone by art which takes the opposite course and returning to the depths where the real has its unknown being, makes us pursue it. It is, of course, a great temptation to recreate true life, to renew impressions. But courage of all kinds is required, even sentimental courage. For it means above all, abrogating our most cherished illusions, ceasing to believe in the objectivity of our own elaborations and, instead of soothing ourselves for the hundredth time with the words "she was very sweet", reading into them "I liked kissing her". Of course what I had experienced in hours of love every other man experiences. But what one has experienced is like certain negatives which show black until they are placed under a lamp and they too must be looked at from the back; we do not know what a thing is until we have approached it with our intelligence. Only when the intelligence illuminates it, when it has intellectualised it, we distinguish, and with how much difficulty, the shape of that which we have felt, and I realised also that the suffering I had formerly experienced with Gilberte in realising that our love has nothing to do with the being who inspires it, is salutary as a supplementary aid to knowledge. (For, however short a time our life may last it is only while we are suffering that our thoughts, in a constant state of agitation and change, cause the depths within us to surge as in a tempest to a height where we see that they are subject to laws which, until then, we could not observe, because the calm of happiness left those depths undisturbed. Perhaps only in the case of a few great geniuses is it possible for this movement to be constantly felt without their suffering turmoil and sadness; but again it is not certain, when we contemplate the spacious and uniform development of their serene achievements that we are not too much taking for granted that the buoyancy of the work implies that of its creator, who perhaps, on the contrary, was continuously unhappy.) But principally because if our love is not only for a Gilberte, what gives us so much pain is not that it is also the love of an Albertine but because it is a more durable part of our soul than the various selves which successively die in us, each of which would selfishly retain it, a part of our soul which must, whatever the pain, detach itself from those beings so that we should understand and constitute their generality and impart the meaning of that love to all men, to the universal consciousness and not to one woman, then to another with which first one, then another of our successive selves has desired to unite.

It was, therefore, necessary for me to discover the meaning of the slightest signs that surrounded me (Guermantes, Albertine, Gilberte, Saint-Loup, Balbec, et cetera) which I had lost sight of owing to habit. We have to learn that to preserve and express reality when we have attained it, we must isolate it from everything that our habit of haste accumulates in opposition to it. Above all, I had, therefore to exclude words spoken by the lips but not by the mind; those humorous colloquialisms which after much social intercourse, we get accustomed to using artificially, which fill the mind with lies, those purely physical words uttered with a knowing smile by the writer who lowers himself by transcribing them, that little grimace which, for instance, constantly deforms the spoken phrase of a Sainte-Beuve, whereas real books must be children not of broad daylight and small-talk but of darkness and silence. And since art minutely reconstructs life round the verities one has apprehended in oneself, an atmosphere of poetry will always float round them, the sweetness of a mystery which is only the remains of twilight through which we have had to pass, the indication, like that of a measuring rod, of the depth of a work. (For that depth is not inherent in certain subjects as is believed by materialist-spiritual novelists, since they cannot penetrate beneath the world of appearances and their lofty intentions, like those virtuous tirades habitual to people who are incapable of the smallest kindly effort, must not prevent our observing that they have not even the mental power to throw off the ordinary banalities acquired by imitation.)

As to the verities which the intellect—even of highly endowed minds—gathers in the open road, in full daylight their value can be very great; but those verities have rigid outlines and are flat, they have no depth because no depths have been sounded to reach them—they have not been recreated. It often happens that writers who no longer exhibit these verities, as they grow old, only use their intelligence which has acquired more and more power; and though for this reason, their mature works are more able they have not the velvety quality of their youthful ones.

Nevertheless, I felt that the truths the intellect extracts from immediate reality are not to be despised for they might enshrine, with matter less pure but, nevertheless, vitalised by the mind, intuitions the essence of which, being common to past and present, carries us beyond time, but which are too rare and precious to be the only elements in a work of art. I felt a mass of truths pressing on my notice, relative to passions, characters and habits which could be thus used. We can, perhaps, attach every creature who has caused us unhappiness to a divinity of which she is only the most fragmentary reflection, a divinity the contemplation of whom in the realm of idea will give us immediate happiness instead of our former pain. The whole art of living is to regard people who cause us suffering as, in a degree, enabling us to accept its divine form and thus to populate our daily life with divinities. The perception of these truths gave me joy albeit it reminded me that if I had discovered more than one of them through suffering, I had discovered as many in the course of the most commonplace indulgences. Then a new light arose in me, less brilliant indeed than the one that had made me perceive that a work of art is the only means of regaining lost time. And I understood that all the material of a literary work was in my past life, I understood that I had acquired it in the midst of frivolous amusements, in idleness, in tenderness and in pain, stored up by me without my divining its destination or even its survival, as the seed has in reserve all the ingredients which will nourish the plant. Like the seed I might die when the plant had developed and I might find I had lived for it without knowing it, without my life having ever seemed to require contact with the books I wanted to write and for which when I formerly sat down at my table, I could find no subject.

Thus all my life up to that day might have been or might not have been summed up under the title: "A vocation?" In one sense, literature had played no active part in my life. But, in another, my life, the memories of its sorrows, of its joys, had been forming a reserve like albumen in the ovule of a plant. It is from this that the plant draws its nourishment in order to transform itself into seed at a time when one does not yet know that the embryo of the plant is developing though chemical phenomena and secret but very active respirations are taking place in it. Thus my life had been lived in constant contact with the elements which would bring about its ripening. And those who would later derive nourishment from it would be as ignorant of the process that supplied it as those who eat the products of grain are unaware of the rich aliments it contains though they have manured the soil in which it was grown and have enabled it to reach maturity. In this connection the comparisons which are false if one starts from them may be true if one ends by them. The writer envies the painter, he would like to make sketches and notes and, if he does so, he is lost. Yet, in writing, there is not a gesture of his characters, a mannerism, an accent, which has not impregnated his memory; there is not a single invented character to whom he could not give sixty names of people he has observed, of whom one poses for a grimace, another for an eyeglass, another for his temper, another for a particular movement of the arms. And the writer discovers that if his aspiration to be a painter could not be consciously realised, he has nevertheless filled his notebook with sketches without being aware of it. For, owing to his instinct, the writer long before he knew he was going to be one, habitually avoided looking at all sorts of things other people noticed, and was, in consequence, accused by others of absent-mindedness and by himself of being incapable of attention and observation, while all the time he was ordering his eyes and his ears to retain for ever what to others seemed puerile, the tone in which a phrase had been uttered, the facial expression and movement of the shoulders of a particular person at a particular moment perhaps years ago, who was otherwise unknown to him, and this because he had heard that tone before or felt he might hear it again, that it was a recurrent and permanent characteristic. It is the feeling for the general in the potential writer, which selects material suitable to a work of art because of its generality. He only pays attention to others, however dull and tiresome, because in repeating what their kind say like parrots, they are for that very reason prophetic birds, spokesmen of a psychological law. He recalls only what is general. Through certain ways of speaking, through a certain play of features and through certain movements of the shoulders even though they had been seen when he was a child, the life of others remains within himself and when later on he begins writing, that life will help to recreate reality, possibly by the use of that movement of the shoulders common to many people. This movement is as true to life as though it had been noted by an anatomist, but the writer expresses thereby a psychological verity by grafting on to the shoulders of one individual the neck of another, both of whom had only posed to him for a moment.

It is uncertain whether in the creation of a literary work the imagination and the sensibility are not interchangeable and whether the second, without disadvantage, cannot be substituted for the first just as people whose stomach is incapable of digesting entrust this function to their intestines. An innately sensitive man who has no imagination could, nevertheless write admirable novels. The suffering caused him by others and the conflict provoked by his efforts to protect himself against them, such experiences interpreted by the intelligence might provide material for a book as beautiful as if it were imagined and invented and as objective, as startling and unexpected as the author's imaginative fancy would have been, had he been happy and free from persecution. The stupidest people unconsciously express their feelings by their gestures and their remarks and thus demonstrate laws they are unaware of which the artist brings to light. On account of this, the vulgar wrongly believe the writer to be mischievous for the artist sees an engaging generality in an absurd individual and no more imputes blame to him than a surgeon despises his patient for being affected with a chronic ailment of the circulation. Moreover, no one is less inclined to scoff at absurd people than the artist. Unfortunately he is more unhappy than mischievous where his own passions are concerned; though he recognises their generality just as much in his own case, he escapes personal suffering less easily. Obviously, we prefer to be praised rather than insulted and still more when a woman we love deceives us, what would we not give that it should be otherwise. But the resentment of the affront, the pain of the abandonment would in that event have been worlds we should never have known, the discovery of which, painful as it may be for the man, is precious for the artist. In spite of himself and of themselves, the mischievous and the ungrateful must figure in his work. The publicist involuntarily associates the rascals he has castigated with his own celebrity. In every work of art we can recognise the man the artist has most hated, and alas, even the women he has most loved. They were posing for the writer at the very moment when, against his will, they were making him suffer the most. When I was in love with Albertine I fully realised she did not love me and I had to resign myself to her only teaching me the pain of love even at its dawn. And when we try to extract generality from our sorrow so as to write about it we are a little consoled, perhaps for another reason than those I have hitherto given, which is, that thinking in a general way, writing is a sanitary and indispensable function for the writer and gives him satisfaction in the same way that exercise, sweating and baths do a physical man. To tell the truth I revolted somewhat against this. However much I might believe that the supreme truth of life is in art, however little I was capable of the effort of memory needed to feel love for Albertine again as to mourn my grandmother anew, I asked myself whether, nevertheless a work of art of which neither of them was conscious could be for those poor dead the fulfilment of their destiny. My grandmother whom I had watched with so much indifference while she lay near me in her last agony. Ah! could I, when my work is done, wounded beyond remedy, suffer, in expiation, long hours of abandonment by all as I lie dying! Moreover, I had an infinite pity for beings less dear, even indifferent to me and of how many destinies had my thought used the sufferings, even only the absurdities in my attempts to understand them. All those beings who revealed truths to me and who were no longer there, seemed to me to have lived a life from which I alone profited and as though they had died for me. It was sad for me to think that in my book, my love which was once everything to me, would be so detached from a being that various readers would apply it textually to the love they experienced for other women. But why should I be horrified by this posthumous infidelity, that this man or that should offer unknown women as the object of my sentiment, when that infidelity, that division of love between several beings began with my life and long before I began writing? I had indeed suffered successively through Gilberte, through Mme. de Guermantes, through Albertine. Successively also I had forgotten them and only my love, dedicated at different times to different beings, had lasted. I had anticipated the profanation of my memories by unknown readers. I was not far from being horrified with myself as, perhaps, some nationalist party might be in whose name hostilities had been provoked and who alone had benefited from a war in which many noble victims had suffered and died without even knowing the issue of the struggle which, for my grandmother, would have been such a complete reward. And the single consolation she never knew, that at last I had set to work, was, such being the fate of the dead, that though she could not rejoice in my progress she had at least been spared consciousness of my long inactivity, of the frustrated life which had been such a pain to her. And certainly there were many others besides my grandmother and Albertine from whom I had assimilated a word, a glance, but of whom as individual beings I remembered nothing; a book is a great cemetery in which, for the most part, the names upon the tombs are effaced. Sometimes, on the other hand, one writes a well remembered name without knowing whether anything else survives of the being who bore it. That young girl with the deep sunken eyes, with the haunting voice, is she there? And if she is, in which part, where are we to look for her under the flowers? But since we live remote from individual lives, since we no longer retain our deepest feelings such as my love for my grandmother and for Albertine, since they are now no more than meaningless words, since we can talk about these dead with people in society to whose houses it still gives us pleasure to go after the death of all we loved, if there is yet a means of learning to understand those forgotten words, should we not use it even though we had first to find a universal language in which to express them so that, thus rendered permanent, they would form the ultimate essence of those who are gone and remain an acquisition in perpetuity of every soul? Indeed, if we could explain that law of change which has made those words of the dead unintelligible to us, might not our inferiority become a new force? Furthermore the work in which our sorrows have collaborated, may perhaps be interpreted as an indication both of atrocious suffering and of happy consolation in the future. Indeed, if we say that the loves, the sorrows of the poet have served him, that they have aided him to construct his work, that the unknown women who least suspected, one with her mischief-making, the other with her raillery, that they were each contributing their stone towards the building of the monument they would never see, one does not sufficiently reflect that the life of the writer is not finished with that work, that the same nature which caused him the sorrow that coloured his work, will remain his after the work is finished, will cause him to love other women in circumstances which would be similar if they were not slightly changed by time which modifies conditions in the subject himself, in his appetite for love and in his resistance to suffering. From this first point of view his work must be considered only as an unhappy love which inevitably presages others and which causes his life to resemble it, so that the poet hardly needs to continue writing, so completely will he discover the semblance of what will happen anticipated in what he has written. Thus my love for Albertine and the degree in which it differed was already engrossed in my love for Gilberte in the midst of those joyous days when for the first time I heard Albertine's name mentioned by her aunt, without suspecting that that insignificant germ would one day develop and spread over my whole life. But from another point of view, work is an emblem of happiness because it teaches us that in all love the general has its being close beside the particular and passes from the second to the first by a gymnastic which strengthens the writer against sorrow through making him pass over its cause in order to probe to its essence. In fact, as I was to experience thereafter, when I had realised my vocation, even at a time of anguish caused by love, the object of one's passion becomes so completely merged in the universal during one's working hours, that for the time being, one forgets her existence and only feels one's heartache as a physical pain. It is true that it is a question of moments and that the effect seems to be the contrary if work comes afterwards. For when beings, who by their badness, their insignificance, succeed, in spite of ourselves, in destroying our illusions, are themselves reduced to impotence by being separated from the amorous chimera we had forged for ourselves, if we then put ourselves to work, our spirit raises them anew, identifies them, for the needs of self-analysis, with beings we once loved and in this case, literature doing over again the work undone by disillusion bestows a sort of survival on sentiments which have ceased to exist. Certainly we are obliged to relive our particular suffering with the courage of a physician who tries over again upon himself an experiment with a dangerous serum. But we ought to think of it under a general form which enables us to some extent to escape from its control by making all men co-partners in our sorrow and this is not devoid of a certain gratification. Where life closes round us, intelligence pierces an egress, for if there is no remedy for unrequited love, one emerges from the verification of suffering if only by drawing its relevant conclusions. The intellect does not recognise situations in life which have no issue. And I had to resign myself, since nothing can last except by becoming general (unless the mind lies to itself) by accepting the idea that even those beings who were dearest to the writer have ultimately only posed to him as to painters. Sometimes when a painful section has remained at the stage of a sketch, a new tenderness, a new suffering comes which enables us to finish it and fill it out. One has no need to complain of the lack of new and helpful sorrows for plenty are forthcoming and one will not have to wait long for them. All the same, it is necessary to hasten to profit by them for they do not last very long; either we console ourselves or if they are too strong and the heart is not too sound, one dies. In love our successful rival, as well call him our enemy, is our benefactor. He immediately adds to a being who only excited in us an insignificant physical desire, an enormously enhanced value which we confuse with it. If we had no rivals, physical gratification would not be transformed into love, that is to say, if we had no rivals or believed we had none, for they need not actually exist. That illusory life which our suspicion and jealousy give to rivals who have no existence, is sufficient for our good. Happiness is salutary for the body but sorrow develops the powers of the spirit. Moreover, does it not on each occasion reveal to us a law which is no less indispensable for the purpose of bringing us back to truth, of forcing us to take things seriously by pulling up the weeds of habit, scepticism, frivolity and indifference. It is true that that truth which is incompatible with happiness, with health, is not always compatible with life itself. Sorrow ends by killing. At each fresh overmastering sorrow one more vein projects and develops its mortal sinuousness across our brows and under our eyes. Thus, little by little, those terribly ravaged faces of Rembrandt, of Beethoven, are made, at which people once mocked. And those pockets under the eyes and wrinkles in the forehead would not be there if there had not been such suffering in the heart. But since forces can change into other forces, since heat which has duration becomes light and the electricity in a lightning-flash can photograph, since our heavy heartache can with each recurrent sorrow raise above itself like a flag, a visible and permanent symbol, let us accept the physical hurt for the sake of the spiritual knowledge and let our bodies disintegrate, since each fresh fragment which detaches itself now becomes more luminously revealing so that we may complete our task at the cost of suffering not needed by others more gifted, building it up and adding to it in proportion to the emotions that destroy our life. Ideas are substitutes for sorrows; when the latter change into ideas they lose part of their noxious action on our hearts and even at the first instant their very transformation disengages a feeling of joy. Substitutes only in the order of time, however, for it would seem that the first element is idea and that sorrow is only the mode in which certain ideas first enter us. But there are many families in the group of ideas, some are immediately joys. These reflections made me discover a stronger and more accurate sense of the truth of which I had often had a presentiment, notably when Mme. de Cambremer was surprised that I could abandon a remarkable man like Elstir for the sake of Albertine. Even from the intellectual point of view I felt she was wrong but I did not know that what she was misunderstanding were the lessons through which one makes one's apprenticeship as a man of letters. The objective value of the arts has little say in the matter; what it is necessary to extract and bring to light are our sentiments, our passions, which are the sentiments and passions of all men. A woman we need makes us suffer, forces from us a series of sentiments, deeper and more vital than a superior type of man who interests us. It remains to be seen, according to the plane on which we live, whether we shall discover that the pain the infidelity of a woman has caused us is a trifle when compared with the truths thereby revealed to us, truths that the woman delighted at having made us suffer would hardly have grasped. In any case, such infidelities are not rare. A writer need have no fear of undertaking a long labour. Let the intellect get to work; in the course of it there will be more than enough sorrows to enable him to finish it. Happiness serves hardly any other purpose than to make unhappiness possible. When we are happy, we have to form very tender and strong links of confidence and attachment for their rupture to cause us the precious shattering called misery. Without happiness, if only that of hoping, there would be no cruelty and, therefore, no fruit of misfortune. And more than a painter who needs to see many churches in order to paint one church, a writer, to obtain volume, consistency, generality and literary reality, needs many beings in order to express one feeling, for if art is long and life is short one can say on the other hand, that if inspiration is short, the sentiments it has to express are not much longer. Our passions shape our books, repose writes them in the intervals. When inspiration is reborn, when we are able to take up our work again, the woman who posed to us for our sentimental reaction can no longer make us feel it. We must continue to paint her from another model and if that is a treachery to the first, in a literary sense, thanks to the similarity of our sentiments which make a work at one and the same time a memory of our past loves and the starting point of new ones, there is no great disadvantage in the exchange. That is one of the reasons why studies in which an attempt is made to guess whom an author has been writing about, are fatuous. For even a direct confession is at the very least intercalated between different episodes in the life of the author, the early ones which inspired it, the later ones which no less inspired the successive loves whose peculiarities were a tracing of the preceding ones. For we are not as faithful to the being we have most loved as we are to ourselves and sooner or later we forget her—since that is one of our characteristics—so as to start loving another. At the very most, she whom we have so much loved has given a particular form to that love which will make us faithful to her even in our infidelity. We should feel a need to take the same morning walks with her successor and to bring her home in the same fashion in the evening and we should give her also much too much money. (That circulation of money we give to women is curious; because of it, they make us miserable and so help us to write books—one might almost say that works of literature are like artesian wells, the deeper the suffering, the higher they rise.) These substitutions add something disinterested and more general to work, and are also a lesson in austerity; we ought not to attach ourselves to beings, it is not beings who exist in reality and are amenable to description, but ideas. And we must not lose time while we can still dispose of these models. For those who pose for happiness are not, as a rule, able to spare us many sittings. But those who pose to us for sorrow give us plenty of sittings in the studio we only use at those periods. That studio is within ourselves. Those periods are a picture of our life with its divers sufferings. For they contain others and just when we think we are calm, a new one is born, new in all senses of the word; perhaps because unforeseen situations force us to enter into deeper contact with ourselves, the painful dilemmas in which love places us at every instant, instruct us, disclose to us successively the matter of which we are made.

Moreover, even when suffering does not supply by its revelation the raw material of our work, it helps us by stimulating us to it. Imagination, thought, may be admirable mechanisms but they can also be inert. Suffering alone sets them going. Thus when Françoise, noticing that Albertine came in by any door of the house that happened to be open as a dog would, spreading disorder wherever she went, ruining me, causing me infinite unhappiness, she said (for at that time I had already done some articles and translations), "Ah, if only Monsieur had engaged a well-educated little secretary who would have put all Monsieur's rolls of paper in order instead of that girl who only wastes his time," perhaps I was wrong in thinking she was talking good sense. Perhaps Albertine had been more useful to me, even from the literary point of view, in making me lose my time and in causing me sorrow than a secretary who would have arranged my papers. But all the same, when a creature is so badly constituted (perhaps in nature that being is man) that he cannot love unless he suffers and that he must suffer to learn truth, the life of such a being becomes in the end very exhausting. The happy years are those that are wasted; we must wait for suffering to drive us to work. The idea of preliminary suffering is associated with that of work, we dread every fresh undertaking because we are thereby reminded of the pain in store for us before we can conceive it. And, realising that suffering is the best thing life has to offer, we think of death without horror and almost as a deliverance. And yet, if that thought was somewhat repellent to me, we have to be sure we have not played with life and profited by other people's lives to write books but the exact opposite. The case of the noble Werther was, alas, not mine. Without believing an instant in Albertine's love, twenty times I wanted to kill myself for her; I had ruined myself and destroyed my health for her. When it is a question of writing, we have to be scrupulous, look close and cast out what is not true. But when it is only a question of our own lives, we ruin ourselves, make ourselves ill, kill ourselves for the sake of lies. Of a truth, it is only out of the matrix of those lies (if one is too old to be a poet) that we can extract a little truth. Sorrows are obscure and hated servitors against whom we contend, under whose sway we fall more and more, sinister servitors whom we cannot replace but who by strange and devious ways lead us to truth and to death. Happy those who have encountered the former before the latter and for whom, closely as one may follow the other, the hour of truth sounds before the hour of death.

Furthermore, I realised that the most trivial episodes of my past life had combined to give me the lesson of idealism from which I was now going to profit. Had not my meetings with M. de Charlus, for instance, even before his Germanophilism had given me the same lesson, and better than my love for Mme. de Guermantes or for Albertine, better than the love of Saint-Loup for Rachel, proved to me how little material matters, that everything can be made of it by thought, a verity that the phenomenon of sexual inversion, so little understood, so idly condemned, enhances even more than that of love of women, instructive as that is; the latter shows us beauty flying from the woman we no longer love and residing in a face which others consider extremely ugly, which indeed might have displeased us and probably will later on; but it is still more remarkable to observe such a face under the cap of an omnibus conductor, receiving all the homage of a *grand seigneur*, who has for that abandoned a beautiful princesse. Did not my astonishment each time that I again saw the face of Gilberte, of Mme. de Guermantes, of Albertine in the Champs Elysées, in the street, on the shore, prove that a memory can only be prolonged in a direction which diverges from the impression with which it formerly coincided and from which it separates itself more and more. The writer must not mind if the invert gives his heroines a masculine visage. This peculiar aberration is the only means open to the invert of applying generality to what he reads. If M. de Charlus had not given Morel's face to the unfaithful one over whom Musset sheds tears in the *Nuit d'Octobre* or in the *Souvenir*, he would neither have wept nor understood since it was by that road alone, narrow and tortuous though it might be, that he had access to the verities of love. It is only through a custom which owes its origin to the insincere language of prefaces and dedications that a writer says "my reader". In reality, every reader, as he reads, is the reader of himself. The work of the writer is only a sort of optic instrument which he offers to the reader so that he may discern in the book what he would probably not have seen in himself. The recognition of himself in the book by the reader is the proof of its truth and *vice-versa*, at least in a certain measure, the difference between the two texts being often less attributable to the author than to the reader. Further, a book may be too learned, too obscure for the simple reader, and thus be only offering him a blurred glass with which he cannot read. But other peculiarities (like inversion) might make it necessary for the reader to read in a certain way in order to read well; the author must not take offence at that but must, on the contrary, leave the reader the greatest liberty and say to him: "Try whether you see better with this, with that, or with another glass."

If I have always been so much interested in dreams, is it not because, compensating duration with intensity they help us to understand better what is subjective in love? And this by the simple fact that they render real with prodigious speed what is vulgarly called *nous mettre une femme dans la peau* to the point of falling passionately in love for a few minutes with an ugly one, which in real life would require years of habit, of union and—as though they had been invented by some miraculous doctor—intravenal injections of love as they can also be of suffering; with equal speed the amorous suggestion is dissipated and sometimes not only the nocturnal beloved has ceased to be such and has again become the familiar ugly one but something more precious is also dissipated, a whole picture of ravishing sentiments, of tenderness, of delight, of regrets, vaguely communicated to the mind, a whole shipload of passion for Cythera of which we should take note against the moment of waking up, shades of a beautiful truth which are effaced like a painting too dim to restore. Well, perhaps it was also because of the extraordinary tricks dreams play with time! that they fascinated me so much. Had I not in a single night, in one minute of a night, seen days of long ago which had been relegated to those great distances where we can distinguish hardly any of the sentiments we then felt, melt suddenly upon me, blinding me with their brightness as though they were giant aeroplanes instead of the pale stars we believed, making me see again all they had once held for me, giving me back the emotion, the shock, the vividness of their immediate nearness, then recede, when I woke, to the distance they had miraculously traversed, so that one believes, mistakenly however, that they are one of the means of recovering lost Time.

I had realised that only grossly erroneous observation places everything in the object while everything is in the mind; I had lost my grandmother in reality many months after I had lost her in fact, I had seen the aspect of people vary according to the idea that I or others formed of them, a single person become many according to the number of people who saw him (the various Swanns at the beginning of this work according to who met him; the Princesse de Luxembourg according to whether she was seen by the first President or by me) even according to a single person over many years (the variations of Guermantes and Swann in my own experience). I had seen love endow another with that which is only in the one who loves. And I had realised all this the more because I had stretched to its extreme limits the distance between objective reality and love; (Rachel from Saint-Loup's point of view and from mine, Albertine from mine and from Saint-Loup's, Morel or the omnibus conductor or other people from M. de Charlus' point of view). Finally, in a certain measure the Germanophilism of M. de Charlus, like the gaze of Saint-Loup at the photograph of Albertine, had helped me for a moment to detach myself, if not from my Germanophobia at least from my belief in its pure objectivity and to make me think that perhaps it was with hate as with love and that in the terrible sentence which France is now pronouncing on Germany, whom she regards as outside the pale of humanity, there is an objectivity of feeling like that which made Rachel and Albertine seem so precious, the one to Saint-Loup, the other to me. What made it seem possible, in fact, that this wickedness was not entirely intrinsic to Germany was that I myself had experienced successive loves at the end of which the object of each one appeared to have no value and I had also seen my country experience successive hates which had caused to appear as traitors—a thousand times worse than the Germans to whom these traitors were supposed to be betraying France—Dreyfusards like Reinach with whom patriots were now collaborating against a country every member of which was necessarily a liar, a ferocious beast and an imbecile except, of course, those Germans who had espoused the French cause such as the King of Roumania and the Empress of Russia. It is true that the anti-Dreyfusard, would have replied: "It is not the same thing." But, as a matter of fact, it never is the same thing, any more than it is the same person; were that not so, in the presence of an identical phenomenon he who is its dupe could not believe that qualities or defects are inherent in it and would only blame his own subjective condition.

The intellect has no difficulty, then, in basing a theory upon this difference (the teaching of the congregations according to Radicals, is against nature, it is impossible for the Jewish race to assimilate nationalism, the secular hatred of the Germans for the Latin race, the yellow races being momentarily rehabilitated). That subjective influence was equally marked among neutral Germanophiles who had lost the faculty of understanding or even of listening, the instant the German atrocities in Belgium were spoken of. (And, after all, there were real ones.) I remarked that the subjective nature of hatred as in vision itself, did not prevent the object possessing real qualities or defects and in no way caused reality to disappear in a pure "relativeness". And if, after so many years and so much lost time, I felt the stirring of this vital pool within humanity even in international relationships, had I not apprehended it at the very beginning of my life when I read one of Bergotte's novels in the Combray garden and even if to-day I turn those forgotten pages, and see the schemes of a wicked character, I cannot lay down the book until I assure myself, by skipping a hundred pages, that towards the end the villain is duly humiliated and lives long enough to know that his sinister purposes have been foiled. For I could no longer recall what happened to the characters, in that respect not unlike those who will be seen this afternoon at Mme. de Guermantes', the past life of whom, at all events of many of them, is as shadowy as though I had read of them in a half-forgotten novel.

Did the Prince of Agrigente end by marrying Mlle. X—? Or was it not the brother of Mlle. X— who was to marry the sister of the Prince of Agrigente, or was I confusing them with something I had once read or dreamed? The dream remained one of the facts of my life which had most impressed me, which had most served to convince me of the purely mental character of reality, a help I should not despise in the composition of my work. When I lived for love in a somewhat more disinterested fashion, a dream would bring my grandmother singularly close to me, making her cover great spaces of lost time, and so with Albertine whom I began to love again because, in my sleep, she had supplied me with an attenuated version of the story of the laundress. I believed that dreams might sometimes in this way be the carriers of truths and impressions that my unaided effort or encounters in the outside world could not bring me, that they would arouse in me that desire or yearning for certain non-existent things which is the condition for work, for abstraction from habit and for detaching oneself from the concrete. I should not disdain this second, this nocturnal muse, who might sometimes replace the other.

I had seen aristocrats become vulgar when their minds (like that of the Duc de Guermantes for instance) were vulgar. "You aren't shy?" he asked, as Cottard might have done. In medicine, in the Dreyfus affair, during the war, I had seen people believe that truth is a thing owned and possessed by ministers and doctors, a yea or a nay which has no need of interpretation, which-enables a radiographic plate to indicate, without interpretation, what is the matter with an invalid, which enables those in power to know that Dreyfus was guilty, to know (without despatching Roques to investigate on the spot) whether Sarrail had the necessary resources to advance at the same time as the Russians. There had not been an hour of my life which might not have thus served to teach me, as I have said, that only crudely erroneous perception places everything in the object; while, to the contrary, everything is in the mind. In short, if I reflected, the matter of my experience came to me from Swann, not simply through what concerned himself and Gilberte. It was he who, ever since the Combray days, had given me the desire to go to Balbec, where, but for him, my parents would never have had the notion of sending me and but for which I should never have known Albertine. True, I associated certain things with her face as I saw her first, gazing towards the sea. In one sense I was right in associating them with her for if I had not walked by the sea that day, if I had not known her, all those ideas would not have developed (unless, at least, they had been developed by another). I was wrong again because that inspiring pleasure we like to identify retrospectively with the beautiful countenance of a woman, comes from our senses and, in any case, it was quite certain that Albertine, the then Albertine, would not have understood the pages I should write. But it was just on that account, (and that is a warning not to live in too intellectual an atmosphere) because she was so different from me that she had made me productive through suffering, and, at first, even through the simple effort required to imagine that which differs from oneself. Had she been able to understand these pages, she would have been unable to inspire them. But without Swann I should not even have known the Guermantes, since my grandmother would not have rediscovered Mme. de Villeparisis, I should not have made the acquaintance of Saint-Loup and of M. de Charlus which in turn caused me to know the Duchesse de Guermantes and, through her, her cousin, so that my very presence at this moment at the Prince de Guermantes' from which suddenly sprang the idea of my work (thus making me owe Swann not only the matter but the decision) also came to me from Swann, a rather flimsy pedestal to support the whole extension of my life. (In that sense, this Guermantes side derived from Swann's side.) But very often the author of a determining course in our lives is a person much inferior to Swann, in fact, a completely indifferent individual. It would have sufficed for some schoolfellow or other to tell me about a girl it would be nice for me to meet at Balbec (where in all probability I should not have met her) to make me go there. So it often happens that later on one runs across a schoolfellow one does not like and shakes hands with him without realising that the whole subsequent course of one's life and work has sprung from his chance remark: "You ought to come to Balbec." We feel no gratitude toward him nor does that prove us ungrateful. For in uttering those words he in no wise foresaw the tremendous consequences they might entail for us. The first impulse having been given, one's sensibility and intelligence exploited the circumstances which engendered each other without his any more foreseeing my union with Albertine than the masked ball at the Guermantes'. Doubtless, his agency was necessary and, through it, the exterior form of our life, even the raw material of our work sprang from him. Had it not been for Swann, my parents would never have had the idea of sending me to Balbec but that did not make him responsible for the sufferings which he indirectly caused me; these were due to my own weakness as his had been responsible for the pain Odette caused him. But in thus determining the life I was to lead, he had thereby excluded all the lives I might otherwise have lived. If Swann had not told me about Balbec I should never have known Albertine, the hotel dining-room, the Guermantes. I should have gone elsewhere; I should have known other people, my memory like my books would have been filled with quite different pictures, which I cannot even imagine but whose unknowable novelty allures me and makes me sorry I was not drawn that way and that Albertine, the Balbec shore, Rivebelle and the Guermantes did not remain unknown to me for ever.

Jealousy is a good recruiting sergeant who, when there is an empty space in our picture, goes and finds the girl we want in the street. She may not be pretty at first, but she soon fills the blank and becomes so when we get jealous of her.

Once we are dead we shall get no pleasure from our picture being so complete. But this thought is in no way discouraging for we feel that life is rather more complex than is generally supposed, likewise circumstances and and there is a pressing need of proving this complexity. Jealousy is not necessarily born from a look, from something we hear or as the result of reflection; we can find it ready for us between the leaves of a directory — what in Paris is called *Tout-Paris* and in the country *The Annuaire des Châteaux*. Absent-mindedly, we had heard that a certain pretty girl we no longer thought about, had gone to pay a visit of some days to her sister in the Pas-de-Calais. With equal indifference it had occurred to us previously that, possibly, this pretty girl had been made love to by M. E. whom she never saw now because she no longer frequented the bar where she used to meet him. Who and what might her sister be, a maid perhaps? From discretion, we had never asked her. And now, lo and behold! Opening by chance the *Annuaire des Châteaux* we discover that M. E. owns a country house in the Pas-de-Calais near Dunkerque.

There is no further room for doubt; to please the pretty girl, he has taken her sister as a maid, and if the pretty girl does not see him any more in the bar it is because he has her come to his house and, though he lives in Paris nearly the whole year round, he cannot dispense with her even while he is in the Pas-de-Calais. The paint-brushes, drunk with rage and love, paint and paint. But supposing, after all, it is not that, supposing that really M. E. did not any longer see the pretty girl and had only recommended her sister to his brother who lives the whole year round in the Pas-de-Calais, so that, by chance, she has gone to see her sister at a time when M. E. is not there, seeing that they had ceased to care for each other. Unless indeed the sister is nota maid in the Château or anywhere else but that her family happens to live in the Pas-de-Calais. Our original distress surrenders to the latest supposition which soothes our jealousy. But what does that matter? Jealousy buried within the pages of the *Annuaire des Châteaux* has come just at the right moment, for now the empty space in the canvas has been filled and the whole picture has been capitally composed, thanks to jealousy having evoked the apparition of the pretty girl whom we neither care for nor are jealous of.

At that moment the butler came to tell me that the first piece was over and that I could leave the library and enter the drawing-rooms. That reminded me of where I was. But I was in no wise disturbed in my argument by the fact that a fashionable entertainment, a return into society, provided the point of departure towards a new life I had been unable to find the way to in solitude. There was nothing extraordinary about this, an influence which had roused the eternal man in me being no more necessarily linked to solitude than to society (as I had once believed, as perhaps was the case formerly, as perhaps it might still have been, if I had developed harmoniously instead of having suffered that long break which only now seemed to be reaching its end). For, as I only felt that impression of beauty when there was imposed upon the actual sensation however insignificant, another akin to it which, spontaneously reborn in me, expanded the first one simultaneously over several periods and filled my soul, in which my ordinary single sensations left a void, with a generalising essence, there was no reason why I should not just as well receive such sensations from society as from nature, since they occur haphazard, provoked doubtless by a peculiar excitement owing to which, on days when one happens to be outside the normal course of one's life, even the most simple things begin to cause reactions which habit spares our nervous system. My purpose was to discover the objective reason of its being exactly and only that class of sensations which must lead to a work of art, by pursuing the reflections I had been bent on linking together in the library, for I felt that the emancipation of my spiritual life was now complete enough for me to be able to sustain my thought in the midst of guests in the drawing-room just as well as alone in the library; I should know how to preserve my solitude from that point of view even in the midst of that numerous company. Indeed, for the same reason that great events in the outer world have no influence upon our mental powers and that a mediocre writer living in an epic period will, nevertheless, remain a mediocre writer what was dangerous in society was the worldly disposition one brought to it. But, of itself, it will no more make us mediocre than a war of heroes can make a bad poet sublime. In any case, whether it was theoretically advantageous or not that a work of art should be thus constituted, and awaiting the further examination of that question, it was undeniable so far as I was concerned, that when any really aesthetic intuitions came to me it had always been as a result of sensations of that nature. True, they had been rare enough in my life but they dominated it, and I could recover from the past some of those heights I had mistakenly allowed myself to lose sight of (and I did not mean to do so again). This much I could now say, that if in my case this was an idiosyncrasy due to the exclusive significance it had for me, I was reassured by discovering that it was related to characteristics less marked yet discernible and fundamentally analogous in the case of certain writers. Is not the most beautiful part of the *Mémoires d'Outre-Tombe* assimilable with my sensations relative to the madeleine: "Yesterday evening I was walking alone.... I was drawn from my reflections by the warbling of a thrush perched upon the highest branch of a birch tree. At that instant the magical sound brought my paternal home before my eyes; I forgot the catastrophes of which I had been a witness and, transported suddenly into the past, I saw again that country where I had so often heard the thrush sing." And is not this, one of the two or three most beautiful passages in the *Mémoires*: "A delicate and subtle odour of heliotrope was exhaled by a cluster of scarlet runners in flower; that odour was not brought us by a breeze from the homeland but by a wild Newfoundland wind, without relation to the exiled plant, without sympathy with memory and joy. In that perfume which beauty had not breathed nor purified in its breast nor spread abroad upon its path, in that perfume permeated by the light of dawn, of culture and of life, there was all the melancholy of regret, of exile and of youth." One of the masterpieces of French literature *Sylvie* by Gérard de Nerval, contains, in regard to Combourg, just like the *Mémoires d'Outre-Tombe*, a sensation of the same order as the taste of the madeleine and the warbling of the thrush. Finally, in the case of Baudelaire, such reminiscences are still—more numerous, evidently less fortuitous and consequently, in my opinion, decisive. It is the poet himself who with greater variety and leisure seeks consciously in the odour of a woman, of her hair and of her breast, those inspiring analogies which evoke for him *"l'azur du ciel immense et rond"* and *"un port rempli de flammes et de mâts"*. I was seeking to recall those of Baudelaire's verses which are based upon the transposition of such sensations, so that I might place myself in so noble a company and thus obtain confirmation that the work I no longer had any hesitation in undertaking, merited the effort I intended to consecrate to it, when, reaching the foot of the staircase leading from the library, I found myself all of a sudden in the great salon and in the midst of a fête which seemed to me entirely different from those I had formerly attended and which began to disclose a peculiar aspect and to assume a new significance. From the instant I entered the great salon, in spite of my firmly retaining within myself the point I had reached in the project I had been forming, a startlingly theatrical sensation burst upon my senses which was to raise the gravest obstacles to my enterprise. Obstacles I should, doubtless, surmount but which, while I continued to muse upon the conditions of a work of art, were about to interrupt my reasoning by the repetition a hundred times over of the consideration most calculated to make me hesitate. At the first moment I did not understand why I failed to recognise the master of the house and his guests, why they all appeared to have "made a head", generally powdered, which completely changed them. The Prince, receiving his guests, still preserved that air of a jolly king of the fairies he suggested to my mind the first time I saw him, but now, having apparently submitted to the disguise he had imposed upon his guests, he had tricked himself out in a white beard and dragged his feet heavily along as though they were soled with lead. He seemed to be representing one of the ages of man. His moustache was whitened as though the hoarfrost in Tom Thumb's forest clung to it. It seemed to inconvenience his stiffened mouth and once he had produced his effect, he ought to have taken it off. To tell the truth, I only recognised him by reasoning out his identity with himself from certain familiar features. I could not imagine what that little Lezensac had put on his face, but while others had grown white, some as to half of their beard, some only as to their moustaches, he had found means, without the help of dyes, to cover his face with wrinkles and his eyebrows with bristling hairs; moreover, all this suited him ill, his countenance seemed to have hardened and bronzed and he wore an appearance of solemnity that aged him so much that he could no longer be taken for a young man. At the same moment I was astonished to hear addressed as Duc de Châtellerault a little old man with the silver moustache of an ambassador of whom only the slightest likeness reminded me of the young man whom I had once met calling on Mme. de Villeparisis. In the case of the first person whom I succeeded in identifying by abstracting his natural features from his travesty by an effort of memory, my first thought ought to have been and perhaps was, for an instant, to congratulate him on being so marvellously made up that, at first, one had the same sort of hesitation in recognising him as is felt by an audience which, though informed by the programme, remains for a moment dumbfounded and then bursts into applause when some great actor, taking a part in which he looks completely different from himself, walks on to the stage. From that point of view the most extraordinary of all was my personal enemy M. d'Argencourt; he was, verily, the *clou* of the party. Not only had he replaced a barely silvered beard by one of incredible whiteness, he had so tricked himself out by those little material changes which reconstitute and exaggerate personality and, more than that, apparently modify character, that this man, whose pompous and starchy stiffness still lingered in my memory, had changed into an old beggar who inspired no respect, an aged valetudinarian so authentic that his limbs trembled and the swollen features, once so arrogant, kept on smiling with silly beatitude. Pushed to this degree, the art of disguise becomes something more, it becomes a transformation. Indeed, some trifles might certify that it was actually M. d'Argencourt who offered this indescribable and picturesque spectacle, but how many successive facial states should I not have had to trace if I wanted to reconstruct the physiognomy of M. d'Argencourt whom I had formerly known and who had now succeeded, although he only had the use of his own body, in producing something so entirely different. It was obviously the extreme limit that haughtiest of faces could reach without disintegration, while that stiffest of figures was no more than a boiled rag shaking about from one spot to another. It was only by the most fleeting memory of a particular smile which formerly sometimes tempered for an instant M. d'Argencourt's arrogant demeanour, that one realised the possibility that this smile of an old, broken-down, second-hand clothes-dealer might represent the punctilious gentleman of former days. But even admitting it was M. d'Argencourt's intention to use the old meaning smile, the prodigious transformation of his face, the very matter of the eye with which he expressed it had become so different that the expression was that of another. I almost burst into laughter as I looked at this egregious old guy, as emolliated in his comical caricature of himself as M. de Charlus, paralysed and polite, was tragical. M. d'Argencourt, in his incarnation of a moribund buffoon by Regnard, exaggerated by Labiche, was as easy of access, as urbane as was the King Lear of M. de Charlus who uncovered himself with deference before the most commonplace acquaintance who saluted him. All the same, I refrained from expressing my admiration for the remarkable performance. It was less my former antipathy which prevented me than his having reached a condition so different from himself that I had the illusion of standing before another as amiable, disarming and inoffensive as the Argencourt of former days was supercilious, hostile and nefarious. So entirely a different personage that, watching this snow-man imitating General Dourakine falling into second childhood, grinning so ineffably comic and white, it seemed to me that a human being could undergo metamorphoses as complete as those of certain insects. I had the impression of observing through the glass of a showcase in a natural history museum what the sharpest and most stable features of an insect had turned into and I could no longer feel the sentiments which M. d'Argencourt had always inspired in me when I stood looking at this soft chrysalis which rather vibrated than moved. So I kept my silence, I did not congratulate M. d'Argencourt on offering a spectacle which seemed to assign the limits within which the transformation of the human body can operate. Certainly, in the wings of a theatre or during a costume ball, politeness inclines one to exaggerate the difficulty, even to go so far as to affirm the impossibility of recognising the person in travesty. Here, on the contrary an instinct warned me that dissimulation was demanded, that these compliments would have been the reverse of flattering because such a transformation was not intended and I realised what I had not dreamed of when I entered this drawing-room, that every entertainment, however simple, when it takes place long after one has ceased to go into society and however few of those one has formerly known it brings together, gives the effect of a costume ball and the most successful one of all, at which one is truly puzzled by others, for the heads have been in the making for a long time without their wishing it and cannot be got rid of by toilet operations when the party is over. Puzzled by others! Alas! We ourselves puzzle them. The difficulty I experienced in putting the required name to the faces around me seemed to be shared by all those who perceived mine, for they paid no more attention to me than if they had never seen me before or were trying to disentangle from my appearance the memory of someone else.

M. d'Argencourt's success with this astonishing "turn", certainly the most striking picture in his burlesque I could possibly have of him, was like an actor who makes a last appearance on the stage before the curtain falls amidst roars of laughter. If I no longer felt any antagonism to him, it was because he had returned to the innocence of babyhood and had no recollection of his contemptuous opinion of me, no recollection of having seen M. de Charlus suddenly leave go of my arm, whether because none of those sentiments survived in him or because in order to reach me they would have been so deformed by physical refractions that their meaning would have completely changed on the way, so that M. d'Argencourt appeared to have become amiable because he no longer had the power to express his malevolence and to curb his chronic and irritating hilarity. To compare him with an actor is an overstatement for, having no conscious mind at all, he was like a shaky doll with a woollen beard stuck on his face pottering about the room, like a scientific or philosophical marionette mimicking a part in a funeral ceremony or a lecture at the Sorbonne, simultaneously illustrating the vanity of all things and representing a natural history specimen. A Punch and Judy show of puppets, of which one could only identify those one had known by viewing them simultaneously at several levels graded in the background, which gave them depth and forced one to the mental effort of combining eye and memory as one gazed at these old phantoms. A Punch and Judy show of puppets bathed in the immaterial colours of years, of puppets which exteriorised Time, Time usually invisible, which to attain visibility seeks and fastens on bodies to exhibit wherever it can, with its magic lantern. Immaterial like Golo on the door-handle of my room at Combray, the new and unrecognisable M. d'Argencourt was a revelation of Time by rendering it partially visible. In the new elements composing M. d'Argencourt's face and personality one could read a sum of years, one could recognise the symbolical figure of life, not permanent as it appears to us, but as it is, a constantly changing atmosphere in which the haughty nobleman caricatures himself in the evening as an old clothes-dealer.

In the case of others these changes, these positive transformations seemed to proceed from the sphere of natural history and it was surprising to hear a name applied to a person, not, as in the case of M. d'Argencourt, with the characteristics of a new and different species but with the exterior features of another person altogether. As in the case of M. d'Argencourt there were unsuspected potentialities which time had elicited from such and such a young girl, and though these potentialities were purely physiognomical or corporeal, they seemed to have moral implications. If the features of a face change, if they unite differently, if they contract slowly but continuously, they assume, with that changed aspect, another significance. Thus, a particular woman who had formerly given one an impression of aridity and shallowness and who had now acquired an enlargement of the cheeks and an unforeseeable bridge on her nose occasioned the same surprise, often an agreeable one, as a sensitive and thoughtful remark, a fine and highminded act which one would never have expected of her. Unhoped for horizons opened around that new nose. Kindness and tenderness, formerly undreamed of became possible with those cheeks. From that chin one might hope for things unimaginable from the preceding one. These new facial features implied altered traits of character; the hard, scraggy girl had become a buxom, generous dowager. It was not in the zoological sense like M. d'Argencourt, but in the social and moral sense that one could say she had become a different person. In all these ways an afternoon party such as this was something much more valuable than a vision of the past for it offered me something better than the successive pictures I had missed of the past separating itself from the present, namely, the relationship between the present and the past; it was like what used to be called a panopticon but a panopticon of years, a view not of a monument but of a person situated in the modifying perspective of Time.

The woman whose lover M. d'Argencourt had been, was not much changed, if one reckoned the time that had passed, that is, her face was not so completely demolished into that of a creature which has continuously disintegrated throughout his journey into the abyss, the direction of which we can only express by equally vain comparisons since we can only borrow them from the world of space and which, whether we estimate them in terms of height or length or depth have only the merit of conveying to us that this inconceivable yet perceptible dimension exists. The need, so as to give a name to a face, of what amounted to climbing up the years, compelled me later to reconstruct retrospectively the years about which I had never thought, so as to give them their proper order. From this point of view and so as not to allow myself to be deceived by the apparent identity of space, the perfectly new aspect of a being like M. d'Argencourt was a striking revelation of the reality of the era which generally seems an abstraction, in the same way as dwarf trees or giant baobabs illustrate a change of latitude. Then life appears to us like a fairyland where one can watch the baby becoming adolescent, man becoming mature and inclining to the grave. And, since it is through perpetual change that one grasps that these beings, observed at considerable intervals, are so different, one realises that one has been obeying the same law as these creatures which are so transformed that they no longer resemble, though they have never ceased to be—just because they have never ceased to be—what we thought them before,

A young woman I had formerly known, now snow-white and reduced to a little malevolent old woman, seemed to prove that, in the final act, it was necessary that characters should be made up to be unrecognisable. But her brother had remained so erect, so exactly as he was, that the whitening of his upturned moustache seemed surprising on so young a face. The snowy whiteness of beards which had been completely black made the human landscape of that afternoon party melancholy as do the first brown leaves of a summer one has hardly begun enjoying when autumn comes. Thus I who from infancy, had lived from day to day, with a sort of fixed idea of myself derived from others as well as myself, perceived for the first time, after witnessing the metamorphosis of all these people, that the time which had gone by for them, had gone by for me also and this revelation threw me into consternation. Indifferent as their ageing was to me, now that theirs heralded the approach of my own, I was disconsolate. This approach was indeed announced by one verbal blow after another at intervals, which sounded to my ears like blasts from the trumpets of Judgment Day. The first was uttered by the Duchesse de Guermantes; I had just seen her pass between a double row of gaping people who, without realising how the marvellous artifice of her dress and aesthetic worked on them, moved by the sight of her scarlet head, her salmon-like flesh strangled with jewels just emerging from its black lace fins, gazed at the hereditary sinuosity of her figure as they might have done at some ancient jewel-bedecked fish in which the protective genius of the Guermantes' family was incarnated. "Ah!" she exclaimed on seeing me, "what a joy to see you, you my oldest friend!" In my youthful vanity of Combray days which never permitted me to count myself among her friends who actually shared that mysterious Guermantes' life, one of her accredited friends like M. de Bréauté or M. de Forestille or Swann, like so many who were dead, I might have been flattered but, instead, I was extremely miserable. "Her oldest friend!" I thought, "She's exaggerating, perhaps one of the oldest but am I really—" At that moment one of the Prince's nephews came up to me and remarked: "You who are an old Parisian." An instant later a note was brought me. I had, on my arrival, seen one of the young Létourvilles whose relationship to the Duchesse I could not remember but who knew me a little. He had just left Saint-Cyr and thinking to myself he would be a charming acquaintance like Saint-Loup, who could initiate me into military affairs and their incidental changes, I had told him I would find him later so that we could arrange to dine together, for which he thanked me effusively. But I had remained dreaming in the library too long and the note he had left was to tell me that he was not able to wait and gave me his address. This coveted comrade ended his letter thus: "With respectful regard, your young friend, Létourville". "Young friend!" Thus I used formerly to address people thirty years older than myself, Legrandin, for instance. That sub-lieutenant whom I was regarding as a comrade called himself my young friend. So it was not only military methods which had changed since then and from M. de Létourville's standpoint I was not a comrade but an old gentleman and I was separated from M. de Létourville to whom I imagined that I appeared as I did to myself as though by the opening arms of an invisible compass which placed me at such a distance from that young sub-lieutenant that to him who called himself my young friend I was an elderly gentleman.

Almost immediately afterwards someone spoke of Bloch and I asked if they were talking of young Bloch or his father (of whose death during the war I was unaware). It was said he died of emotion when France was invaded. "I did not know that he had any children, not even that he was married," said the Duchesse, "but evidently it is the father we're talking about for there's nothing young about him." She added, laughing, "He might have grown-up sons." Then I realised she was talking about my old friend. As it happened, he came in a few minutes later and I had difficulty in recognising him. He had now adopted the name of Jacques du Rozier, under which it would have needed the nose of my grandfather to scent the sweet valley of Hebron and the bond of Israel which my friend seemed to have finally broken. A modish Englishness had completely changed his appearance and every thing that could be effaced was moulded into the semblance of a plaster cast. His former curly hair was now smoothed out flat, was parted in the middle and shone with cosmetics. His nose was still red and prominent and appeared to be swollen by a sort of permanent catarrh which perhaps explained the nasal accent with which he lazily drawled his phrases, for, he had discovered, in addition to a way of doing his hair to suit his complexion, a voice to the former nasal tone of which he had added an air of peculiar disdain to suit the inflamed contours of his nose. And thanks to hairdressing, to the elimination of his moustache, to his smartness of style and to his will, that Jewish nose had disappeared as a hump can almost be made to look like a straight back by being carefully disguised. But the significance of Bloch's physiognomy was changed above all by a redoubtable eyeglass. The mechanical effect produced in Bloch's face by this monocle enabled him to dispense with all those difficult duties to which the human countenance must submit, that of looking amiable, of expressing humour, good nature and effort. Its mere presence in Bloch's face made it unnecessary to consider whether it was good-looking or not, like when a shop-assistant shows you an English object and says it is "le grand chic", and you don't dare consider whether you like it or not. And then he installed himself behind his glass in a haughty, distant and comfortable attitude as though it were an eight-fold mirror, and by making his face suit his flat hair and his eyeglass his features no longer expressed anything whatever. On that face of Bloch's were super-imposed that vapid and self-opinionated expression, those feeble movements of the head which soon find their point of stasis, and with which I should have identified the out-worn learning of a complacent old gentleman if I had not at last recognised that the man facing me was an old friend, whom my memories had endowed with the continuous vigour of youth which he seemed now completely to lack. I had known him on the threshold of life, he had been my school-fellow and unconsciously, I was regarding him, like myself, as though we were both living in the period of our youth. I heard it said that he looked quite his age and I was surprised to notice some familiar signs of it in his face. Then I realised that, in fact, he was old and that life makes its old men out of adolescents who last many years.

Someone hearing I was not well asked if I was not afraid to catch the "grippe" which was raging at that time while another benevolent individual reassured me by remarking: "Don't be afraid, it only attacks the young, people of your age don't run much risk of it." I noticed that the servants had recognised me and whispered my name, and a lady said she had heard them remark in their vernacular: "There goes old—" (This was followed by my name.)

On hearing the Duchesse de Guermantes say, "Of course! I knew the Marshal? But I knew others who were much more representative, the Duchesse de Galliera, Pauline de Périgord, Mgr. Dupanloup," I naïvely regretted not having known those she called relics of the *ancien régime*. I ought to have remembered that we call *ancien regime* what we have only known the end of; what is perceived thus on the horizon assumes a mysterious grandeur and seems the last chapter of a world we shall never see again; but as we go on it is soon we ourselves who are on the horizon for the generations behind us, the horizon continues to recede and the world which seemed finished begins again. "When I was a young girl," added Mme. de Guermantes, "I even saw the Duchesse de Dino. I'm no longer twenty-five, you know." Her last words displeased me; she need not have said that, it would have been all right for an old woman. "As to yourself," she continued, "you're always the same, you haven't, so to speak, changed at all," and that gave me almost more pain than if she had said the contrary for it proved, by the mere fact of being remarkable, how much time had passed. "You're astonishing, my dear friend. You're always young," a melancholy remark since there is only sense in it when we have, in fact, if not in appearance, become old. And she gave me a final blow by adding: "I've always regretted you did not get married. But, who knows! After all, perhaps you're happier as it is. You would have been old enough to have sons in the war and if they had been killed like poor Robert Saint-Loup (I often think of him) with your sensitiveness, you would not have survived them." And I could see myself as in the first truth-telling mirror I might encounter in the eyes of old men who had in their own opinion remained young as I believed I had, and who when I offered myself as an example of old age, in order that they should deny it, would by the look they gave me, show not the slightest pretence that they saw me otherwise than they saw themselves. For we do not see ourselves as we are, our age as it is, but each of us sees it in the other as though in a mirror. And, no doubt, many would have been less unhappy than I to realise they were old. At first, some face age as they do death, with indifference, not because they have more courage than others but because they have less imagination. But a man who, since boyhood has had one single idea in his mind, whose idleness and delicate health, just because they cause the postponement of its realisation, annul each wasted day because the disease which hastens the ageing of his body retards that of his spirit, such a man is more overwhelmed when he realises that he has never ceased living in Time than another who, having no inner life, regulates himself by the calendar and does not suddenly discover the aggregate of years he has been daily though unconsciously adding up. But there was a graver reason for my pain; I discovered that destructive action of Time at the very moment when I wanted to elucidate, to intellectualise extra-temporal realities in a work of art.

In the case of certain people present at this party, the successive substitution of cellules had brought about so complete a change during my absence from society, such an entire metamorphosis, that I could have dined opposite them in a restaurant a hundred times without any more imagining I had formerly known them than I could have guessed the royalty of an incognito sovereign or the vice of a stranger. The comparison is inadequate in the matter of names, for one can imagine an unknown seated in front of you being a criminal or a king whilst those I had known, or rather, the people I had known who bore their name, were so different that I could not believe them the same. Nevertheless, as I would have done in taking the idea of sovereignty or of vice as a starting-point which soon makes us discern in the stranger (whom one might so readily have treated with amiability or the reverse while one was blindfolded) a distinguished or suspicious appearance, I applied myself to introducing into the face of a woman entirely unknown to me the idea that she was Mme. Sazerat. And I ended by establishing my former notion of this face which would have remained utterly unknown to me, entirely that of another woman, as it had lost as fully the human attributes I had known as though it were that of a man changed into a monkey, were it not that the name and the statement of her identity put me in the way of solving the problem in spite of its difficulty. Sometimes, however, the old picture came to life with sufficient precision for me to confront the two and like a witness in the presence of an accused person, I had to say: "No, I do not recognise her."

A young woman asked me: "Shall we go and dine together at a restaurant?" and when I replied: "With pleasure, if you don't mind dining alone with a young man," I heard the people round me giggle and I added hastily, "or rather with an old one." I realised that the words which caused the laughter were of the kind my mother might have used in speaking of me; for my mother I always remained a child and I perceived that I was looking at myself from her point of view. Had I registered, as she did, changes since my childhood, they would have been very old ones for I had stopped at the point where people once used to say, almost before it was true, "Now he really is almost a young man." That was what I was now thinking but tremendously late. I had not perceived how much I had changed but how did the people who laughed at me know? I had not a grey hair, my moustache was black. I should have liked to ask them how this awful fact revealed itself. And now I understood what old age was—old age, which, of all realities, is perhaps the one of which we retain a purely abstract notion for the longest time, looking at calendars, dating our letters, seeing our friends get married, the children of our friends, without realising its significance, whether through dread or through idleness, until the day when an unknown effigy like M. d'Argencourt teaches us that we are living in a new world; until the when we, who seem to him like his grandfather, treat the grandson of one of our women friends as a comrade and he laughs as though at a joke. And then I understood what is meant by death, love, joys of the mind, usefulness of sorrow and vocation. For if names had lost their meaning for me, words had unfolded it. The beauty of images is lodged at the back of things, that of ideas in front, so that the first no longer cause us wonder when we reach them and we only understand the second when we have passed beyond them.

The cruel discovery I had now made regarding the lapse of Time could only enrich my ideas and add to the material of my book. Since I had decided that it could not consist only of pure intuitions, namely those beyond Time, amongst the verities with which I intended to frame them, those which are concerned with Time, Time, in which men, societies and nations bathe and change, would have an important place. I should not be mindful only of those alterations to which the aspect of human beings must submit, of which new examples presented themselves at every moment, for still considering my work now begun with decision strong enough to resist temporary distraction, I continued to say, "How do you do?" and talk to people I knew. Age, moreover, had not marked all of them in similar fashion. Someone asked my name and I was told it was M. de Cambremer. To show he had recognised me he inquired: "Do you still suffer from those feelings of suffocation?" On my replying in the affirmative, he went on: "You see that that does not prevent longevity," as though I were a centenarian. I was speaking to him with my eyes fixed upon two or three features which my thought was reducing to a synthesis of my memories of his personality quite different from what he now represented. He half turned his head for a moment and I then perceived that he had become unrecognisable owing to the adjunction to his cheeks of enormous red pockets which prevented him from opening his mouth and his eyes properly, so much so that I stood stupefied not wanting to show that I noticed this sort of anthrax to which it was more becoming that he should allude first. But since, like a courageous invalid, he made no allusion to it and laughed, I feared to seem lacking in feeling if I did not inquire and in tact if I did. "But don't they come more rarely as one grows old?" he asked, referring to the suffocated feeling. I told him not. "Well, my sister has them much less now than formerly," he remarked with an air of contradiction, as though it must be the same in my case, as though age were a remedy which had been good for Mme. de Gaucourt and therefore salutary for me. Mme. de Cambremer-Legrandin now approached and I felt more and more afraid of seeming insensitive in not deploring what I remarked on her husband's face and yet I did not dare speak first. "You must be pleased to see him again," she said. "Is he well?" I answered hesitatingly. "As you see," she replied. She had never even noticed the growth which offended my vision and which was only another of the masks which Time had attached to the Marquis' face, but so gradually and progressively that the Marquise had noticed nothing. When M. de Cambremer had finished questioning me about my attacks of suffocation it was my turn to ask someone, in a whisper, if the Marquis' mother was still alive. She was. In appreciating the passage of time, it is only the first step that counts. At first it is painful to realise that so much time has passed, afterwards one is surprised it is not more. One begins by being unable to realise that the thirteenth century is so far away and afterwards finds difficulty in believing that any churches of that period survive though they are innumerable in France. In a few instants that slower process had taken place in me which happens to those who can scarcely believe a person they know is sixty and fifteen years later are equally incredulous when they hear he is still alive and no more than seventy-five. I asked M. de Cambremer how his mother was. "Splendid as ever," he answered, using an adjective which to the contrary of those tribes which treat aged parents without pity applies in certain families to old people whose use of the physical faculties, such as hearing, walking to church and bearing bereavement without feeling depressed, endows them with extreme moral beauty in the eyes of their children.

If certain women proclaimed their age by make-up, certain men on whose faces I had never noticed cosmetics accentuated their age by ceasing to use them, now that they were no longer concerned to charm. Amongst these was Legrandin. The disappearance of the pink in his lips and cheeks which I had never suspected of being an artifice, gave his skin a grey hue and his long-drawn and mournful features the sculptured and lapidary precision of an Egyptian God. A God! More like one who had come back from the dead. He had not only lost the courage to paint himself but to smile, to put life into his manner and to talk with animation. It was astonishing to see him so pale, so beaten, only emitting a word now and then which had the insignificance of those uttered by the dead when they are evoked. One wondered what prevented him from being lively, talkative and entertaining, as at a séance, one is struck by the insignificant replies of the spirit of a man who was brilliant when he was alive, to questions susceptible of interesting developments. And one realised that old age had substituted a pale and tenuous phantom for the highly-coloured and alert Legrandin. Certain people's hair had not gone white. I noticed this when the Prince de Guermantes' old footman went to speak to his master. The ample whiskers which stood out from his cheeks had like his neck retained that red-pink which he could not be suspected of obtaining by dye like the Duchesse de Guermantes. But he did not seem less old on that account. One only felt that there are species of man like mosses and lichens in the vegetable kingdom which do not change at the approach of winter.

In the case of guests whose faces had remained intact, age showed itself in other ways; they only seemed to be inconvenienced when they had to walk; at first, something seemed wrong with their legs, later only, one grasped that age had attached soles of lead to their feet. Some, like the Prince of Agrigente, had been embellished by age. This tall, thin, dispirited-looking man with hair which seemed to remain eternally red, had, by means of a metamorphosis analogous to that of insects, been succeeded by an old man whose red hair, like a worn-out table-cloth had been replaced by white. His chest had assumed an unheard of and almost warrior-like protuberance which must have necessitated a regular bursting of the frail chrysalis I had known; a self-conscious gravity tinged his eyes which beamed with a newly acquired benevolence towards all and sundry. And as, in spite of the change in him, there was still a certain resemblance between the vigorous prince of now and the portrait my memory preserved, I was filled with admiration of the recreative power of Time which, while respecting the unity of the being and the laws of life, finds means of thus altering appearance and of introducing bold contrasts in two successive aspects of the same individual. Many people could be immediately identified but like rather bad portraits of themselves in which an unconscientious and malevolent artist had hardened the features of one, taken away the freshness of complexion or slight-ness of figure of another and darkened the look of a third. Comparing these images with those retained by my memory, I liked less those displayed to me now, in the same way as we dislike and refuse the photograph of a friend because we don't consider it a pleasant likeness. I should have liked to say to each one of them who showed me his portrait: "No, not that one, it doesn't do you justice, it isn't you." I should not have ventured to add: "Instead of your beautiful straight nose you have now got the hooked nose of your father"; it was, in fact, a new familial nose. In short, the artist Time had produced all these models in such a way as to be recognisable without being likenesses, not because he had flattered but because he had aged them. That particular artist works very slowly. Thus the replica of the face of Odette, a barely outlined sketch of which I perceived in that of Gilberte on the day I first saw Bergotte, had been worked by time into the most perfect resemblance (as will be seen shortly) like painters who keep a work a long time and add to it year by year. In several cases I recognised not only the people themselves but themselves as they used to be, like Ski, for instance, who was no more changed than a dried flower or fruit, a type of those amateur "celibates of art" who remain ineffectual and unfulfilled in their old age. Ski had, in thus remaining an incomplete experiment, confirmed my theories about art. Others similarly affected were in no sense amateurs; they were society people interested in nothing, whom age had not ripened and if it had drawn a curve of wrinkles round their faces and given them an arch of white hair, they yet remained chubby and retained the sprightliness of eighteen. They were not old men but extremely faded young men of eighteen. Little would have been needed to efface the withering effects of years, and death would have had no more trouble in giving youth back to their faces than is needed to restore a slightly soiled portrait to its original brightness. I reflected also on the illusion which dupes us into crediting an aged celebrity with virtue, justice and loveliness of soul, my feeling being that such famous people, forty years earlier, had been terrible young men and that there was no reason to suppose that they were not just as vain, cunning, self-sufficient and tricky now.

Yet in complete contrast with these last I was surprised when I conversed with men and women who were formerly unbearable, to discover that they had almost entirely lost their defects, whether because life had disappointed or satisfied their ambitions and thus freed them from presumption or from bitterness. A rich marriage which makes both effort and ostentation unnecessary, perhaps too the influence of a wife, a slowly-acquired sense of values other than those in which light-headed youth exclusively believes had enlarged their characters and brought out their qualities. With age such individuals seemed to have acquired a different personality like trees which seem to assume a new character with their autumnal tints. In their case age manifested itself as a form of morality they used not to possess, in the case of others it was physical in character and so new to me that a particular person such as Mme. de Souvré, for instance, seemed simultaneously familiar and a stranger. A stranger for I could not believe it was she and, in responding to her bow, I could not help letting her notice my mental effort to establish which of three or four people (of whom Mme. de Souvré was not one) I was bowing to with a warmth which must have astonished her for, in fear of being too distant if she were an intimate friend, I had made up for the uncertainty of my recognition by the warmth of my smiling handshake. On the other hand, her new aspect was familiar to me. It was one I had, in the course of my life, often observed in stout, elderly women without then suspecting that, many years before, they might have resembled Mme. de Souvré. So different was this aspect from the one I had known in the past that I might have thought her a character in a fairy story which first appears as a young girl, then as a stout matron and finally, no doubt, turns into a tottering, bowbacked old woman. She looked like an exhausted swimmer far from shore who painfully manages to keep her head above the waves of time which were submerging her. After looking long at her irresolute face, wavering like a treacherous memory which cannot retain former appearances, I succeeded somehow in recovering something by indulging in a little game of eliminating the squares and hexagons which age had affixed to those cheeks. But it was by no means always geometrical figures that it affixed to the faces of the women. In the Duchesse de Guermantes' cheeks which had remained remarkably unchanged though they now seemed compounded of nougat, I distinguished a trace of verdigris, a tiny bit of crushed shell and a fleshiness difficult to define because it was slighter than a mistletoe-berry and less transparent than a glass bead.

Some men walked lame and one knew it was not on account of a carriage accident but of a stroke and that they had, as people say, one foot in the grave. This was gaping for half-paralysed women like Mme. de Franquetot who seemed to be unable to pull away their raiment caught in the stones of the vault, as though they could not recover their footing, with their heads held low, their bodies bent into a curve like the one between life and death they were now descending to their final extinction. Nothing could resist the movement of the parabola which was carrying them off, trying tremblingly to rise, their quivering fingers failed them. Certain faces under the hood of their white hair wore the rigidity, the sealed eyelids of those about to die, their constantly moving lips seemed to be mumbling the prayer of the dying.

If a face retained its linear form, white hair replacing blond or black sufficed to make it look like that of another. Theatrical costumiers know that a powdered wig so dis-guises a person as to make him unrecognisable. The young Marquis de Beausergent whom I had met in Mme. de Cambremer's box when he was a sub-lieutenant on the day when Mme. de Guermantes was in her sister's box, still had perfectly regular features, even more so, because the physiological rigidity of arteriosclerosis exaggerated the impassive physiognomy of the dandy and gave his features the intense and almost grimacing immobility of a study by Mantegna or Michael Angelo. His formerly brick-red skin had become gravely pale; silver hair, slight stoutness, Doge-like dignity and a chronic fatigue which gave him a constant longing for sleep, combined to produce a new and impressive majesty. A rectangle of white beard had replaced a similar rectangle of blond so perfectly that, noticing that my former sub-lieutenant now had five stripes, my first thought was to congratulate him not on having been promoted Colonel but on being one so completely that he seemed to have borrowed not only the uniform but also the solemn and serious appearance of his father the Colonel. In the case of another man, a white beard had succeeded a blond one but as his face had remained gay, smiling and youthful, it made him appear redder and more active and by increasing the brightness of his eyes, gave this worldling who had remained young the inspired appearance of a prophet. The transformation which white hair and other elements had effected, particularly in women, would have claimed my attention less if it had involved a change of colour only, for that may charm the eyes whereas a change of personality troubles the mind. Actually to recognise someone, more still, to identify him you have been unable to recognise, is to think two contradictory things under a single denomination, it is the same as saying that he who was here, the being we recall, is here no longer and that he who is here is one we never knew, that means piercing a mystery almost as troubling as that of death of which it is indeed the preface and the herald. For I knew what these changes meant and what they preluded and so that whitening of the women's hair in addition to so many other changes deeply moved me. Somebody mentioned a name and I was stupefied to know it applied at one and the same time to my former blonde dance-partner and to the stout elderly lady who moved ponderously past me. Except for a certain pinkness of complexion their name was perhaps the only thing in common between these two women who differed so much—the one in my memory and this one at the Guermantes' reception—the young *ingénue* and the theatrical dowager. That my dancer had managed to annex that huge carcass, that she had succeeded in slowing down her cumbersome movements like a metronome, that all she should have preserved of her youth were her cheeks, fuller certainly but freckled as ever, that for the erstwhile dainty blonde there should have been substituted this old pot-bellied Marshal, life must have achieved more destruction and reconstruction than is needed to replace a spire by a dome and when one remembered that the operation had been carried out not upon inert matter but upon flesh which only changes insensibly, the overwhelming contrast between this apparition and the being I remembered removed her into a past which, rather than remote, was almost incredible. It was difficult to reunite the two aspects, to think of the two creatures under the same denomination; for in the same way that one has difficulty in realising that a dead body was alive or that he who was alive is dead to-day, it is almost as difficult, and the difficulty is the same (for the annihilation of youth, the destruction of a personality full of strength and vitality is the beginning of a void), to conceive that she who was young is old, when the aspect of this old woman juxtaposed on that of the young one seems so completely to exclude it that in turn it is the old woman, then the young one, then again the old one which appear to you as in a dream and one cannot believe that this was ever that, that the matter of that one is herself which had not escaped elsewhere, but thanks to the adroit manipulations of time, had become this one, that the same matter has never left the same body—if one did not have the name as an indication as well as the affirmative testimony of friends to which the copperas, erstwhile exiguous between the gold of the wheat ears to-day buried beneath the snow, alone gives an appearance of credibility. One was terrified on considering the periods which must have passed since such a revolution had been accomplished in the geology of the human countenance, to observe the erosions that had taken place beside the nose, the immense deposits on the cheeks which enveloped the face with their opaque and refractory mass. I had always thought of our own individuality at a given moment in time as a polypus whose eye, an independent organism, although associated with it, winks at a scatter of dust without orders from the mind, still more, whose intestines are infected by an obscure parasite without the intelligence being aware of it, and similarly of the soul as a series of selves juxtaposed in the course of life but distinct from each other which would die in turn or take turn about like those different selves which alternately took possession of me at Combray when evening came. But I had also observed that these moral cellules which constitute a being are more durable than itself. I had seen the vices and the bravery of the Guermantes return in Saint-Loup, as I had seen the strange and swift defects and then the loyal semitism of Swann. I could see it again in Bloch. After he had lost his father the idea, besides the strong familial sentiment which often exists in Jewish families, that his father was superior to everyone, had given the form of a cult to his love for him. He could not bear losing him and had shut himself up for nearly a year in a sanatorium. He had replied to my condolences in a deeply felt but almost haughty tone, so enviable did he consider me for having been acquainted with that distinguished man whose carriage and pair he would have gladly given to a historical museum. And at his family table (for contrary to what the Duchesse de Guermantes believed, he was married) the same anger which animated M. Bloch senior against M. Nissim Bernard animated Bloch against his father-in-law. He made the same attacks on him. In the same way when I listened to the talk of Cottard, Brichot and so many others I had felt that by culture and fashion a single undulation propagates identical modes of speech and thought in the whole expanse of space, and in the same way, throughout the duration of time, great fundamental currents raise from the depths of the ages the same angers, the same sorrows, the same boasts, the same manias, throughout superimposed generations, each section accepting the criteria of various levels of the same series and reproducing, like shadows upon successive screens, pictures similar to though often less insignificant than that which brought Bloch and his father-in-law, M. Bloch senior and M. Nissim Bernard and others I never knew, to blows.

There were men I knew there with whose relations I was also acquainted without ever realising that they had a feature-in common; in admiring the white-haired old hermit into whom Legrandin had changed, I suddenly observed, I could say discovered with a zoologist's satisfaction, in his ironed-out cheeks, the same construction as in those of his young nephew, Léonor de Cambremer, who-however, did not seem to bear any resemblance to him; to this preliminary common feature I added another I had not until now remarked, then others, none of which composed the synthesis his youthfulness ordinarily offered me, so that soon I had a sort of caricature of him, deeper and more lifelike than a literal resemblance would have been; his uncle now seemed to me young Cambremer who, for fun, had assumed the appearance of the old man he would eventually be, so completely indeed that it was not only what youth of the past had become but what youth of to-day would change into that had given me such an intensified sense of Time.

Women tried to keep touch with the particular charm which had most distinguished them but the fresh matter that time had added to their faces would not permit of it. The features moulded by beauty, having disappeared in roost cases, they tried to construct another one with the relics. By displacing the centre of perspective if not of gravity in the face and recomposing its features to accord with the new character, they began building up a new sort of beauty at fifty as a man takes up a new profession late in life or as soil no longer good for the vine is used to produce beetroot. This caused a new youth to flower round the new features. But those who had been too beautiful or too ugly could not accommodate themselves to these transformations. The former modelled like marble on definitive lines which cannot be changed, crumbled away like a statue, the latter who had some facial defect had even an advantage over them. To start with it was only they whom one immediately recognised. One knew there were not two mouths in Paris like theirs which enabled me to distinguish them in the course of a party at which I had recognised nobody. And they did not even appear to have aged. Age is human and being monsters they had no more changed than whales. There were other men and women who did not seem to have aged; their outlines were as slim, their faces as young as ever. But, if one approached them closely so as to talk to them, the face with its smooth skin and delicate contours appeared different and as happens when one examines a vegetable body under a microscope, watery or ensanguined spots exuded. I observed sundry greasy marks on skin I had believed to be smooth which gave me a feeling of disgust. The outline did not resist this enlargement; at a close view that of the nose had been deflected and rounded, had been invaded by the same oily patches as the rest of the face and when it met the eyes, the latter disappeared into pockets which destroyed the resemblance with the former face one thought one had rediscovered. Thus those guests who had an appearance of youth at a distance, became old as one got near to them and could observe the enlargement and distribution of the facial planes. In fact their age seemed to depend upon the spectator so placing himself as to envisage them as young by observing them only at a distance which, deprived of the glass supplied to a long-sighted person by an optician, diminishes the object; their age, like the presence of infusoria in a glass of water, was brought about less by the progress of years than by the scale of enlargement in the observer's vision.

In general the amount of white hair was an index of depth in time like mountain summits which appear to be on the same level as others until the brilliance of their snowy whiteness reveals their height above them. And even that could not always be said, especially about women. Thus the Princesse de Guermantes' locks, when they were grey, had the brilliance of silvery silk round her protuberant brow but now having determined to become white seemed to be made of wool and stuffing and resembled soiled snow. It also occurred that blonde dancing girls had not merely annexed, together with their white hair, the friendship of duchesses they had not previously known, but having formerly done nothing but dance, art had touched them with its grace. And, like those illustrious ladies in the eighteenth century who became religious, they lived in flats full of cubist paintings, with a cubist painter working only for them and they living only for him.

Old men whose features had changed attempted to fix on them permanently the fugitive expressions adopted for a pose, thinking they would secure a better appearance or palliate its defects; they seemed to have become unchangeable snapshots of themselves.

All these people had taken so much time to make up their disguises that, as a rule, they escaped the notice of those who lived with them, indeed often a reprieve was granted them and, during the interval, they had been able to remain themselves until quite late in life. But this deferred disguise was then accomplished more quickly and was, in any case, inevitable. Thus I had always known Mme. X— charming and erect and for long she remained so, too long indeed, for like a person who must not forget to put on her Turkish disguise before dark, she had waited till the last moment and precipitately transformed herself into the old Turkish lady her mother formerly resembled.

At the party I discovered one of my early friends whom I had formerly seen nearly every day during ten years. Someone reintroduced us to each other. As I went near to him, he said with a voice I well remembered: "What a joy for me after so many years!" but what a surprise for me! His voice seemed to be proceeding from a perfected phonograph for though it was that of my friend, it issued from a great greyish man whom I did not know and the voice of my old comrade seemed to have been housed in this fat old fellow by means of a mechanical trick. Yet I knew that it was he, the person who introduced us after all that time not being the kind to play pranks. He declared that I had not changed by which I grasped that he did not think he had. Then I looked at him again and except that he had got so fat, he had kept a good deal of his former personality. Nevertheless, I found it impossible to realise it and I tried to recall him. In his youth he had blue eyes that were always smiling and moving, apparently searching for something I was unaware of, which may have been disinterested truth, perhaps pursued in perpetual doubt with a boy's fugitive respect for family friends. Having become an influential politician, capable and despotic, those blue eyes which had never succeeded in finding what they were after had become immobilised and this gave them a sharp expression like a frowning-eye-brow, while gaiety, unconsciousness and innocence had changed into design and disingenuousness. Emphatically he had changed into another person—then suddenly, in reply to a word of mine, he burst into laughter, the jolly familiar laugh of former days which suited the perpetual gay mobility of his glance. Musical fanatics hold that Z's music orchestrated by X becomes something absolutely different. These are shades which ordinary people cannot grasp, but the wild stifled laugh of a child beneath an eye pointed like a well-sharpened blue pencil, though a little on one side, is something more than a difference in orchestration. When his laughter ceased I would have liked to reconstruct my friend, but like Ulysses in the Odyssey, throwing himself upon the body of his dead mother, like a medium vainly trying to obtain from an apparition a reply which shall identify it, like a visitor to an electrical exhibition who cannot accept the voice from a phonograph as the spontaneous utterance of a human being, I ceased to recognise my friend.

It is necessary, however, to make this reserve that the beat of time itself can in certain cases be accelerated or slowed down. Four or five years before, I had by chance, met in the street Vicomtesse de St. Fiacre (daughter-in-law of the Guermantes' friend). Her sculptured features had seemed to assure her eternal youth and indeed she still was young. But now, in spite of her smiles and greetings, I failed to recognise her in a lady whose features had so gone to pieces that the outline of her face could not be restored. What had happened was that for three years she had been taking cocaine and other drugs. Her eyes deeply and darkly rimmed were haggard, her mouth had a strange twitch. She had, it seems, got up for this reception though she was in the habit of remaining in bed or on a sofa for months. Time has these express and special trains which bring about premature old age but on a parallel line return trains circulate which are almost as rapid. I took M. de Courgivaux for his son; he looked younger and though he must have been past fifty, appeared to be no more than thirty. He had found an intelligent doctor, had avoided alcohol and salt and so had become thirty again, hardly even that because he had had his hair cut that morning.

A curious thing is that the phenomenon of age seemed in its modalities to take note of certain social customs. Great gentlemen who had been in the habit of wearing the plainest alpaca and old straw hats which a bourgeois would not have put on his head, had aged in the same way as the gardeners and peasants in the midst of whom they had lived. Their cheeks were stained brown inl patches and their faces had grown yellow and had sunk flat like a book. And I thought, too, of those who were not there because they could not be, of how their secretary, in an attempt to give them the illusion of survival, would excuse them by one of those telegrams the Princess received on occasion from such as had been ill or dying for years, who can rise no more nor even move and, surrounded by frivolous or assiduous visitors, the former attracted like inquisitive tourists, the latter by the faith of pilgrims, lie, with closed eyes clasping their breviary, their bedclothes partly thrown back like a mortuary shroud, chiselled into a skeleton beneath the pale, distended skin like marble on a tomb.

Certainly, some women were recognisable because their faces had remained almost the same and they wore their grey hair to harmonise with the season like autumn leaves. But in others and in some men their identity was so impossible to establish—for instance between the dark voluptuary one remembered and the old monk of now—that their transformation made one think, rather than of the actor's art, of that of the amazing mimic of whom Fregoli remains the prototype. That old woman yonder is about to weep because she knows that the indefinable and melancholy smile which was formerly her charm cannot even irradiate the surface of the mask old age has affixed to her. Now, discouraged from attempts to please she more adroitly resigns herself to using it as though it were a theatrical mask to make people laugh. But in the case of nearly all the women there was no limit to their efforts to fight against age; they held the mirror of their faces towards beauty, vanishing like a setting sun whose last rays they passionately long to retain. Some sought to smooth out, to extend the white surface, renouncing the piquancy of menaced dimples, quelling the resistance of a smile doomed and disarmed, while others, realising that their beauty had finally departed, took refuge in expression, as one compensates the loss of the voice by the art of diction, and hung on to a pout, to a smirk, to a pensive gaze, or to a smile to which muscular inco-ordination gave the appearance of weeping.

A stout lady bade me good afternoon during the moment that these varied thoughts were pressing upon my mind. For an instant I hesitated to reply to her, fearing she might be taking me for someone else, then her confidence making me think the contrary and fearing she was someone with whom I might at one time have been intimate, I exaggerated the affability of my smile while my gaze still sought in her features the name I could not find. Thus an uncertain candidate for matriculation searches the face of the examiner for the answer he would be wiser to seek in his own memory. So I smiled and stared at the features of the stout lady. They appeared to be those of Mme. de Forcheville and my smile became tinged with respect and my indecision began to cease when a second later, the stout lady said: "You were taking me for mamma, I know I'm getting to look exactly like her," and I recognised Gilberte.

Moreover, even among men who had been subjected to only a slight change, whose moustaches only had become white, one felt that the change was not purely material. One saw them as through a coloured mist or glass which affected their facial aspect with a sort of fogginess and revealed what they allowed one to observe as if it were life-size though in reality it was far away, not in the sense of space, but, fundamentally, like being on another shore whence they had as much trouble in recognising us as we them. Perhaps Mme. de Forcheville who looked to me as though she had been injected with paraffin which swells the skin and prevents it from sagging, was unique in presenting the appearance of a courtesan of an earlier period who had been embalmed for eternity. "You took me for my mother," Gilberte had said and it was true. For that matter it was a compliment to the daughter. Moreover, it was not only in the last-named that familiar features had reappeared, as invisible till then in her face as the inturned parts of a seed-pod, the eventual opening out of which would never be suspected. Thus the enormous maternal bridge in one as in the other transformed towards the fifties a nose till then inflexibly straight. In the case of another daughter of a banker, her complexion of flower-like freshness had become copper-coloured through the reflection of the gold which the father had so freely manipulated. Some even ended by resembling the quarter where they lived, bearing upon their countenances a sort of reflection of the Rue de l'Arcade or the Avenue du Bois or the Rue de l'Elysée. But they reproduced more than anything else the features of their parents.

One starts with the idea that people have remained the same and one discovers that they have got old. But if one starts by thinking them old, one does not find them so bad. In Odette's case it was not merely that; her appearance, when one knew her age and expected her to be an old woman seemed a more miraculous challenge to the laws of chronology than the conservation of radium to those of nature. If I had not recognised her at first, it was not because she had changed but because she had not. Having realised in the course of the last hour what additions time made to people and the subtraction that was needed to rediscover their personalities, I rapidly added to the old Odette the number of years which had passed over her with the result that I found someone before my eyes who could not possibly be her precisely because this someone was the Odette of former days.

Which was the effect of paint and which of dye? With her flat golden hair arranged at the back like the ruffled chignon of a doll surmounting a face with a doll-like expression of surprise and superimposed upon that an equally flat sailor hat of straw of the period of the 1878 Exhibition (in which she certainly had figured and if she had then been as old as now, she would have been one of its choicest features) she looked as though she were a young woman playing a part in a Christmas revue featuring the Exhibition of 1878.

Close to us, a minister of the pre-Boulangist period who had again become a minister, passed by, bowing right and left to ladies with a tremulous and distant smile, as though imprisoned in the past like a little phantom figure manipulated by an unseen hand which had reduced his size and changed his substance so that he looked like a pumice-stone reproduction of himself. This former Prime Minister, now cultivated by the Faubourg Saint-Germain, had once been the object of criminal proceedings and had been execrated by society and by the populace. But thanks to the renewal of the social elements in both groupings and the extinction of individual passions, memories disappear, no one remembered and he was honoured. There is no disgrace great enough to make a man lose heart if he bears in mind that at the end of a certain number of years our buried mistakes will be but invisible dust upon which nature's flowers will smile peacefully. The individual momentarily under a cloud, through the equilibrium brought about by Time between the new and the old social strata, will easily assert his authority over them and be the object of their deference and admiration. Only, this is Time's business; and at the moment of his troubles, he was inconsolable because the young milkmaid opposite had heard the crowd call him a swindler and shake their fists at him when he was in the soup. The young milk-maid does not see things on the plane of time and is unaware that men to whom the morning paper offers the incense of flattery were yesterday of bad repute and that the man who just now escaped prison, while perhaps, he was thinking of that young milk-maid, and who had not the humility to utter conciliatory words which might have secured him sympathy, will one day be glorified by the press and sought after by duchesses. Time also heals family quarrels. At the Princesse de Guermantes' there was a couple, each of whom had had an uncle; these two uncles were not content merely to fight a duel but each had sent the other his concierge or his butler as his representative for the occasion, so as to humiliate him by showing he was not fit to be treated as a gentleman. Such tales were asleep in the papers of thirty years ago and nobody knew anything about them. Thus the Princesse de Guermantes' salon illuminated and forgetful, flowered like a peaceful cemetery. There Time had not only disintegrated those of the past, it had made possible and created new associations.

To return to our politician. In spite of the change in his physical substance, a change as complete as the moral transformation he now roused in the public, in a word, in spite of the many years gone by since he was Prime Minister, he had become a Minister again. The present Prime Minister had given the one of forty years ago a post in the new Cabinet much as theatrical managers entrust a part to one of their earlier women associates who has been long in retirement but whom they consider more capable than younger ones of performing it with delicacy, of whose embarrassed situation they are, moreover, aware and who, at nearly eighty, still shows that age has scarcely impaired an artistic integrity which amazes the public within a few days of her death.

Mme. de Forcheville presented an appearance so miraculous that one would have said not that she had grown young, but that, with all her carmine and rouge, she had reflowered. Even more than an incarnation of the Universal Exhibition of 1878, she could have been the chief attraction of a horticultural exhibition to-day. To me, at all events, she did not seem to be saying: "I am the Exhibition of 1878" but "I am the *Allée des Acacias* of 1892." To me it was as though she were still part of it. And, because she had not changed, she seemed hardly to be living, she was like a sterilised rose. When I wished her good afternoon, she tried for a moment vainly to put a name to my face. I gave it her and at once, thanks to its evocative magic, I ceased to wear the appearance of Arbousier or of Kangouroo apparently bestowed on me by age, and she began talking to me with that peculiar voice, applauded in the smaller theatres, which enchanted people so much when they were invited to meet her at lunch and discovered that they could have as much as they liked of it with every word she uttered. That voice had retained the same futile cordiality, the same slight English accent. And yet, just as her eyes seemed to be looking at me from a distant shore, her voice was sad, almost appealing like that of the dead in the Odyssey. Odette ought to have gone on acting. I paid her a compliment on her youth. She answered: "You are charming, my dear, thanks." And as it was difficult for her to express any sentiment, however sincere, without revealing her anxiety to be fashionable, she repeated several times: "Thanks so much, thanks so much." And I, who had formerly made long journeys only to catch a glimpse of her in the Bois, who, when first I went to her house, had listened to the words that fell from her lips as though they were pearls, found the moments now spent with her interminable; I knew not what to say and I left her. Alas, she was not always to remain thusy Less than three years afterwards, I was to see her at an evening party given by Gilberte, not fallen into second childhood but somewhat decayed, no longer able to hide under a mask-like face what she was thinking—thinking is saying too much—what she was feeling, moving her head about, pursing her lips, shaking her shoulders at everything she felt, like a drunken man or a child or like certain inspired poets who, unconscious of their surroundings, compose their poems when they are in company or at table, and, to the alarm of their astonished hostess, knit their brows and make grimaces. Mme. de Forcheville's feelings—except the one that brought her to Gilberte's party, tenderness for her beloved child, her pride in so brilliant an entertainment, a pride which could not veil the mother's melancholy that she no longer counted—these feelings were never happy and were inspired by her perpetual self-defence against rudeness meted out to her, the timid defence of a child. One constantly heard people say: "I don't know if Mme. de Forcheville recognises me, perhaps I ought to be introduced over again." "You can dispense with that," (someone replied at the top of his voice neither knowing nor caring that Gilberte's mother could hear every word) "you won't get any fun out of it. Leave her alone. She's a bit daft." Furtively, Mme. de Forcheville cast a glance from her still beautiful eyes at the insulting speakers, then quickly looked away, for fear of seeming to have heard, while, bowing beneath the blow, she restrained her weak resentment with quivering head and heaving breast, and glanced towards another equally ruthless guest. Nor did she seem too greatly overwhelmed for she had been ailing several days and had hinted to her daughter to postpone the party which the latter had refused. Mme. de Forcheville did not love her the less; the presence of the Duchesses, the admiration the company manifested for the new mansion, flooded her heart with joy, and when the Marquise de Sebran was announced, this lady representing, with much effort, the highest peak of fashion, Mme. de Forcheville felt she had been a good and far-seeing mother and that her maternal task had been accomplished. A fresh lot of contemptuous guests brought on another solitary colloquy if a mute language only expressed by gesticulation can be called talking. Beautiful still, she had become as never previously, an object of infinite sympathy for now the whole world betrayed her who had once betrayed Swann and the rest; now that the rôles were reversed, she had become too weak to defend herself against men. And soon she would be unable to defend herself against death. After that anticipation, let us go back three years, to the reception at the Prince de Guermantes'.

Bloch, having asked me to introduce him to the master of the house I did not make a shadow of difficulty. The embarrassment I had felt the first time at the Prince de Guermantes' evening party seemed natural enough then but now it seemed as simple a matter to introduce one of his guests to him as to bring someone to his house who had not been invited. Was this because, since those far distant days, I had become an intimate though a long-forgotten intimate, of a society in which I was once a stranger or was it because, not being a true man of the world, what causes that type embarrassment had no existence for me, now my shyness had passed? Or, again, was it because these people had little by little shed their first, their second and their third fictitious aspects in my presence and that I sensed, under the Prince's disdainful manner, a human longing to know people, to make the acquaintance of those even whom he affected to despise? Finally, was it because the Prince had changed like those others, arrogant in their youth and in their maturity, whom old age had softened (the more so that they had for long known by sight men against whose antecedents they had reacted and whom they now knew to be on good terms with their own acquaintances) especially if old age is assisted by virtues or vices which broaden social relationships or by a social revolution which causes a political conversion such as the Prince's to Dreyfusism?

Bloch interrogated me as I formerly did others when I first entered society, and as I still did, about people I formerly knew socially and who were now as far away, as isolated, as those Combray folk I had often wanted to place. But Combray was so distinct from and impossible to reconcile with the outer world that it was like a piece of a jig-saw puzzle that could not be fitted into the map of France. "Then I can't have any idea of what the Prince de Guermantes used to be like from my knowledge of Swann or M. de Charlus?" Bloch asked. For some time I used to borrow his way of putting things and now he often imitated mine. "Not the least." "But how did they actually differ?" "You would have had to hear them talk together to grasp it. Now Swann is dead and M. de Charlus is not far from it. But the difference was enormous." And while Bloch's eye gleamed as he thought of what the conversation of these marvellous people must have been, I was thinking that I had exaggerated my pleasure in their society, having never got any until I was alone and could differentiate them in my imagination. Did Bloch realise this? "Perhaps you've coloured it all a bit too much," he remarked. "Look at our hostess, the Princesse de Guermantes, I know she's no longer young but, after all, it isn't so very long ago that you spoke of her incomparable charm and her marvellous beauty. Certainly I admit she has the grand manner and she also has the extraordinary eyes you described to me, but I don't see that she's so wonderful as all that. Obviously she's high-bred but still...." I had to explain to Bloch that we weren't alluding to the same person. The Princesse de Guermantes was dead and the Prince, ruined by the German defeat, had married ex-Mme. Verdurin whom Bloch had not recognised. "You're mistaken, I've looked up the Gotha of this year," Bloch naïvely confessed, "and I found that the Prince de Guermantes was living in this very mansion and had married someone of great importance. Wait a minute, now I've got it, Sidonie, Duchesse de Duras, *née* des Beaux." This was a fact, for Mme. Verdurin, shortly after her husband's death married the old ruined Duc de Duras, who thus made her the Prince de Guermantes' cousin and died after they had been married two years. He had supplied a very useful means of transition for Mme. Verdurin who by a third marriage had become Princesse de Guermantes and now occupied a great position in the Faubourg Saint-Germain which would have much astonished Combray where the ladies of the Rue de l'Oiseau, Mme. Goupil's daughter and Mme. Sazerat's daughter-in-law had said with a laugh, years before Mme. Verdurin became Princesse de Guermantes: "The Duchesse de Duras!" as though Mme. Verdurin were playing a part at the theatre. The caste principle maintained that she should die Mme. Verdurin and that the title which, in their eyes, could never confer any new social prestige, merely produced the bad effect of getting herself "talked about"; that expression which in all social categories is applied to a woman who has a lover, was also applied in the Faubourg Saint-Germain to people who published books and in the Combray bourgeoisie to those who make marriages which for one reason or another are considered unsuitable. When Mme. Verdurin married the Prince de Guermantes they must have said he was a sham Guermantes, a swindler. For myself, the realisation that a Princesse de Guermantes still existed, who had nothing to do with her who had so much charmed me and who was now no more, whom death had left defenceless, was intensely saddening as it was to witness the objects once owned by Princesse Hedwige such as her Château and everything else, pass to another. Succession to a name is sad like all successions and seems like an usurpation; and the uninterrupted stream of new Princesses de Guermantes would flow until the millennium, the name held from age to age by different women would always be that of one living Princesse de Guermantes, a name that ignored death, that was indifferent to change and heartaches and which would close over those who had worn it like the sea in its serene and immemorial placidity.

But, in contradiction to that permanence, the former *habitués* asserted that society had completely changed, that people were now received who in their day would never have been and that, as one says, was "true and not true". It was not true because they were not taking the curve of time into consideration, the result of which is that the present generation see the new people at their point of arrival whereas those of the past saw them at their point of departure. And when the latter entered society, there were new arrivals whose point of departure was remembered by others. One generation brings about a change while it took the bourgeois name of a Colbert centuries to become noble. On the other hand, it was true, for if the social position of people changes, the most ineradicable ideas and customs (as also fortunes, marriages and national hatreds) change also, amongst them even that of only associating with fashionable people. Not only does snobbishness change its form but it might be forgotten like the war and Radicals and Jews be admitted to the Jockey Club.

Certainly even the exterior change in faces I had known was only the symbol of an internal change effected day by day. Perhaps these people continued doing the same things every day but the idea they had about these things and about the people they associated with having a little life in it, resulted after some years, in those things and people being different under the same names and it would have been strange if the faces of the latter had not changed.

If in these periods of twenty years, the conglomerates of coteries had been demolished and reconstructed to suit new stars, themselves destined to disappear and to reappear, crystallisations and dispersals followed by new crystallisations had taken place in people's souls. If the Duchesse de Guermantes had been many people to me, such and such a person had been a favourite of Mme. de Guermantes or of Mme. Swann at a period preceding the Dreyfus Affair, and a fanatic or imbecile afterwards because the Dreyfus Affair had changed their social valuations and regrouped people round parties which had since been unmade and remade. Time serves us powerfully by adding its influence to purely intellectual affinities; it is the passage of time that causes us to forget our antipathies, our contempts, and the very causes which gave birth to them. If anyone had formerly analysed the modish elegance of young Mme. Léonor de Cambremer, he would have discovered that she was the niece of the shopkeeper in our courtyard, to wit, Jupien, and that what had especially added to her prestige was that her father procured men for M. de Charlus. Yet, in combination, all this had produced an effect of brilliance, the now distant causes being unknown to most of the newcomers in society and forgotten by those who had been aware of them and valued to-day's effulgence more highly than yesterday's disgrace, for we always take a name at its present-day valuation. So the interest of these social transformations was that they, too, were an effect of lost time and a phenomenon of memory.

Amongst the present company, there was a man of considerable importance who in a recent notorious trial, had given evidence depending for its value on his high moral probity, in deference to which Judge and Counsel had unanimously bowed and the conviction of two people had been brought about. There was a general movement of interest and respect when he entered. It was Morel. I was perhaps the only one present who knew that he had first been kept by M. de Charlus, then by Saint-Loup and simultaneously by a friend of Saint-Loup. In spite of our common recollections, he wished me good day with cordiality though with a certain reserve. He recalled the time when we met at Balbec and those memories represented for him the beauty and melancholy of youth.

But there were people whom I failed to recognise because I had not known them, for time had exercised its chemistry on the composition of society as it had upon people themselves. The milieu, the specific nature of which was defined by affinities which attracted to it the great princely names of Europe and by the repulsion which separated from it any element which was not aristocratic, where I had found a material refuge for that name of Guermantes to which it lent its ultimate reality, had itself been subjected to a profound modification in the essential constitution which I had believed stable. The presence of people whom I had seen in quite other social groupings and who, it had seemed to me, could never penetrate into this one, astonished me less than the intimate familiarity with which they were received and called by their first names; a certain *ensemble* of aristocratic prejudices, of snobbery which until recently automatically protected the name of Guermantes from everything that did not harmonise with it, had ceased to function.

Certain foreigners of distinction, who, when I made my *début* in society, gave grand dinner-parties to which they only invited the Princesse de Guermantes, the Duchesse de Guermantes and the Princesse de Parme, and when they went to those ladies' houses were accorded the place of honour, passing for what was most illustrious in the society of the time, which perhaps they were, had disappeared without leaving a trace. Were they on a diplomatic mission or were they remaining at home? Perhaps a scandal, a suicide, a revolution had prevented their return to society or were they perhaps German? Anyhow, their name only derived its lustre from their former position and was no longer borne by anyone: people did not even know to whom I was alluding and if I tried to spell out their names believed they were "rastaquouères".

The best friends of those who, according to the old social code, ought not to have been there, were to my great astonishment, extremely well-born people who only bothered to come to the Princesse de Guermantes' for their new acquaintances' sake. What most characterised this new society was its prodigious aptitude for breaking up class distinctions.

The springs of a machine which had been strained were bent or broken and no longer worked, a thousand strange bodies penetrated it, deprived it of its homogeneity, its distinction, its colour. The Faubourg Saint-Germain, like a senile duchesse, responded with timid smiles to the insolent servants who invaded its drawing-rooms, drank its orangeade and introduced their mistresses to it. Again I had that sense of time having drained away, of the annihilation of part of my vanished past presented to me less vitally by the destruction of this coherent unity (which the Guermantes' salon had been) of elements whose presence, recurrence and co-ordination were explained by a thousand shades of meaning, by a thousand reasons, than by the fact that the consciousness of those shades and meanings which caused one who was present to be there because he belonged there, because he was there by right while another who elbowed him was a suspicious newcomer, had been itself destroyed. That ignorance was not '. only social but political and of every kind. For the memory of individuals is not coincident with their lives and the younger ones who had never experienced what their elders remembered, now being members of society, very legitimately in the nobiliary sense, the beginnings of certain people being unknown or forgotten, took them where they found them, at the point of their elevation or fall, believing it had always been so, that the Princesse de Guermantes and Bloch had always occupied the highest position and that Clemenceau and Viviani had always been Conservatives. And, as certain facts have greater historic duration than others, the execrated memory of the Dreyfus Affair lingered vaguely in their minds owing to what their fathers had told them and if they were informed that Clemenceau had been a Dreyfusard they replied: "It's not possible; you're making a mistake, he was on the other side." Ministers with a shady past and former prostitutes were held to be paragons of virtue. Someone having asked a young man of good family if there had not been something equivocal in the past of Gilberte's mother, the young aristocrat answered that, as a matter of fact, she had, early in life, married an adventurer called Swann, but afterwards she had married one of the most prominent men in society, the Comte de Forcheville. Doubtless some people in that drawing-room, the Duchesse de Guermantes for instance, would have smiled at this statement (the denial of social qualifications to Swann seeming preposterous to me although formerly at Combray I had believed in common with my great-aunt, that Swann could not possibly know princesses) and so would other women who might have been there, but who now hardly ever went into society, the Duchesses de Montmorency, de Mouchy, de Sagan, who had been Swann's intimate friends, though they had never caught sight of Forcheville who was unknown in society when they frequented it. But society as it was only existed like faces which have changed and blonde hair now white, in the memory of people whose numbers diminished every day. During the war Bloch gave up going about and frequenting his former haunts where he cut a poor figure. On the other hand, he kept on publishing works, the sophistry of which I made a point of repudiating, so as not to be beguiled by it, but which, nevertheless, gave young men and ladies in society the impression of uncommon intellectual depth, even of a sort of genius. It was only after making a complete break between his earlier and his present worldliness that he had entered on a new phase of his life and presented the appearance of a famous and distinguished man in a reconstructed society. Young men were, of course, unaware of his early beginnings in society and the few names he recalled were those of former friends of Saint-Loup which gave a sort of retrospective and undefined elasticity to his present prestige. In any case, he seemed to them one of those men of talent who at all periods have flourished in good society and no one thought he had ever been otherwise.

After I had finished talking to the Prince de Guermantes, Bloch took possession of me and introduced me to a young woman who had often heard the Duchesse de Guermantes speak of me. If those of the new generation considered the Duchesse de Guermantes nothing particular because she knew actresses and others, the ladies of her family, now old, always regarded her as exceptional, partly because they were familiar with her high birth and heraldic distinction and her intimacies with what Mme. de Forcheville would have called in her pseudo-English, "royalties", but also because she disdained going to family parties, was terribly bored by them and they knew they could never count on her. Her theatrical and political associations, which were completely misunderstood, only increased her preciousness in their eyes and, therefore, her prestige. So that whereas in the political and artistic spheres she was a somewhat indefinable being, a sort of *défroquée* of the Faubourg Saint-Germain who goes about with under-secretaries of State and theatrical stars, if anyone in the Faubourg Saint-Germain gave a grand party, they said: "Is it any use inviting Marie Sosthènes? She won't come. Still, for the sake of appearances—but she won't turn up." And if, late in the evening, Marie Sosthènes appeared in a brilliant dress and stood in the doorway with a look of hard contempt for all her relations, if, maybe, she remained an hour, it was a most important party for the dowager who was giving it, in the same way as in early days, when Sarah Bernhardt promised a theatrical manager her assistance upon which he did not count, and not only came but with infinite compliance and simplicity recited twenty pieces instead of one. The presence of Marie Sosthènes, to whom Ministers spoke condescendingly though she, nevertheless, continued to cultivate more and more of them (that being the way of the world) classified the dowager duchess's evening party attended by only the most exclusive ladies above all the other parties given by all the other dowager duchesses that "season" (as again Mme. de Forcheville would have said) at which Marie Sosthènes, one of the most fashionable women of the day, had not taken the trouble to put in an appearance. The name of the young woman to whom Bloch had introduced me was entirely unknown to me and those of the different Guermantes could not be very familiar to her, for she asked an American woman how Mme. de Saint-Loup came to be so intimate with the most distinguished people at the reception. This American was married to the Comte de Furcy, an obscure relative of the Forchevilles who to her represented everything that was most brilliant in society. So she answered in a matter-of-course way: "It's only because she was born a Forcheville, nothing is better than that." Although Mme. de Furcy naïvely believed the name of Forcheville to be superior to that of Saint-Loup, at least she knew who the latter was. But of this, the charming friend of Bloch and of the Duchesse de Guermantes was absolutely ignorant and being somewhat bewildered, when a young girl presently asked her how Mme. de Saint-Loup was related to their host, the Prince de Guermantes, she replied in good faith: "Through the Forchevilles", a piece of information which that young woman passed on, as though she knew all about it, to one of her friends who, having a bad temper and an excitable disposition, got as red as a turkey-cock when a gentleman told her it was not through the Forchevilles that Gilberte belonged to the Guermantes, while he, thinking he had made a mistake, adopted her version and did not hesitate to propagate it. For this American woman, dinner-parties and social functions were a sort of Berlitz school. She repeated names she heard without any knowledge of their significance. Some-one was explaining to someone else that Gilberte had not inherited Tansonville from her father, M. de Forcheville, that it was a family property of her husband's, being close to the Guermantes' estate and originally in the possession of Mme. de Marsantes, but owing to its being heavily mortgaged, had been bought back by Gilberte as a marriage dowry. Finally, a gentleman of the old school reminiscing about Swann being a friend of the Sagans and the Mouchys and Bloch's Amer-ican friend asking him how I came to know Swann, Bloch informed her that I had met him at Mme. de Guermantes', not being aware that I had known him through his being our neighbour in the country and through his being known to my grandfather as a boy. Such mistakes, which are considered serious in all conservative societies, have been made by the most famous men. St.-Simon, to prove that Louis XIV's ignorance was so great that "it caused him sometimes to commit himself in public to the grossest absurdities" only gives two examples of it; the first was that the King being unaware that Rénel belonged to the family of Clermont-Gallerande and that St.-Hérem belonged to that of Montmorin, treated them as men of no standing. So far as St.-Hérem was concerned we are consoled by knowing that the King did not die in error, for he was put right "very late" by M. de la Rochefoucauld. "Moreover," adds St.-Simon with some pity, "he had to explain (to the King) what these families were whose name conveyed nothing to him." The oblivion which so quickly buries the recent past combined with general ignorance, result reactively in erudition being attributed to some little knowledge, the more precious for its rarity, concerning people's genealogies, their real social position, whether such and such a marriage was for love, for money or otherwise; this knowledge is much esteemed in societies where a conservative spirit prevails and my grandfather possessed it to a high degree regarding the bourgeoisdom of Combray and of Paris. St.-Simon esteemed this knowledge so much that, in hold-ing up the Prince de Conti's remarkable intelligence to admiration, before even mentioning the sciences, or rather as as though it were the most important one, he eulogised him for possessing "a very beautiful mind, luminous, just, exact, com-prehensive, infinitely well-stored, which forgot nothing, which was acquainted with genealogy, its chimeras and realities, of distinguished politeness, respecting rank and merit, showing in every way what princes of the blood ought to be and what they no longer are. He even went into details regarding their usurpations and through historical literature and conversations, derived the means of judging what was commendable in their birth and occupation." In less brilliant fashion but with equal accuracy, my grandfather was familiar with everything concerning the *bourgeoisie* of Combray and of Paris and savoured it with no less appreciation. Epicures of that kind who knew that Gilberte was not Forcheville nor Mme. de Cambremer Méséglise nor the youngest a Valintonais were few in number. Few, and perhaps not even recruited from the highest aristocracy (it is not necessarily the devout or even Catholics who are most learned in the Golden Legend or the stained windows of the thirteenth century) but often forming a secondary aristocracy, keener about that with which it hardly has any contact and which on that account it has the more leisure for studying, its members meeting and making each other's acquaintance with satisfaction, enjoying succulent repasts at which genealogies are discussed like the Society of Bibliophiles or the Friends of Rheims. Ladies are not asked to such gatherings, but when the husbands go home, they say to their wives: "I have been to a most interesting dinner; M. de la Raspelière was there and charmed us by explaining that that Mme. de Saint-Loup with the pretty daughter was not born Forcheville at all. It's a regular romance."

The young woman who was a friend of Bloch and of the Duchesse de Guermantes was not only elegant and charming, she was also intelligent and conversation with her was agreeable but was a matter of difficulty to me because not only was the name of my questioner new to me but also those of many to whom she referred and who now apparently formed the basis of society. On the other hand, it was a fact that, in compliance with her wish that I should tell her things, I referred to many who meant nothing to her; they had fallen into oblivion, at all events, those who had shone only with the lustre of their personality and had not the generic permanence of some celebrated aristocratic family the exact title of which the young woman rarely knew, making inaccurate assumptions as to the birth of those whose names she had heard the previous evening at a dinner-party and which, in most cases, she had never heard before, as she only began to go into society some years after I had left it, (partly because she was still young, but also because she had only been living in France a short time and had not got to know people immediately). So, if we had a vocabulary of names in common, the individuals we fitted to them were different. I do not know how the name of Mme. Leroi fell from my lips, but by chance, my questioner had heard it mentioned by some old friend of Mme. de Guermantes who was making up to her. Not as it should have been, however, as was clear from the disdainful answer of the snobbish young woman: "Oh! I know who Mme. Leroi is! She was an old friend of Bergotte's," in a tone which implied "A person I should not want at my house." I knew that Mme. de Guermantes' old friend, as a thorough society man imbued with the Guermantes' spirit, of which one characteristic was not to seem to attach importance to aristocratic intercourse, had not been so ill-bred and anti-Guermantes as to say: "Mme. Leroi who knew all the Highnesses and Duchesses" but had referred to her as "rather an amusing woman. One day she said so and so to Bergotte." But for people who know nothing about these matters, such conversational information is equivalent to what the press gives to the public which believes, according to its paper, alternatively that M. Loubet or M. Reinach are robbers or honourable citizens. In the eyes of my young questioner Mme. Leroi had been a sort of Mme. Verdurin during her first period but with less prestige and the little *clan* limited to Bergotte. By pure chance, this young woman happened to be amongst the last who were likely to hear the name of Mme. Leroi. Today nobody knows anything about her which actually is quite as it should be. Her name does not even figure in the index of Mme. de Villeparisis' posthumous memoirs although Mme. Leroi had been much in her mind. The Marquise did not omit mentioning Mme. Leroi because the latter had not been particularly amiable to her during her life-time but because neither Mme. Leroi's life nor her death were of interest so that the Marquise's silence was dictated less by social umbrage than by literary tact. My conversation with Bloch's smart young friend was agreeable but the difference between our two vocabularies made her uneasy though it was instructive to me. In spite of our knowing that the years go by, that old age gives place to youth, that the most solid fortunes and thrones vanish, that celebrity is a passing thing, our way of rendering this knowledge conscious to ourselves and, so to speak, of accepting the impress of this universe whirled along by time upon our mental retina, is static. So that we always see as young those we knew young and those whom we knew as old people we embellish retrospectively with the virtues of old age, so that we unreservedly pin our faith to the credit of a millionaire and to the protection of a king though our reason tells us that both may be powerless fugitives tomorrow. In the more restricted field of society as in a simple problem which leads up to a more complex one of the same order, the unintelligibleness resulting from my conversation with this young woman owing to our having lived in a particular society at an interval of twenty-five years, impressed me with the importance of history and may have strengthened my own sense of it. The truth is that this ignorance of the real situation which every ten years causes the newly-elected to rise and seem as though the past had never existed, which prevents an American who has just landed knowing that M. de Charlus occupied the highest social position in Paris at a period when Bloch had none whatever, and that Swann who put himself about for M. Bontemps had been the Prince of Wales's familiar friend, that ignorance exists not only among new-comers but also amongst contiguous societies, and, in the case of the last named as in the case of the others is also an effect (now exercised upon the individual instead of on the social curve) of Time. Doubtless we may change our milieu and our manner of life, but our memory retaining the thread of our identical personality attaches to itself, at successive periods, the memory of societies in which we lived, were it forty years earlier. Bloch at the Prince de Guermantes' perfectly remembered the humble Jewish environment in which he had lived when he was eighteen, and Swann, when he no longer loved Mme. Swann but a woman who served tea at Colombin's which, for a time Mme. Swann considered fashionable as she had the Thé de la Rue Royale, perfectly well knew his own social value for he remembered Twickenham and knew why he preferred going to Colombin's rather than to the Duchesse de Broglie's and knew equally well, had he been a thousand times less *"chic"*, that would not have prevented him going to Colombin's or to the Hotel Ritz since anyone can go there who pays. Doubtless too Bloch's or Swann's friends remembered the obscure Jewish society and the invitations to Twickenham and thus friends, like more shadowy selves, of Swann and Bloch did not in their memory separate the elegant Bloch of to-day from the sordid Bloch of formerly or the Swann who went to Colombin's in his old age from the Swann of Buckingham Palace. But, in life, those friends were, in some measure, Swann's neighbours, their lives had developed sufficiently near his for their memory to contain him; whereas in the case of others further away from Swann, not exactly socially but in intimacy, who had known him more vaguely and whose meetings with him had been rarer, memories as numerous had given rise to more superficial views of his personality. And, such strangers, after thirty years, remember nothing accurately enough about a particular individual's past to modify what he represents to their view in the present. I had heard people in society say of Swann in his last years, as though it were his title to celebrity: "Are you talking about the Swann who goes to Colombin's?" Now, I heard people who ought to have known better, remark in alluding to Bloch, "Do you mean the Guermantes Bloch, the intimate friend of the Guermantes?" These mistakes, which cut a life in two and, isolating him in the present, construct another man, a creation of yesterday, a man who is the mere compendium of his present-day habits (whereas he bears within himself the continuity which links him to his past) these mistakes are also the effect of time, but they are not a social phenomenon, they are a phenomenon of memory. At that instant an example presented itself of a quite different kind, it is true, but on that account the more striking, of those oblivions which modify our conception of people. Mme. de Guermantes' young nephew, the Marquis de Villemandois, had formerly displayed a persistent insolence towards me which had induced me, in a spirit of reprisal, to adopt so offensive an attitude towards him that we had tacitly become enemies. Whilst I was reflecting about time at this afternoon party at the Princesse de Guermantes' he asked to be introduced to me and then told me he was under the impression that I had been acquainted with his parents, that he had read some of my articles and wanted to make or remake my acquaintance. It is true that with increasing age he, like many overbearing people of a weightier sort, had become less supercilious and, moreover, I was being talked about in his set because of articles (of small importance for that matter) I had been writing. But these grounds for his cordiality and advances were only accessory. The chief one, or at least the one which brought others into play, was that, either because he had a worse memory than I or attached less significance to my reprisals than I to his attacks, owing to my being less important in his eyes than he in mine, he had entirely forgotten our hostility. At most, my name recalled to his mind that he had seen me or somebody belonging to me at one of his aunt's houses and not being quite certain whether he had met me before or not, he at once started talking about his aunt at whose house he thought he might have met me, remembering he had often heard me spoken of there but not remembering our quarrel. Often a name is all that remains to us of a being, not only when he is dead but even while he is alive. And our memories about him are so vague and peculiar, correspond so little to the reality of the past that though we entirely forget that we nearly fought a duel with him, we remember that, when he was a child, he wore odd-looking yellow gaiters in the Champs Elysées, of which, although we remind him of them, he has no recollection. Bloch had come in, leaping like a hyena. I thought, "He's coming into a drawing-room which he could never have penetrated twenty years ago." But he was also twenty years older and he was nearer death, what good will it do him? Looking at him closely, I perceived in the face upon which the light now played, which from further away and when less illumined seemed to reflect youthful gaiety whether because it actually survived there or I evoked it, the almost alarming visage of an old Shylock anxiously awaiting in the wings the moment to appear upon the stage, reciting his first lines under his breath. In ten years he would limp into these drawing-rooms dragging his feet over their heavy piled carpets, a master at last, and would be bored to death by having to go to the La Trémouilles. How would that profit him?

I could the better elicit from these social changes truths sufficiently important to serve as a unifying factor in a portion of my work that they were not, as I might at first have been tempted to believe, peculiar to our period. At the time when I had hardly reached the point of entering the Guermantes' circle, I was more of a new-comer than Bloch himself to-day and I must then have observed human elements which, though integrated in it, were entirely foreign to it, recently assembled elements which must have seemed strangely new to the older set from whom I did not differentiate them and who, believed by the dukes to have always been members of the faubourg, had either themselves been *parvenus* or if not they, their fathers or grandfathers. So it was not the quality of its members which made that society brilliant but its power to assimilate more or less completely people who fifty years later would appear just as good as those who now belonged to it. Even in the past with which I associated the name of Guermantes in order to do it honour in the fullest measure, with reason moreover, for under Louis XIV the semi-royal Guermantes were more supreme than to-day, the phenomenon I had studied was equally apparent. For instance, had they not then allied themselves by marriage with the Colbert family, to-day Considered of high degree, since a Rochefoucauld considers a Colbert a good match. But it was not because the Col-berts, then plain bourgeois, were noble that the Guermantes formed alliances with them, it was they who became noble by marrying into the Guermantes family. If the name of Haussonville is extinguished with the death of the present representative of that family, he will perhaps derive his distinction from being descended from Mme. de Staël, while, before the Revolution, M. d'Haussonville, one of the first gentlemen in the kingdom, gratified his vanity as towards M. de Broglie by not deigning to know M. de Staël's father and by no more condescending to introduce him to M. de Broglie than the latter would have done to M. d'Haussonville, never imagining that his own son would marry the daughter, his friend's son the grand-daughter of the authoress of *Corinne*. I realised from the way that the Duchesse de Guermantes talked to me that I might have cut a figure in society as an untitled man of fashion who is accepted as having always belonged to the aristocracy like Swann in former days and after him M. Lebrun and M. Ampère, all of them friends of the Duchesse de Broglie who herself at the beginning was, so to speak, hardly in the best society. The first times I had dined at Mme. de Guermantes' how often I must have shocked men like M. de Beaucerfeuil, less by my presence than by remarks showing that I was entirely ignorant of the associations which constituted his past and gave form to his social experience. Bloch would, when very old, preserve memories of the Guermantes' salon as it appeared to him now ancient enough for him to feel the same surprise and resentment as M. de Beaucerfeuil at certain intrusions and ignorances. And besides, he would have acquired and dispensed amongst those about him qualities of tact and discretion which I had believed to be the particular gift of men like M. de Norpois and which are incarnated in those who seem to us most likely to be deficient in them. Moreover, I had supposed myself exceptional in being admitted into the Guermantes set. But when I got away from myself and my immediate ambient, I observed that this social phenomenon was not as isolated as it first seemed and that from the Combray basin where I was born many jets of water had risen, like myself, above the liquid pool which was their source. Of course, circumstances and individual character have always a share in the matter and it was in quite different ways that Legrandin (by the curious marriage of his nephew) had in his turn penetrated this *milieu*, that Odette's daughter had become related to it, that Swann and finally I myself, had entered it. To myself who had been enclosed within my life, seeing it from within, Legrandin's way appeared to have no relevance to mine and to have gone in another direction, in the same way as one who follows the course of a river through a deep valley does not see that, in spite of its windings, it is the same stream. But, from the bird's eye view of a statistician who ignores reasons of sentiment and the imprudences which lead to the death of an individual and only counts the number of people who die in a year, one could observe that many people starting from the same environment as that with which the beginning of this narrative has been concerned reach another quite different and it is likely that, just as in every year there are an average number of marriages, any other well-to-do and refined bourgeois *milieu* would have furnished about the same proportion of people like Swann, like Legrandin, like myself and like Bloch, who would be rediscovered in the ocean of "Society". Moreover they are recognisable, for if young Comte de Cambremer impressed society with his grace, distinction and modishness, I recognised in those qualities as in his good looks and ardent ambition, the characteristics of his uncle Legrandin, that is to say, an old and very bourgeois friend of my parents, though one who had an aristocratic bearing.

Kindness, which is simply maturity, ends in sweetening natures originally more acid than Bloch's, and is as prevalent as that sense of justice which, if we are in the right, should make us fear a prejudiced judge as little as one who is our friend. And Bloch's grand-children would be well-mannered and discreet from birth. Bloch had perhaps not reached that point yet. But I remarked that he who formerly affected to be compelled to take a two hours' railway-journey to see someone who hardly wanted to see him, now that he received many invitations not only to luncheon and to dinner but to come and spend a fortnight here and there, refused many of them without talking about it or boasting he had received them. Discretion in action and in words had come to him with age and social position, a sort of social old-age, one might say. Undoubtedly Bloch was formerly as indiscreet as he was incapable of kindness and friendly service. But certain defects and certain qualities belong less to one or another individual from the social point of view than to one or another period of his life. They are almost exterior to individuals who pass through the projection of their light as at varying solstices which are pre-existent, universal and inevitable. Doctors who want to find out whether a particular medicine has diminished or increased the acidity of the stomach, whether it quickens or lessens its secretions, obtain results which differ, not according to the stomach from the secretions of which they have extracted a little gastric juice, but according to the effects disclosed at an early or late stage through the action of the medicine upon it.

Thus at each of the moments of its duration the name of Guermantes considered as a unity of all the names admitted within and about itself suffered some dispersals, recruited new elements like gardens where flowers only just in bud yet about to replace others already faded, are indistinguishable from the mass which seems the same save to those who have not observed the new-comers and keep in their mind's eye the exact picture of those that have disappeared.

More than one of the persons whom this afternoon party had collected or whose memory it evoked, provided me with the successive appearances he had presented under widely dissimilar circumstances. The individual rose before me again as he had been and, in doing so, called forth the various aspects of my own life, like different perspectives in a countryside where a hill or a castle seems at one moment to be to the right, at another to the left, to dominate a forest or emerge from a valley, thus reminding the traveller of changes of direction and altitude in the road he has been following. As I went further and further back I finally discovered pictures of the same individual, separated by such long intervals, represented by such distinct personalities, with such different meanings that, as a rule, I eliminated them from my field of recollection when I believed I had made contact with them, and often ceased believing they were the same people I had formerly known. Chance illumination was required for me to be able to attach them, like in an etymology, to the original significance they had for me. Mlle. Swann throwing some thorny roses to me from the other side of the hedge, with a look I had retrospectively attributed to desire; the lover, according to Combray gossip, of Mme. Swann, staring at me from behind that same hedge with a hard look which also did not warrant the interpretation I gave to it then and who had changed so completely since I failed to recognise him at Balbec as the gentleman looking at a notice near the casino, and whom I happened to think of once every ten years, saying to myself: "That was M. de Charlus, how curious!", Mme. de Guermantes at Dr. Percepied's wedding, Mme. Swann in pink at my great-uncle's, Mme. de Cambremer, Legrandin's sister, who was so smart that he was afraid we should want him to introduce us to her, and so many more pictures of Swann, Saint-Loup, etc. which, when I recalled them, I liked now and then to use as a frontispiece on the threshold of my relations with these different people but which actually seemed to me mere fancies rather than impressions left upon my mind by the individual with whom there was no longer any link. It is not only that certain people have the power of remembering and others not (without living in a state of permanent oblivion like Turkish ambassadors) which always enables the latter to find room—the new precedent having vanished in a week or the following one having exorcised it— for a fresh item of news contradicting the last. Even if memories are equal, two persons do not remember the same things. One would hardly notice an act which another would feel intense remorse about while he will grasp at a word almost unconsciously let fall by the other as though it were a characteristic sign of good-will. Self-interest implicit in not being wrong in our prejudgment limits the time we shall remember it and encourages us to believe we never indulged in it. Finally, a deeper and more unselfish interest diversifies memories so thoroughly that a poet who has forgotten nearly all the facts of which one reminds him retains a fugitive impression of them. As a result of all this, after twenty years' absence one discovers involuntary and unconscious forgiveness instead of anticipated resentments and on the other hand, hatreds the cause of which one cannot explain (because one has forgotten the bad impression one had made). One forgets dates as one does the history of people one has known best. And because twenty years had passed since Mme. de Guermantes had first seen Bloch, she would have sworn that he was born in her set and had been nursed by the Duchesse de Chartres when he was two years old.

How many times these people had returned to my vision in the course of their lives, the differing circumstances of which seemed to offer identical characteristics under diverse forms and for various ends; and the diversity of my own life at its turning-points through which the thread of each of these lives had passed was compounded of lives seemingly the most distant from my own as if life itself only disposed of a limited number of threads for the execution of the most varied designs. What, for instance, were more separate in my various pasts than my visits to my Uncle Adolphe, than the nephew of Mme. de Villeparisis, herself cousin of the Marshal, than Legrandin and his sister, than the former waistcoat maker, Françoise's friend in the court-yard of our home. And now all these different threads had been united to produce here, the woof of the Saint-Loup *ménage*, there, that of the young Cambremers, not to mention Morel and so many others the conjunction of which had combined to form circumstances so compact that they seemed to make a unity of which the personages were mere elements. And my life was already long enough for me to have found in more than one case a being to complete another in the conflicting spheres of my memory. To an Elstir whose fame was now assured I could add my earliest memories of the Verdurins, of the Cottards, of conversations in Rivebelle restaurant on the morning when I first met Albertine and many others. In the same way, a collector who is shown the wing of an altar screen, remembers the church or museum or private collection in which the others are dispersed (as also, by following sale-catalogues or searching among dealers in antiques, he finally discovers the twin object to the one he possesses which makes them a pair and thus can mentally reconstitute the predella and the entire altar-piece). As a bucket let down or hauled up a well by a windlass touches the rope or the sides every now and then, there was not a personage, hardly even an event in my life, which had not at one time or another played different parts. If, after years I rediscovered the simplest social relationship or even a material object in my memory, I perceived that life had been ceaselessly weaving threads about it which in the end became a beautiful velvet covering like the emerald sheath of a water-conduit in an ancient park.

It was not only in appearance that these people were like dream-figures, their youth and love had become to themselves a dream. They had forgotten their very resentments and hatreds and, to be sure that this individual was the one they had not spoken to for ten years, they would have needed a register which even then would have had the vagueness of a dream in which an insult has been offered them by one unknown. Such dreams account for those contrasts in political life where people who once accused each other of murder and treason are members of the same Government. And dreams become as opaque as death in the case of old men on days following those of love-making. On such days no one was allowed to ask the President of the Republic any questions; he had forgotten everything. After he had been allowed to rest for some days, the recollection of public affairs returned to him fortuitously as in a dream. Sometimes it was not a single image only that presented itself to my mind of one whom I had since known to be so different. It was during the same years that Bergotte had seemed a sweet, divine old man to me that I had been paralysed at the sight of Swann's grey hat and his wife's violet cloak, by the glamour of race which surrounded the Duchesse de Guermantes even in a drawing-room as though I stood gazing at ghosts; almost fabulous origins of relationships subsequently so banal which these charming myths lengthened into the past with the brilliance projected into the heavens by the sparkling tail of a comet. And even relations such as mine with Mme. de Souvré, which had not begun in mystery, which were to-day so hard and worldly, revealed themselves at their beginnings in a smile, calm, soft and flatteringly expressed in the fulness of an afternoon by the sea, on a spring evening in Paris in the midst of smart equipages, of clouds of dust, of sunshine moving like water. And perhaps Mme. de Souvré would not have been worth while if she had been detached from her frame like those monuments—the Salute for instance—which, without any great beauty of their own are so perfectly adapted to their site, and she had her place in a collection of memories which I estimated at a certain price, taking one with another, without going too closely into the particular value of Mme. de Souvré's personality.

A thing by which I was more impressed, in the case of people who had undergone physical and social change was the different notion they had of each other. In old days Legrandin despised Bloch and never spoke to him; now he was most amiable to him. It was not in the least owing to Bloch's more prominent position which in this case was negligible, for social changes inevitably bring about respective changes in position amongst those who have been subjected to them. No. It was that people, that is, people as we see them, do not retain the uniformity of a picture when we look back on them. They evolve in relation to our forgetfulness. Sometimes we even go so far as to confuse them with others. "Bloch, that's the man who came from Combray," and when he said Bloch, the person meant me. Inversely Mme. Sazerat was convinced that a historical thesis on Philippe II was by me whereas it was by Bloch. Apart from these substitutions one forgets the bad turns people have done us, their unpleasantness, one forgets that last time we parted without shaking hands and, in contrast, we remember an earlier period when we were on good terms. Legrandin's affability with Bloch was referable to that earlier period, whether because he had forgotten a phase of his past or that he judged it better to ignore it, a mixture, in fact, of forgiveness, forgetfulness and indifference which is also an effect of Time. Moreover, even in love, the memories we have of each other are not the same. I had known Albertine to remind me in the most remarkable way of something I had said to her during the early days of our acquaintance which I had completely forgotten while she had no recollection whatever of another fact implanted in my head like a stone for ever. Our parallel lives resemble paths bordered at intervals by flower-vases placed symmetrically but not facing each other. It is still more comprehensible that one hardly remembers who the people were one knew slightly or one remembers something else about them further back, something suggested by those amongst whom one meets them again who have only just made their acquaintance and endow them with qualities and a position they never had but which the forgetful person wholly accepts.

Doubtless life, in casting these people upon my path on different occasions, had presented them in surrounding circumstances which had shrunk my view of them and prevented my knowing their essential characters. Of those Guermantes even, who had been the subject of such wonderful dreams, at my first approach to them, one had appeared in the guise of an old friend of my grandmother's, another in that of a gentleman who had stared at me so unpleasantly in the grounds of the casino (for, between us and other beings there is a borderland of contingencies, as, from my readings at Combray, I knew there was one of perceptions which prevent reality and mind being placed in absolute contact). So that it was only after the event, by relating them to a name, that my acquaintance with them had become to me acquaintance with the Guermantes. But perhaps it was that very thing which made life seem more poetic to me when I thought about that mysterious race with the piercing eyes and beaks of birds, that pink, golden, unapproachable race which the force of blind and differing circumstances had presented so naturally to my observation, to my intercourse, even to my intimacy, that when I wanted to know Mlle. de Stermaria or to have dresses made for Albertine, I applied to the Guermantes, as to my most helpful friends. Certainly it bored me at times to go and see them as to go and see others I knew in society. The charm of the Duchesse de Guermantes, even, like that of certain of Bergotte's pages, was only discernible to me at a distance and disappeared when I was near her, for it lay in my memory and in my imagination, and yet, the Guermantes, like Gilberte, were different from other people in society in that their roots were plunged more deeply in my past when I dreamed more and believed more in individuals. That past filled me with weariness while talking to one or the other of them, for it was associated with those imaginings of my childhood which had once seemed the most beautiful and inaccessible and I had to console myself by confusing the value of their possession with the price at which my desire had appraised them like a merchant whose books are in disorder. But my past relations with other beings were magnified by dreams more ardent and hopeless with which my life opened so richly, so entirely dedicated to them that I could hardly understand how it was that what they yielded was this exiguous, narrow, mournful ribbon of a despised and unloved intimacy in which I could discover no trace of what had once been their mystery, their fever and their loveliness.

* * *

"What has become of the Marquise d'Arpajon?" asked Mme. de Cambremer. "She's dead," answered Bloch. "You're confusing her with the Comtesse d'Arpajon who died last year," the Princesse de Malte joined the discussion. The young widow of a very wealthy old husband, the bearer of a great name, she had been much sought in marriage and from that had derived a great deal of self-assurance. "The Marquise d'Arpajon died too about a year ago." "I can assure you it isn't a year," answered Mme. de Cambremer. "I was at a musical party at her house less than a year ago." Bloch could no more take part in the discussion than a society gigolo for all these deaths of aged people were too far away from him, whether owing to the great difference in age or to his recent entry into a different society which he approached, as it were, from the side, at a period of its decline into a twilight in which the memory of an unfamiliar past could not illuminate it. And for those of the same age and of the same society death had lost its strange significance. Moreover every day people were at the point of death of whom some recovered while others succumbed, so that one was not certain whether a particular individual one rarely saw had recovered from his cold on the chest or whether he had passed away. Deaths multiplied and lives became increasingly uncertain in those aged regions. At these crossroads of two generations and two societies which for different reasons were ill-placed for identifying death, it became confused with life, the former had been socialised and become an incident, which qualified a person more or less without the tone in which it was mentioned signifying that this incident ended everything so far as that person was concerned. So people said: "You've forgotten. So and so is dead," as they might have said: "He's decorated, he's a member of the Academy," or—which came to the same thing as it prevented his coming to parties—"he has gone to spend the winter in the south," or "he's been ordered to the mountains." In the case of well-known men, what they left helped people to remember they were dead. But in the case of ordinary members of society, people got muddled about whether they were dead or not, partly because they did not know them well and had forgotten their past but more because they bothered little about the future one way or the other. And the difficulty people had in sorting out marriages, absences, retirements to the country and deaths of old people in society equally illustrated the insignificance of the dead and the indifference of the living.

"But if she's not dead how is it one doesn't see her any more nor her husband either?" asked an old maid who liked to be thought witty. "I tell you," answered her mother who, though fifty years old, never missed a party, "it's because they're old and at that age people don't go out." It was as though there lay in front of the cemetery a closed city of the aged with lamps always alight in the fog. Mme. de Sainte-Euverte closed the debate by saying that the Comtesse d'Arpajon had died the year before after a long illness, but the Marquise d'Arpajon had also died suddenly "from some quite trifling cause," a death which thus resembled the lives of them all and, in the same fashion, explained that she had passed away without anyone being aware of it and excused those who had made a mistake. Hearing that Mme. d'Arpajon was really dead, the old maid cast an alarmed glance at her mother fearing that the news of the death of one of her contemporaries might be a shock to her; she imagined in anticipation people alluding to her own mother's death by explaining that "she died as the result of a shock through the death of Mme. d'Arpajon." But on the contrary, her mother's expression was that of having won a competition against formidable rivals whenever anyone of her own age passed away. Their death was her only means of being agreeably conscious of her own existence. The old maid, aware that her mother had not seemed sorry to say that Mme. d'Arpajon was a recluse in those dwellings from which the aged and tired seldom emerge, noticed that she was still less upset to hear that the Marquise had entered that ultimate abode from which no one returns. This affirmation of her mother's indifference aroused the caustic wit of the old maid. And, later on, to amuse her friends, she gave a humorous imitation of the lively fashion with which her mother rubbed her hands as she said: "Goodness me, so that poor Mme. d'Arpajon is dead." She thus pleased even those who did not need death to make them glad they were alive. For every death is a simplification of life for the survivors; it relieves them of being grateful and of being obliged to make visits. Nevertheless, as I have said, M. Verdurin's death was not thus welcomed by Elstir.

* * *

A lady went out for she had other afternoon receptions to go to and she was to take tea with two queens. She was the society courtesan I formerly knew, the Princesse de Nissau. Apart from her figure having shrunk—which gave her head the appearance of being lower than it was formerly, of having what is called "one foot in the grave"—one would have said that she had hardly aged. She remained, with her Austrian nose and delightful mien a Marie-Antoinette preserved, embalmed, thanks to a thousand cunningly combined cosmetics which gave her face the hue of lilac. Her face wore that regretful soft expression of being compelled to go with a sweet half-promise to return, of inconspicuous withdrawal because of numerous exclusive invitations. Born almost on the steps of a throne, married three times, protected long and luxuriously by great bankers, the confused memories of her innumerable pasts, not to speak of the caprices she had indulged, weighed on her as lightly as her beautiful round eyes, her painted face and her mauve dress. As, taking French leave, she passed me, I bowed and she, taking my hand, fixed her round violet orbs upon me as if to say: "How long since we met, do let us talk of it next time." She pressed my hand, not quite sure whether there had or had not been a passage between us that evening she drove me from the Duchesse de Guermantes'. She merely took a chance by seeming to suggest something that had never been, which was not difficult for she looked tender over a strawberry-tart and assumed, about her compulsion to leave before the music was over, an attitude of despairing yet reassuring abandonment. Moreover, in her uncertainty about the incident with me, her furtive pressure did not detain her long and she did not say a word. She only looked at me in a way that said: "How long! How long!" as there passed across her vision her husbands, the different men who had kept her, two wars—and her star-like eyes, like astronomic dials carved in opal, registered in quick succession all those solemn hours of a far-away past she conjured back each time she uttered a greeting which was always an excuse. She left me and floated to the door so as not to disturb me, to show me that if she did not stop and talk to me it was because she had to make up the time she had lost pressing my hand so as not to keep the Queen of Spain waiting. She seemed to go through the door at racing-pace. And she was, as a fact, racing to her grave.

Meanwhile, the Princesse de Guermantes kept repeating in an excited way in the metallic voice caused by her false teeth: "That's it, we'll form a group. I love the intelligence of youth, it so co-operates! Ah, what a 'mugician' you are." She was talking with her large eyeglass in a round eye which was partly amused and partly excusing itself for not being able to keep it up but till the end she decided to "co-operate" and "form a group".

* * *

I sat down by the side of Gilberte de Saint-Loup. We talked a great deal about Robert. Gilberte alluded to him deferentially as to a superior being whom she wanted me to know she admired and understood. We reminded each other that many of the ideas he had formerly expressed about the art of war (for he had often exposed the same theses at Tansonville as at Doncières and later) had been verified by the recent one. "I can't tell you how much the slightest thing he told me at Doncières strikes me now as it did during the war. The last words I heard him say when we parted never to meet again were that he was expecting of Hindenburg, a Napoleonic General, a type of Napoleonic battle the object of which is to separate two adversaries, perhaps, he said, the English and ourselves. Now scarcely a year after Robert's death a critic whom he much admired and who obviously exercised great influence on his military ideas, M. Henri Bidou, said that Hindenburg's offensive in March, 1918 was 'a battle of separation by one adversary massed against two in line, a manœuvre which the Emperor successfully executed in 1796 on the Apennines and failed with in 1815 in Belgium'. Some time before that Robert was comparing battles with plays in which it is sometimes difficult to know what the author means because he has changed his plot in the course of the action. Now, as to this interpretation of the German offensive of 1918, Robert would certainly not be of M. Bidou's opinion. But other critics think that Hindenburg's success in the direction of Amiens, then his forced halt then his success in Flanders, then again the halt, accidentally made Amiens and afterwards Boulogne objectives he had not previously planned. And as everyone can reconstruct a play in his own way, there are those who see in this offensive the threat of a terrific march on Paris, others disordered hammer blows to annihilate the English Army. And even if the General's orders are opposed to one or the other conception, critics will always be able to say, as Mounet-Sully did to Coquelin who affirmed that the 'Misanthrope' was not the depressing drama he made it appear (for Molière's contemporaries testify that his interpretation was comic and made people laugh): 'Well, then, Molière made a mistake.'"

"And you remember," Gilberte replied, "what he said about aeroplanes, he expressed himself so charmingly, every army must be an Argus with a hundred eyes. Alas, he did not live to see the verification of his predictions." "Oh, yes, he did," I answered, "he knew very well that, at the battle of the Somme, they were beginning to blind the enemy by piercing his eyes, destroying his aeroplanes and captive balloons." "Oh yes! So they did." Since she had taken to living in her mind, she had become somewhat pedantic. "And it was he who foretold a return to the old methods. Do you know that the Mesopotamian expeditions in this war" (she must have read this at the time in Brichot's articles) "keep reminding one of the retreat of Xenophon; to get from the Tigris to the Euphrates the English Commander made use of canoes, long narrow boats, the gondolas of that country, which the ancient Chaldeans had made use of." Her words gave me that feeling of stagnation in the past which is immobilised in certain places by a sort of specific gravity to such a degree that one finds it just as it was. I avow that, thinking of my readings at Balbec, not far from Robert, I had been much impressed—as I was when I discovered Mme. de Sévigné's intrenchment in the French countryside—to observe, in connection with the siege of Kut-el-Amara (Kut-the-Emir just as we say Vaux-le-Vicomte, Boilleau-l'Evêque, as the curé of Combray would have said if his thirst for etymology had extended to Oriental languages) the recurrence, near Bagdad, of that name Bassorah about which we hear so much in the *Thousand and One Nights*, whence, long before General Townsend, Sinbad the Sailor, in the times of the Caliphs, embarked or disembarked whenever he left or returned to Bagdad.

"There was a side of the war he was beginning to perceive," I said, "which is that it is human, that it is lived like a love or a hatred, can be recounted like a romance, and consequently if people keep on repeating that strategy is a science, it does not help them to understand it because it is not strategic. The enemy no more knows our plans than we know the motive of a woman we love, and perhaps we do not know ours either. In the offensive of March, 1918 was the object of the Germans to take Amiens? We know nothing about it. Perhaps they did not either and it was their advance westwards towards Amiens which determined their plan. Even admitting that war is scientific it is still necessary to paint it like Elstir painted the sea, by the use of another sense and using imagination and beliefs as a starting-point, to rectify them little by little as Dostoevski narrated a life. Moreover, it is but too obvious that war is rather medical than strategic since it brings in its train unforeseen accidents the clinician hopes to avoid, such as the Russian Revolution."

Throughout this conversation, Gilberte had spoken of Robert with a deference which seemed rather addressed to my former friend than to her dead husband. She seemed to be saying: "I know how much you admired him, believe me, I knew and understood what a superior creature he was." And yet the love she certainly no longer felt for his memory may perhaps have been the distant cause of the peculiarities in her present life. For Andrée was now Gilberte's inseparable friend. Although the former had for some time, chiefly because of her husband's talent, begun to enter, not, of course, the Guermantes set but an infinitely more fashionable society than that which she formerly frequented, people were astonished that the Marquise de Saint-Loup condescended to become her best friend. That fact seemed to be a sign of Gilberte's preference for what she believed to be an artistic life and for a positive social forfeiture. That may be the true explanation. Another, however, came to my mind, always convinced that images assembled somewhere are generally the reflection or in some fashion the effect of a former grouping different from though symmetrical with other images extremely distant from the second group. I thought that if Andrée, her husband and Gilberte were seen together every evening it was possibly because many years earlier Andrée's future husband had lived with Rachel and then left her for Andrée. It is probable that Gilberte lived in a society too far removed from and above theirs to know anything about it. But she must have learned of it later when Andrée went up and she came down enough for them to meet. Then the woman for whom a man had abandoned Rachel although she, Rachel, preferred him to Robert, must have been dowered with much prestige in the eyes of Gilberte.

In the same way, perhaps, the sight of Andrée recalled to Gilberte the youthful romance of her love for Robert and also inspired her respect for Andrée who was still loved by the man so adored by Rachel whom Gilberte knew Saint-Loup had preferred to herself. Perhaps, on the other hand, these memories played no part in Gilberte's predilection for this artistic couple and it was only the result, as in many other cases, of the development of tastes common amongst society women for acquiring new experience and simultaneously lowering themselves. Perhaps Gilberte had forgotten Robert as completely as I had Albertine and even if she knew it was Rachel whom the artist had left for Andrée she never thought about it because it never played any part in her liking for them. The only way of ascertaining whether my first explanation was either possible or true would have been through the evidence of the interested parties and then only if they proffered their confidence with clarity and sincerity. And the first is rarely met with, the second never.

"But how is it that you are here at this crowded reception?" asked Gilberte. "It's not like you to come to a massacre like this. I might have expected to meet you anywhere rather than in one of these omnium-gatherums of my aunt; she is my aunt you know," she added subtly; for having become Mme. de Saint-Loup considerably before Mme. Verdurin entered the family, she considered herself a Guermantes from the beginning of time and, in consequence, affected by the *mésalliance* of her uncle with Mme. Verdurin whom, it is true, she had heard the family laugh at a thousand times whereas, of course, it was only when she was not there that they alluded to the *mesalliance* of Saint-Loup and herself. She affected, moreover the greater disdain for this undistinguished aunt because the Princesse de Guermantes, owing to a sort of perversity which impels intelligent people to escape from the bondage of fashion, also owing to the need displayed by ageing people of memories that will form a background to their newly acquired position, would say about Gilberte: "That's no new relationship for me, I knew the young woman's mother very well; why, she was my cousin Marsantes' great friend. It was at my house she met Gilberte's father. As to poor Saint-Loup, I used to know all his family, his uncle was once an intimate friend of mine at La Raspelière." "You see, the Verdurins were not Bohemians at all," people said to me when they heard the Princesse de Guermantes talk in that way, "they were old friends of Mme. de Saint-Loup's family." I was, perhaps, the only one who knew, through my grandfather, that indeed the Verdurins were not Bohemians, but it was not exactly because they had known Odette. But it is as easy to give accounts of the past which nobody knows anything about as it is of travels in countries where no one has ever been. "Well," concluded Gilberte, "as you do sometimes emerge from your ivory tower, would not a little intimate party at my house amuse you? I should invite sympathetic souls who would be more to your taste. A big affair like this is not for you. I saw you talking to my Aunt Oriane who may have the best qualities in the world but we shouldn't be libelling her, should we, if we said she doesn't belong to the *élite* of the mind?" I could not impart to Gilberte the thoughts which had occupied me during the last hour but I thought she might provide me with distraction which, however, I should not get from talking literature with the Duchesse de Guermantes nor with her either. Certainly I intended to start afresh from the next day to live in solitude but, this time, with a real object. Even at my own house I should not let people come to see me during my working hours, for my duty to my work was more important than that of being polite or even kind. Doubtless, those who had not seen me for a long time would come, and believing me restored to health, would be insistent. When their day's work was finished or interrupted, they would insist on coming, having need of me as I once had of Saint-Loup, because, as had happened at Combray when my parents reproached me just when, unknown to them, I was forming the most praiseworthy resolution, the internal timepieces allotted to mankind are not all regulated to the same hour; one strikes the hour of rest when another strikes that of work, one that of a judge's sentence when the guilty has repented and that of his inner perfectioning has struck long before. But to those who came to see me or sent for me, I should have the courage to answer that I had an urgent appointment about essential matters it was necessary for me to regulate without further delay, an appointment of capital importance with myself. And yet, though indeed there be little relation between our real self and the other—because of their homonymy and their common body, the abnegation which makes us sacrifice easier duties, pleasures even, seems to others egoism. Moreover, was it not to concern myself with them that I was going to live far apart from those who would complain that they never saw me, to concern myself with them more fundamentally than I could have done in their presence, so that I might reveal them to themselves, make them realise themselves. How would it have profited if, for years longer, I had wasted my nights by letting the words they had just uttered fade into an equally vain echo of my own, for the sake of the sterile pleasure of a social contact which excludes all penetrating thought? Would it not be better I should try to describe the curve, to elicit the law that governed their gestures, their words, their lives, their nature? Unhappily, I should be compelled to fight against that habit of putting myself in another's place which, though it may favour the conception of a work retards its execution. For, through an excess of politeness it makes us sacrifice to others not merely our pleasure but our duty even though putting oneself in the place of others, duty, whatever form it may take, even, were it helpful, that of remaining at the rear when one can render no service at the front, appears contrary to the truth, to be our pleasure. And far from believing myself unhappy because of a life without friends, without conversation, as some of the greatest have believed, I realised that the force and elation spent in friendship are a sort of false passport to an individual intimacy that leads nowhere and turns us back from a truth to which they might have conducted us. But anyhow, should intervals of repose and social intercourse be necessary to me, I felt that instead of the intellectual conversations which society people believe interesting to writers, light loves with young flowering girls would be the nourishment I might, at the most, allow my imagination, like the famous horse which was fed on nothing but roses. All of a sudden I longed again for what I had dreamed of at Balbec, when I saw Albertine and Andrée disporting themselves with their friends on the sea-shore before I knew them. But alas, those I now so much longed for, I could find no more. The years which had transformed all those I had seen to-day including Gilberte herself must, beyond question, have made of the other survivors as, had she not perished, of Albertine, women very different from the girls I remembered. I suffered at the thought of their attaint for time's changes do not modify the images in our memory. There is nothing more painful than the contrast between the alteration in beings and the fixity of memory, than the realisation that what our memory keeps green has decayed and that there can be no exterior approach to the beauty within us which causes so great a yearning to see it once more. The intense desire for those girls of long ago which my memory excited, could never be quenched unless I sought its satisfaction in another being as young. I had often suspected that what seems unique in a creature we desire does not belong to that individual. But the passage of time gave me completer proof, since after twenty years I now wanted, instead of the girls I had known, those possessing their youth. Moreover, it is not only the awakening of physical desire that corresponds to no reality because it ignores the passing of time. At times I prayed that, by a miracle, my grandmother and Albertine had, in spite of my reason, survived and would come to me. I believed I saw them, my heart leaped towards them. But I forgot that, if they had been alive, Albertine would almost have the appearance of Mme. Cottard at Balbec and that my grandmother at ninety-five would not exhibit the beautiful, calm, smiling face I still imagined hers as arbitrarily as we picture God the Father with a beard or as, in the seventeenth century, the heroes of Homer were represented in the company of noblemen with no regard to chronology. I looked at Gilberte and I did not think, "I should like to see you again." But I told her it would certainly give me pleasure if she invited me to meet young girls, of whom I should ask no more than to evoke reveries and sorrows of former days, perhaps, on some unlikely day, to allow me the privilege of one chaste kiss. As Elstir loved to see incarnated in his wife the Venetian beauty he so often painted in his works, I excused myself for being attracted through a certain aesthetic egoism towards beautiful women who might cause me suffering, and I cultivated a sort of idolatry for future Gilbertes, future Duchesses de Guermantes and Albertines who I thought might inspire me like a sculptor in the midst of magnificent antique marbles. I ought, nevertheless, to have remembered that each experience had been preceded by my sense of the mystery which pervaded them and that, instead of asking Gilberte to introduce me to young girls I should have done better to journey to those shores where nothing binds them to us, where an impassable gulf lies between them and us, where, though they are about to bathe two paces away on the beach, they are separated from us by the impossible. It was thus that my sentiment of mystery had enshrined first Gilberte, then the Duchesse de Guermantes, Albertine, so many others. True, the unknown and almost unknowable had become the common, the familiar, the indifferent or the painful, yet it retained something of its former charm. And, to tell the truth, (as in those calendars the postman brings us when he wants his Christmas box,) there was not one year of my life that did not have the picture of a woman I then desired as its frontispiece or interleaved in its days; a picture sometimes the more arbitrary that I had not even seen her, as for instance, Mme. Putbus' maid, Mlle. d'Orgeville or some other girl whose name I had noticed in a society column amongst those of other charming dancers. I imagined her beautiful, I fell in love with her, I created an ideal being, queen of the provincial country-side where, I gleaned from the *Annuaire des Châteaux*, her family owned an estate. In the case of women I had known, that countryside was at least a double one. Each one of them emerged at a different point of my life, standing like protective local divinities first in the midst of the countryside of my dreams, a setting which patterned my life and to which my imagination clung; then perceived by the memory in the various places where I had known her, places she recalled because of her association with them; for though our life wanders, our memory is sedentary and, project ourselves as we may, our memories riveted to places from which we are detached, remain at home like temporary acquaintances made by a traveller in some city in which he leaves them to live their lives and finish their days as though he were still standing beside the church, in front of the door, beneath the trees in the avenue. Thus the shadow of Gilberte lengthened from the front of a church in l'Ile de France where I had imagined her to the drive of a park on the Méséglise side, that of Mme. de Guermantes from the damp path over which red and violet grapes hung in clusters to the morning-gold of a Paris pavement. And this second personality, not born of desire but of memory, was not in either case the only one. I had known each in different circumstances and periods and in each she was another for me or I was another, bathed in dreams of another colour. And the law which had governed the dreams of each year now gathered round them the memories of the woman I had each time known, that which concerned the Duchesse de Guermantes of my child-hood was concentrated by magnetic energy round Combray and that which con-cerned the Duchesse de Guermantes who invited me to luncheon about a sensitive being of a different kind; there were several Duchesses de Guermantes as there had been several Mme. Swanns since the lady in pink, separated from each other by the colourless ether of years and I could no more jump from one to the other than I could fly from here to another planet. Not only separated but different, decked out with dreams at different periods as with flora indiscoverable in anoth-er planet. So true was this that, having decided not to go to luncheon either with Mme. de Forcheville or with Mme. de Guermantes, so completely would that have transported me into another world, I could only tell myself that the one was the Duchesse de Guermantes, descendant of Geneviève de Brabant and the other was the lady in pink, because within me an educated man asserted the fact with the same authority as a scientist who stated that a nebulous Milky Way was composed of particles of a single star. In the same way Gilberte, whom I nevertheless, asked absent-mindedly to introduce me to girls like her former self, was now nothing more to me than Mme. de Saint-Loup. As I looked at her, I did not start dreaming of the part my admiration of Bergotte, whom she had also forgotten, had formerly played in my love of her for I now only thought of Bergotte as the author of his books, without remembering, except during rare and isolated flashes, my emotion when I was introduced to him, my disappointment, my astonishment at his con-versation in the drawing-room with the white rugs, full of violets, where such a number of lamps were brought so early and placed upon so many different tables. All the memories which composed the original Mlle. Swann were, in fact, fore-shortened by the Gilberte of now, held back by the magnetic attraction of another universe, united to a sentence of Bergotte and bathed in the perfume of hawthorn. The fragmentary Gilberte of to-day listened smilingly to my request and setting herself to think, she became serious and appeared to be searching for something in her head. Of this I was glad as it prevented her from noticing a group seated not far from us, the sight of which would not have been agreeable to her. The Duchesse de Guermantes was engaged in an animated conversation with a horrible old woman whom I stared at without having the slightest idea who she was. "How extraordinary to see Rachel here," Bloch passing at that moment, whispered in my ear. The magic name instantly broke the spell which had laid the disguise of this unknown and foul old woman upon Saint-Loup's mistress and I recognised her at once. In this case as in others, as soon as names were supplied to faces I could not recognise, the spell was broken and I knew them. All the same, there was a man there I could not recognise even when I was supplied with his name and I believed it must be a homonym for he bore no sort of likeness to the one I had formerly known and come across afterwards. It was the same man, after all, only greyer and fatter but he had removed his moustache and with it, his personality. It was indeed Rachel, now a celebrated actress, who was to recite verses of Musset and La Fontaine during the reception, with whom Gilberte's aunt, the Duchesse de Guermantes, was then talking. The sight of Rachel could in no case have been agreeable to Gilberte and I was annoyed to hear she was going to recite because it would demonstrate her intimacy with the Duchesse. The latter, too long conscious of being the leader of fashion, (not realising that a situation of that kind only exists in the minds of those who believe in it and that many newcomers would not believe she had any position at all unless they saw her name in the fashion-columns and knew she went everywhere) nowadays only visited the Faubourg Saint-Germain at rare intervals, saying that it bored her to death and went to the other extreme by lunching with this or that actress whose company pleased her.

The Duchesse still hesitated to invite Balthy and Mistinguette, whom she thought adorable, for fear of a scene with M. de Guermantes, but in any case Rachel was her friend. From this the new generation concluded, notwithstanding her name, that the Duchesse de Guermantes must be a *demi-castor* who had never been the "real thing". It is true that Mme. de Guermantes still took the trouble to ask certain sovereigns for whose friendship two other great ladies were her rivals, to luncheon. But they rarely came to Paris and knew people of no particular position, and as the Duchesse, owing to the Guermantes partiality for old forms (for though well-bred people bored her, she liked good manners) announced, "Her Majesty has commanded the Duchesse de Guermantes, has deigned, et cetera," the newcomers, ignorant of these formulas, assumed that the Duchesse's position had diminished. From Mme. de Guermantes' standpoint, her intimacy with Rachel might indicate that we were mistaken in believing her condemnation of fashion to be a hypocritical pose at a time when her refusal to go to Mme. de Sainte-Euverte's seemed to be due to snobbishness rather than to intelligence and her objection to the marquise on the ground of stupidity to be attributable to the latter's failure to attain her snobbish ambitions. But this intimacy with Rachel might equally signify that the Duchesse's intelligence was meagre, unsatisfied and desirous, very late, of expressing itself, combined with a total ignorance of intellectual realities and a fanciful spirit which makes ladies of position say, "What fun it will be" and finish their evenings in what actually is the most excruciating boredom, forcing themselves on someone to whom they have nothing to say so as to stand a moment by his bedside in an evening cloak, after which, observing that it is very late, they go off to bed.

It may be added that for some little time, the versatile Duchesse had felt a strong antipathy towards Gilberte which might make her take particular pleasure in receiving Rachel, which moreover enabled her to proclaim one of the Guermantes' maxims, namely, that they were too numerous to take up a quarrel or to go into mourning among themselves, a sort of "it's not my business" independence which it had been expedient to adopt in regard to M. de Charlus who, had they espoused his cause, would have made them quarrel with everybody. As to Rachel, if she had actually taken a good deal of trouble to make friends with the Duchesse (trouble which the Duchesse had been unable to detect in the affected disdain and pretentious rudeness which made her believe the actress was not at all a snob) doubtless it came about from the fascination exercised upon society people by hardened bohemians which is parallel to that which bohemians feel about people in society, a double reaction which corresponds, in the political order, to the reciprocal curiosity and desire to be allies displayed by nations who have fought against each other. But Rachel's wish to be friends with the Duchesse might have a more peculiar reason. It was at the house of Mme. de Guermantes and from Mme. de Guermantes herself that she once suffered her greatest humiliation. Rachel had not forgotten though, little by little, she had pardoned it but the singular prestige the Duchesse had derived from it in her eyes, would never be effaced. The colloquy from which I wanted to draw Gilberte's attention was fortunately interrupted, for the mistress of the house came to fetch Rachel, the moment having come for her recitation, so she left the Duchesse and appeared upon the platform.

While these incidents were taking place a spectacle of a very different kind was to be seen at the other end of Paris. La Berma had asked some people to come to tea with her in honour of her daughter and her son-in-law but the guests were apparently in no hurry to arrive. Having learned that Rachel was to recite poems at the Princesse de Guermantes' (which greatly shocked la Berma, a great artist to whom Rachel was still a courtesan given minor parts, because Saint-Loup paid for her stage-wardrobe, in plays in which la Berma took the principal rôle, more shocked still by the report in town that though the invitations were sent in the name of the Princesse de Guermantes, it was Rachel who was receiving there) la Berma had written insistently to some of her faithful friends not to fail to come to her tea party, knowing they were also friends of the Princesse de Guermantes when she was Mme. Verdurin. But the hours passed and no one arrived. When Bloch was asked to go he replied naïvely: "No, I prefer going to the Princesse de Guermantes'." And, alas, everyone else had made up his mind to do likewise. La Berma, attacked by a mortal disease which prevented her from going into society except on rare occasions, had become worse, since, in order to satisfy her daughter's demand for luxuries which her ailing and idle son-in-law could not provide, she had again gone on the stage. She knew she was shortening her life, but only cared to please her daughter to whom she brought the great prestige of her fame as to her son-in-law whom she detested but flattered because, as she knew her daughter adored him, she feared, if she did not conciliate him, he would, out of spite, keep them apart. La Berma's daughter, who was not entirely cruel and was secretly loved by the doctor who was attending her mother, allowed herself to be persuaded that these performances of Phèdre were not very dangerous to the invalid. In a measure she had forced the doctor to say so and had retained only that out of the many things he forbade and which she ignored; in reality the doctor had said that there was no harm in la Berma's performances, to please the young woman whom he loved, and perhaps through ignorance as well, knowing that the disease was incurable anyhow, on the principle that one readily accepts the shortening of the sufferings of invalids when in doing so one is the gainer, perhaps also through stupidly supposing it would please la Berma herself and must, therefore, do her good, a foolish notion in which he felt justified when, a box being sent him by la Berma's children for which he left all his patients in the lurch, he had found her as full of life on the stage as she had appeared moribund in her own house. And our habits do, indeed, in large measure, enable even our organisms to accommodate themselves to an existence which at first seemed impossible. We have all seen an old circus performer with a weak heart accomplish acrobatic tricks which no one would believe his heart could stand. La Berma was in the same degree a stage veteran to whose exactions her organs so much adapted themselves that forfeiting prudence, she could, without the public discerning it, produce the illusion of health only affected by an imaginary nervous ailment. After the scene of Hippolyte's declaration, though la Berma well knew the terrible night to which she was returning, her admirers applauded her to the echo and declared her more beautiful than ever. She went back in a state of horrible suffering but happy to bring her daughter the bank-notes which, with the playfulness of a former child of the streets, she was in the habit of tucking into her stocking whence she proudly extracted them, hoping for a smile or a kiss. Unhappily, these notes only enabled son-in-law and daughter to add new decorations to their house adjoining that of their mother, in consequence of which, incessant hammering interrupted the sleep which the great tragedian so much needed. To conform to changes of fashion and to the taste of Messrs, de X— or de Y—, whom they hoped to entertain, they redecorated every room in the house. La Berma, realising that the sleep which alone could have calmed her suffering, had fled, resigned herself to not sleeping any more, not without a secret contempt for elegancies which were hastening her death and making her last days a torture. Doubtless she despised such decrees of fashion owing to a natural resentment of things that injure us which we are powerless to avoid. But it was also because, conscious of the genius within her, she had acquired in her early youth the realisation of their futility and had remained faithful to the tradition she had always reverenced and of which she was the incarnation, which made her judge things and people as she would have done thirty years earlier—Rachel, for instance, not as the fashionable actress she had become but as the little prostitute she had been. In truth, la Berma was no better than her daughter; it was from her heredity and from the contagion of example which admiration had rendered more, effective, that her daughter had derived her egotism, her pitiless raillery, her unconscious cruelty. But, la Berma, in thus saturating her daughter with her own defects, had delivered herself. And even if la Berma's daughter had not had workmen in her house she would have exhausted her mother through the ruthless and irresponsible force of attraction of youth which infects old age with the madness of trying to assimilate it. Every day there was a luncheon party and they would have considered la Berma selfish to deny them that pleasure, or even not to be there as they counted on the magical presence of the illustrious mother to attract, not without difficulty, new social relationships which had to be hauled in by the ears. They "promised" her to these new acquaintances for some party elsewhere so as to show them "civility". And the poor mother, engaged in a grave colloquy with death who had taken up his abode in her, had to get up and go out. The more so that, at this period, Réjane, in all the lustre of her talent, was giving performances abroad with enormous success and the son-in-law anxious that la Berma should not be eclipsed, wanted as profuse an effulgence for the family and forced la Berma to make tours during which she had to have injections of morphia which might cause her death at any moment because of the state of her kidneys. The same magnet of fashion and social prestige had on the day of the Princesse de Guermantes' party, acted as an air-pump and had drawn la Berma's most faithful habitués there with the power of hydraulic suction, while at her own house there was absolute void and death. One young man had come, being uncertain whether the party at la Berma's would be equally brilliant or not. When she saw the time pass and realised that everyone had thrown her over, she had tea served and sat down to table as though to a funereal repast. There was nothing left in la Berma's face to recall her whose photograph had so deeply moved me one mid-Lenten evening long ago; death, as people say, was written in it. At this moment she verily resembled a marble of Erechtheum. Her hardened arteries were half petrified, long sculptural ribbons were traced upon her cheeks with a mineral rigidity. The dying eyes were relatively living in contrast with the terrible ossified mask and shone feebly like a serpent asleep in the midst of stones. Nevertheless, the young man who had sat down to the table out of politeness was continually looking at the time, attracted as he was to the brilliant party at the Guermantes'. La Berma had no word of reproach for the friends who had abandoned her naïvely hoping she was unaware they had gone to the Guermantes'. She only murmured: "Fancy a Rachel giving a party at the Princesse de Guermantes'; one has to come to Paris to see a thing like that!" and silently and with solemn slowness ate forbidden cakes as though she were observing some funeral rite. The tea-party was the more depressing that the son-in-law was furious that Rachel, whom he and his wife knew well, had not invited them. His despair was the greater that the young man who had been invited, told him he knew Rachel well enough, if he went to the Guermantes' at once, to ask her to invite the frivolous couple at the last moment. But la Berma's daughter knew the low level to which her mother relegated Rachel and that, to solicit an invitation from the former prostitute, would have been tantamount to killing her, and she told the young man and her husband that such-a thing was out of the question. But she revenged herself during tea by adopting an air of being deprived of amusement and bored by that tiresome mother of hers. The latter pretended not to notice her daughter's sulkiness and every now and then addressed an amiable word to the young man, their only guest, in a dying voice. But soon the whirlwind which was blowing everybody to the Guermantes' and had blown me there prevailed; he got up and left, leaving Phèdre or death, one did not know which, to finish eating the funereal cakes with her daughter and her son-in-law.

The conversation Gilberte and I were having was interrupted by the voice of Rachel who had just stood up. Her performance was intelligent, for it assumed the unity of the poem as pre-existent apart from the recital and that we were only listening to a fragment of it, as though we were for a moment within earshot of an artist walking along a road. But the audience was bewildered at the sight of the woman bending her knees and throwing out her arms as though she were holding some invisible being in them, before she uttered a sound, and then becoming suddenly bandy-legged and starting to recite very familiar lines in a tone of supplication.

The announcement of a poem which nearly everybody knew had given satisfaction. But when they saw Rachel before beginning, peering about like one who is lost, lifting imploring hands and giving vent to sobs with every word everyone felt embarrassed and shocked by the exaggeration. No one had ever supposed that reciting verses was this sort of thing. But, by degrees, one gets accustomed to it and one forgets the first feeling of discomfort; one begins analysing the performance and mentally comparing various forms of recitation so as to say to oneself that one thing or the other is better or worse. It is like when, on seeing a barrister the first time in an ordinary lawsuit stand forward, lift his arm from the folds of his gown and begin in a threatening tone, one does not dare look at one's neighbours. One feels it is ridiculous, but perhaps, after all, it is magnificent and one waits to see. Everybody looked at each other, not knowing what sort of face to put on; some of the younger ones whose manners were less restrained stifled bursts of laughter. Each person cast a stealthy look at the one next to him, that furtive look one bestows on a guest more knowing than oneself at a fashionable dinner when at the side of one's plate one observes a strange instrument, a lobster fork or a sugar-sifter one does not know how to wield, hoping to watch him using it so that one can copy him. One behaves similarly when someone quotes a verse one does not know but wants to appear to know and which, like giving way to someone else at a door, one leaves to a better-informed person the pleasure of identifying as though we were doing him a favour. Thus those who were listening waited with bent head and inquisitive eye for others to take the initiative in laughter, criticism, tears or applause. Mme. de Forcheville, come expressly from Guermantes whence the Duchesse, as we shall see later on, had been virtually expelled, adopted an attentive and strained appearance which was all but positively disagreeable, either to show she knew all about it and was not present as a mere society woman, or out of hostility to those less versed in literature who might talk to her about something else or because she was trying by complete concentration, to make up her mind whether she liked it or not because though, perhaps, she thought it "interesting", she did not "approve" the manner in which certain verses were delivered. This attitude might more properly have been adopted one would have thought, by the Princesse de Guermantes. But as it was her own house and she had become as miserly as she had rich she made up her mind to give just five roses to Rachel and see to the *claque* for her. She excited enthusiasm and created general approval by her loud exclamations of delight. Only in that respect did she become a Verdurin again; she conveyed the impression of listening to the verses for her own pleasure, of really preferring them to be recited to her alone and of its being a matter of chance that five hundred people had come by her permission to share her pleasure in secrecy. I noticed, however, without its affording my vanity any satisfaction since she had become old and ugly, that Rachel gave me a surreptitious wink. Throughout the recital she let me perceive by a subtly conveyed yet expressive smile that she was soliciting my acquiescence in her advances. But certain old ladies, unaccustomed to poetic recitations, remarked *sotto voce* to their neighbours: "Did you see that?" alluding to the actress's tragi-comic miming which was too much for them. The Duchesse de Guermantes sensed the wavering of opinion and determining to assure the performer's triumph, exclaimed "marvellous!" in the very middle of a poem which she believed finished. Upon this several guests emphasised the exclamation with a gesture of appreciation, less with the object of displaying their approval of the recital than the terms they were on with the Duchesse. When the poem was finished, we were close to Rachel who thanked Mme. de Guermantes and as I was with the latter, took advantage of the opportunity to address me graciously. I then realised that, unlike the impassioned gaze of M. de Vaugoubert's son which I had assumed to be a salutation intended for another, Rachel's significant smile, instead of being meant as an invitation was only intended to provoke my recognition and the bow I now made to her. "I am sure he does not know me," the actress remarked to the Duchesse in a mincing manner. "On the contrary," I asserted, "I recognised you immediately."

If, while that woman was reciting some of La Fontaine's most beautiful verses, she had only been thinking, whether out of goodwill, stupidity or embarrassment, of the awkwardness of approaching me, during the same time Bloch had only thought of how he could bound, like one who is escaping from a beleaguered city, if not over the bodies at all events on the feet of his neighbours, to congratulate the actress the moment the recital was over, whether from a mistaken sense of obligation or from a desire to show off. "It was beautiful," he said to her and, having thus relieved himself, he turned his back on her and made such a noise in resuming his seat that Rachel had to wait several minutes before she could begin her second poem. It was the *Deux pigeons* and when it was over, Mme. de Monrieuval went up to Mme. de Saint-Loup who, she knew, was well-read but did not remember that she had her father's subtle and sarcastic wit, and asked her: "It's one of La Fontaine's fables, isn't it?" thinking so but not being sure, for she only knew the fables slightly and believed they were children's tales unsuitable for recitation in society. Doubtless the good woman supposed that, to have such a success, the artist must have parodied them. Gilbert, till then impassive, confirmed the notion, for as she disliked Rachel and wanted to convey that with such a diction nothing of the fables remained, her answer was given with that tinge of malice which left simple people uncertain what Swann really meant. Though she was Swann's daughter, she was more modern than he—like a duck hatched by a chicken—and being as a rule rather *lakist*, would have contented herself with saying: "I thought it most moving, a charming sensibility", but Gilberte answered Mme. de Monrieuval in Swann's fanciful fashion which people often made the mistake of taking literally: "A quarter is the interpreter's invention, a quarter crazy, a quarter meaningless, the rest La Fontaine," which enabled Mme. de Monrieuval to assert that what people had been listening to was not the *Deux pigeons* of La Fontaine, but a composition of which at the most a quarter was La Fontaine, at which nobody was surprised owing to their extraordinary ignorance.

But one of Bloch's friends having arrived late, the former painted a wonderful picture of Rachel's performance, getting a peculiar pleasure out of exaggerating its merits and holding forth to someone about modernist diction though it had not given him the slightest satisfaction. Then Bloch again congratulated Rachel with overdone emotion in a squeaky voice, told her she was a genius and introduced his friend who declared he had never admired anyone so much and Rachel, who now knew ladies in the best society and unconsciously copied them, answered: "I am flattered, honoured, by your appreciation." Bloch's friend asked Rachel what she thought of la Berma. "Poor woman! It appears she's in a state of poverty. I will not say she had no talent, though it was not real talent for, at bottom, she only liked horrors, but certainly she was useful, she played in a lively fashion and she was a well-meaning, generous creature and has ruined herself for others. She has made nothing for a long time because the public no longer cares for the things she plays in. To tell the truth," she added with a laugh, "I must tell you that my age did not enable me to hear her till her last period when I was too young to form an opinion." "Didn't she recite poetry well?" Bloch's friend ventured the question to flatter her: "As to that," she replied, "she never could recite a single line, it was prose, Chinese, Volapuk, anything you like except verse. Moreover, as I tell you, I hardly heard her and only quite at the last," to appear youthful, "but I've been told she was no better formerly, rather the reverse."

I realised that the passing of time does not necessarily bring about progress in the arts. And in the same way that a seventeenth century writer who was without knowledge of the French Revolution, scientific discoveries and the war, can be superior to another of this period and that Fagon was, perhaps, as great a physician as du Boulbon (the superiority of genius compensating in this case the inferiority of knowledge) so la Berma was a hundred times greater than Rachel and time, by placing her at the top of the tree together with Elstir, had consecrated her genius.

One must not be surprised that Saint-Loup's former mistress sneered at la Berma, she would have done so when she was young, so how would she not do so now. Let a society woman of high intelligence and of amiable disposition become an actress, displaying great talent in her new profession and meeting with nothing but success, if one happened to be in her company some time later, one would be surprised at hearing her talk a language which was not hers but that of people of the theatre, assume their peculiar kind of coarse familiarity towards their colleagues and all the rest of the habits acquired by those who have been on the stage for thirty years. Rachel behaved similarly without having been in society.

Mme. de Guermantes, in her decline, had felt new curiosities rising within her. Society had nothing more to give her. The fact that she occupied the highest position in it was, as we have seen, as plain to her as the height of the blue sky above the earth. She did not consider that she had to assert a position she regarded as unassailable. On the other hand, she wanted to extend her reading and attend more performances. As in former days, all the choicest and most exclusive spirits gathered familiarly in the little garden to drink orangeade amidst the perfumed breezes and clouds of pollen, to be entertained of an evening by her taste for and understanding of what was best in society, now another sort of appetite made her want to know the reasons of some literary controversy, to make the acquaintance of its protagonists and of actresses. Her tired mind demanded a new stimulant. To know such people, she now made advances to women with whom formerly she would not have exchanged cards, and who made much of their intimacy with the director of some review or other in the hope of getting hold of the Duchesse. The first actress she invited believed herself to be the only one admitted to a wonderful social milieu which seemed less wonderful to the second when the latter saw who had preceded her. The Duchesse believed her position to be unchanged because she received royalties at some of her evening parties. In reality she, the only representative of stainless blood, herself a born Guermantes, who could sign "Guermantes" when she did not sign "Duchesse de Guermantes", she who represented to her own sisters-in-law something infinitely precious, like a Moses saved from the waters, a Christ escaped into Egypt, a Louis XVII fled from the Temple, purest of pure breeds, now sacrificed it all, doubtless, for the sake of that congenital need of mental nourishment which caused the social desuetude of Mme. de Villeparisis and had herself become a sort of Mme. de Villeparisis at whose house snobbish women were afraid of meeting this person or that and whom young men, observing the accomplished fact without knowing what had preceded it, believed to be a Guermantes of inferior vintage, of a poor year, a *déclassée* Guermantes. In her new environment she remained what she had been more than she supposed and went on believing that being bored implied intellectual superiority and expressed this sentiment with a violence that made her voice sound harsh. When I talked about Brichot to her she said: "He bored me enough for twenty years," and when Mme. de Cambremer suggested her re-reading "what Schopenhauer said about music," she commented on the remark with asperity: "Re-read! That's a gem! Please not that." Then old Albon smiled because he recognised one of the forms of the Guermantes' spirit.

"People can say what they like, it's admirable, there's the right note and character in it, it's an intelligent rendering, nobody ever recited verses like it," the Duchesse said of Rachel, for fear Gilberte would sneer at her. The latter moved away to another group to avoid conflict with her aunt who, indeed, was extremely dull when she talked about Rachel. But considering the best writers cease to display any talent with increase of age or from excess of production, one can excuse society women for having less sense of humour as they get old. Swann missed the Princesse des Laumes' delicacy in the hard wit of the Duchesse de Guermantes. Late in life, tired by the slightest effort, Mme. de Guermantes gave vent to an immense number of stupid observations. It is true that every now and then, even in the course of this very afternoon, she was again the woman I once knew and talked about society matters with her former verve. But in spite of the sparkling words and the accompanying charm which for so many years had held under their sway the most distinguished men in Paris, her wit scintillated, so to speak, in a vacuum. When she was about to say something funny, she paused the same number of seconds as she used to but when the jest came, there was no point in it. However, few enough people noticed it. The continuity of the proceeding made them think the spirit survived like people who have a fancy for particular kinds of cakes and go to the same shop for them without noticing that they have deteriorated. Even during the war the Duchesse had shown signs of this decay. If anyone used the word culture, she stopped, smiled, her beautiful face lighted up and she ejaculated: "la K K K Kultur" and made her friends, who were fervents of the Guermantes' spirit, roar with laughter. It was, of course, the same mould, the same intonation, the same smile that had formerly delighted Bergotte, who, for that matter, had he lived, would have kept his pithy phrases, his interjections, his periods of suspense, his epithets, to express nothing. But newcomers were sometimes taken aback and if they happened to turn up on a day when she was neither bright nor in full possession of her faculties, they said, "What a fool she is." Moreover, the Duchesse so timed her descent into a lower sphere as not to allow it to affect those of her family from whom she drew aristocratic prestige. If, to play her part as protectress of the arts, she invited a minister or a painter to the theatre and he asked her naïvely whether her sister-in-law or her husband were in the audience, the Duchesse intimidated him by a show of audacity and answered disdainfully: "I don't know. When I go out I don't bother about my family. For politicians and artists I'm a widow." In this way she prevented the too obtrusive parvenu from getting rebuffs—and herself reprimands—from M. de Marsantes and Basin.

I told Mme. de Guermantes I had met M. de Charlus. She thought him more deteriorated than he was, it being the habit of people in society to see differences of intelligence in various people in their world amongst whom it is about uniform and also in the same person at different periods of his life. She added: "He was always the very image of my mother-in-law and the likeness is more striking than ever." There was nothing remarkable in that. We know, as a matter of fact, that certain women are reproduced in certain men with complete fidelity, the only mistake being the sex. We cannot qualify this as *felix culpa*, for sex reacts upon personality and feminism becomes effeminacy, reserve susceptibility and so on. This does not prevent a man's face, even though bearded, from being modelled on lines transferable to the portrait of his mother. There was nothing but a ruin of the old M. de Charlus left but under all the layers of fat and rice powder one could recognise the remnants of a beautiful woman in her eternal youth.

"I can't tell you how much pleasure it gives me to see you," the Duchesse continued, "goodness, when was it we last met?" "Calling upon Mme. d'Agrigente where I often used to see you." "Ah, of course, I often went there, my dear friend, as Basin was in love with her then. I could always be found with his particular friend of the moment because he used to say: 'Mind you go and see her.' I must confess that sort of 'digestion-call' he made me pay when he had satisfied his appetite was rather troublesome. I got accustomed to that, but the tiresome part was being obliged to keep these relationships up after he had done with them. That always made me think of Victor Hugo's verse '*Emporte le bonheur et laisse-moi l'ennui.*' I accepted it smilingly like poetry but it wasn't fair. At least he might have let me be fickle about his mistresses; making-up his accounts with the series he had enough of didn't leave me an afternoon to myself. Well, those days seem sweet compared to the present. I can consider it flattering that he has started being unfaithful to me again because it makes me feel young. But I prefer his earlier manner. I suppose it was so long since he had done that sort of thing that he didn't know how to set about it. But all the same, we get on quite well together. We talk together and rather like each other." The Duchesse said this for fear I might think they had completely separated and, just as people say when someone is very ill: "He still likes to talk, I was reading to him for an hour this morning," she added: "I'll tell him you're here, he'd like to see you," and went up to the Duc who was sitting on a sofa talking to a lady. But when he saw his wife approaching him, he looked so angry that she had no alternative but to retire. "He's engaged; I don't know what he is up to, we shall see presently," Mme. de Guermantes said, leaving me to make what I liked of the situation. Bloch approached us and asked us in the name of his American friend who the young Duchesse over there was. I told him she was the niece of M. de Bréauté, about whom Bloch, who had never heard his name, wanted particulars. "Ah, Bréauté!" exclaimed Mme. de Guermantes, addressing me, "you remember! Goodness, how long ago it is!" Then turning to Bloch, "He was a snob if you like; his people lived near my mother-in-law. That won't interest you, it's amusing for my old friend," she indicated me, "he used to know all about them in old days as I did." These words and many things in Mme. de Guermantes' manner showed the time that had passed since then. Her friendships and opinions had so changed since the time she was referring to that she had come to thinking her charming Babel a snob. He, on the other hand, had not only receded in time, but, a thing I had not realised when I entered society and believed him one of those notabilities of Paris which would always be associated with his social history like with that of Colbert in the reign of Louis XIV, he also had a provincial label as a country neighbour of the old Duchesse and it was in that capacity that the Princesse des Laumes had been associated with him. Nevertheless, this Bréauté, barren of his one time wit, relegated to a past which dated him and proved he had since been completely forgotten by the Duchesse and her circle, formed a link between the Duchesse and myself which I could never have believed that first evening at the Opéra Comique when he had appeared to me like a nautical God in his marine cave, because she recalled that I had known him, consequently that I had been her friend, if not of the same social circle as herself, that I had frequented that circle for a far longer time than most of the people present; she recalled him and yet not clearly enough to remember certain details which were then my vital concern, that I was not invited to the Guermantes' place in the country and was only a small bourgeois of Combray when she came to Mlle. Percepied's marriage mass, that, in spite of all Saint-Loup's requests, she did not invite me to her house during the year following Bréauté's appearance with her at the Opéra Comique. To me that was of capital importance for it was exactly then that the life of the Duchesse de Guermantes seemed to me like a paradise I could not enter, but for her it was the same indifferent existence she was accustomed to, and owing to my having often dined at her house later on, and to my having, even earlier, been her aunt's and her nephew's friend, she no longer remembered at what period our intimacy had begun nor realised the anachronism of making it start several years too early. For that made it seem as though I had known the Mme. de Guermantes of that marvellous Guermantes name, that I had been received by the name of golden syllables in the Faubourg Saint-Germain when I had merely dined with a lady who was even then nothing more to me than a lady like any other and who had invited me not to descend into the submarine kingdom of the Nereids but to spend the evening in her cousin's box. "If you want to know all about Bréauté, who isn't worth it," she added to Bloch, "ask my friend who is worth a hundred of him. He has dined fifty times at my house with Bréauté. Wasn't it at my house that you met him? Anyhow, you met Swann there." And I was as surprised that she imagined I might have met M. de Bréauté elsewhere than at her house and frequented that circle before I knew her as I was to observe that she imagined I had first known Swann at her house. Less untruthfully than Gilberte when she said that Bréauté was "one of my old neighbours in the country; I like talking to him about Tansonville," whereas he did not in those days go to the Swann's at Tansonville, I might have remarked: "He was a country neighbour who often came to see us in the evening," in reference to Swann, who in truth, recalled something very different from the Guermantes, "It's rather difficult to explain," she continued. "He was a man to whom Highnesses meant everything. He told a lot of rather funny stories about Guermantes people and my mother-in-law and Mme. de Varambon before she was in attendance on the Princesse de Parme. But who cares about Mme. de Varambon now? My friend here knew about all this, but it's done with now, they're people whose names are forgotten and, for that matter, they didn't deserve to survive." And I realised, in spite of that unified thing society seems to be, where, in fact, social relationships reach their greatest concentration, where everything gets known about everybody, that areas of it remain in which time causes changes that cannot be grasped by those who only enter it when its configuration has changed. "Mme. de Varambon was an excellent creature who said unbelievably stupid things," continued the Duchesse, insensitive to that poetry of the incomprehensible which is an effect of time, and concerned only with extracting human elements assimilable with literature of the Meilhac kind and with the Guermantes spirit, "at one time she had a mania for constantly chewing cough drops called"—she laughed to herself as she recalled the name so familiar formerly, so unknown now to those she was addressing—"Pastilles Géraudel. 'Mme. de Varambon,' my mother-in-law said to her, "'if you go on swallowing those Géraudel pastilles, you'll get a stomach-ache.' 'But, Mme. la Duchesse,' answered Mme. de Varambon, 'how can I hurt my stomach since they go into the bronchial tubes?' It was she who said, 'The Duchesse has got such a beautiful cow that it looks like a stallion.'" Mme. de Guermantes would have gladly gone on telling stories about Mme. de Varambon of which we knew hundreds but the name did not evoke in Bloch's memory any of those associations rekindled in us by the mention of Mme. de Varambon, of M. de Bréauté, of the Prince d'Agrigente, who perhaps, on that account, exercised a glamour in his eyes I knew to be exaggerated but understood, though not because I had felt it, since our own weaknesses and absurdities seldom make us more indulgent to those of others even when we have thrust them into the light.

The past had been so transformed in the mind of the Duchesse or the demarcations which existed in my own had always been so absent from hers, that what had been an important event for me had passed unperceived by her and she endowed me with a social past which she made recede too far. For the Duchesse shared that notion of time past which I had just acquired, and contrary to my illusion which shortened it, she lengthened it, notably in not reckoning with that undefined line of demarcation between the period when she represented a name to me, then the object of my love—and the period during which she had become merely a woman in society like any other. Moreover, I only went to her house during that second period when she had become another to me. But these differences escaped her eyes and she would not have thought it more singular that I should have been at her house two years earlier because she did not know that she was then another person to me, her personality not appearing to her, as to me, discontinuous.

I told the Duchesse that Bloch believed it was the former Princesse de Guermantes who was receiving to-day, "That reminds me of the first evening when I went to the Princesse de Guermantes' and believed I was not invited and that they were going to turn me out, when you wore a red dress and red shoes." "Gracious, how long ago that is!" she answered, thus emphasising the passage of time. She gazed sadly into the distance but particularly insisted on the red dress. I asked her to describe it to me, which she did with complaisance. "Those dresses aren't worn nowadays. They were the fashion then." "But it was pretty, wasn't it?" She was always afraid of saying anything that might not be to her advantage. "Yes, I thought it very pretty. It isn't the fashion now but it will be again. All fashions come back, in dress, in music, in painting," she added with emphasis, imagining something original in this philosophy. But the sadness of growing old gave her a lassitude belied by her smile. "You're sure they were red shoes; I thought they were gold ones?" I assured her that my memory was exact on the point without detailing the circumstances which enabled me to be so certain. "You're charming to remember," she said tenderly, for women call those charming who remember their beauty as artists do those who remember their works. Moreover, however distant the past, so determined a woman as the Duchesse is unlikely to forget it. "Do you remember," she said, as she thanked me for remembering her dress and her shoes, "Basin and I brought you back that evening and there was a girl coming to see you after midnight. Basin laughed heartily about your having visitors at that time of night." I did, indeed, remember that Albertine came to see me that night after the evening party at the Princesse de Guermantes'. I remembered it quite as well as the Duchesse, I to whom Albertine was now as indifferent as she would have been to Mme. de Guermantes, had the latter known that the young girl on whose account I had not gone to their house, was Albertine. Long after our hearts have forsaken the poor dead, their indifferent dust remains, like an alloy, mingled with events of the past and, though we love them no more, when we evoke a room, a path, a road they lived in or traversed with us, we are compelled, so that the place they occupied may not remain untenanted, to think of them though we neither regret nor name nor identify them. (Mme. de Guermantes did not identify the girl who was to come that evening, had never known her name and only referred to her because of the hour and the circumstances.) Those are the final and least enviable forms of survival.

If the opinions the Duchesse subsequently expressed regarding Rachel were indifferent in themselves, they interested me because they, too, marked a new hour on the dial. For the Duchesse had no more forgotten her evening party in which Rachel figured than had the latter and the memory had not undergone the slightest transformation. "I must tell you," she said, "that I am the more interested to hear her recite and to witness her success that I discovered her, appreciated her, treasured her, imposed her, at a time when she was ignored and laughed at. You may be surprised, my dear friend, to know that the first time she was heard in public was at my house. Yes, while all the would-be advanced people like my new cousin"—she ironically indicated the Princesse de Guermantes who to her was still Mme. Verdurin, "would have let her starve without condescending to listen to her. I considered her interesting and gave her the prestige of performing at my house before the smartest audience we could get together. I can say, though it sounds stupid and pretentious, for fundamentally talent doesn't need protection, that I launched her. Of course she didn't need me." I made a gesture of protest and observed that Mme. de Guermantes was quite ready to welcome it. "You evidently think talent has need of support? Perhaps, after all, you're right. You're repeating what Dumas formerly told me. In this case, I am extremely flattered if I do count for something, however little, not in the talent, of course, but in the reputation of an artist like her." Mme. de Guermantes preferred to abandon her idea that talent bursts like an abscess because it was more flattering for herself, but also because for some time now, she had been receiving new people and being rather worn out, she had practised humility by seeking information and asking others their opinion in order to form one. "It isn't necessary for me to tell you," she resumed, "that this intelligent public which is called society saw nothing in it. They objected to her and scoffed at her. I might tell them it was original and curious, something different from what-had been done before, no one believed me, as they never did believe me in anything. It was the same with the thing she recited, a piece by Maeterlinck. Now it's well known, but then everyone laughed at it though I considered it admirable. It surprises even myself considering I was only a peasant with the education of a country-girl, that I spontaneously admired things of that kind. I could not, of course, have explained why, but it gave me pleasure, it moved me. Why, Basin, who is anything but sensitive, was struck by its effect on me. At that time, he said: 'I don't want you to listen to these absurdities any more, they make you ill,' and it was true. They take me for a hard woman and really I am a bundle of nerves."

At this moment an unexpected incident occurred. A footman came to tell Rachel that la Berma's daughter and son-in-law wanted to speak to her. We have seen that the daughter had opposed her husband when he wanted to get an invitation from Rachel. But, after the departure of the young man, the boredom of the young couple left alone with their mother had grown, the thought that others were amusing themselves tormented them; in brief, availing themselves of la Berma's retirement to her bedroom to spit blood, they had quickly put on their smartest clothes, called a carriage and had arrived at the Princesse de Guermantes' without being invited. Rachel hardly grasped the situation, but secretly flattered, adopted an arrogant tone and told the footman she could not be disturbed, they must write and explain the object of their unusual proceeding. The footman came back with a card on which la Berma's daughter had scribbled that she and her husband could not resist the pleasure of hearing Rachel recite and asked her to let them come in. Rachel gloated over the pretext and her own triumph and replied that she was very sorry but that the recitation was over. In the anteroom, the footmen were winking at each other while the couple in vain awaited admission. The shame of their humiliation, the consciousness of the insignificance, the nullity of Rachel in her mother's eyes, pushed la Berma's daughter into pursuing to the end the step she had risked simply for amusement. She sent a message to Rachel that she would take it as a favour, even if she could not hear her recite, to be allowed to shake hands with her. Rachel at the moment, was talking to an Italian Prince who was said to be after her large fortune, the source of which her social relationships somewhat concealed. She took stock of the reversal of situations which now placed the children of the illustrious Berma at her feet. After informing everyone about the incident in the most charming fashion, she sent the young couple a message to come in, which they did without being asked twice, ruining la Berma's social prestige at one blow as they had previously destroyed her health. Rachel had realised that her condescension would result in her being considered kinder and the young couple baser than her refusal. So she received them with open arms and with the affectation of a patroness in the limelight who can put aside her magnificence, said: "But of course, I'm delighted to see you, the Princesse will be charmed". As she did not know that at the theatre she was supposed to have done the inviting, she may have feared, if she refused entry to la Berma's children, that they might have doubted not her goodwill for that would have been indifferent to her—but her influence. The Duchesse de Guermantes moved away instinctively, for in proportion to anyone's appearing to court society, he diminished in her esteem. At the moment she only felt it for Rachel's kindness and would have turned her back on la Berma's children if they had been introduced to her. Meanwhile, Rachel was composing the gracious phrases with which she, the following day, would overwhelm la Berma in the wings: "I was harrowed, distressed that your daughter should have been kept waiting in the anteroom. If I had only known! She sent me card after card." She was enchanted to offer this insult to la Berma. Perhaps, had she known it would be a mortal blow, she might have hesitated. People like to persecute others but without exactly putting themselves in the wrong and without hounding them to death. Moreover, where was she wrong? She might say laughingly a few days later: "That's pretty thick, I meant to be far nicer to her children than she ever was to me, and now they nearly accuse me of killing her. I take the Duchesse to witness." It seems as though the children of great actors inherit all the evil and pretence of stage-life without accomplishing the determined work that springs from it as did this mother. Great actresses frequently die the victims of domestic plots which are woven round them, as happens so often at the close of dramas they play in.

Gilberte, as we have seen, wanted to avoid a conflict with her aunt on the subject of Rachel. She did well; it was not an easy matter to undertake the defence of Odette's daughter in opposition to Mme. de Guermantes, so great was her animosity owing to what the Duchesse told me about the new form the Duc's infidelity had·taken, which, extraordinary as it might appear to those who knew her age, was with Mme. de Forcheville.

When one remembered Mme. de Forcheville's present age, it did, indeed, seem extraordinary. But Odette had probably begun the life of a courtesan very young. And we encounter women who reincarnate themselves every ten years in new love affairs and sometimes drive some young wife to despair because of her husband's deserting her for them when one actually thought they were dead.

The life of the Duchesse was a very unhappy one, and one reason for it simultaneously brought about the lowering of M. de Guermantes' social standard. He, sobered by advancing age though still robust, had long ceased being unfaithful to Mme. de Guermantes, but had suddenly become infatuated with Mme. de Forcheville without knowing how he had got involved in the liaison.

It had assumed such proportions that the old man, in this last love affair, imitating his own earlier amative proceedings, so secluded his mistress that, if my love for Albertine had been a multiple variation of Swann's for Odette, M. de Guermantes' recalled mine for Albertine. She had to take all her meals with him and he was always at her house. She boasted of this to friends who, but for her, would never have known the Duc and who came to her house to make his acquaintance, as people visit a courtesan to get to know the king who is her lover. It is true that Mme. de Forcheville had been in society for a long time. But beginning over again, late in life, to be kept by such a haughty old man who played the most important part in her life, she lowered herself by ministering only to his pleasure, buying peignoirs and ordering food he liked, flattering her friends by telling them that she had spoken to him about them, as she told my great-uncle she had spoken about him to the Grand-Duke who then sent him cigarettes, in a word, she once more tended, in spite of the position she had secured in society, to become, owing to force of circumstances, what she had been to me when I was a child, the lady in pink. Of course, my Uncle Adolphe had been dead many years. But does the substitution of new people for old prevent us from beginning the same life over again? Doubtless she adapted herself to the new conditions out of cupidity, but also because, somewhat sought after socially when she had a daughter to marry, she had been left in the background when Gilberte married Saint-Loup. She knew that the Duc would do what she liked, that he would bring her any number of duchesses who would not be reluctant to score off their friend Oriane and, perhaps, was stimulated into the bargain by the prospect of gratifying her feminine sentiment of rivalry at the expense of the outraged Duchesse. The Duc de Guermantes' exclusive Courvoisier nephews, Mme. de Marsantes, the Princesse de Trania, went to Mme. de Forcheville's in the expectation of legacies without troubling whether or no this caused pain to Mme. de Guermantes, about whom Odette, stung by Mme. de Guermantes' disdain, said the most evil things. This liaison with Mme. de Forcheville, which was only an imitation of his early ones, caused the Duc de Guermantes to miss for the second time being elected President of the Jockey Club and honorary member of the Académie des Beaux Arts just as M. de Charlus' public association with Jupien was the cause of his failure to be elected President of the Union Club and of the Society of Friends of Old Paris. Thus the two brothers, so different in their tastes, had fallen into disrepute on account of the same indolence and lack of will, more pleasantly observable in the case of their grandfather, a member of the French Academy, which led to the normal proclivities of one and the abnormal habits of the other degrading both.

The old Duc did not go out any more, he spent his days and evenings at Odette's. But to-day, as she herself had come to the Princesse de Guermantes' party, he had dropped in to see her for a moment, in spite of the annoyance of meeting his wife. I dare say I should not have recognised him if the Duchesse had not drawn my attention to him. He was now nothing but a ruin, but a splendid one; grander than a ruin, he had the romantic beauty of a rock beaten by a tempest. Scourged from every side by the waves of suffering, by rage at his suffering, his face, slowly crumbling like a block of granite almost submerged by the towering seas, retained the style, the suavity I had always admired. It was defaced like a beautiful antique head we are glad to possess as an ornament in a library. But it seemed to belong to an earlier period than it did, not only because its matter had acquired a rude brokenness in the place of its former grace but also because an involuntary expression caused by failing health, resisting and fighting death, by the arduousness of keeping alive, had replaced the old delicacy of mien and exuberance. The arteries had lost all their suppleness and had imprinted a sculptured hardness on the once expressive features. And, unconsciously, the Duc revealed by the contours of his neck, his cheeks, his brow, a being forced to hold on grimly to every moment and as though tossed by a tragic storm, his sparse white locks dashed their spray over the invaded promontory of his visage. And like the weird and spectral reflection an approaching storm sweeping everything before it, gives to rocks till then of another colour, I knew that the leaden grey of his hard, worn cheeks, the woolly whiteness of his unkempt hair, the wavering light which lingered in his almost unseeing eyes, were the but too real pigment borrowed from a fantastic palette with which was inimitably painted the prophetic shadows of age and the terrifying proximity of death. The Duc only stayed a few moments but long enough for me to see that Odette made fun of him to her younger aspirants. But it was strange that he who used to be almost ridiculous when he assumed the pose of a stage-king, was now endowed with a noble mien, resembling in that his brother whom also old age had relieved of accessories. And like his brother, once so arrogant, though in a different way, he seemed almost respectful. For he had not suffered the eclipse of M. de Charlus, reduced to bowing with a forgetful invalid's politeness to those he had formerly disdained, but he was very old and when he went through the door and wanted to go down the stairs to go away, old age, that most miserable condition which casts men from their high estate as it did the Kings of Greek tragedy, old age gripped him, forced him to halt on that road of the cross which is the life of an impotent menaced by death, so that he might wipe his streaming brow and tap to find the step which escaped his foothold because he needed help to ensure it, help against his swimming eyes, help he was unknowingly imploring ever so gently and timidly from others. Old age had made him more than august, it had made him a suppliant.

Thus in the Faubourg Saint-Germain the apparently impregnable positions of the Duc and Duchesse de Guermantes and of the Baron de Charlus had lost their inviolability as everything changes in this world through the action of an interior principle which had never occurred to them; in the case of M. de Charlus it was the love of Charlie who had enslaved him to the Verdurins and then gradual decay, in the case of Mme. de Guermantes a taste for novelty and for art, in the case of M. de Guermantes an exclusive love, as he had had so many in his life, rendered more tyrannical by the feebleness of old age to which the austerity of the Duchesse's salon where the Duc no longer put in an appearance and which, for that matter, had almost ceased functioning, offered no resistance by its power of rehabilitation. Thus the face of things in life changes, the centre of empires, the register of fortunes, the chart of positions, all that seemed final, are perpetually remoulded and during his life-time a man can witness the completest changes just where those seemed to him least possible.

Unable to do without Odette, always at her house and in the same armchair from which old age and gout made it difficult for him to rise, M. de Guermantes let her receive her friends who were only too pleased to be introduced to the Duc, to give him the lead in conversation, and listen to his talk of former society, of the Marquise de Villeparisis and of the Duc de Chartres.

At moments, beneath the old pictures collected by Swann which, with this *Restauration* Duc and his beloved courtesan, completed the old-fashioned picture, the lady in pink interrupted him with her chatter and he stopped short, and stared at her with a ferocious glare. Possibly he had discovered that she, as well as the duchesse, occasionally made stupid remarks, perhaps an old man's fancy made him think that one of Mme. de Guermantes' intemperate passages of humour had interrupted what he was saying and he thought himself back in the Guermantes' mansion as caged beasts may imagine themselves free in African wilds. Raising his head sharply, he fixed his little yellow eyes, which once had the gleam of a wild animal's, on her in one of those sustained scowls which made me shiver when Mme. de Guermantes told me about them. Thus the Duc glared at the audacious lady in pink, but she held her own, did not remove her eyes from him and at the end of a moment which seemed long to the spectators, the old wild beast, tamed, remembered he was no longer at large in the Sahara of his own home, but in his cage in the Jardin des Plantes at Mme. de Forcheville's and he withdrew his head, from which still depended a thick fringe of blonde-white hair, into his shoulders and resumed his discourse. Apparently he had not understood what Mme. de Forcheville said, which as a rule, meant little. He permitted her to ask her friends to dinner with him. A mania which was a relic of his former love affairs and did not surprise Odette, accustomed as she was to the same habit in Swann and which reminded me of my life with Albertine, was to insist on people going early so that he could say good-night to Odette last. It is unnecessary to add that the moment he had gone she invited other people. But the Duc had no suspicion of that, or preferred not to seem to suspect it; the vigilance of old men diminishes with their sight and hearing. After a certain age Jupiter inevitably changes into one of Molière's characters—into the absurd Géronte—not into the Olympian lover of Alcmene. And Odette deceived M. de Guermantes and took care of him with neither charm nor generosity of spirit. She was commonplace in that as in everything else. Life had given her good parts but she could not play them and, meanwhile, she was playing at being a recluse. It was a fact that whenever I wanted to see her, I could not, because M. de Guermantes, desirous of reconciling the exactions of his hygiene with those of his jealousy, only allowed her to have parties in the day time and on the further condition that there was no dancing. She frankly avowed the seclusion in which she lived and this for various reasons. The first was that she imagined, although I had only published a few articles and studies, that I was a well-known author which caused her to remark naïvely, returning to the past when I went to see her in the Avenue des Acacias and later at her house: "Ah, if I could have then foreseen that that boy would one day be a great writer." And having heard that writers are glad to be with women in order to document themselves and hear love stories, she readopted her rôle of courtesan to entertain me: "Fancy, once there was a man who was crazy about me and I adored him. We were having a divine time together. He had to go to America and I was to go with him. On the eve of his departure I thought it would be more beautiful not to risk that such a wonderful love should come to an end. We spent our last evening together. He believed I should go with him. It was a delirious night of infinite voluptuousness and despair, for I knew I should never see him again. In the morning I gave my ticket to a traveller I did not know. He wanted to buy it but I answered: 'No, you are rendering me such service in accepting it that I do not want the money.'" There was another story: "One day I was in the Champs Elysées. M. de Bréauté, whom I had only seen once, looked at me so significantly that I stopped and asked him how he dared look at me like that. He answered: 'I'm looking at you because you've got an absurd hat on.' It was true. It was a little hat with pansies on it and the fashions of that period were awful. But I was furious and I said to him: 'I don't permit you to talk to me like that.' It began to rain and I said: 'I might forgive you if you had a carriage.' 'Oh, well, that's all right, I've got one and I'll accompany you home.' 'No, I shall be glad to accept your carriage but not you.' I got into the carriage and he departed in the rain. But that evening he came to my house. We had two years of wild love together. Come and have tea with me," she went on "and I'll tell you how I made M. de Forcheville's acquaintance. Really," with a melancholy air, "my life has been a cloistered one, for I've only had great loves for men who were terribly jealous of me. I don't speak of M. de Forcheville; he was quite indifferent and I only cared for intelligent men, but, you see, M. Swann was as jealous as this poor Duc for whose sake I sacrifice my life because he is unhappy at home. But it was M. Swann I loved madly, and one can sacrifice dancing and society and everything to please a man one loves or even to spare him anxiety. Poor Charles, he was so intelligent, so seductive, exactly the kind of man I liked." Perhaps it was true. There was a time when Swann pleased her and it was exactly when she was not "his kind". To tell the truth, she never had been "his kind", then or later. And yet he had loved her so long and so painfully. He was surprised afterwards when he realised the contradiction of it. But there would be none if we consider how great a proportion of suffering women who aren't "their kind" inflict on men. That is probably due to several causes; first because they are not our kind, we let ourselves be loved without loving; through that we adopt a habit we should not acquire with a woman who is our kind. The latter, knowing she was desired, would resist and only accord occasional meetings and thus would not gain such a foothold in our lives that if, later on, we came to love her and then, owing to a quarrel or a journey, we found ourselves alone and without news of her, she would deprive us not of one bond but a thousand. Again this habit is sentimental because there is no great physical desire at its base and if love is born, the brain works better; romance takes the place of a physical urge. We do not suspect women who are not our kind, we allow them to love us and if we afterwards love them we love them a hundred times more than the others, without getting from them the relief of satisfied desire. For these reasons and many others, the fact that we experience our greatest sorrows with women who are not our kind, is not only due to that derisive illusion which permits the realisation of happiness only under the form that pleases us least. A woman who is our kind is rarely dangerous, for she does not care about us, satisfies us, soon abandons us and does not install herself in our lives. What is dangerous and produces suffering in love is not the woman herself, it is her constant presence, the eagerness to know what she is doing every moment; it is not the woman, it is habit. I was coward enough to say that what she told me about Swann was kind, not to say noble on her part, but I knew it was not true and that her frankness was mixed up with lies. I reflected with horror, as little by little she told me her adventures, on all that Swann had been ignorant of and of how much he would have suffered, for he had associated his sensibility with that creature and had guessed to the point of certainty, from nothing but her glance at an unknown man or woman, that they attracted her. Actually she told me all this only to supply what she believed was a subject for novels. She was wrong, not because she could not at any time have furnished my imagination with abundant material but it would have had to be in less intentional fashion and by my agency disengaging, unknown to her, the laws that governed her life.

M. de Guermantes kept his thunders for the Duchesse to whose mixed gatherings Mme. de Forcheville did not hesitate to draw the irritated attention of the Duc. Moreover, the Duchesse was very unhappy. It is true that M. de Charlus to whom I had once spoken about it, suggested that the first offence had not been on his brother's side, that the legend of the Duchesse's purity was in reality composed of an incalculable number of skilfully dissimulated adventures. I had never heard of them. To nearly everyone Mme. de Guermantes was nothing of the sort and the belief that she had always been irreproachable was universal. I could not decide which of the two notions was true for truth is nearly always unknown to three-quarters of the world. I recalled certain azure and fugitive glances of the Duchesse de Guermantes in the nave of the Combray church but, in truth, they refuted neither of these opinions for each could give a different and equally acceptable meaning to them. In the madness of boyhood I had for a moment taken them as messages of love to myself. Later, I realised that they were but the benevolent glances which a suzeraine such as the one in the stained windows of the church bestowed on her vassals. Was I now to believe that my first idea was the right one, and that if the Duchesse never spoke to me of love, it was because she feared to compromise herself with a friend of her aunt and of her nephew rather than with an unknown boy she had met by chance in the church of St. Hilaire de Combray?

The Duchesse might have been pleased for the moment that her past seemed more consistent for my having shared it, but she resumed her attitude of a society woman who despises society in replying to a question I asked her about the provincialism of M. de Bréauté, whom at the earlier period I had placed in the same category as M. de Sagan or M. de Guermantes. As she spoke, the Duchesse took me round the house. In the smaller rooms, the more intimate friends of the hosts were sitting apart to enjoy the music. In one of them, a little Empire salon where one or two frock-coated gentlemen sat upon a sofa listening, there was a couch curved like a cradle placed alongside the wall close to a Psyche leaning upon a Minerva, in the hollow of which a young woman lay extended. Her relaxed and—languid attitude, which the entrance of the Duchesse in no way disturbed, contrasted with the brilliance of her Empire dress of a glittering silk beside which the most scarlet of fuchsias would have paled, encrusted with a pearl tissue in the folds of which the floral design appeared to be embedded. She slightly bent her beautiful brown head to salute the Duchesse. Although it was broad daylight, she had had the heavy curtains drawn to give herself up to the music, and the servants had lighted an urn on a tripod to prevent people stumbling. In answer to my question the Duchesse told me she was Mme. de Sainte-Euverte and I wanted to know what relation she was of the Mme. de Sainte-Euverte I had known. She was the wife of one of her great-nephews and Mme. de Guermantes appeared to suggest that she was born a La Rochefoucauld but emphasised that she herself had never known the Sainte-Euvertes. I recalled to her mind the evening party, of which, it is true, I was only aware by hearsay, when, as Princesse des Laumes, she had renewed her acquaintance with Swann. Mme. de Guermantes affirmed she had never been to that party but she had always been rather a liar and had become more so. Madame de Sainte-Euverte's salon—somewhat faded with time—was one she preferred ignoring and I did not insist. "No," she said, "the person you may have met at my house because he was amusing, was the husband of the woman you refer to. I never had any social relations with her." "But she was a widow?" "You thought so because they were separated; he was much nicer than she." At last I realised that a huge, extremely tall and strong man with snow-white hair, whom I met everywhere but whose name I never knew, was the husband of Mme. de Sainte-Euverte and had died the year before. As to the niece, I never discovered whether she lay extended on the sofa listening to the music without moving for anyone because of some stomach trouble or because of her nerves or phlebitis or a coming accouchement or a recent one which had gone wrong. The likely explanation was that she thought she might as well play the part of a Récamier figure on her couch in that shimmering red dress. She little knew that she had: given birth to a new development of that name of Sainte-Euverte which, at so many intervals, marked the distance and continuity of Time. It was Time she was rocking in that cradle where the name of Sainte-Euverte flowered in a fuchsia-red silk in the Empire style. Mme. de Guermantes declared that she had always detested Empire style; that meant, she detested it now, which was true, because she followed the fashions though not closely. Without complicating the matter by alluding to David of whose work she knew something, when she was a girl she considered Ingres the most boring of draughtsmen, then suddenly the most beguiling of new masters, so much so that she detested Delacroix. By what process she had returned to this creed of reprobation matters little, since such shades of taste are reflected by art-critics ten years before these superior women talk about them. After criticising the Empire style, she excused herself for talking about such insignificant people as the Sainte-Euvertes and of rubbish like Bréauté's provincialism for she was as far from realising the interest they had for me as Mme. de Sainte-Euverte de la Rochefoucauld looking after her stomach or her Ingres pose, was from suspecting that her name was my joy, her husband's name, not the far more famous one of her family, and that to me it represented the function of cradling time in that room full of temporal associations. "How can all this nonsense interest you?" the Duchesse remarked. She uttered these words under her breath and nobody could have caught what she said. But a young man (who was to be of interest to me later because of a name much more familiar to me formerly than Sainte-Euverte) rose with an exaggerated air of being disturbed and went further away to listen in greater seclusion. They were playing the Kreutzer Sonata but he, having read the programme wrong, believed it was a piece by Ravel which he had been told was as beautiful as Palestrina but difficult to understand. In his abrupt change of place, he knocked, owing to the half darkness, against a tea-table which made a number of people turn their heads and thus afforded them an agreeable diversion from the suffering they were undergoing in listening religiously to the Kreutzer Sonata. And Mme. de Guermantes and I who were the cause of this little scene, hastened into another room. "Yes," she continued, "how can such nonsense interest a man with your talent? Like just now when I saw you talking to Gilberte de Saint-Loup, it isn't worthy of you. For me that woman is just nothing, she isn't even a woman; she's unimaginably pretentious and bourgeoise," for the Duchesse mixed up her aristocratic prejudices with her championship of truth. "Indeed, ought you to come to places like this? To-day, after all, it may be worth while because of Rachel's recitation. But, well as she did it, she doesn't extend herself before such an audience. You must come and lunch alone with her and then you'll see what a wonderful creature she is. She's a hundred times superior to everyone here. And after luncheon she shall recite Verlaine to you and you'll tell me what you think of it." She boasted to me specially about these luncheon parties to which X and Y always came. For she had acquired the characteristic that distinguishes the type of woman who has a "Salon" whom she formerly despised (though she denied it to-day), the chief sign of whose superior eclecticism is to have "all the men" at their houses. If I told her that a certain great lady who went in for a "salon" spoke ill of Mme. Rowland, the Duchesse burst out laughing at my simplicity and said: "Of course, she had 'all *the* men' at her house and the other tried to take them away from her." Mme. de Guermantes continued: "It passes my comprehension that you can come to this sort of thing—unless it's for studying character," she added the last words doubtfully and suspiciously, afraid to go too far because she was not sure what that strange operation consisted of.

"Don't you think," I asked her, "it's painful for Mme. de Saint-Loup to have to listen, as she did just now, to her husband's former mistress?" I observed that oblique expression coming over Mme. de Guermantes' face which connects what someone has said with unpleasant factors. These may remain unspoken but words with serious implications do not always receive verbal or written answers. Only fools solicit twice an answer to a foolish letter which was a *gaffe*; for such letters are only answered by acts and the correspondent whom the fool thinks careless, will call him Monsieur the next time he meets him instead of by his first name. My allusion to Saint-Loup's liaison with Rachel was not so serious and could not have displeased Mme. de Guermantes more than a second by reminding her that I had been Robert's friend, perhaps his confidant about the mortification he had been caused when he obtained the Duchesse's permission to let Rachel appear at her evening party. Mme. de Guermantes' face did not remain clouded and she answered my question about Mme. Saint-Loup: "I may tell you that I believe it to be a matter of indifference to her, for Gilberte never loved her husband. She is a horrible little creature. All she wanted was the position, the name, to be my niece, to get out of the slime to which her one idea now is to return. I can assure you all that pained me deeply for poor Robert's sake because though he may not have been an eagle, he saw it all and a good many things besides. Perhaps I ought not to say so because, after all, she's my niece and I've no proof that she was unfaithful to him, but there were all sorts of stories about her. But supposing I tell you that I know Robert wanted to fight a duel with an officer of Méséglise. And it was on account of all that that Robert joined up. The war was a deliverance from his family troubles and if you care for my opinion, he was not killed, he took care to get himself killed. She feels no sort of sorrow, she even astonishes me by the cynicism with which she displays her indifference, and that greatly pains me because I was very fond of Robert. It may perhaps surprise you because people don't know me, but I still think of him. I forget no one. He told me nothing but he knew I guessed it all. But, dear me, if she loved her husband ever so little, could she bear with such complete indifference being in the same drawing-room with a woman whose passionate lover he was for years, indeed one might say always, for I know for certain it went on even during the war. Why, she would spring at her throat," the Duchesse cried, quite forgetting that she herself had acted cruelly by inviting Rachel and staging the scene she regarded as inevitable if Gilberte loved Robert. "No!" she concluded, "that woman is a pig." Such an expression was possible in the mouth of Mme. de Guermantes owing to her easy and gradual descent from the Guermantes environment to the society of actresses and with this she affected an eighteenth century manner she considered refreshing on the part of one who could afford herself any liberty she chose. But the expression was also inspired by her hatred of Gilberte, by the need of striking her in effigy in default of physically. And she thought she was thereby equally justifying her action towards Gilberte or rather against her, in society, in the family, even in connection with her interest in Robert's inheritance. But sometimes facts of which we are ignorant and which we could not imagine supply an apparent justification of our judgments. Gilberte, who doubtless inherited some of her mother's traits (and I dare say I had unconsciously surmised this when I asked her to introduce me to girls) after reflecting on my request and so that any profits that might accrue should not go out of the family, a conclusion the effrontery of which was greater than I could have imagined, came up to me presently and said: "If you'll allow me, I'll fetch my young daughter, she's over there with young Mortemart and other youngsters of no importance. I'm sure she'll be a charming little friend for you." I asked her if Robert had been pleased to have a daughter. "Oh, he was very proud of her but, of course, it's my belief, seeing what his tastes were," Gilberte naïvely added, "he would have preferred a boy." This girl, whose name and fortune doubtless led her mother to hope she would marry a prince of the blood and thus crown the whole edifice of Swann and of his wife, later on married an obscure man of letters, for she was quite unsnobbish, and caused the family to fall lower in the social scale than the level from which she originated. It was afterwards very difficult to convince the younger generation that the parents of this obscure household had occupied a great social position.

The surprise and pleasure caused me by Gilberte's words were quickly replaced while Mme. de Saint-Loup disappeared into another room, by the idea of past Time which Mlle. de Saint-Loup had brought back to me in her particular way without my even having seen her. In common with most human beings, was she not like the centre of cross-roads in a forest, the point where roads converge from many directions? Those which ended in Mlle. de Saint-Loup were many and branched out from every side of her. First of all, the two great sides where I had walked so often and dreamt so many dreams, came to an end in her—through her father, Robert de Saint-Loup, the Guermantes side and through Gilberte, her mother, the side of Méséglise which was Swann's side. One, through the mother of the young girl and the Champs Elysées, led me to Swann, to my evenings at Combray, to the side of Méséglise, the other, through her father, to my afternoons at Balbec where I saw him again near the glistening sea. Transversal roads already linked those two main roads together. For through the real Balbec where I had known Saint-Loup and wanted to go, chiefly because of what Swann had told me about its churches, especially about the Persian church and again through Robert de Saint-Loup, nephew of the Duchesse de Guermantes I reunited Combray to the Guermantes' side. But Mlle. de Saint-Loup led back to many other points of my life, to the lady in pink who was her grandmother and whom I had seen at my great-uncle's house. Here there was a new cross-road, for my great-uncle's footman who had announced me that day and who, by the gift of a photograph, had enabled me to identify the lady in pink, was the uncle of the young man whom not only M. de Charlus but also Mlle. de Saint-Loup's father had loved and on whose account her mother had been made unhappy. And was it not the grandfather of Mlle. de Saint-Loup, Swann, who first told me about Vinteuil's music as Gilberte had first told me about Albertine? And it was through speaking to Albertine about Vinteuil's music that I had discovered who her intimate girl-friend was and had started that life with her which had led to her death and to my bitter sorrows. And it was again Mlle. de Saint-Loup's father who had tried to bring back Albertine to me. And I saw again all my life in society, whether at Paris in the drawing-rooms of the Swanns and the Guermantes', or in contrast, at the Verdurins' at Balbec, uniting the two Combray sides with the Champs Elysées and the beautiful terraces of the Raspelière. Moreover, whom of those we have known are we not compelled inevitably to associate with various parts of our lives if we relate our acquaintance with them? The life of Saint-Loup described by myself would be unfolded in every kind of scene and would affect the whole of mine, even those parts of it to which he was a stranger, such as my grandmother or Albertine. Moreover, contrast them as one might, the Verdurins were linked to Odette through her past, with Robert de Saint-Loup through Charlie and how great a part had Vinteuil's music played in their home! Finally, Swann had loved the sister of Legrandin and the latter had known M. de Charlus whose ward young Cambremer had married. Certainly, if only our hearts were in question, the poet was right when he spoke of the mysterious threads which life breaks. But it is still truer that life is ceaselessly weaving them between beings, between events, that it crosses those threads, that it doubles them to thicken the woof with such industry that between the smallest point in our past and all the rest, the store of memories is so rich that only the choice of communications remains. It is possible to say, if I tried to make conscious use of it and to recall it as it was, that there was not a single thing that served me now which had not been a living thing, living its own personal life in my service though transformed by that use into ordinary industrial matter. And my introduction to Mlle. de Saint-Loup was going to take place at Mme. Verdurin's who had become Princesse de Guermantes! How I thought back on the charm of those journeys with Albertine, whose successor I was going to ask Mlle. de Saint-Loup to be—in the little tram going towards Douville to call on Mme. Verdurin, that same Mme. Verdurin who had cemented and broken the love of Mlle. de Saint-Loup's grandfather and grandmother before I loved Albertine. And all round us were the pictures of Elstir who introduced me to Albertine and as though to melt all my pasts into one, Mme. Verdurin, like Gilberte, had married a Guermantes.

We should not be able to tell the story of our relations with another, however little we knew him without registering successive movements in our own life. Thus every individual—and I myself am one of those individuals—measured duration by the revolution he had accomplished not only round himself but round others and notably by the positions he had successively occupied with relation to myself.

And, without question, all those different planes, upon which Time, since I had regained it at this reception, had exhibited my life, by reminding me that in a book which gave the history of one, it would be necessary to make use of a sort of spatial psychology as opposed to the usual flat psychology, added a new beauty to the resurrections my memory was operating during my solitary reflections in the library, since memory, by introducing the past into the present without modification, as though it were the present, eliminates precisely that great Time-dimension in accordance with which life is realised.

I saw Gilberte coming towards me. I, to whom Saint-Loup's marriage and all the concern it then gave me (as it still did) were of yesterday, was astonished to see beside her a young girl whose tall, slight figure marked the lapse of time to which I had, until now, been blind.

Colourless, incomprehensible time materialised itself in her, as it were, so that I could see and touch it, had moulded her into a graven masterpiece while upon me alas, it had but been doing its work. However, Mlle. de Saint-Loup stood before me. She had deep cleanly-shaped, prominent and penetrating eyes. I noticed that the line of her nose was on the same pattern as her mother's and grandmother's, the base being perfectly straight, and though adorable, was a trifle too long. That peculiar feature would have enabled one to recognise it amongst thousands and I admired Nature for having, like a powerful and original sculptor, effected that decisive stroke of the chisel at exactly the right point as it had in the mother and grandmother. That charming nose, protruding rather like a beak had the Saint-Loup not the Swann curve. The soul of the Guermantes' had vanished but the charming head with the piercing eyes of a bird on the wing was poised upon her shoulders and threw me, who had known her father, into a dream. She was so beautiful, so promising. Gaily smiling, she was made out of all the years I had lost; she symbolised my youth.

Finally, this idea of Time had the ultimate value of the hand of a clock. It told me it was time to begin if I meant to attain that which I had felt in brief flashes on the Guermantes' side and during my drives with Mme. de Villeparisis, that indefinable something which had made me think life worth living. How much more so now that it seemed possible to illuminate that life lived in darkness, at last to make manifest in a book the truth one ceaselessly falsifies. Happy the man who could write such a book. What labour awaited him. To convey its scope would necessitate comparison with the noblest and most various arts. For the writer, in creating each character, would have to present it from conflicting standpoints so that his book should have solidity, he would have to prepare it with meticulous care, perpetually regrouping his forces as for an offensive, to bear it as a load, to accept it as the object of his life, to build it like a church, to follow it like a régime, to overcome it like an obstacle, to win it like a friendship, to nourish it like a child, to create it like a world, mindful of those mysteries which probably only have their explanation in other worlds, the presentiment of which moves us most in life and in art. Parts of such great books can be no more than sketched for time presses and perhaps they can never be finished because of the very magnitude of the architect's design. How many great cathedrals remain unfinished? Such a book takes long to germinate, its weaker parts must be strengthened, it has to be watched over, but afterwards it grows of itself, it designates our tomb, protects it from evil report and somewhat against oblivion. But to return to myself. I was thinking more modestly about my book and it would not even be true to say that I was thinking of those who would read it as my readers. For, as I have already shown, they would not be my readers, but the readers of themselves, my book being only a sort of magnifying-glass like those offered by the optician of Combray to a purchaser. So that I should ask neither their praise nor their blame but only that they should tell me if it was right or not, whether the words they were reading within themselves were those I wrote (possible devergencies in this respect might not always arise from my mistake but sometimes because the reader's eyes would not be those to whom my book was suitable). And, constantly changing as I expressed myself better and got on with the task I had undertaken, I thought of how I should devote myself to it at that plain white table, watched over by Françoise. As all those unpretentious creatures who live near us have a certain intuition of what we are trying to do and as I had so far forgotten Albertine that I forgave Françoise for her hostility to her, I should work near her and almost like her (at least as she used to formerly for now she was so old that she could hardly see), for it would be by pinning supplementary leaves here and there that I should build up my book, so to speak, like a dress rather than like a cathedral. When I could not find all the sheets I wanted, all my *"paperoles"* as Françoise called them, when just that one was missing that I needed, Françoise would understand my apprehension, for she always said she could not sew if she had not got the exact thread-number and sort of button she wanted and because, from living with me, she had acquired a sort of instinctive understanding of literary work, more right than that of many intelligent people and still more than that of stupid ones. Thus when I used to write my articles for the *Figaro*, while the old butler with that exaggerated compassion for the severity of toil which is unfamiliar, which cannot be observed, even for a habit he had not got himself like people who say to you, "How it must tire you to yawn like that," honestly pitied writers and said: "What a head-breaking business it must be," Françoise, to the contrary, divined my satisfaction and respected my work. Only she got angry when I told Bloch about my articles before they appeared, fearing he would forestall me and said: "You aren't suspicious enough of all these people, they're copyists." And Bloch, in fact, did offer a prospective alibi by remarking each time that I sketched something he liked: "Fancy! that's curious, I've written something very much like that; I must read it to you." (He could not then have read it to me because he was going to write it that evening.)

In consequence of sticking one sheet on another, what Françoise called my *paperoles* got torn here and there. In case of need she would be able to help me mend them in the same way as she patched worn parts of her dresses, or awaiting the glazier as I did the printer, when she stuck a bit of newspaper in a window instead of the glass pane. Holding up my copy-books devoured like worm-eaten wood, she said: "It's all moth-eaten, look, what a pity, here's the bottom of a page which is nothing but a bit of lace," and, examining it like a tailor: "I don't think I can mend it, it's done for, what a shame; perhaps those were your most beautiful ideas. As they said at Combray, there are no furriers who know their job as well as moths, they always go for the best materials."

Moreover, since individualities (human or otherwise) would in this book be constructed out of numerous impressions which, derived from many girls, many churches, many sonatas, would serve to make a single sonata, a single church and a single girl, should I not be making my book as Françoise made that *bœuf à la mode*, so much savoured by M. de Norpois of which the jelly was enriched by many additional carefully selected bits of meat? And at last I should achieve that for which I had so much longed and believed impossible during my walks on the Guermantes' side as I had believed it was impossible, when I came home, to go to bed without embracing my mother, or later, that Albertine loved women, an idea I finally accepted unconsciously, for our greatest fears like our greatest hopes are not beyond our capacity and it is possible to end by dominating the first and realising the second. Yes, this newly-formed idea of time warned me that the hour had come to set myself to work. It was high time. The anxiety which had taken possession of me when I entered the drawing-room and the made-up faces gave me the notion of lost time, was justified. Was there still time? The mind has landscapes at which it is only given us to gaze for a time. I had lived like a painter climbing a road which overlooks a lake hidden by a curtain of rocks and trees. Through a breach he perceives it, it lies before him, he seizes his brushes, but already darkness has come and he can paint no longer, night upon which day will never dawn again.

A condition of my work as I had conceived it just now in the library was that I must fathom to their depths impressions which had first to be recreated through memory. And my memory was impaired. Therefore as I had not yet begun, I had reason for apprehension, for even though I thought, in view of my age, that I had some years before me, my hour might strike at any moment. I had, in fact, to regard my body as the point of departure, which meant that I was constantly under the menace of a two-fold danger, without and within. And even when I say this it is only for convenience of expression. For the internal danger as in that of cerebral haemorrhage is also external, being of the body. And the body is the great menace of the mind. We are less justified in saying that the thinking life of humanity is a miraculous perfectioning of animal and physical life than that it is an imperfection in the organisation of spiritual life as rudimentary as the communal existence of protozoa in colonies or the body of the whale etc., so imperfect, indeed, that the body imprisons the spirit in a fortress; soon the fortress is assailed at all points and in the end the spirit has to surrender. But in order to satisfy myself by distinguishing the two sorts of danger which threatened my spirit and beginning by the external one, I remembered that it had often already happened in the course of my life, at moments of intellectual excitement when some circumstance had completely arrested my physical activity, for instance when I was leaving the restaurant of Rivebelle in a half-intoxicated condition in order to go to a neighbouring casino, that I felt the immediate object of my thought with extreme vividness and realised that it was a matter of chance not only that the object had not yet entered my mind but that its survival depended upon my physical existence. I cared little enough then. In my light-hearted gaiety I was neither prudent nor apprehensive. It mattered little to me that this happy thought flew away in a second and disappeared in the void. But now it was no longer so because the joy I experienced was not derived from a subjective nervous tension which isolates us from the past, but, on the contrary, from an extension of the consciousness in which the past, recreated and actualised, gave me, alas but for a moment, a sense of eternity. I wished that I could leave this behind me to enrich others with my treasure. My experience in the library which I wanted to preserve was that of pleasure but not an egoistical pleasure or at all events it was a form of egoism which is useful to others (for all the fruitful altruisms of Nature develop in an egoistical mode; human altruism which is not egoism, is sterile, it is that of a writer who interrupts his work to receive a friend who is unhappy, to accept some public function or to write propaganda articles).

I was no longer indifferent as when I returned from Rivebelle; I felt myself enlarged by this work I bore within me (like something precious and fragile, not belonging to me, which had been confided to my care and which I wanted to hand over intact to those for whom it was destined). And to think that when, presently, I returned home, an accident would suffice to destroy my body and that my lifeless mind would have for ever lost the ideas it now contained and anxiously preserved within its shaky frame before it had time to place them in safety within the covers of a book. Now, knowing myself the bearer of such a work, an accident which might cost my life was more to be dreaded, was indeed (by the measure in which this work seemed to me indispensable and permanent) absurd, when contrasted with my wish, with my vital urge, but not less probable on that account since accidents due to material causes can take place at the very moment when an opposing will, which they unknowingly annihilate, renders them monstrous, like the ordinary accident of knocking over a water-jug placed too near the edge of a table and thus disturbing a sleeping friend one acutely desires not to waken.

I knew very well that my brain was a rich mineral basin where there was an enormous and most varied area of precious deposits. But should I have the time to exploit them? I was the only person capable of doing so, for two reasons. With my death not only would the one miner capable of extracting the minerals disappear, but with him, the mineral itself. And the mere collision of my automobile with another on my way home would suffice to obliterate my body and my spirit would have to abandon my new ideas for ever. And by a strange coincidence, that reasoned fear of danger was born at the very moment when the idea of death had become indifferent to me. The fear of no longer existing had formerly horrified me at each new love I experienced,—for Gilberte, for Albertine—because I could not bear the thought that one day the being who loved them might not be there; it was a sort of death. But the very recurrence of this fear led to its changing into calm confidence.

If the idea of death had cast a shadow over love, the memory of love had for long helped me not to fear death. I realised that death is nothing new, ever since my childhood I had been dead numbers of times. To take a recent period, had I not cared more for Albertine than for my life? Could I then have conceived my existence without my love for her? And yet I no longer loved her, I was no longer the being who loved her but a different one who did not love her and I had ceased to love her when I became that other being. And I did not suffer because I had become that other, because I no longer loved Albertine; and certainly it did not seem to me a sadder thing that one day I should have no body than it had formerly seemed not to love Albertine. And yet how indifferent it all was to me now. These successive deaths, so feared by the self they were to destroy, so indifferent, so sweet, were they, once they were accomplished, when he who feared them was no longer there to feel them, had made me realise how foolish it would be to fear death. And now that it had been for a while indifferent to me I began fearing it anew, in another form, it is true, not for myself but for my book for the achievement of which that life, menaced by so many dangers, was, at least, for a period, indispensable. Victor Hugo says: "The grass must grow and children die." I say that the cruel law of art is that beings die and that we ourselves must die after we have exhausted suffering so that the grass, not of oblivion but of eternal life, should grow, fertilised by works upon which generations to come will gaily picnic without care of those who sleep beneath it. I have spoken of external dangers but there were internal ones also. If I were preserved from an accident without, who knows whether I might not be prevented from profiting from my immunity by an accident within, by some internal disaster, some cerebral catastrophe, before the months necessary for me to write that book, had passed. A cerebral accident was not even necessary. I had already experienced certain symptoms, a curious emptiness in the head and a forgetfulness of things I only found by luck as one does on going through one's things and finding something one had not been looking for; I was a treasurer from whose broken coffer his riches were slipping away. When presently I went back home by the Champs Elysées who could say that I should not be struck down by the same evil as my grandmother when, one day she came for a walk with me which was to be her last, without her ever dreaming of such a thing, in that ignorance which is our lot when the hand of the clock reaches the moment when the spring is released that strikes the hour. Perhaps the fear of having already almost traversed the minute that precedes the first stroke of the hour, when it is already preparing to strike, perhaps the fear of that blow which was about to crash through my brain was like an obscure foreknowledge of what was coming to pass, a reflection in the consciousness of a precarious state of the brain whose arteries are about to give way, which is no less possible than the sudden acceptance of death by the wounded who, if their lucidity remains and both doctor and will to live deceive them, yet see what is coming and say: "I am going to die, I am ready," and write their last farewells to their wife.

That obscure premonition of what had to be came to me in a singular form before I began my book. One evening I was at a party and people said I was looking better than ever and were astonished that I showed so little signs of age. But that evening I came near falling three times going downstairs. I had only gone out for a couple of hours but when I got home, my memory and power of thought had gone and I had neither strength nor life in me. If they had come to proclaim me King or arrest me, I should have allowed them to do what they liked with me without saying a word, without even opening my eyes, like those who at the extreme point of sea-sickness, crossing the Caspian Sea, would offer no resistance if they were going to be thrown into the sea. Properly speaking I was not ill but I was as incapable of taking care of myself as old people active the evening before, who have fractured their thigh and enter a phase of existence which is only a preliminary, be it short or long, to inevitable death. One of my selves the one that recently went to one of those barbaric feasts which are called dinners in society attended by white cravated men and plumed, half-nude women whose values are so topsy-turvy that a person who does not go to a dinner to which he has accepted an invitation or only puts in an appearance at the roast commits in their eyes a greater crime than the most immoral acts as lightly discussed in the course of it as illness and death which provide the only excuse for not being there, as long as the hostess has been informed in time to notify the fourteenth guest that someone has died,—that self had kept its scruples and lost its memory. On the other hand, the other self, the one who conceived this work, remembered I had received an invitation from Mme. Molé and had heard that Mme. Sazerat's son was dead. I had made up my mind to use an hour of respite after which I should not be able to utter a word or swallow a drop of milk, tongue-tied like my grandmother during her death agony, for the purpose of excusing myself to Mme. Molé and expressing my condolences to Mme. Sazerat. But shortly afterwards, I forgot I had to do it. Happy oblivion! For the memory of my work was on guard and was going to use that hour of survival to lay my first foundations. Unhappily, taking up a copy-book, Mme. Molé's invitation card slipped out of it. Instantly, the forgetful self which dominates the other in the case of all those scrupulous savages who dine out, put away the copy-book and began writing to Mme. Molé (who would doubtless have thought more of me had she known that I had put my reply to her invitation before my architectural work). Suddenly, as I was answering, I remembered that Mme. Sazerat had lost her son, so I wrote her too and having thus sacrificed the real duty to the fictitious obligation of proving my politeness and reasonableness, I fell lifeless, closed my eyes and for a whole week was only able to vegetate. Yet, if all my useless duties to which I was prepared to sacrifice the real one, went out of my head in a few minutes, the thought of my edifice never left me for an instant. I did not know whether it would be a church where the faithful would gradually learn truth and discover the harmony of a great unified plan or whether it would remain, like a Druid monument on the heights of a desert island, unknown for ever. But I had made up my mind to consecrate to it the power that was ebbing away, reluctantly almost, as though to leave me time to elaborate the structure before the entrance to the tomb was sealed. I was soon able to show an outline of my project. No one understood it. Even those who sympathised with my perception of the truth I meant later to engrave upon my temple, congratulated me on having discovered it with a microscope when, to the contrary, I had used a telescope to perceive things which were indeed very small because they were far away but every one of them a world. Where I sought universal laws I was accused of burrowing into the "infinitely insignificant". Moreover, what was the use of it all, I had a good deal of facility when I was young and Bergotte had highly praised my schoolboy efforts. But instead of working I had spent my time in idleness and dissipation, in being laid up and taken care of and in obsessions and I was starting my work on the eve of death without even knowing my craft. I had no longer the strength to face either my human obligations or my intellectual ones, still less both. As to the first, forgetfulness of the letters I had to write somewhat simplified my task. Loss of memory helped to delete social obligations which were replaced by my work. But, at the end of a month, association of ideas suddenly brought back remorseful memories and I was overwhelmed by my feeling of impotence. I was surprised at my own indifference to criticisms of my work but from the time when my legs had given way when I went downstairs I had become indifferent to everything; I only longed for rest until the end came. It was not because I counted on posthumous fame that I was indifferent to the judgments of the eminent to-day. Those who pronounced upon my work after my death could think what they pleased of it. I was no more concerned about the one than the other. Actually, if I thought about my work and not about the letters which I ought to have answered, it had ceased to be because I considered the former so much more important as I did at the time when I was idle and afterwards when I tried to work, up to the day when I had had to hold on to the banisters of the stair-case. The organisation of my memory, of my preoccupations, was linked to my work perhaps because, while the letters I received were forgotten an instant later, the idea of my work was continuously in my mind, in a state of perpetual becoming. But it too had become importunate.

My work was like a son whose dying mother must still unceasingly labour in the intervals of inoculations and cuppings. She may love him still but she only realises it through the excess of her care of him. And my powers as a writer were no longer equal to the egoistical exactions of the work. Since the day on the staircase, nothing in the world, no happiness, whether it came from friendships, from the progress of my work or from hope of fame, reached me except as pale sunlight that had lost its power to warm me, to give me life or any desire whatever and yet was too brilliant in its paleness for my weary eyes which closed as I turned towards the wall. As much as I could tell from the movement of my lips, I might have had a very slight smile in the corner of my mouth when a lady wrote me: "I was surprised not to get an answer to my letter," Nevertheless, that reminded me and I answered it. I wanted to try, so as not to be thought ungrateful, to be as considerate to others as they to me. And I was crushed by imposing these super-human fatigue's on my dying body.

This idea of death installed itself in me definitively as love does. Not that I loved death, I hated it. But I dare say I had thought of it from time to time as one does of a woman one does not yet love and now the thought of it adhered to the deepest layer of my brain so thoroughly that I could not think of anything without its first traversing the death zone and even if I thought of nothing and remained quite still, the idea of death kept me company as incessantly as the idea of myself. I do not think that the day when I became moribund, it was the accompanying factors such as the impossibility of going downstairs, of remembering a name, of getting up, which had by unconscious reasoning given me the idea that I was already all but dead, but rather that it had all come together, that the great mirror of the spirit reflected a new reality. And yet I did not see how I could pass straight from my present ills to death without some warning. But then I thought of others and how people die every day without it seeming strange to us that there should be no hiatus between their illness and their death. I thought even that it was only because I saw them from the inside (far more than through deceitful hope) that certain ailments did not seem to me necessarily fatal, taken one at a time, although I thought I was going to die, just like those who certain that their time has come, are nevertheless easily persuaded that their not being able to pronounce certain words has nothing to do with apoplexy or heart failure but is due to the tongue being tired, to a nerve condition akin to stammering, owing to the exhaustion consequent on indigestion.

In my case it was not the farewell of a dying man to his wife that I had to write, it was something longer and addressed to more than one person. Long to write! At best I might attempt to sleep during the day-time. If I worked it would only be at night but it would need many nights perhaps a hundred, perhaps a thousand. And I should be harassed by the anxiety of not knowing whether the Master of my destiny, less indulgent than the Sultan Sheriar, would, some morning when I stopped work, grant a reprieve until the next evening. Not that I had the ambition to reproduce in any fashion the *Thousand and One Nights*, anymore than the *Mémoires of Saint-Simon*, they too written by night, nor any of the books I had so much loved and which superstitiously attached to them in my childish simplicity as I was to my later loves, I could not, without horror, imagine different from what they were. As Elstir said of Chardin, one can only recreate what one loves by repudiating it. Doubtless my books, like my fleshly being, would, some day, die. But one must resign oneself to death. One accepts the thought that one will die in ten years and one's books in a hundred. Eternal duration is no more promised to works than to men. It might perhaps be a book as long as the *Thousand and One Nights* but very different. It is true that when one loves a work one would like to do something like it but one must sacrifice one's temporal love and not think of one's taste but of a truth which does not ask what our preferences are and forbids us to think of them. And it is only by obeying truth that one may some day encounter what one has abandoned and having forgotten the *Arabian Nights* or the *Mémoires of Saint-Simon* have written their counterpart in another period. But had I still time? Was it not too late?

In any case, if I had still the strength to accomplish my work, the circumstances, which had to-day in the course of the Princesse de Guermantes' reception simultaneously given me the idea of it and the fear of not being able to carry it out, would specifically indicate its form of which I had a presentiment formerly in Combray church during a period which had so much influence upon me, a form which, normally, is invisible, the form of Time. I should endeavour to render that Time-dimension by transcribing life in a way very different from that conveyed by our lying senses. Certainly, our senses lead us into other errors, many episodes in this narrative had proved to me that they falsify the real aspect of life. But I might, if it were needful, to secure the more accurate interpretation I proposed, be able to leave the locality of sounds unchanged, to refrain from detaching them from the source the intelligence assigns to them, although making the rain patter in one's room or fall in torrents into the cup from which we are drinking is, in itself, no more disconcerting than when as they often have, artists paint a sail or a peak near to or far away from us, according as the laws of perspective, variation in colour and ocular illusion make them appear, while our reason tells us that these objects are situated at enormous distances from us.

I might, although the error would be more serious, continue the fashion of putting features into the face of a passing woman, when instead of nose and cheeks and chin there was nothing there but an empty space in which our desire was reflected. And, a far more important matter, if I had not the leisure to prepare the hundred masks suitable to a single face, were it only as the eyes see it and in the sense in which they read its features, according as those eyes hope or fear or, on the other hand, as love and habit which conceal changes of age for many years, see them, indeed, even if I did not undertake, in spite of my liaison with Albertine proving that without it everything is fictitious and false, to represent people not from outside but from within ourselves where their smallest acts may entail fatal consequences, and to vary the moral atmosphere according to the different impressions on our sensibility or according to our serene sureness that an object is insignificant whereas the mere shadow of danger multiplies its size in a moment, if I could not introduce these changes and many others (the need for which, if one means to portray the truth has constantly been shown in the course of this narrative) into the transcription of a universe which had to be completely redesigned, at all events I should not fail to depict therein man, as having the extension, not of his body but of his years, as being forced to the cumulatively heavy task which finally crushes him, of dragging them with him wherever he goes. Moreover, everybody feels that we are occupying an unceasingly increasing place in Time, and this universality could only rejoice me since it is the truth, a truth suspected by each one of us which it was my business to try to elucidate. Not only does everyone feel that we occupy a place in Time but the most simple person measures that place approximately as he might measure the place we occupy in space. Doubtless we often make mistakes in this measurement but that one should believe it possible to do it proves that one conceives of age as something measurable.

And often I asked myself not only whether there was still time but whether I was in a condition to accomplish my work. Illness which had rendered me a service by making me die to the world (for if the grain does not die when it is sown, it remains barren but if it dies it will bear much fruit), was now perhaps going to save me from idleness as idleness had preserved me from facility. Illness had undermined my strength and, as I had long noticed, had sapped the power of my memory when I ceased to love Albertine. And was not the recreation of the memory of impressions it was afterwards necessary to fathom, to illuminate, to transform into intellectual equivalents, one of the conditions, almost the essential condition, of a work of art such as I had conceived just now in the library? Ah, if I only still had the powers that were intact on the evening I had evoked when I happened to notice François le Champi. My grandmother's lingering death and the decline of my will and of my health dated from that evening of my mother's abdication. It was all settled at the moment when, unable to await the morning to press my lips upon my mother's face, I had taken my resolution, I had jumped out of bed and had stood in my nightshirt by the window through which the moonlight shone, until I heard M. Swann go away. My parents had accompanied him, I had heard the door open, the sound of bell and closing door. At that very moment, in the Prince de Guermantes' mansion, I heard the sound of my parents' footsteps and the metallic, shrill, fresh echo of the little bell which announced M. Swann's departure and the coming of my mother up the stairs; I heard it now, its very self, though its peal rang out in the far distant past. 'Then thinking of all the events which intervened between the instant when I had heard it and the Guermantes' reception I was terrified to think that it was indeed that bell which rang within me still, without my being able to abate its shrill sound, since, no longer remembering how the clanging used to stop, in order to learn, I had to listen to it and I was compelled to close my ears to the conversations of the masks around me. To get to hear it close I had again to plunge into myself. So that ringing must always be there and with it, between it and the present, all that indefinable past unrolled itself which I did not know I had within me. When it rang I already existed and since, in order that I should hear it still, there could be no discontinuity, I could have had no instant of repose or of non-existence, of non-thinking, of non-consciousness, since that former instant clung to me, for I could recover it, return to it, merely by plunging more deeply into myself. It was that notion of the embodiment of Time, the inseparableness from us of the past that I now had the intention of bringing strongly into relief in my work. And it is because they thus contain the past that human bodies can so much hurt those who love them, because they contain so many memories, so many joys and desires effaced within them but so cruel for him who contemplates and prolongs in the order of time the beloved body of which he is jealous, jealous to the point of wishing its destruction. For after death Time leaves the body and memories—indifferent and pale—are obliterated in her who exists no longer and soon will be in him they still torture, memories which perish with the desire of the living body.

I had a feeling of intense fatigue when I realised that all this span of time had not only been lived, thought, secreted by me uninterruptedly, that it was my life, that it was myself, but more still because I had at every moment to keep it attached to myself, that it bore me up, that I was poised on its dizzy summit, that I could not move without taking it with me.

The day on which I heard the distant, far-away sound of the bell in the Combray garden was a land-mark in that enormous dimension which I did not know I possessed. I was giddy at seeing so many years below and in me as though I were leagues high.

I now understood why the Duc de Guermantes, whom I admired when he was seated because he had aged so little although he had so many more years under him than I, had tottered when he got up and wanted to stand erect—like those old Archbishops surrounded by acolytes, whose only solid part is their metal cross— and had moved, trembling like a leaf on the hardly approachable summit of his eighty-three years, as though men were perched upon living stilts which keep on growing, reaching the height of church-towers, until walking becomes difficult and dangerous and, at last, they fall. I was terrified that my own were already so high beneath me and I did not think I was strong enough to retain for long a past that went back so far and that I bore within me so painfully. If at least, time enough were allotted to me to accomplish my work, I would not fail to mark it with the seal of Time, the idea of which imposed itself upon me with so much force to-day, and I would therein describe men, if need be, as monsters occupying a place in Time infinitely more important than the restricted one reserved for them in space, a place, on the contrary, prolonged immeasurably since, simultaneously touching widely separated years and the distant periods they have lived through—between which so many days have ranged themselves—they stand like giants immersed in Time.

THE END

Lector House believes that a society develops through a two-fold approach of continuous learning and adaptation, which is derived from the study of classic literary works spread across the historic timeline of literature records. Therefore, we aim at reviving, repairing and redeveloping all those inaccessible or damaged but historically as well as culturally important literature across subjects so that the future generations may have an opportunity to study and learn from past works to embark upon a journey of creating a better future.

This book is a result of an effort made by Lector House towards making a contribution to the preservation and repair of original ancient works which might hold historical significance to the approach of continuous learning across subjects.

HAPPY READING & LEARNING!

LECTOR HOUSE LLP
E-MAIL: lectorpublishing@gmail.com